America's Best Day Hiking Series

Hiking
KENTUCKY

BROOK ELLIOTT

BARBARA ELLIOTT

Human Kinetics

D1127297

Library of Congress Cataloging-in-Publication Data

Elliott, Brook, 1944-
    Hiking Kentucky / Brook Elliott, Barbara Elliott ; [illustrator,
Tim Shedelbower].
       p.   cm. -- (America's best day hiking series)
    ISBN 0-88011-812-1 (pbk.)
    1. Hiking--Kentucky--Guidebooks.   2. Parks--Kentucky--Guidebooks.
3. Trails--Kentucky--Guidebooks.   4. Kentucky--Guidebooks.
I. Elliott, Barbara, 1944- . II. Title.   III. Series.
   GV199.42.K4E56   1998   98-9398
   917.6904'43--dc21   CIP

ISBN: 0-88011-812-1

Acquisitions Editor: Patricia Sammann
Managing Editor: Coree Schutter
Copyeditors: Joyce Sexton and Denelle Eknes
Proofreader: Sue Fetters
Graphic Designer: Robert Reuther
Graphic Artist: Francine Hamerski
Cover Designer: Jack Davis
Photographer (cover): The Stock Market/J.T. Miller
Photographers (interior): Barbro Foto
Illustrator: Tim Shedelbower
Printer: United Graphics

Maps Adapted From—**Daniel Boone National Forest:** Parks #8, #9, #10, #16, #17, #19, #21, #22; **Kentucky Department of Parks:** Parks #1, #2, #4, #6, #7, #12, #13, #15, #18, #23, #24, 30, #34, #38, #39, #46, #49, #50, #51; **Kentucky State Nature Preserves Commission:** Parks #3, #5, #14, #27, #29, #35, #45, #53; **National Park Service:** Parks #11, #25; **Trails Illustrated:** Park #20; **Lost River Valley:** Park #26; **City of Ft. Thomas:** Park #31; **Lexington Parks and Recreation Dept.:** Park #32; **Lexington Convention and Visitors Bureau:** Park #33; **Lexington Cemetery Co.:** Park #33; **National Audubon Society:** Park #36; **Central Kentucky Wildlife Refuge:** Park #37; **Bernheim Arboretum and Research Forest:** Park #40; **Louisville Waterfront Development Corp.:** Park #41; **Greenspace Inc.:** Park #42; **U.S. Army Armor Center:** Park #43; **Otter Creek Park:** Park #44; **Daviess County Parks and Recreation Dept.:** Parks #47, #48; **Tennessee Valley Authority:** Park #52; **The Nature Conservancy—Kentucky Chapter:** Park #53

Human Kinetics books are available at special discounts for bulk purchase. Special editions or book excerpts can also be created to specification. For details, contact the Special Sales Manager at Human Kinetics.

Printed in the United States of America   10 9 8 7 6 5 4 3 2

Human Kinetics
Web site: http:∥www.humankinetics.com/

United States: Human Kinetics, P.O. Box 5076, Champaign, IL 61825-5076
1-800-747-4457

Canada: Human Kinetics, 475 Devonshire Road, Unit 100, Windsor, ON N8Y 2L5
1-800-465-7301 (in Canada only)

Europe: Human Kinetics, P.O. Box IW14, Leeds LS16 6TR, United Kingdom
+44 (0)113-278 1708

Australia: Human Kinetics, 57A Price Avenue, Lower Mitcham, South Australia 5062
(08) 82771555

New Zealand: Human Kinetics, P.O. Box 105-231, Auckland Central
09-523-3462

*For Nick and Helene
And Sam and Marion,
who gave us life
And for Carlton Greenbaum,
who gave us the green world to live it in.*

Acknowledgments

A book like this cannot be written without the help of dozens of naturalists, park staffers, tourism directors, volunteer trail workers, and friends too numerous to mention. Although our names are on the cover, this is really their book.

We would like to single out Lela Shaw, backcountry specialist at J & H Lanmark Store, in Lexington, Kentucky, for a special "attaboy." Her advice on places to hike and equipment to use has always been invaluable. Without her help, this book would be less than it is.

The good folks at Rollatape Measuring Systems, in Spokane, Washington, assured accurate trail distances by providing solid advice about measuring trails and a precision wheel to measure them with.

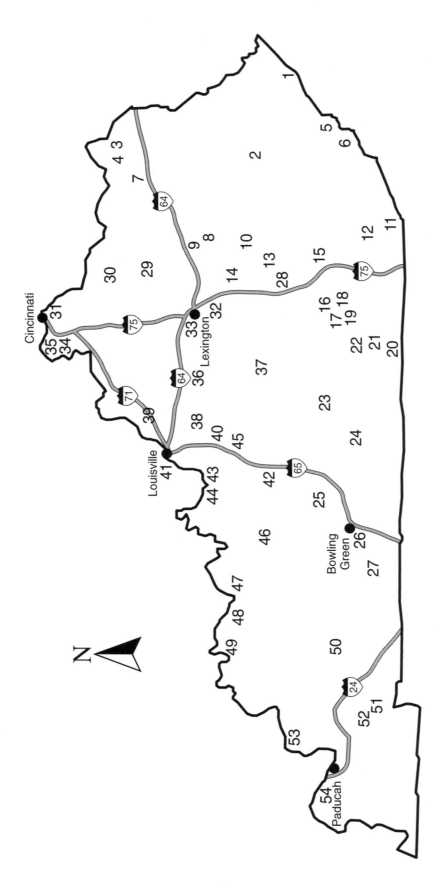

Contents

How to Use This Book

easiest   1   2   3   4   5   most difficult

Hiking is an antidote to modern life. It gives the body some much-needed (and enjoyable) exercise, and it gives the mind both rest and stimulation. It even lifts the spirit to connect again with this earth that we're a part of but seldom have time to think about. With the America's Best Day Hiking Series, we hope to provide you with an incentive to start or continue hiking, for the pleasure and the challenge of it.

Each book in the series offers information on more than 100 of the most interesting and scenic trails in a particular state, as well as notes about recreational, historical, and sightseeing destinations located near the trails. The assortment of trails ranges from short, easy hikes for occasional hikers and families with young children to longer, more rugged ones for the experienced trailblazer. None of the trails takes more than a day to hike, although some trails may be linked together to create a hike of several days.

The trails in *Hiking Kentucky* are divided into four main areas—Eastern Highlands, Scenic Wonderlands, Bluegrass Heartlands, and Western Waterlands. Within each area, trails are listed from east to west. Divider pages signal the beginning of each new area, and those pages include information on the local topography, major rivers and lakes, flora and fauna, weather, and best features of the area.

The innovative format is designed to make exploring new parks and trails easy. Information on each park or other nature area always appears on a right-hand page. It begins with the park's name and a small state map that shows the park's general location. Bulleted highlights then point out the trails' most interesting features. A description of the park's history and terrain comes next, with practical information on how to get to the park and the park's hours, available facilities, permits and rules, and the address and phone number of a contact who can give you more information. The section entitled "Other Points of Interest" briefly mentions nearby parks and recreational opportunities, with phone numbers to call for more information.

After the general information follows a selected list of trails in the park. The length and difficulty of hiking each is given, along with a brief description of its terrain. The difficulty rating, shown by boot icons, ranges from one (the easiest) to five (the most difficult).

On the other side of the page is a full-sized map of the park. Our book's larger format allows us to provide clear, readable maps that are easy to follow.

The next right- and left-hand pages are usually descriptions of the two best hikes in that park, along with a trail map at the bottom of each page (a few parks have only one hike, with just one map that primarily shows the trail). Each hike begins with information on the length and difficulty of the trail, and the estimated time to walk it, plus cautions to help you avoid possible annoyances or problems. The description of the trail provides more than directions; it's a guided tour of what you will see as you hike along. The scenery, wildlife, and history of the trail are all brought to life. Points of interest along the trail are numbered in brackets within the text, and those numbers are shown on the trail map to guide you. The approximate distance from the trailhead to each point of interest is given.

The park descriptions, maps, and trails are all kept as a unit within an even number of pages. Parks for which only one trail is highlighted take up only two pages; those with the regular two trails cover four pages. We've perforated the book's pages so you can remove them if you like, or you can copy them for your personal use. If you carry the pages with you as you hike, you might want to use a plastic sleeve to protect them from the elements. You also can make notes on these pages to remind you of your favorite parts of the park or trail.

If you want to find a park or trail quickly, use the trail finder that appears on the next pages. It gives essential information about each highlighted trail in the book, including the trail's length, difficulty, special features, and park facilities.

We hope the books in the America's Best Day Hiking Series inspire you to get out and enjoy a wide range of outdoor experiences. We've tried to find interesting trails from all parts of each state. Some are unexpected treasures—places you'd never dream exist in the state. Some may be favorites that you've already hiked and recommended to friends. But whether you live in a city or in the country, are away vacationing or are at home, some of these trails will be near you. Find one you like, strap on your hiking boots, and go!

Trail Finder

KEY

RV camping	tent camping	swimming	canoeing
fishing	boating	picnicking	biking

Trail Sites and Trails	Park Facilities	Miles	Trail Difficulty Rating	Hills	Prairie/Grass	Forest	Lake	Wetlands	Overlook	River/Stream	Page #
1 Breaks Interstate Park	RV, tent camping										
Chestnut Ridge Nature Trail	swimming, fishing	.66	🥾🥾🥾🥾	✓		✓			✓	✓	5
Overlook Trail	boating, picnicking, biking	1.50	🥾🥾🥾	✓		✓			✓		6
2 Jenny Wiley State Resort Park	RV, tent camping										
Steve Brackett Memorial Trail	swimming, fishing	2.43	🥾🥾🥾	✓		✓					9
Moss Ridge Hiking Trail	boating, picnicking	1.33	🥾🥾🥾	✓		✓	✓				10
3 Jesse Stuart State Nature Preserve											
Loop Trail		1.52	🥾🥾🥾	✓	✓	✓					12
4 Greenbo Lake State Resort Park	RV, tent camping										
Fern Valley Trail	swimming, canoeing	.87	🥾🥾🥾🥾	✓		✓	✓			✓	15
Michael Tygart Trail A	fishing, picnicking	7.2	🥾🥾🥾🥾	✓	✓	✓	✓	✓		✓	16
Michael Tygart Trail B	boating, biking	5.56	🥾🥾🥾	✓		✓					16
5 Bad Branch State Nature Preserve											
Waterfall Trail		2	🥾🥾🥾🥾🥾	✓		✓				✓	18
6 Kingdom Come State Park											
Lake/Laurel/Powerline/ Raven Rock/Groundhog/ Pine Trail Loop	tent camping, fishing, boating, picnicking	2	🥾🥾🥾🥾	✓		✓	✓			✓	21
Log Rock Trail		.5	🥾🥾🥾🥾	✓		✓			✓		22
7 Carter Caves State Resort Park	RV, tent camping, swimming, canoeing										
Red Trail	fishing, boating	3.2	🥾🥾🥾🥾🥾🥾	✓		✓	✓		✓		25
Cascade Cave Nature Trail	picnicking	.61	🥾🥾🥾🥾	✓		✓					26

Continued ☞

Continued ☞

Terrain/Landscape

#	Trail Sites and Trails	Park Facilities	Miles	Trail Difficulty Rating	Hills	Prairie/Grass	Forest	Lake	Wetlands	Overlook	River/Stream	Page #
16	**Bee Rock Recreation Area**											
	Rockcastle Narrows West		4.62	🥾🥾🥾🥾	✓		✓		✓		✓	63
	Bee Rock Overlook Loop		2.25	🥾🥾🥾🥾🥾	✓		✓			✓	✓	64
17	**Rockcastle Recreation Area**											
	Scuttle Hole Trail		1.9	🥾🥾🥾🥾	✓		✓		✓	✓		67
	Dutch Branch Trail		.75	🥾🥾🥾🥾🥾🥾	✓		✓		✓		✓	68
18	**Cumberland Falls State Resort Park**											
	Eagle Falls (Trail #9)		2.1	🥾🥾🥾🥾🥾	✓		✓				✓	71
	CCC Memorial Trail		.87	🥾🥾🥾	✓		✓					72
19	**Natural Arch Scenic Area**											
	Natural Arch Trail and Shawnee Nature Path		1.27	🥾🥾🥾	✓		✓			✓		75
	Chimney Arch Trail		2.44	🥾🥾	✓		✓					76
20	**Big South Fork National River and Recreation Area**											
	Blue Heron Loop		6.4	🥾🥾🥾	✓	✓	✓			✓	✓	81
	Catawba Overlook		3.5	🥾🥾🥾	✓		✓			✓	✓	82
21	**Beaver Creek Wilderness**											
	Three Forks of Beaver Loop		1.9	🥾🥾🥾	✓	✓	✓			✓	✓	85
	Bowman Ridge/Middle Ridge/Beaver Creek Wilderness Loop		4.06	🥾🥾🥾🥾	✓	✓	✓				✓	86
22	**Alpine Recreation Area**											
	Alpine Loop		1.1	🥾🥾🥾	✓	✓	✓				✓	89
	Alpine Spur		.69	🥾🥾🥾	✓		✓					90
23	**Lake Cumberland State Resort Park**											
	Lake Bluff Nature Trail (Short Loop)		2.1	🥾🥾🥾	✓		✓	✓		✓	✓	93
	Lake Bluff Nature Trail (Long Loop)		3.8	🥾🥾🥾🥾	✓		✓	✓		✓	✓	94
24	**Barren River Lake State Resort Park**											
	Lena Madison Phillips Trail		.6	🥾🥾🥾	✓		✓				✓	97
	Lewis Hill (Connell) Nature Trail		1.29	🥾🥾🥾🥾	✓	✓	✓	✓			✓	98

Continued ☞

	Trail Sites and Trails	Park Facilities	Miles	Trail Difficulty Rating	Hills	Prairie/Grass	Forest	Lake	Wetlands	Overlook	River/Stream	Page #
25	**Mammoth Cave National Park**	(icons)										
	Green River Bluffs Trail		1.8	🥾🥾🥾	✓	✓	✓			✓	✓	101
	River Styx Spring Trail		1.4	🥾🥾🥾🥾	✓		✓			✓	✓	102
26	**Lost River Valley and Cave**											
	Lost River Nature Trail		1.8	🥾🥾🥾	✓	✓	✓				✓	105
	Nature Trail/Cedar Trail Loop		.96	🥾🥾🥾	✓		✓				✓	106
27	**Logan County Glade State Nature Preserve**											
	Logan Glade Nature Trail		.53	🥾🥾	✓	✓	✓					108
28	**Berea College Forest**	(icons)										
	West Pinnacle Trail		2.9	🥾🥾🥾🥾🥾	✓		✓			✓	✓	113
	Indian Fort Lookout Trail		1.84	🥾🥾🥾🥾🥾	✓		✓			✓	✓	114
29	**Quiet Trails State Nature Preserve**											
	Challenger/Sassafras/Prairie Vista Loop		1.15	🥾🥾 or 🥾🥾🥾	✓	✓	✓				✓	117
	Deep Hollow/Challenger Loop		1.2	🥾🥾🥾	✓	✓	✓				✓	118
30	**Kincaid Lake State Park**	(icons)										
	Ironwood Trail		2.2	🥾🥾🥾🥾	✓	✓	✓	✓	✓		✓	121
	Spicebush Trail		1.76	🥾🥾🥾	✓		✓		✓		✓	122
31	**Fort Thomas Landmark Tree Trail**											
	Fort Thomas Landmark Tree Trail		.82	🥾🥾🥾	✓		✓				✓	124
32	**Raven Run Nature Sanctuary**	(icons)										
	Red Trail		4.2	🥾🥾🥾	✓	✓	✓			✓	✓	127
	Freedom Trail		.62/.45	🥾	✓	✓	✓				✓	128
33	**City of Lexington**	(icons)										
	Lexington Walk Tour		1.77	🥾🥾	✓							131
	Lexington Cemetery Tree Walk		1.22	🥾		✓						132
34	**Big Bone Lick State Park**	(icons)										
	Big Bone Creek (Diorama) Trail		.8	🥾🥾	✓	✓					✓	135
	Bison Trace Loop		1.1	🥾🥾	✓	✓					✓	136

Continued ☞

	Trail Sites and Trails	Park Facilities	Miles	Trail Difficulty Rating	Terrain/Landscape							
					Hills	Prairie/Grass	Forest	Lake	Wetlands	Overlook	River/Stream	Page #
35	**Boone County Cliffs State Nature Preserve**											
	Long Loop Trail		1.69	🥾🥾🥾🥾	✓		✓			✓	✓	139
	Short Loop Trail		.68	🥾🥾🥾🥾	✓		✓				✓	140
36	**Clyde E. Buckley Wildlife Sanctuary**	(camp, picnic)										
	Red Trail		1.5	🥾🥾🥾	✓	✓	✓				✓	143
	Blue Trail		1.06	🥾🥾	✓	✓	✓	✓			✓	144
37	**Central Kentucky Wildlife Refuge**	(camp, picnic)										
	Circle Trail		2.8	🥾🥾🥾🥾	✓	✓	✓	✓			✓	147
	Wildflower Trail		.5	🥾		✓	✓				✓	148
38	**Taylorville Lake State Park**	(RV, tent, boat, fishing, camp, picnic)										
	Beech Creek Loop A		2.6	🥾🥾🥾🥾🥾	✓	✓	✓		✓	✓	✓	150
39	**E.P. "Tom" Sawyer State Park**	(swim, picnic, bike)										
	Goose Creek Nature Trail		2.1	🥾🥾			✓	✓	✓		✓	152
40	**Bernheim Arboretum and Research Forest**	(fishing, boat, camp, picnic)										
	Jackson Hollow Loop		.88	🥾🥾🥾	✓	✓				✓	✓	155
	Double Cabin Hollow Loop		2.25	🥾🥾🥾🥾	✓		✓				✓	156
41	**City of Louisville**	(RV, tent, swim, boat, fishing, camp, picnic, bike)										
	Louisville Riverwalk		5.1	🥾						✓	✓	158
42	**Freeman Lake Park**	(boat, camp, picnic, bike)										
	Freeman Lake Trail		4.47	🥾🥾	✓	✓	✓	✓	✓		✓	161
	John Cox Pirtle Nature Trail		.38	🥾🥾	✓	✓	✓				✓	162
43	**Tioga Trails**	(camp, picnic)										
	Tioga Falls Trail		2.1	🥾🥾🥾	✓	✓	✓				✓	165
	Bridges to the Past		2.1	🥾🥾	✓	✓					✓	166
44	**Otter Creek Park**	(RV, tent, swim, fishing, camp, picnic, bike)										
	Yellow Trail		3.8	🥾🥾🥾🥾🥾	✓	✓	✓			✓	✓	169
	Red Trail		3.3/4.25	🥾🥾🥾🥾	✓	✓	✓		✓	✓	✓	170
45	**Vernon Douglas State Nature Preserve**											
	Vernon Douglas Nature Trail		3.4	🥾🥾🥾	✓	✓	✓				✓	172

Continued ☞

	Trail Sites and Trails	Park Facilities	Miles	Trail Difficulty Rating	Hills	Prairie/Grass	Forest	Lake	Wetlands	Overlook	River/Stream	Page #
46	**Rough River Dam State Resort Park**											
	Marina Trail		1.49	🥾🥾🥾	✓		✓	✓		✓	✓	175
	Folklore Nature Trail		.71	🥾🥾🥾	✓	✓	✓				✓	176
47	**Yellow Creek Park**											
	Adventure Trail (Blue)		1.2	🥾🥾	✓	✓	✓		✓	✓	✓	181
	Hidden Valley Trail		.58	🥾🥾	✓		✓			✓	✓	182
48	**Panther Creek Park**											
	Nature Center Trail		.61	🥾	✓		✓		✓		✓	184
49	**John James Audubon State Park**											
	Backcountry Loop		2+(1.4)	🥾🥾🥾🥾	✓		✓	✓	✓		✓	187
	Coffeetree/Woodpecker/ Warbler Road Loop		.96	🥾🥾🥾	✓		✓				✓	188
50	**Pennyrile Forest State Resort Park**											
	Lake Trail		2.7	🥾🥾🥾	✓		✓	✓	✓	✓		191
	Indian Bluffs/Clifty Creek Combined Loop		.93	🥾🥾🥾	✓		✓	✓			✓	192
51	**Lake Barkley State Resort Park**											
	Blue Springs Trail		1.6	🥾🥾🥾	✓	✓	✓	✓	✓		✓	195
	Lena Madesin Phillips Trail		1.25	🥾 & 🥾🥾🥾🥾	✓	✓	✓	✓	✓		✓	196
52	**Land Between the Lakes**											
	Hematite Lake Trail		2.4	🥾🥾🥾	✓		✓	✓	✓		✓	199
	Center Furnace Trail		.3	🥾🥾🥾	✓		✓					200
53	**Mantle Rock Nature Preserve**											
	Mantle Rock Trail		1.9	🥾🥾🥾	✓	✓	✓				✓	202
54	**Metropolis Lake State Nature Preserve**											
	Metropolis Lake Nature Trail		.72	🥾🥾🥾	✓		✓	✓			✓	204

Eastern Highlands

Kentucky's rough Eastern Highlands are enclosed by Tennessee and Virginia on the southeast, West Virginia on the northwest, the Ohio River on the north, and an imaginary line extending north from Tennessee west of I-75 to Crab Orchard, then on a jagged diagonal to Vanceburg on the Ohio River.

Topography

When Kentuckians say "mountains," they mean the Appalachian Plateau area of eastern Kentucky. Although superficially resembling the valley-ridge province of the Appalachian and Blue Ridge Mountains, the mountains of the Bluegrass state are not part of those chains.

Technically, eastern Kentucky is not composed of mountains at all. It is an eroded plain, similar to the Catskills in New York. The Appalachian Plateau has never undergone the metamorphic stresses typical of mountain building. Instead, it is a folded and faulted uplifting of carboniferous sediments that were deposited in shallow seas, lakes, and streambeds during the Mississippian and Pennsylvanian periods. The Cincinnati Arch uplifted these sediments, forcing them high above the Interior Low Plateaus and the Gulf Coastal Plain, which make up the rest of the state.

The extreme eastern and southeastern sections are underlain with vast seams of coal, much of which was extracted by open-pit mining. Under new laws, the land must be restored to its original contour, but the scarring and erosion of the hills is still evident in coal country.

The Pottsville Escarpment marks the western edge of the Appalachian Plateau, and its resistant sandstones, eroded by wind, rain, and the numerous creeks that flow through the region, have created the valley-ridge appearance. Rock formations here are typified by scarps (gentle slopes on one side, dropping off precipitously on the other), sheer cliffs, natural bridges, and rock-shelters—cavelike openings in the ridges that, given enough time, may become natural bridges.

The Knobs Physiographic Region is separate from the Pottsville Escarpment, although the topography is similar. The Knobs are individual sedimentary humps, which form a line down the western edge of the Pottsville Escarpment—similar to foothills. A great valley, running on a northeast and southwest line, divides the Knobs from the Escarpment.

It's the rock-shelters and natural bridges, however, that give the region its flavor. Most are formed when streams, eroding headward, cut into the softer rock underlying the resistant sandstone caps. Eventually, a rock-shelter forms.

If two rock-shelters form on opposing sides of a ridge, they eventually meet, forming a lighthouse. As the lighthouse enlarges, it is reclassified as an arch, but there is no established point when that happens.

Streams in the area—most of which are intermittent—lack the steep gradients expected in such terrain. Because of the ongoing uplifting of the Cincinnati Arch, the land is rising through the creeks, which, seeking to maintain their natural level, are flat and level.

Major Rivers

Although the Ohio River borders the Eastern Highlands, it is relatively unimportant to it. The Big Sandy, Licking, Kentucky, and Cumberland Rivers provide the major watersheds of the region. All four play important historical and geological roles in Kentucky's development; the Licking and Big Sandy watersheds formed the most popular natural paths into the interior for early settlers and explorers.

The preeminent stretch of white water in America is found here. The Levisa Branch of the Russell Fork, of the Big Sandy River, is Class IV and V water its entire length.

None of the watersheds in eastern Kentucky can be considered free running, as they all have been dammed for flood control, navigation, or hydroelectric generation purposes. This has, in turn, created large impoundments, including Paintsville, Fishtrap, Cave Run, Carr Fork, Grayson, Laurel, Woods Creek, and Buckhorn Lakes, among others. These lakes are available for recreational purposes, primarily fishing and recreational boating.

Common Plant Life

The Eastern Highlands have been extensively lumbered, usually by clear-cutting, over the past 150 years. Today they are typified by second-growth oak/hickory forests. Many trees have reached climax forest stage and are easily confused with old-growth.

Most of the 84 tree species that grow in Kentucky can be seen in the Eastern Highlands, with tulip poplar, sugar maple, beech, hackberry, and ash dominating. Among conifers are Virginia pine, white and red cedar, and hemlock. The understory is primarily redbud and flowering dogwood, but you'll also find vast areas where various magnolias predominate—including the umbrella magnolia, whose leaves stretch more than three feet long and two feet wide.

Rhododendron and mountain laurel grow profusely in large thickets, referred to locally as rhody hells.

More than 300 of the 400 wildflowers found in the Bluegrass state grow in the Eastern Highlands. Many are rarely or never seen outside the area.

Poison ivy is common in the Eastern Highlands, and many trails in the region are bordered by it. The hairy-vine form is, perhaps, more common and less recognized.

Common Birds and Mammals

More than 250 species of birds have been counted in the Eastern Highlands, ranging from cardinals, robins, and hummingbirds, to pileated woodpeckers and various hawks and owls. Blue jays, which had almost disappeared for a time, are once again common.

Eastern wild turkey, perhaps the greatest conservation story of the century, are common throughout the mountains.

Wood ducks and mallards are common in the region. There's also a large population of Canada geese in the Cave Run Lake area.

Resident mammals include white-tailed deer, raccoon, opossum, skunk, and predators such as red fox and coyote. Black bear, once common, had been eradicated, but are starting a comeback, notably in the southeast where they have migrated from Virginia. The best sighting possibility is anywhere on Pine Mountain, with Kingdom Come State Park offering the most likely spot to see the ursines.

Timber rattlers and copperheads are common in the region but are rarely seen on the trails. Cross-country travelers should take proper precautions. Black snakes, green racers, cow suckers, and several other varieties of nonpoisonous snakes inhabit the region. Except for garter snakes, these are rarely seen by most visitors.

Climate

Overall, Kentucky's climate is classed as humid, continental, hot summer. The elevation of the Eastern Highlands moderates this somewhat. Summers are cooler and moister than the rest of the state, and winters see more ice and snow.

The cooler winter temperatures combine with the scarps to produce dramatic icicles that hang 20 to 50 feet off the drip lines. Frozen waterfalls are another sight much looked for by wintertime hikers.

Rarely do summer temperatures rise above 90 degrees. Winter lows can extend into the single digits, but temperatures in the teens and 20s are more likely.

Best Features

- Hundreds of natural arches and bridges.
- Pine Mountain, extending more than 125 miles along the Virginia border.
- Cumberland Gap.
- Microhabitats with subtropical plants.
- High cliffs and rock-shelters.
- Red River Gorge Geologic Area.
- Pilot Knob.

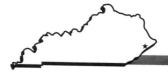

1. Breaks Interstate Park

- Descend into Breaks Gorge, the largest canyon east of the Mississippi River.
- Explore the human history of the region at the permanent outdoor exhibit near the Visitor Center.
- Try to discover John Swift's secret silver mine, said to be somewhere near The Towers.
- See rare plants, such as yellow lady's slipper.

Park Information

The 4,500 acres of Breaks Interstate Park sprawl across the Kentucky/Virginia border, along the Russell Fork of the Big Sandy River. Jointly administered by the two states, the park contains the largest canyon east of the Mississippi River. The gorge, carved through Pine Mountain by the Russell Fork, stretches more than 5 miles long and is as much as 1,600 feet deep—guarded by sheer walls most of the way. It's often called "the Grand Canyon of the South." The park takes its name from this gorge, which forms a "break" in Pine Mountain.

Crown jewel of the park is The Towers, an imposing pyramid of rocks more than a half mile long and a third of a mile wide, where the river describes a white water-filled horseshoe.

Because of elevation and moisture differences, the park contains various biospheres, ranging from oak/hickory climax forests on the drier ridgetops to a laurel/hemlock environment in the bottoms and along the creeks. This biodiversity results in an amazing display of spring wildflowers, including rare plants like yellow lady's slipper and Catawba rhododendron.

Caves, balanced rocks, "hidden" springs, and towering sandstone cliffs abound in this mountainous country, while white-water enthusiasts run the river almost every month of the year.

Rich in human history, the region was a hunting ground for Cherokee and Shawnee Indians. Pioneers like Daniel Boone and Simon Kenton explored here in the last quarter of the 18th century. The area around The Towers is said to contain the lost silver mine of Englishman John Swift.

In the late 1700s, Swift supposedly had one or more silver mines that were subsequently lost. He spent the last part of his life trying to refind them. The lost mines are one of the great—and recurring—legends of southeastern Kentucky. If you're interested, you can buy a genuine map of their locations, drawn by John Swift himself.

Directions: From Elkhorn City, take KY-80 south to the Virginia border. Follow VA-80 to the park gates at VA-702. Breaks is 7 miles south of Elkhorn City and 8 miles north of Haysi, Virginia.

Hours Open: Open year-round.

Facilities: Lodge, restaurant, Visitor Center, swimming pool, horseback stable, campground, picnic shelters.

Permits and Rules: Permit necessary for overnight use of the backcountry.

Further Information: Contact Breaks Interstate Park, P.O. Box 100, Breaks, VA 24607; 703-865-4413.

Other Points of Interest

Bad Branch State Nature Preserve (see park #5) and **Kingdom Come State Park** (see park #6) are within 1 1/2 hours southeast. **Jenny Wiley State Resort Park** (see park #2) is 1 1/2 hours north.

Pikeville, 45 minutes north, is the locale of the infamous Hatfield-McCoy feud. Contact the Pike Country Tourism Commission (606-432-5063) for details.

Park Trails

There are 12 miles of hiking trails in the park, most of them moderate to difficult.

Cold Spring Trail 🥾🥾🥾—.5 miles each way—follows a streambed from the Cold Spring to Laurel Branch Trail.

River Trail 🥾🥾🥾🥾🥾—1 mile each way—leads from the ridge level down to the river, and follows it. The first half is extremely strenuous.

Laurel Branch Trail 🥾🥾🥾🥾—1.25 miles each way—follows the stream it is named for throughout its length; the last half mile is steep, rocky, and uneven.

Prospector's Trail 🥾🥾🥾—1.5 miles each way—follows the base of the cliffs more than 350 feet below the major overlooks.

Breaks Interstate Park

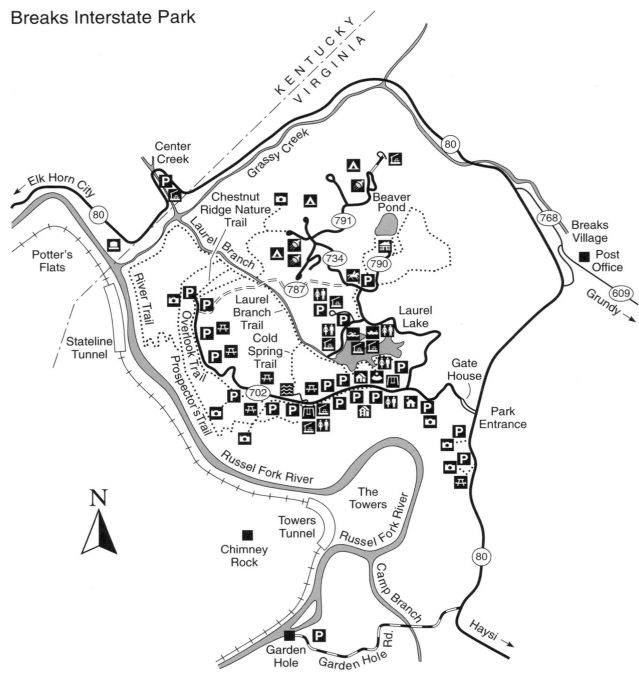

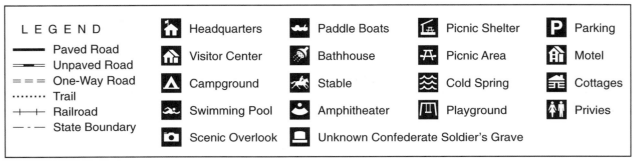

LEGEND

— Paved Road
=== Unpaved Road
= = = One-Way Road
⋯⋯ Trail
+++ Railroad
–·–·– State Boundary

🏠 Headquarters
🏠 Visitor Center
⛺ Campground
🏊 Swimming Pool
📷 Scenic Overlook

🛶 Paddle Boats
🚿 Bathhouse
🐎 Stable
♟ Amphitheater
▪ Unknown Confederate Soldier's Grave

⛺ Picnic Shelter
⛺ Picnic Area
〜 Cold Spring
🎠 Playground

🅿 Parking
🏨 Motel
🏢 Cottages
👫 Privies

Chestnut Ridge Nature Trail

Distance Round-Trip: .66 miles

Estimated Hiking Time: 60 to 90 minutes

Cautions: Watch for exposed rocks and roots. You will do some rock hopping and stream crossing.

Trail Directions: Chestnut Ridge Nature Trail uses a short section of Laurel Branch Trail to connect the Ridge and Geologic Trails into a well-interpreted loop, with 30 identified sites along the route.

The trailhead **[1]** is at the State Line Overlook parking lot. A short path through an oak/hickory climax forest leads to the junction of the Ridge and Geologic Trails. Go straight, following the ridgeline. Along the way you'll see oaks, magnolias, laurel, rhododendron, and sassafras, until mile .17, where the trail starts descending steeply **[2]**. The plant communities change, as you descend, to hemlock, basswood, yellow birch, and sugar maple.

At mile .21 are the remains of a chestnut log **[3]**. Chestnuts covered the Appalachian hillsides until a blight wiped them out. This log is mute evidence of an imported disease that killed every chestnut in America.

The trail levels out at mile .23, where, on your left, is a 40-foot-wide minicanyon **[4]**. Barely a crack in the earth where you stand, the gorge widens and deepens as it descends to its own floor. You'll soon be lower than that apparent bottom.

The trail descends again, through a laurel thicket that arches overhead, forming a cool, green tunnel. You'll bottom out on the banks of Laurel Branch Creek at mile .27 **[5]**. Listen carefully to the rocks here, trying to tune out the creek. There's a spring there that during the dry months does not exit the cliff, but you can hear it flowing along its hidden passages.

Turn left, and follow the creek—sometimes wading in it—to the Geologic Trail at mile .34 **[6]**. Until now, flora—the changing plant communities and the wildflowers that grow in profusion—have been the appealing feature of the trail. You'll still see plants and trees. But their interest pales in comparison to the rocks and geologic formations that predominate as you ascend back to the ridge.

Turn left onto the Geologic Trail. Although very rocky, it climbs more gradually than the Ridge Trail. At mile .4, look down and to the left, where you'll see a vaguely nose-shaped rock **[7]**. Give it several

thousand more years, and one of two things will happen: wind and water will carve a full face into the cliff, or the nose will break off and tumble down the slope. For now, let your imagination shape the face that nature is carving.

A short distance further, at mile .406, is a fossilized logjam **[8]** in the rock above you. The imprints of a seed fern and a horsetail tree are clearly evident. These trees were carried downstream and deposited here about 250 million years ago. You might have seen modern trees forming a similar jam down on Laurel Branch Creek.

A few steps further you'll pass through some high rocks. Look behind you to see the twin towers, putting you in mind of Tolkien's *Rings* trilogy. The bare starkness of the surrounding rocks easily transports you "to the land of Mordor, where the shadows lie."

The shadows lie even deeper at mile .5 as you pass under a natural tunnel **[9]**. Sometime in the geologic past, the roof fractured. Later, a spearhead-shaped rock dropped straight into the crack, point downward. Despite its appearance, there is no danger of the spearhead's falling; it's wedged solidly in place.

At mile .55, the darkness is brightened by a splash of color on the rocks **[10]**. Mosses and lichens have produced a dark green wash, and the shadows seem to lift and dissipate. The trail continues climbing gradually from here until mile .6, where you ascend a wooden stairway **[11]** and return to the trailhead.

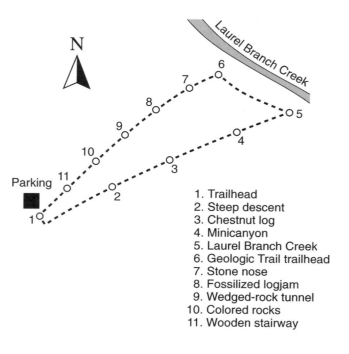

1. Trailhead
2. Steep descent
3. Chestnut log
4. Minicanyon
5. Laurel Branch Creek
6. Geologic Trail trailhead
7. Stone nose
8. Fossilized logjam
9. Wedged-rock tunnel
10. Colored rocks
11. Wooden stairway

Overlook Trail 👢👢👢

Distance Round-Trip: 1.50 miles

Estimated Hiking Time: 60 to 90 minutes

Cautions: Be careful on high cliffs; watch for exposed rocks and roots.

Trail Directions: The Overlook Trail runs along the edge of the cliffs, providing almost continuous views into Breaks Gorge, the largest canyon east of the Mississippi River. There are frequent changes in grade, and many of the edges have no railings.

The trailhead **[1]** is at the State Line Overlook. From there you look down into the canyon, with the Russell Fork River almost 1,000 feet below you. The railroad tunnel slightly to your right marks the Kentucky/Virginia border. If your timing is right, you'll see (and hear) coal trains—multi-engined diesels hauling as many as 100 gondolas filled with coal to heat the world.

Seeing that, you have to agree with Dave Brower, former director of the Sierra Club, who always felt that while a road though the wilderness was a sacrilege, a rail line somehow fit.

Follow the green blazes south along the cliff edge. At mile .32 you'll reach the Pinnacle Overlook **[2]**. It's amazing the difference in perspective a few feet can make. From here, parallel ridges stretch out forever. The railroad is a faint rusty line along the river, while the mouth of State Line Tunnel is an arched black shadow against the paving stones. Midstream, a large column—Pinnacle Rock—rises from the water.

At mile .5, the trail touches the park road **[3]**, then climbs steeply on railroad-tie steps back to the cliff edge. The trail plays leapfrog with the road several times like this until mile .64, where it reaches the parking lot **[4]** for Clinchfield Overlook. From there it's still quite some distance, down multiple wooden stairways, to Clinchfield Overlook **[5]** at mile .75.

By now you'd think the views into the canyon would be old hat. Such is not the case. The changes in angle and light conditions provide never-quite-the-same vistas, while cloud shadows play Johnny-on-the-pony with the serrated ridges.

From Clinchfield, too, are close-up views of carved and shaped rock outcrops, projecting from the cliff edges. You can dream these rocks into all sorts of real and fanciful figures, a game that can be even better than dreaming the clouds.

Retrace your steps, or follow the park road, back to the trailhead.

1. Trailhead
2. Pinnacle Overlook
3. Park road
4. Clinchfield Overlook parking lot
5. Clinchfield Overlook

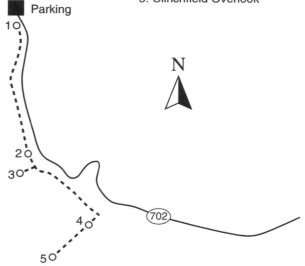

2. Jenny Wiley State Resort Park

- Walk in the footsteps of a pioneer heroine who escaped Indian captivity and made her way home alone.

- Experience the totality of a moist Appalachian environment that includes Christmas fern, ground cedar, pawpaws, and numerous wildflowers in addition to the dominant trees like maples, hemlocks, and tulip poplars.

- Watch wildlife, including deer, wild turkey, and small mammals, undisturbed on the park's little-used hiking trails.

Park Information

Jenny Wiley State Resort Park is named for Virginia Sellards "Jenny" Wiley, a pioneer woman who was captured by Cherokees in 1789 at Ab's Valley, Virginia, after seeing most of her family slain. After several months, she escaped while camped along Little Mud Lick Creek, near Paintsville, and made her way home in the spring of 1790. This saga is considered one of the two most dramatic captivity tales in Kentucky history—the other being the rescue of Jemima Boone and the Callaway girls from Shawnee raiders in July 1776.

Later, Jenny and her husband moved to the Paintsville area and raised a family there. Her grave is in a small cemetery in nearby River, Kentucky. The trailhead and 4 miles of the 164-mile-long Jenny Wiley Trail, which retraces the route of her captivity and escape, lie within the park, with the terminus on the Ohio River at South Portsmouth.

Nestled in the heart of the eastern Kentucky coalfields, the park flows along the shore of Dewey Lake, a 1,100-acre flood-control impoundment offering fishing, camping, picnicking, and water sports—including a Corps of Engineers campground accessible only by boat. The lake was formed by the damming of Johns Creek, a tributary of the Levisa Fork, America's most challenging white water.

Visitors can get an overview of the park and surrounding mountains by taking the sky lift to the top of Sugar Camp Mountain. Unfortunately, it is open only from mid-May to Labor Day, then on weekends in September and October.

Directions: From the Martin/Hazard exit of US-23 near Prestonsburg, take KY-302 north 3.8 miles to the park entrance; then go another mile to May Lodge.

Hours Open: Open year-round, but some facilities have seasonal days and hours. Trails close at dusk.

Facilities: Lodge and restaurant, cottages, Conference Center, campground, outdoor theater, swimming pool, picnic grounds, golf, boating, sky lift.

Permits and Rules: Only foot travel on trails.

Further Information: Contact Jenny Wiley State Resort Park, HC 66 Box 200, Prestonsburg, KY 41653; 606-886-2711.

Other Points of Interest

The Mountain Homeplace (606-297-1521) at Paintsville Lake State Park is a living-history museum that recreates a post-Civil War farmstead.

Pikeville was the site of the infamous Hatfield-McCoy feud. Contact the Pike County Tourism Commission (606-432-5063) for details.

Butcher Hollow (606-789-3397), in nearby Van Lear, is the birthplace of country singing star Loretta Lynn. Also near Van Lear is the **Coal Camp Museum** (606-789-4759), which depicts life in the coal camps during the 1920s and 1930s.

Park Trails

There are approximately 9 miles of hiking trails in the park, many of them fairly strenuous. Because of the trail difficulty and remoteness, do not hike the Jenny Wiley Trail alone. Most visitors are oriented to the lake and resort activities, so the trails see relatively little use. As a result, wildlife watching can be an especially rewarding experience.

Jenny Wiley Trail 👢👢👢👢👢—4.5 miles each way—starts in the park and continues for 164 miles to the Ohio River, along the route taken by Jenny Wiley's Indian captors.

Lakeshore Hiking Trail 👢👢👢—2.5-mile loop—follows the shore of Dewey Lake, then returns via the park road.

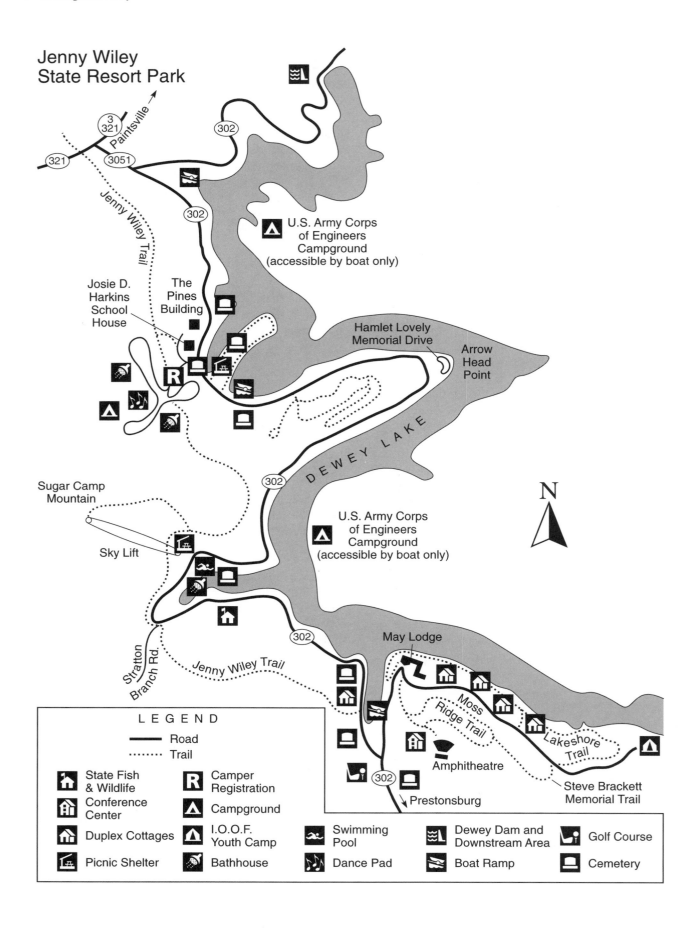

Jenny Wiley State Resort Park

LEGEND

— Road

····· Trail

State Fish & Wildlife

Conference Center

Duplex Cottages

Picnic Shelter

R Camper Registration

Campground

I.O.O.F. Youth Camp

Bathhouse

Swimming Pool

Dance Pad

Dewey Dam and Downstream Area

Boat Ramp

Golf Course

Cemetery

Steve Brackett Memorial Trail

Distance Round-Trip: 2.43 miles

Estimated Hiking Time: 1.5 to 2 hours

Cautions: Watch for drop-offs and exposed rocks and roots.

Trail Directions: To find the trailhead, drive from the lodge, past the cabins, to the Oddfellows Youth Camp fence, and park there. Walk through the gate and follow the road .27 miles. The walk to the trailhead, combined with the fact that the trail is longer than the park says, makes the total hike almost a mile more than you expect from the official literature.

The trailhead [1] is marked by a monument to Steve Brackett, a well-known eastern Kentucky forester. The trail climbs very steeply, with several switchbacks, through open woods of very young second growth. The shrub layer, in fact, is more interesting than the trees—which is ironic, considering that the trail is named for someone who personally planted more than 6,000 trees.

The slope flattens at mile .38, and during the leafless months there are spectacular views of the mountains [2], with one ridge climbing higher than the next until they fade from view somewhere in West Virginia.

The woods begin to thicken, but still remain open. At mile .5, watch for the burned-out stump and log [3], now a denning site where birds and small mammals make homes in the hollows. The fire that destroyed it (and much of the hillside forest) has left a high-graphic picture behind, with the black soot highlighted by cracks, crevices, and openings in the stump. In the natural world, even destruction can evoke beauty.

At mile .53, a deep hollow appears on your right [4]. Stay particularly alert here for wildlife. Wild turkey, especially, find this an appealing spot. But you're just as likely to spot deer, small mammals, and numerous songbirds. Continue along the edge of this hollow until mile .59, where the trail turns left and climbs. A large patch of royal fern [5] marks the turn, with additional patches on the hillside above. About

a hundred feet further the effects of the burn diminish and some old-growth trees appear, predominantly beeches. The trees grow older as the trail gets higher.

A cubical slump block (a chunk of rock that has fallen from the cliff and migrated) on the left at mile .83 [6] is covered with some unusually long and luxurious moss—long enough, in fact, to wave in any kind of a breeze. This effect, almost like seaweed undulating in a gentle current, is even more apparent on a rotted log flanking the trail on the right.

The trail gets very steep ahead, with erosion steps, until it tops out and levels off. A little further, at mile .93, you reach the chain rocks [7]. Imagine an abandoned logging chain in a world where Paul Bunyan is the smallest man. Instead of rusting, the chain somehow petrifies. It would look exactly like this row of eroded sandstone blocks.

To the right, during leafless months, there's a panoramic view of the mountains forming a horseshoe on three sides. The lake can just be made out, twinkling far below.

A bit further, at mile 1.2, the trail ends at a junction with the Moss Ridge Hiking Trail. Return by retracing your steps.

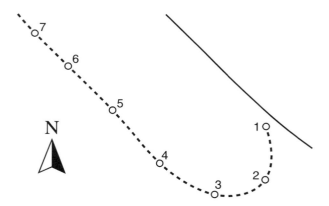

1. Trailhead
2. Mountain views
3. Burned stump
4. Wild turkey hollow
5. Royal ferns
6. Mossy slump block
7. Chain rocks

Moss Ridge Hiking Trail

👢👢👢👢

Distance Round-Trip: 1.33 miles

Estimated Hiking Time: 1 hour

Cautions: Watch for drop-offs and exposed rocks and roots.

Trail Directions: Moss Ridge is a loop trail that takes you to the top of the mountain and back down. The wildlife viewing and bird-watching, frankly, are better than the scenery. Owls and pileated woodpeckers are common, and more than 200 bird species have been counted along this trail.

The trailhead [1] is just beyond the last unit in the lodge. The trail starts as a gravel path through second-growth woods, climbing steadily. The gravel runs out in 150 feet.

At mile .16, a side trail [2] comes in on the left. This is actually the return loop, so stay to the right. Then at mile .2, the trail forms a Y [3]. The path to the right would take you to the park amphitheater. Go left and descend about 800 feet, at which point the trail turns left and climbs steeply.

You'll seem to top out at mile .4, on a moss carpet [4]. Follow this emerald road, and soon enough you will start climbing again. You'll top out at the base of a low sandstone cliff at mile .66 [5]. Lighter than the surrounding rock, this cliff has several small caves, and the extreme base is strongly undercut. Past the cliff the trail climbs again, until you crest out at the junction with the Steve Brackett Trail [6] at mile .71.

You might want to take a side trip on the Steve Brackett Trail to the chain rocks [7], only about 500 feet further at mile .8. Imagine an abandoned logging chain in a world where Paul Bunyan is the smallest man. Instead of rusting, the chain somehow petrifies. The result would look like this row of eroded sandstone blocks.

Be sure to look behind you as well. During leafless months, the mountains can be seen in a giant horseshoe, reflecting in Dewey Lake just visible far below. Return to Moss Ridge Hiking Trail. You can get this same view of the mountains as you follow the trail, until reaching the radio and television antennae at mile .9 [8]. The trail descends more steeply from there, passing through a rock garden 200 feet further that may necessitate some rock hopping.

At mile 1.08, the trail makes a hard right and follows the edge of a large hollow [9] on the left. There are steep drop-offs here, so watch children carefully.

You'll T into the main trail at mile 1.17 [2]. Turn right and return to the trailhead.

As already noted, Moss Ridge is more impressive for its wildlife-watching potential than for its views. So you may want to allow more than the straight walking time in order to take advantage of those possibilities. Moving slowly, you are likely to see deer, wild turkey, and possibly foxes and coyotes as well as birds and small mammals.

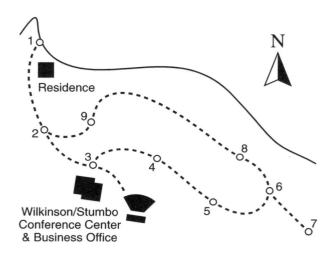

1. Trailhead
2. Return loop
3. Amphitheater Y
4. Moss carpet
5. Sandstone cliff
6. Junction with Steve Brackett Trail
7. Chain rocks
8. Radio and television antennae and rock garden
9. Large hollow

3. Jesse Stuart State Nature Preserve

- Walk in the woods and hollows immortalized by Kentucky poet laureate Jesse Stuart.
- See the natural process of succession, from meadow to climax forest, as it happens.
- Explore the human history of W-Hollow, including the site of Charlie's Cabin and the cabin where Jesse Stuart did some of his writing.

Park Information

Jesse Stuart State Nature Preserve protects 733 acres of the woods and fields that were home, and inspiration, to Kentucky's poet laureate and Pulitzer Prize nominee Jesse Stuart. The preserve protects those places he described so lovingly in books such as *Man With a Bull-Tongue Plow* and *Tales From the Plum Grove Hills*.

The preserve consists of pasture, old fields, and second-growth woods. The management philosophy is to maintain the land in its natural wild state, which is what Stuart envisioned for his land.

The literary aspect of the nature preserve is a major attraction for visitors, many of whom merely want to walk through the woods and experience the actual places the author immortalized in his novels and poetry. Often, people come merely to read his works at the site where they were written.

Directions: From exit 172 off I-64 (15 miles west of Ashland), take KY-1 north 19 miles to the historic marker for W-Hollow. Turn left and go about 1.5 miles to the park entrance.

Hours Open: Open year-round; trails are open from sunrise to sunset.

Facilities: None.

Permits and Rules: No camping or fires.

Further Information: Contact Kentucky State Nature Preserves Commission, 801 Schenkel Lane, Frankfort, KY 40601; 502-573-2886.

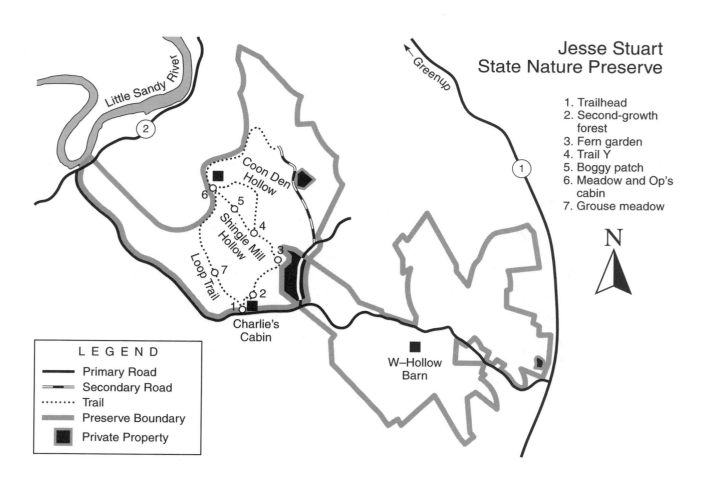

Jesse Stuart
State Nature Preserve

1. Trailhead
2. Second-growth forest
3. Fern garden
4. Trail Y
5. Boggy patch
6. Meadow and Op's cabin
7. Grouse meadow

LEGEND
— Primary Road
═ Secondary Road
····· Trail
▬ Preserve Boundary
■ Private Property

Loop Trail

Distance Round-Trip: 1.52 miles

Estimated Hiking Time: 1 hour

Cautions: Watch for exposed rocks and roots and boggy areas.

Trail Directions: This is a strenuous trail through parts of W-Hollow, a place that inspired Kentucky poet laureate Jesse Stuart and that he immortalized in his writings. "If I could have chosen the spot [to inhabit] in Kentucky, I would have chosen W-Hollow," he wrote. "Where the hills form a semi-circle barrier against roads, and there is only one way to get out."

Stuart loved the deep hollows of this country, which "hid the mayapple, Yellowroot, ginseng, wild sweet Williams, baby tear, and phlox." You'll see all these and more as you climb in and out of several hollows and across the ridges.

The trailhead **[1]** is at a fence gate at the north side of the parking lot, shaded by a crab apple tree. To your right is the site of Charlie's Cabin (which Stuart often wrote about), which is unfortunately no longer standing.

The trail starts through an overgrown meadow. Go right, descending and looping around a large oak. At mile .04, you'll cross a drain on a plank and enter a second-growth hardwood forest **[2]**. Note the mature trees mixed in with the young second-growth oak, hickory, and poplar. The goal of the preserve is to eventually have all the trees mature. The ones you are looking at were, for some reason, spared when the area was logged.

The trail ascends steadily through the hush of cathedral-like trees towering overhead until you reach a fern garden **[3]** at mile .15. You'll soon level out, cross a pipeline right-of-way, and descend, following the lip of a long hollow; you'll bottom out at the lip of a gorge at mile .39. Follow the gorge, switching back left and then right as you descend to a creek and then climb. At mile .56, the trail forms a Y **[4]**. To the right is Coon Den Hollow, named for the many coons Stuart and his friends hunted there. To the left is Shingle Mill Hollow, where for many years a water-operated mill produced wood shingles for surrounding houses. Take that trail.

The trail climbs above the hollow, but follows it until reaching a side hollow and boggy patch at mile .69 **[5]**, where it steepens. This is a particularly good spot for spring wildflowers.

At mile .86, you'll top out in a meadow **[6]**. The Coon Den Hollow trail comes in on the right. Out in the meadow is Op's Cabin—a clapboard shack where Jesse Stuart did much of his writing. It would be nice if the cabin were preserved and maintained as a museum, but such is not the case. It just sits there, in the field, a mute testimony to one man's creativity.

Rejoin the trail, which descends, passing old cedar fence posts and rusty, vine-encrusted barbed wire—another indication of the area's human history. Farms once flourished here. At mile 1.47 **[7]** you'll reach what appears to be an old clear-cut (an area where loggers cut down every tree). It's actually the head of the first meadow, being slowly reclaimed by the forest. Be alert here, as grouse favor this area and you may be treated to an explosive flush as the russet bombshells take off.

Continue through the meadow to the trailhead.

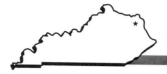

4. Greenbo Lake State Resort Park

- Walk a trail interpreted through the words of Kentucky poet laureate Jesse Stuart, who lived and wrote in the area all his life.
- Explore the remains of cabins and farmsteads dating back to the early 1800s.
- Watch the food chain at work in the lake, as dragonflies catch mosquitoes, baitfish catch the dragonflies, bass catch the baitfish, and people catch the bass—all in a lake the "experts" said couldn't be built.

Park Information

Greenbo Lake State Resort Park got its start back in 1952, when some area sportsmen thought it would be nice to have a local bass lake. Many "experts" fought the idea, claiming that the area wouldn't hold water and that even if it did, the land was too infertile and the banks too steep to provide spawning areas.

Nevertheless, the project went ahead. The Greenbo Lake Association raised $110,000, and the Kentucky Department of Fish and Wildlife Resources kicked in another $125,000 to complete the project. The state then acquired more than 3,300 acres surrounding the 192-acre lake to create the park. Greenbo Lake subsequently produced two state-record largemouth bass. So much for "experts."

The area surrounding the lake is primarily second-growth hardwoods, with many steep hills and hollows. This is Jesse Stuart country. The poet laureate of Kentucky and Pulitzer Prize nominee spent all his life wandering these wooded hillsides, taking inspiration from them, and writing about the land and the people who occupied it.

Much of what is now the park was occupied in the past, and you can still find the remains of old houses and cabins (many of them from the early 1800s) decaying in the woods. The old farm fields provide meadow ecosystems within the deep woods. Deer, wild turkey, and small mammals abound, especially along the edges created where forests and fields meet.

Don't be surprised if the farms surrounding the park look familiar. Change comes slowly to the mountains of eastern Kentucky, and large parts of the settled areas look as though they had come right out of *The Waltons*. Indeed, the star of the show was raised just a few miles to the south. Goodnight, John Boy!

Directions: From exit 172 off I-64 (15 miles west of Ashland), take KY-1 north 14 miles to the park access road; then go 3 miles further to the park itself. Trailheads are located at the lodge and near the lake marina.

Hours Open: Open year-round. Trails close at dusk.

Facilities: Lodge and cabins, campground, picnic areas, golf, swimming pool, beach; boating and fishing on Greenbo Lake.

Permits and Rules: Only foot travel on trails.

Further Information: Contact Manager, Greenbo Lake State Resort Park, HC 60 Box 562, Greenup, KY 41144; 606-473-7324.

Other Points of Interest

Carter Caves State Resort Park (see park #7) is 15 miles west. **Jesse Stuart State Nature Preserve** (see park #3) is 5 miles north.

Grayson Lake State Park (606-474-9727), 35 miles south, has camping, boating, picnicking, a beach, and a nature trail.

Ashland, 15 miles east, has numerous cultural attractions, such as the Kentucky Highlands Museum, Paramount Performing Arts Center, and Indian burial mounds. Contact Ashland Area Convention and Visitors Bureau (606-329-1007) for details.

Park Trails

There are more than 9 miles of trail at Greenbo Lake State Resort Park, most of them on either the Fern Valley Trail or the Michael Tygart Loop Trail.

Segment of Michael Tygart Trail 👢👢👢—3-mile loop—is an abbreviated version of the Michael Tygart Trail that uses the park road to create a loop starting and ending at the lodge.

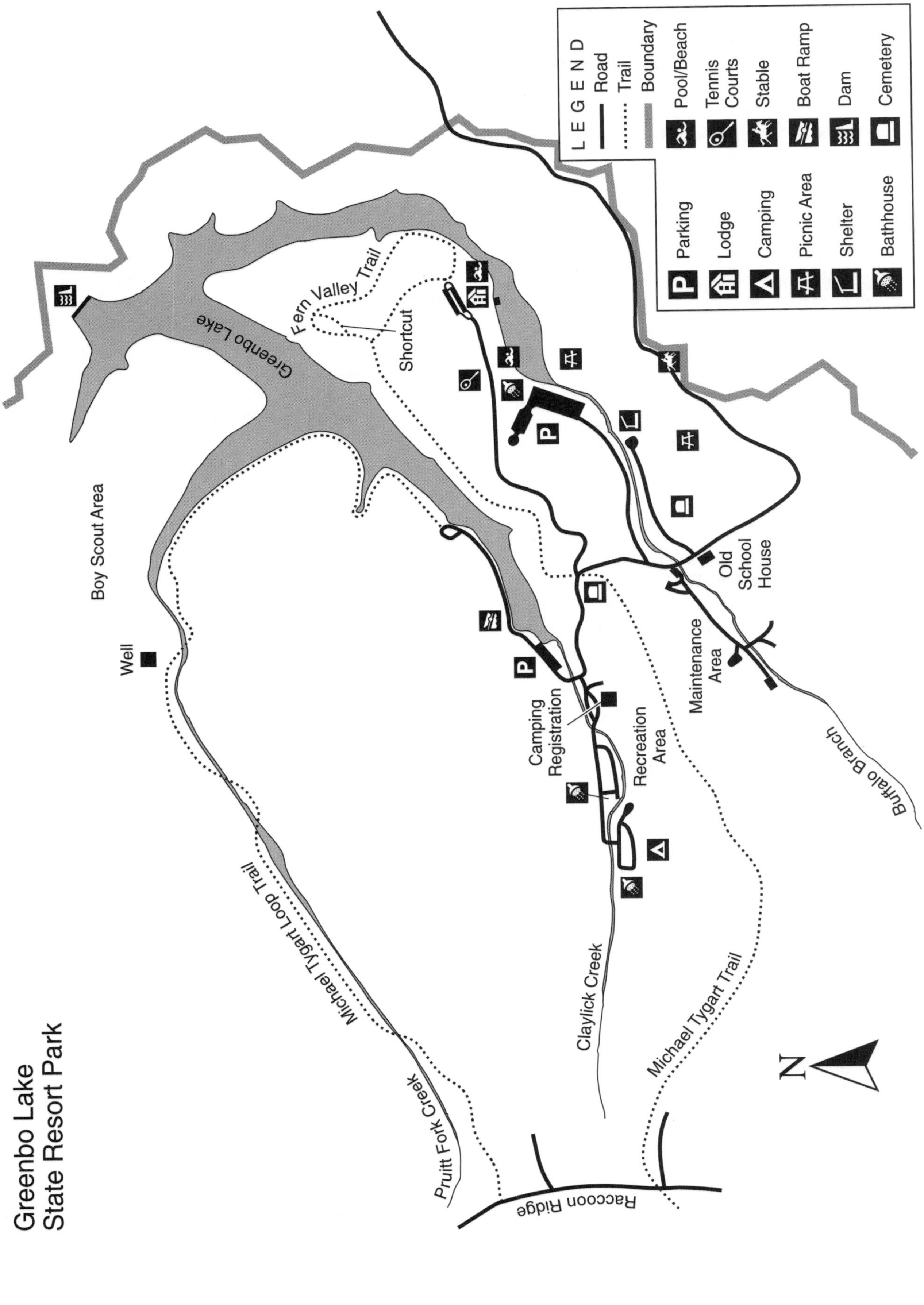

Greenbo Lake
State Resort Park

Greenbo Lake

Fern Valley Trail

Shortcut

Boy Scout Area

Well

Michael Tygart Loop Trail

Pruitt Fork Creek

Camping
Registration

Recreation
Area

Claylick Creek

Michael Tygart Trail

Maintenance
Area

Old
School
House

Buffalo Branch

Raccoon Ridge

N

LEGEND

Road
Trail
Boundary

Parking
Lodge
Camping
Picnic Area
Shelter
Bathhouse

Pool/Beach
Tennis Courts
Stable
Boat Ramp
Dam
Cemetery

Fern Valley Trail 👢👢👢👢

Distance Round-Trip: .87 miles

Estimated Hiking Time: 40 to 60 minutes

Cautions: None.

Trail Directions: A short trail with several steep sections, especially near the trailheads, it is best hiked with a copy of the trail guide available at the lodge desk. The guide uses the words of Kentucky poet laureate Jesse Stuart, along with those of a naturalist, to interpret the land you'll be passing through. There are 16 identified sites. Be sure to return the pamphlet to the lodge. There are only a few copies, and they are provided to hikers on loan.

The trailhead **[1]** is east of Jesse Stuart Lodge. The trail climbs very gradually, with the Buffalo Branch arm of Greenbo Lake just visible through the trees below on your right. Very shortly you'll reach the first interpretive station at mile .08 **[2]**. The prose refers to club moss, a plant dating back 400 million years, which covers the hillside. Jesse Stuart says, "Kentucky is my land. It is a place beneath the wind and sun in the very heart of America." But the club moss was there long before the poet, long before Daniel Boone, long before the Shawnee and Cherokee, and long before any other human being had walked the land.

At mile .22, the trail forms a Y. The Michael Tygart short loop goes left. Fern Valley Trail goes right and climbs steadily, passing more interpretive sites. At site #5, for instance, is a dead beech tree that serves as a denning ground for raccoons, opossums, and squirrels which nest in its hollows. "I hunted the wild game in hunting seasons, Skillful as an Indian . . . ," Stuart recalls of this site. You'll top out at mile .34 near an old family burial plot (site #7) **[3]**. "As I observed the closeness of the tombstones, In the eastern cemeteries, This gave me a feeling that land was scarce . . . ," says the poet. The placement of graves, as the six headstones here demonstrate, was given special consideration. Burying on ridgetops meant that loved ones would be that much closer to heaven.

The trail steepens a bit and then descends into Fern Hollow at mile .46 **[4]**. The hollow (and trail) takes its name from the numerous Christmas ferns that grow on its slopes. Stuart doesn't mention them, concentrating instead on the wildflowers that grow in springtime abundance: "The deep hollows . . . hid the mayapple, Yellowroot, ginseng, wild sweet William's, baby tear and phlox. . . ."

At mile .67, the small creek you've been following enters the lake at a marshy backwater (site #13) **[5]**. "I followed the little streams, That flowed over rocks between the high hills to the rivers, And then somewhere into the unknown world." We spooked a deer here and then watched a bass jump clear of the water to catch a dragonfly that was itself chasing skeeters in the dappling sun. We'd seen that image for years, as part of outdoor calendar art. But this was the first time we'd seen it actually happen.

The trail now follows the lakeshore. The entire watershed of Greenbo Lake lies within the park boundaries, including its three primary feeder streams: Buffalo Branch, Pruitt Fork Creek, and Claylick Creek. This provides a rare opportunity to limit human influence and protect the water quality in the lake. At mile .82 you reach a bench **[6]**. There's a hard climb in front of you, so you might want to rest here for a few minutes, watch the lake, and consider the words of Jesse Stuart and the world he's just described for you.

Shortly after you leave the bench, a false trail continues around the lakeshore. Fern Valley Trail turns hard right and starts climbing very steeply, partially on a set of stairs. At mile .87 you top out at a secondary trailhead, which lies a few feet from the one you entered.

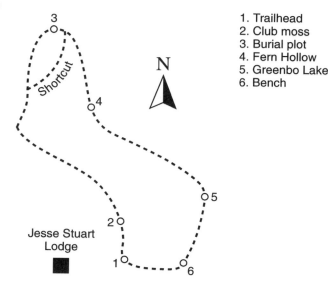

1. Trailhead
2. Club moss
3. Burial plot
4. Fern Hollow
5. Greenbo Lake
6. Bench

Michael Tygart Trail A 👢👢👢👢

Distance Round-Trip: 7.2 miles

Estimated Hiking Time: 4 to 5 hours

Cautions: Watch for fallen trees across the trail, some exposed roots, and possible overgrown sections. There may be stinging insects, so be sure to bring bug repellant along.

Trail Directions: The trail forms a long loop, part of which is the Michael Tygart connector to the Jenny Wiley Trail, 26 miles away. Most of the trail is level, but there are several steep hills near the trailheads.

The trailhead **[1]** is at the end of a turnaround loop near the marina. You'll start in a pine plantation, following the shore of Greenbo Lake. The pines soon peter out as you enter a young second-growth forest and start climbing. Beware of false trails.

After cresting the ridge, you'll descend to the lake. At mile 1.4 you'll pass a large slump block—a chunk of stone that has fallen from the hillside and migrated **[2]**.

Fairly soon the lake ends in a marshy area. Three hundred feet further is a group of three benches surrounding a fire pit. You're welcome to use it, but treat it as the private property it is. A little further, at mile 1.57, you'll wade Pruitt Fork Creek **[3]**.

The trail follows Pruitt Valley, past long-abandoned farmhouses. In fact, the grass and forbs surrounding you are an old farmfield being reclaimed by nature. In the clearing at mile 1.9 lies the foundation of a 19th-century farmhouse **[4]**. If you decide to explore it, be careful. The shrubbery may mask the open mouth of an old well that lies between the trail and the foundation.

Tall grass may obscure the trail as you trek through the clearing. When you reach the creek again, a false trail climbs the hill on your right. Cross the creek and reenter the young, second-growth woods.

At mile 2.75 is a second old homestead **[5]**. Here a cabin is overgrown and has collapsed. Only the front wall and brick chimney remain.

A fern garden appears at mile 3.2 **[6]**, which marks the end of your passage through the valley. The trail climbs very steeply until topping out at a private meadow. Go right until you reach a gravel road at mile 3.6 **[7]**. Retrace your steps and return the way you came.

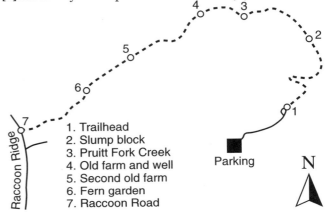

1. Trailhead
2. Slump block
3. Pruitt Fork Creek
4. Old farm and well
5. Second old farm
6. Fern garden
7. Raccoon Road

Michael Tygart Trail B 👢👢👢👢

Distance Round-Trip: 5.56 miles

Estimated Hiking Time: 4 to 5 hours

Cautions: Watch for fallen trees across the trail, some exposed roots, and possible overgrown sections. There may be stinging insects, so be sure to bring bug repellant along.

Trail Directions: The trail forms a long loop, part of which is the Michael Tygart connector to the Jenny Wiley Trail, 26 miles away. Most of the trail is level, but there are several steep hills near the trailheads.

The trailhead **[1]** is just east of the marina access road parking lot. Almost immediately you'll reach Brown cemetery **[2]**.

Cross the cemetery. From here the trail roller-coasters through the woods. The trail is a steep climb up and another steep climb back down.

At mile .68, a side trail leads to old iron ore pits **[3]**. These pits fed the furnace on nearby Buffalo Branch in the 19th century.

At mile 1.54 you'll reach the trail shelter **[4]**. About .14 miles later you'll enter a recovering clear-cut where loggers have cut down every tree **[5]**. During the leafless months there are distant views of the mountains moving off in waves.

Yellow blazes now mark the trail, which follows the ridgetop until reaching Raccoon Ridge at mile 2.78 **[6]**.

Retrace your steps and return the way you came.

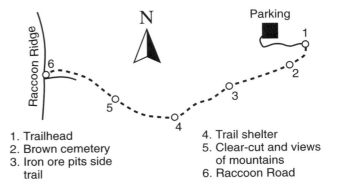

1. Trailhead
2. Brown cemetery
3. Iron ore pits side trail
4. Trail shelter
5. Clear-cut and views of mountains
6. Raccoon Road

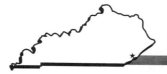

5. Bad Branch State Nature Preserve

- Walk through an environment whose flora are more typical of northern climates or higher elevations.
- See numerous rare species such as small enchanter's nightshade and Fraser's sedge.
- Watch for Kentucky's only known nesting pair of ravens.

Park Information

Bad Branch State Nature Preserve contains 2343 acres of forested slopes surrounding a deep, rugged gorge on the south face of Pine Mountain. It is jointly managed by the Nature Conservancy and the State Nature Preserves Commission.

The natural beauty of the preserve is crowned by a 60-foot waterfall that plunges over a sandstone cliff into a jumble of massive boulders. Bad Branch, noted for its excellent water quality, flows south past hemlock- and rhododendron-lined banks to the Poor Fork of the Cumberland River.

The cold mountain stream and the narrow, shaded gorge maintain conditions that support a large assemblage of species more typical of northern climes. Several rare plants and animals call the area home.

Directions: From Whitesburg, go south for 7 miles on KY-119 to KY-932. Turn left and go 1.7 miles. The preserve is on the left. Note: The sign is recessed, and easy to miss.

Hours Open: Open year-round.

Facilities: None.

Permits and Rules: Only foot travel is permitted (on designated trails); no camping, no fires.

Further Information: Contact Kentucky State Nature Preserves Commission, 801 Schenkel Lane, Frankfort, KY 40601; 502-573-2886.

Other Points of Interest

Kingdom Come State Park (see park #6) and **Breaks Interstate Park** (see park #1) are within an hour of Bad Branch.

The Kentucky Coal Mining Museum (606-848-1530), in nearby Benham, commemorates the history of coal mining in the region.

Park Trails

High Rocks Trail 👢👢👢👢👢—7.24 miles round-trip—is a very strenuous climb.

Waterfall Trail 👢👢👢👢👢

Distance Round-Trip: 2 miles

Estimated Hiking Time: 1.5 to 2 hours

Cautions: You will encounter high banks, exposed rocks and roots, and water flowing across the trail.

Trail Directions: From the trailhead [1] in the parking lot, the trail follows the remains of a logging road built when the virgin forest was cut in the 1940s. A few of the old-growth hemlocks remain.

Bad Branch parallels the trail, with thickets of laurel and rhododendron lining its banks. In the spring an abundance of wildflowers, some of them found nowhere else in Kentucky, grace the trail side.

At mile .1, you cross Bad Branch on a wooden footbridge [2], through a dense laurel/hemlock thicket. A thousand feet further, you'll cross it again, on another footbridge. The trail climbs steadily from there, with lots of exposed roots and rocks.

As the trail ascends, the banks get steeper and steeper until Bad Branch lies as much as 100 feet below you, with steep drop-offs to the boulder-filled waters. A large, light-colored slump block can be seen at mile .5 [3], with pine trees growing from its top.

Four hundred feet further, at mile .56, a large drain crosses the trail [4]. Note the size of the boulders dropped in the drain by water during the rainy seasons. A few steps further, pause and study the flat, moss-covered rock. The parallel lines are mosses growing in the ripple marks left behind by an ancient sea.

At mile .76 is a second drain [5], this one so deep that you have to use the exposed roots of a birch tree as stepping-stones to climb out of it.

The trail forms a Y at mile .85 [6]. The left trail climbs strenuously to the High Rocks area. The right trail takes you to the falls. You'll cross a tributary creek on rocks and climb steeply and steadily, with several switchbacks. The sound of the falls is constantly in your ears, and you always think it's just around the next bend. Not so. You've quite a distance yet to go.

At mile .92 you reach the base of the cliffs forming High Rocks [7]. Follow along the cliffs until mile .96, where the trail loses itself in a boulder garden [8]. Continue along the base of the cliffs. At mile .98 you'll emerge on a high bank [9], with the falls in front of you. The bottom of the falls is about 100 feet down a boulder-strewn bank.

Bad Branch Falls is a double fall of water, dropping 60 feet to massive boulders below. During the rainy seasons, its power is spectacular, as you can imagine from the size of the rocks it has dropped at its own base. During midsummer, it's a delicate cascade. But in winter, when dramatic ice columns the height of the falls are formed, the falls are at their most spectacular.

Return to the trailhead by retracing your steps.

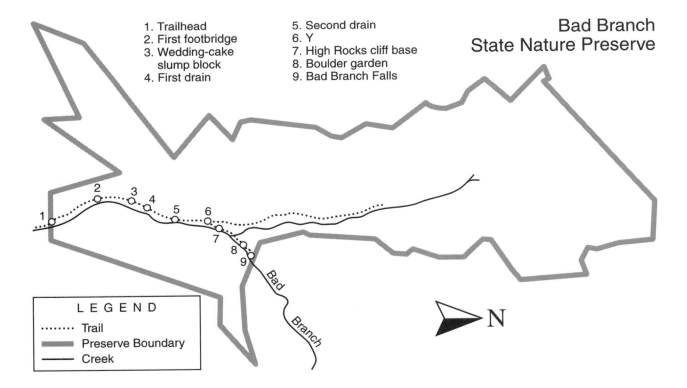

1. Trailhead
2. First footbridge
3. Wedding-cake slump block
4. First drain
5. Second drain
6. Y
7. High Rocks cliff base
8. Boulder garden
9. Bad Branch Falls

Bad Branch
State Nature Preserve

LEGEND
...... Trail
▬ Preserve Boundary
— Creek

Bad Branch

N

6. Kingdom Come State Park

- Explore some of the most extraordinary rock formations in Kentucky, including Log Rock (a natural arch) and Raven Rock (a 290-foot-long rock exposure lying at a 45-degree angle).
- See the unique basin and range topography of southeastern Kentucky from the highest state park in the Bluegrass state.
- Watch for black bears, now rare in Kentucky, which breed in the park.

Park Information

With an elevation of 2,700 feet, Kingdom Come is the highest park in the Kentucky State Park system. As such, it is described as the crown jewel in the crest of Pine Mountain. The spectacular views and unique rock formations found here justify that description.

Pine Mountain, like all those making up the Cumberlands, is not the usual mountain shape. We expect mountains to be conical, but the Cumberlands are long, ridgelike structures, each of which is cut into ridges and valleys of its own.

Pine Mountain is the longest of these, stretching northeast 125 miles from Pineville almost to the Virginia border. From the stone gazebo near the park entrance, you can see Big Black Mountain—at 4,400 feet, Kentucky's highest—and the Cumberland Valley laid out at your feet.

Named after the popular Civil War novel, *The Little Shepherd of Kingdom Come* by Kentucky author John Fox Jr., the park preserves 1,283 acres of the unspoiled wilderness that inspired Fox's writings. The Little Shepherd Trail, a 38-mile hiking/all-terrain vehicle trail traversing the crest of Pine Mountain, is also named after that book. Part of it passes through the park.

In the park, hikers have sighted an increasing number of black bears (rare anywhere in Kentucky), including sows with cubs. For this reason, park officials recommend that you make some noise while on the trails, so the bears know you are there and can avoid confrontations.

Kingdom Come's many overlooks provide spectacular views of the Appalachian Plateau to the north and the Cumberland Mountains to the south. But the greatest appeal is the many special rock formations found there. Raven Rock, a 290-foot-long outcrop of exposed sandstone lying at a 45-degree angle, dominates the park's topography. But numerous unique formations, such as the Log Rock, are found here as well.

Directions: From the junction of KY-160 and KY-1926 in Cumberland, go north .5 miles to the park entrance road, then 1.3 miles to the Visitor Center and trails.

Hours Open: Open year-round, but the Visitor Center hours vary by season.

Facilities: Visitor Center and gift shop, picnic shelters, miniature golf, fishing and boating; primitive camping in designated areas.

Permits and Rules: A permit is required for overnight stays; only foot travel on hiking trails.

Further Information: Contact Kingdom Come State Park, P.O. Box M, Cumberland, KY 40823; 606-589-2479.

Other Points of Interest

Pine Mountain State Resort Park (see park #12), **Cumberland Gap National Historical Park** (see park #11), **Bad Branch State Nature Preserve** (see park #5), and **Breaks Interstate Park** (see park #1) are all within one hour of Kingdom Come.

Lilley Cornett Woods (606-633-5828) near Skyline, Kentucky, preserves 252 acres of remnant virgin forest along with the 90 species of trees and shrubs found within the preserve.

The Kentucky Coal Mining Museum (606-848-1530), in nearby Benham, commemorates the history of coal mining in the region, including the new exhibit, *Coal Miner's Daughter*, dedicated to Loretta Lynn.

Park Trails

A network of 13 trails, none longer than 1 mile, crisscrosses the park. Almost all of them lead to or from Raven Rock, so numerous loops can be constructed.

Nature Haven Trail 🥾🥾🥾🥾—.875 miles each way—is the longest trail in the park.

Saltress Trail 🥾🥾🥾—.25 miles each way—connects with Raven Rock via the Groundhog Trail.

Lake Trail 🥾🥾—.25-mile loop—circles the 3.5-acre mountain lake near the Visitor Center.

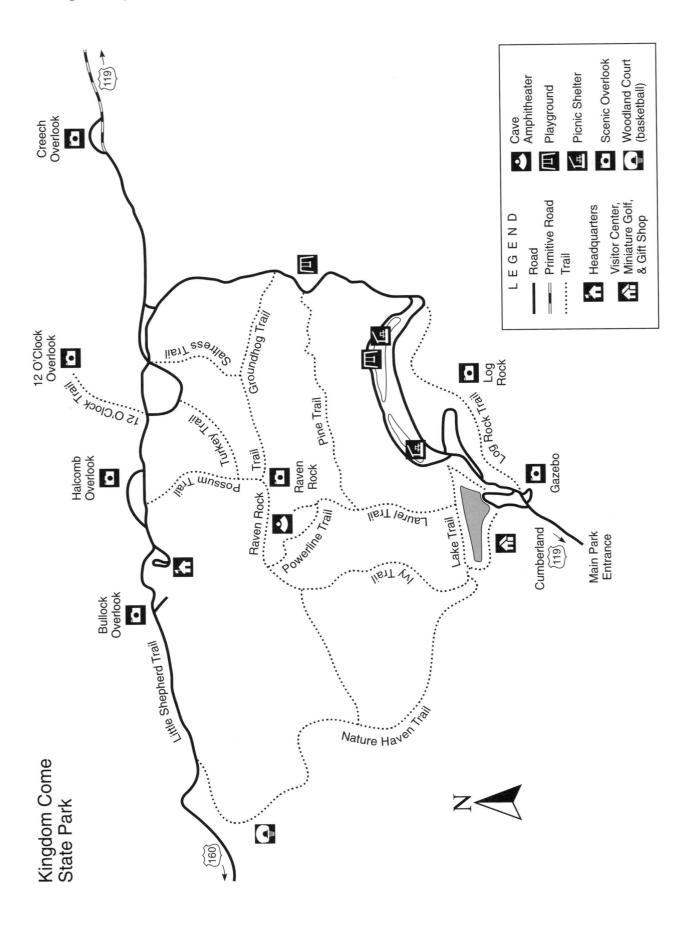

Kingdom Come
State Park

LEGEND

Road
Primitive Road
Trail

Headquarters

Visitor Center,
Miniature Golf,
& Gift Shop

Cave
Amphitheater
Playground
Picnic Shelter
Scenic Overlook
Woodland Court
(basketball)

Creech Overlook

12 O'Clock Overlook

Halcomb Overlook

Bullock Overlook

Little Shepherd Trail

12 O'Clock Trail

Turkey Trail

Possum Trail

Saltress Trail

Groundhog Trail

Pine Trail

Raven Rock Trail

Raven Rock

Powerline Trail

Ivy Trail

Laurel Trail

Lake Trail

Nature Haven Trail

Log Rock Trail

Log Rock

Gazebo

Cumberland

Main Park Entrance

N

Lake/Laurel/Powerline/ Raven Rock/Groundhog/ Pine Trail Loop

Distance Round-Trip: 2 miles

Estimated Hiking Time: 1.5 to 2 hours

Cautions: Watch for drop-offs, exposed rocks and roots—and bears.

Trail Directions: This constructed loop takes you through all the ecosystems found in the park. The trailhead **[1]** is at the northeast corner of the Visitor Center parking lot, by the lake. Start on the Lake Trail, a graveled walking path that circles the lake. About halfway around, at mile .11, you'll climb the bank on an obvious side trail and cross the park road to the Laurel Trail trailhead.

Laurel is a wide, graded, and unobstructed trail, lined with mountain laurel, that follows a creek. At mile .32, Powerline Trail junctions left and Pine Trail goes right **[2]**. Continue straight on a side trip to the amphitheater. Along the way you'll pass a large rock slab; lying on its side, it has created a cavelike recess. Stone stairs lead up to the amphitheater. The exposed sandstone outcrop, looking like a giant water slide without water, is the base of Raven Rock—a 290-foot-long inclined plane, lying at a 45-degree angle. At mile .4 you'll reach the amphitheater **[3]**, a large, deep rock-shelter (a cavelike opening in the cliff) with bleachers installed. Once operated as an actual theater, it is now used by youth groups and park naturalists to conduct programs in a fully natural setting. Return to the Powerline/Pine Trail junction, and turn right onto Powerline Trail.

Powerline Trail climbs steadily, with several switchbacks, through open hardwoods and ferns. Periodically Raven Rock will be visible through the trees. At mile .6 you'll step on a carpet of moss blanketing the trail **[4]**. The thick moss cushions your feet like a shag rug under bare toes. Then, after another switchback or two, you'll reach a trail junction at mile .78 **[5]**. Ivy Trail descends to the left, while Raven Rock Trail turns right, taking you out onto the crest of Raven Rock at mile .79 **[6]**. From here, even in heavy-foliage months, you have an unobstructed view of the Cumberland Mountains and their alternating valleys and serrated ridges, stretching south and east into Virginia.

After crossing Raven Rock, the trail continues through a rich understory. Blueberries grow in profusion along this part of the trail. Keep especially alert for bears, though. The ursine animals consider the berry crop their private property.

At mile .95 you'll pass under an overhanging rock on a plank footbridge. Note the embedded gravels and shales painting an impressionist scene in the sandstone substrate. You'll then pass immediately along the base of what could be an interesting cliff **[7]**. Unfortunately, *Spraypaintus americanis* has been at work even here, and the sheer wall is covered with graffiti. At the end of the cliffs, you'll go up a short set of stairs and join the Groundhog Trail, which ascends.

At mile 1.1 you'll come to an unmarked Y. Saltress Trail climbs left, while the Groundhog Trail descends right through open woods and ferns that line the way. Then, after following limestone cliffs on the right, you'll reach the park road at mile 1.3 **[8]**. Follow it to the right, toward the playground, to the Pine Trail trailhead at mile 1.34 **[9]**. Turn right. Pine Trail climbs steeply through mixed pines, hardwoods, ferns, and laurel.

At mile 1.43 you'll top out at a bench. During the leafless months, the basin and range topography of the Cumberlands is clearly visible as you pause to catch your breath. The trail then descends, through more blueberries. At mile 1.5 you'll pass a ridge of eroded cliffs **[10]** resembling Pine Mountain in miniature. Laurel Trail junctions at mile 1.6. Turn left and retrace your steps to the trailhead.

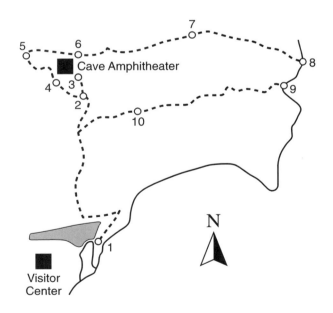

1. Trailhead
2. Trail junction
3. Amphitheater
4. Moss carpet
5. Ivy Trail junction
6. Raven Rock
7. Graffiti wall
8. Park road
9. Pine Trail
10. Eroded cliffs

Log Rock Trail 👢👢👢👢

Distance Round-Trip: .5 miles

Estimated Hiking Time: 30 minutes

Cautions: Be aware of high cliffs and exposed rocks and roots.

Trail Directions: Log Rock Trail follows a cliff line along Pine Mountain, overlooking Cumberland Valley and the mountains to the south and east. The trailhead **[1]** is at the stone gazebo near the park entrance. From here you look out across the valley to Big Black Mountain, Kentucky's highest at 4,400 feet. Like Pine Mountain itself, Black Mountain is not conical. Rather, it's a ridgelike structure stretching on a northeast/southwest heading. But the mountain is cut up into ridges and valleys of its own, so it looks like a mountain range rather than a single entity.

All of the Cumberlands, which include Pine Mountain, Cumberland Mountain, and Powell Mountain among others, follow this design. The result is a basin and range topography, reminiscent of the Rockies.

Time it right, and you'll see the morning mist filling the cuts and valleys with cotton candy while the ridges float like razorback islands in this sea of sugar foam.

From the gazebo, the trail climbs steeply through mixed pines and hardwoods over exposed sandstone outcrops. About 300 feet from the trailhead, there's a limestone slab on your left that's a mini-version of Raven Rock—a bare, inclined plane lying at a 45-degree angle. Then, at mile .12, the trail seems to disappear into a rock outcrop **[2]**. At the end of this exposed sandstone is a panoramic view of Black Mountain and the Cumberlands from a slightly different perspective. Row after row of ridges and valleys stretches out at your feet, disappearing into the Virginia countryside. Mist, like a frothy pudding, swirls through the valleys. Imagine what went through the minds of early explorers who faced these rows of rock walls, with nary a gap to ease their passage.

Follow the outcrop upward and leftward to regain the trail. At mile .15 you'll descend steeply a short distance until you reach Log Rock at mile .17 **[3]**.

Log Rock is a natural stone arch that looks like a weathered tree trunk lying across a gully. The trail follows the 80-foot-long tree trunk, then descends on several sets of stairs to the park road.

Either retrace your steps or follow the road back to the trailhead.

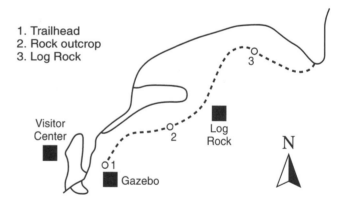

1. Trailhead
2. Rock outcrop
3. Log Rock

7. Carter Caves State Resort Park

- Explore several caves, including Bat Cave (wintering home for thousands of endangered Indiana bats), Saltpetre Cave, and Cascade Caverns.
- Visit a true box canyon with almost perfect corners.
- See the only natural bridge in Kentucky that supports a paved highway.

Park Information

The unique geologic features and numerous caves of Carter Caves State Resort Park have appealed to tourists for many years. Although the area was made a state park in 1946, it had operated as a private tourist attraction since the 1880s and had been used for commercial purposes long before that.

The primary draw was, and remains, the caves. There are 20 caves in the park, and tours are conducted daily throughout the year at 4 of them. Cascade Caverns, the most scenic, contains many formations along with an underground river and waterfall. X Cave takes its name from the configuration of its passages. Saltpetre Cave was the site of mining activity during the War of 1812, and Bat Cave is the winter hibernation ground of the endangered Indiana bat. Tours are not conducted through Bat Cave during the wintering-over season, for obvious reasons. Finally, Laurel Cave is a noncommercial cave that visitors are permitted to explore on their own provided they have proper equipment.

Above-ground geology is another drawing card. The Box Canyon, for instance, is a 60-foot-high sandstone wall with nearly perfect corners. Smokey Bridge is the most massive natural arch in Kentucky, with a 90-foot-high, 220-foot-long tunnel. And Carter Caves Natural Bridge is a 180-foot-long natural tunnel with a paved highway running across the top. Our favorite, though, is Cascade Bridge, which, due to an optical illusion, appears to be a bas-relief carving rather than a true arch.

As a state resort park, Carter Caves offers all the amenities, including a lodge and cabins, golf, tennis, horseback riding, and swimming pools. Fishing and canoeing are available on Smokey Valley Lake, Kentucky's only trophy bass water. Minimum keeper size on the lake is 20 inches.

Caution: Poison ivy is very common at Carter Caves.

Directions: From I-64 exit 161 in Olive Hill, go east on US-60 1.4 miles to KY-182, then 3 miles to the park entrance. For Cascade Caverns and the Cascade Cave Trail, turn left on KY-209 before reaching the park gate; then go 1.5 miles to the cave site.

Hours Open: Open year-round; trails close at dusk.

Facilities: Lodge and cabins, picnic areas, campground, swimming pools, golf, tennis, horseback stables, cave tours.

Permits and Rules: Only foot travel on trails; no rappelling or rock climbing; no motors allowed on Smokey Valley Lake.

Further Information: Contact Manager, Carter Caves State Resort Park, Rural Route 5 Box 1120, Olive Hill, KY 41164; 606-286-4411.

Other Points of Interest

Clear Creek Recreation Area (see park #9), **Pioneer Weapons Hunting Area** (see park #8), **Greenbo Lake State Resort Park** (see park #4), and the **Jesse Stuart State Nature Preserve** (see park #3) are all close by.

Park Trails

There are more than 11 miles of trails at Carter Caves. All of them are hilly, and they may pass near high cliff areas. There are no water sources on any of the trails.

Natural Bridge Trail 👢👢—.25 miles each way—leads from the Welcome Center to Natural Bridge and back.

Green Trail 👢👢👢—.75 miles each way—ascends into a streamless valley, passing a number of cave entrances. This trail is especially rewarding during the spring wildflower season.

The 4Cs 👢👢👢👢—7.2-mile loop—is a strenuous hike to several interesting geologic formations.

Carter Caves State Resort Park

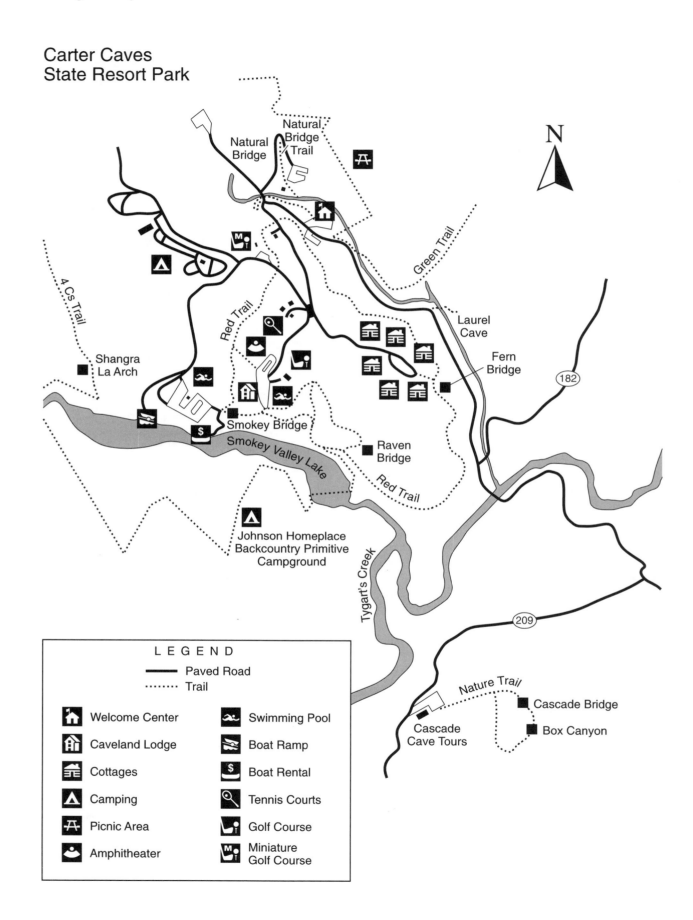

Natural Bridge

Natural Bridge Trail

Green Trail

4 Cs Trail

Red Trail

Laurel Cave

Fern Bridge

182

Shangra La Arch

Smokey Bridge

Smokey Valley Lake

Raven Bridge

Red Trail

Johnson Homeplace Backcountry Primitive Campground

Tygart's Creek

209

Nature Trail

Cascade Bridge

Box Canyon

Cascade Cave Tours

LEGEND

——— Paved Road

.... Trail

Welcome Center

Caveland Lodge

Cottages

Camping

Picnic Area

Amphitheater

Swimming Pool

Boat Ramp

Boat Rental

Tennis Courts

Golf Course

Miniature Golf Course

Red Trail 👢👢👢👢👢

Distance Round-Trip: 3.2 miles plus .75 miles with cave tour

Estimated Hiking Time: 2 to 2.5 hours plus 1.25 hours with cave tour

Cautions: Be careful on high cliffs; watch for exposed rocks and roots, washed-out sections, and poison ivy.

Trail Directions: The trailhead **[1]** is south of Caveland Lodge, down a set of erosion steps that Ts into the actual trail. Go right. A side trail on the left at mile .06 leads, in a few steps, to a natural sandstone overlook above Smokey Valley Lake **[2]**. Smokey Valley is a small lake with a dogleg, so you can never see its entire length.

This section of trail is paved. About 600 feet from the trailhead the pavement continues, but the trail turns right, above a large natural amphitheater. You are actually crossing Smokey Bridge, the largest bridge in the park. It's 220 feet long and more than 90 feet high. About 200 feet further, a side trail at mile .15 leads down a set of stairs into the amphitheater **[3]**. Smokey Bridge looks like a railway tunnel that was hand dug through the ridge, but it's a natural formation. Return to the trail.

From Smokey Bridge the trail climbs steadily and steeply. Stay alert, as this section is particularly good for seeing deer. After crossing the campground road, the trail levels off, then descends rather steeply.

After descending a set of stone stairs, you'll cross a couple of plank footbridges and come to Saltpetre Cave, at mile .88 **[4]**. During the War of 1812, saltpeter was mined here in order to make gunpowder.

The trail climbs from the cave. At mile 1.05 it crosses a natural culvert **[5]**. A crack in the rock leads down, and under the trail, serving as a drain for water cascading off the mountain. The trail now follows the cliff line, crossing a couple of footbridges along the way. Each of them has a seasonal waterfall on the downhill (left) side. You'll soon climb through a laurel thicket. Stay very alert here, because at mile 1.6 **[6]**, the trail seems to continue straight but actually turns sharply right. Going straight leads to a dangerous high cliff in just a few steps.

At mile 1.64, the Red Trail intersects another trail. A sign here has been destroyed by vandals, and it's easy to go astray. Turning right leads you to the cottages. Turning left is the Red Trail. Straight ahead is an unauthorized trail that leads 300 feet to the top of Fern Bridge. Take that trail. When you reach the

bridge, your footfalls will reverberate below you. You're on stone, but you'll be thinking of eggshells. On your right is a large crack where the slab containing the arch has separated from the cliff. On your left is a panoramic view into Cave Branch Valley.

Retrace your steps to the crossroads and turn right, down a set of 58 steep stone steps, through a natural crack in the cliff. At the bottom, turn right along the base of the cliffs. You'll see Fern Bridge ahead, surrounded by a lush floral assemblage of ferns and wildflowers. At mile 1.8 you'll cross a wooden footbridge under Fern Bridge **[7]**. Look up. The crack separating the arch from the cliff is clearly visible.

After about 1,000 feet, you'll leave the cliffs behind and descend into a valley until you reach a junction with the Blue Trail at mile 2.7. This leads to Raven Bridge, another natural arch. If you take it, you'll find that it rejoins the Red Trail later on.

If you stay on the Red Trail you'll soon bottom out at a plank footbridge, at the junction of the 4Cs trail, and then climb again to a large rock outcrop. Note the various color changes in the rock. They're caused by minerals and embedded shales in the sandstone substrate.

From here the trail roller-coasters until reaching the erosion steps leading back to Caveland Lodge.

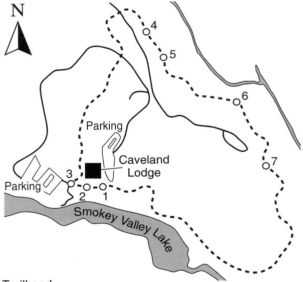

1. Trailhead
2. Smokey Valley Lake overlook
3. Smokey Bridge
4. Saltpetre Cave
5. Natural culvert
6. Cliff drop-off
7. Fern Bridge

Cascade Cave Nature Trail

Distance Round-Trip: .61 miles

Estimated Hiking Time: 40 to 60 minutes

Cautions: There are high cliffs and exposed roots and rocks. You'll do some boulder hopping. Some spots lack trail markers.

Trail Directions: A short but challenging trail, the Cascade Cave Nature Trail has more unique features than any other half mile in Kentucky. The trailhead [1] is at the south end of the parking lot. A short gravel path (130 feet) leads to the trail. Go left, onto the dirt path.

Fifty feet further is the exit from Cascade Cave, which you can tour. The most scenic cave in the park, it has many formations plus an underground river and waterfall. The tour takes about an hour.

The trail ascends steadily, with two major false trails on the right. The first is actually the return loop. After a steep climb, top out at Cascade Bridge, at mile .23 [2]. Cascade Bridge is separated from the cliff by an almost imperceptible crack. But it's a true arch. The effect, when viewed from the front, is of a bas-relief victory arch (complete with sculpture work) carved in the cliff. Note, too, the large "pipes" emerging from the sandstone at the right-hand edge of the arch. These are formed when embedded shales get twisted by the earth's movement.

Follow the cliff line from the arch. There's a sharp drop on your right, so be careful. The sandstone on these cliffs has been bent, twisted, eroded, and dripped, leaving the impression of a huge wedding cake with an ornate frosting design. All that's missing is the bride and groom standing atop the cake.

At mile .3, after squeezing through some slump blocks (large chunks of rock that have broken off the cliffs and migrated), you'll reach the Box Canyon [3]. This is an uncreative name for a unique formation. A box canyon, as any horse opera fan knows, is a cul-de-sac that's surrounded on three sides by unscalable cliffs and has no exit. These formations take their name from the fact that you get boxed in after entering one, rather than from their shape. This box

canyon fits the definition. But it goes a step further; the corners are almost perfectly true—not quite right angles, but close enough to make no difference. With its smooth, sheer walls, the whole thing really does look like a box.

Passing the Box Canyon, you'll have to rock hop over and through fallen boulders and slump blocks for about 100 feet. Stick as close to the cliff face as you can until you regain the trail. This won't make your passage any easier, but it will keep you away from the drop-off.

After climbing steeply though additional exposed rocks, you'll walk through the wind tunnel at mile .38 [4]. Here a set of slump blocks forms a narrow passage through the cliff. You'll have to scramble over some rocks at the end of the tunnel. The trail turns right, at the only marker since the trailhead. Before turning with it, walk a few feet further to see where a new tunnel is being slowly eroded.

Two hundred feet after making the turn, the trail descends steeply, levels out, and then descends again. At mile .53 you'll find yourself at an unmarked T. This is the trail you walked in on. Make a left and return to the trailhead.

If you take the tour of Cascade Caverns, add .75 miles to the hike and about 1.25 hours. Along the way you'll see cave formations, an underground stream, and the only underground waterfall in the region. The fall drops 32 feet down a natural pipe with a travertine-like lining. The viewing platform is actually about halfway up the pipe, thus providing a total view of the fall.

1. Trailhead
2. Cascade Bridge
3. Box Canyon
4. Wind tunnel

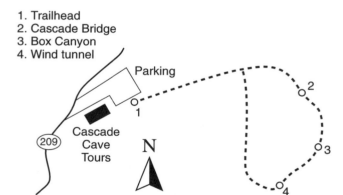

8. Pioneer Weapons Hunting Area

- See the last fire tower remaining in the Daniel Boone National Forest.
- Share the trails with buckskin-clad long hunters, hunting as our pioneering ancestors did.
- Meander Zilpo Scenic Byway, one of the first Forest Service Scenic Byways created by the program that identifies the most scenic drives in the national forests.

Park Information

The Pioneer Weapons Hunting Area is a 7,610-acre tract in the middle of the Morehead Ranger District of the Daniel Boone National Forest, abutting Cave Run Lake.

Created through a cooperative effort between the Kentucky Department of Fish and Wildlife Resources and the Forest Service, it is an area where hunting with modern, breech-loading weapons is prohibited. Only primitive weapons—which include bows and arrows, crossbows, and muzzle-loading flintlock and caplock rifles—are allowed. Many primitive hunters dress the part, as well. So, you may run into a long hunter sharing the trails with you.

Hunting seasons can extend from August (squirrels) through February (grouse and small game) and include a wild turkey season in the spring. So you might encounter hunters any time.

Although managed for multiple use, wildlife management is a major emphasis here. Grassy openings have been created and maintained, water holes developed, and timber management used to create habitat diversity. Thus, it is one of the best areas in the national forest for wildlife watching. Alert hikers are sure to see deer, wild turkey, small game, and possibly ruffed grouse as they walk the numerous trails of the area.

Like much of the Daniel Boone National Forest, the land in the Pioneer Weapons Hunting Area consists of high ridges and deep valleys, so hikers should be prepared for some strenuous trail work. Despite the abundance of creeks and streams, none of the water is considered safe unless filtered or chemically treated. The best bet is to carry your own.

Directions: From Salt Lick, Kentucky, take KY-211 west 3.7 miles to Clear Creek Road (which becomes FS-129 when it enters the national forest). Turn left. Go 4 miles to Zilpo Road. Trails are accessed variously from FS-129 and Zilpo Road.

Hours Open: Open year-round; some facilities are seasonal.

Facilities: Three organized campgrounds, with hookups.

Permits and Rules: Primitive camping no less than 300 feet from roads, trails, or water sources.

Further Information: Morehead Ranger District, Daniel Boone National Forest, 2375 KY 801 South, Morehead, KY 40351, 606-784-6428.

Other Points of Interest

Clear Creek Recreation Area (see park #9) abuts the Pioneer Weapons Wildlife Management Area. **Carter Caves State Resort Park** (see park #7), **Greenbo Lake State Resort Park** (see park #4), **Spencer Morton State Nature Preserve** (see park #14), and **Red River Gorge Geologic Area** (see park#10) are all within one hour of the Pioneer Weapons Hunting Area.

Park Trails

The Pioneer Weapons Hunting Area includes nearly 25 miles of formal trails, plus many undesignated, abandoned forest roads. Many entail stiff climbs from ridgetops to the valleys and back. In general, the area is recommended for experienced hikers in good physical shape. Few loop trails exist, but many trails interconnect so you can create your own loops.

Buckskin Trail 👢👢👢👢—10.3 miles each way—follows the shore of Cave Run Lake from Zilpo Campground to the Clear Creak Recreation Area. It's part of the Sheltowee Trace Trail.

Buck Creek Trail 👢👢👢👢—4 miles each way—begins at Clear Creek Recreation Area and ends at Cave Run Lake, climbing up and over several ridges along the way.

Hog Pen Trail 👢👢👢👢—3 miles each way—shortens the distance along the Buckskin Trail but entails stiff climbing, with a 460-foot elevation change.

Pioneer Weapons Hunting Area

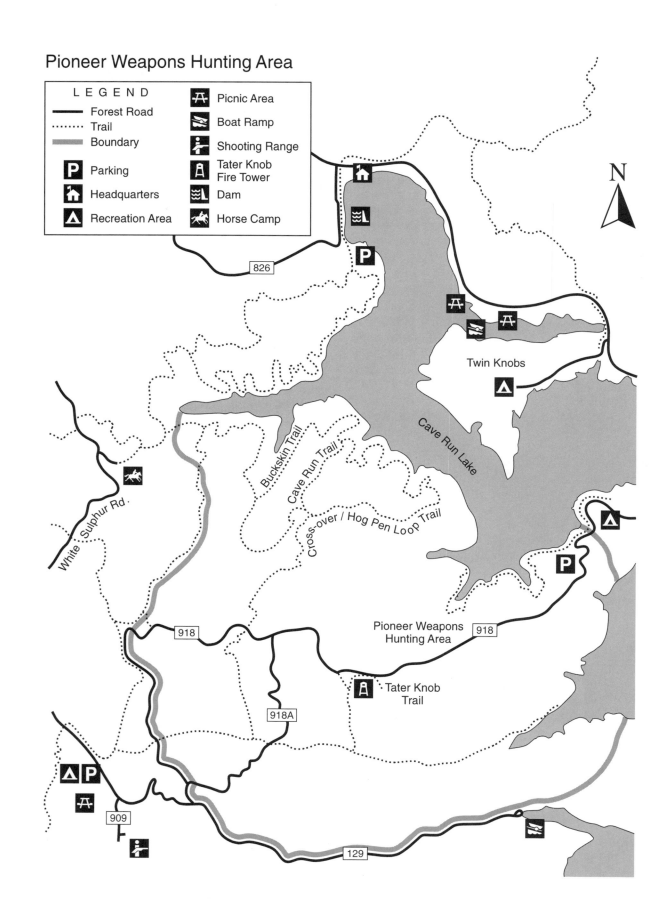

LEGEND

— Forest Road
···· Trail
▬ Boundary

P Parking
🏠 Headquarters
△ Recreation Area

🏕 Picnic Area
🚤 Boat Ramp
🎯 Shooting Range
🔥 Tater Knob Fire Tower
🌊 Dam
🐎 Horse Camp

N

826

Twin Knobs

Buckskin Trail

Cave Run Trail

Cross-over / Hog Pen Loop Trail

Cave Run Lake

White Sulphur Rd.

918

918

Pioneer Weapons
Hunting Area

918A

Tater Knob
Trail

909

129

Crossover/Cave Run/ Buckskin/Hog Pen Trails Loop

Distance Round-Trip: 8.2 miles

Estimated Hiking Time: 3.5 to 4 hours

Cautions: Be on the lookout for drop-offs, exposed rocks and roots, and horses.

Trail Directions: This is a moderate loop, with one stiff climb. Otherwise, although long, it is not difficult.

The trailhead **[1]** is at FS-1225, on Zilpo Road, 3.5 miles from FS-129. The trail starts immediately left of the gate.

Seven hundred feet later the trail turns sharply left at mile .14. Note the remains of an old wagon road **[2]** below you on the right. You'll rejoin FS-1225 at a small meadow **[3]** at mile .25. This is the first of several wildlife clearings you'll pass along the way. Stay alert for deer and turkey, who come into these openings to feed.

Follow the road, through a second gate and beyond. During the leafless months you'll see surrounding mountains and deep hollows. Otherwise, you'll be walking through a green tunnel, with a profusion of sassafras and grapevines—which are especially attractive to ruffed grouse.

You'll juncture with Cave Run Trail **[4]** at mile 1.6. Turn left. In a few feet you'll join a traffic circle, where several trails come together. Follow the light blue diamonds. At mile 1.75 you'll get your first glimpse of Cave Run Lake **[5]**, with the surrounding mountains reflecting in its clear, clean waters. The trail parallels, then joins an old logging road, and descends, until mile 1.86 where it turns right. The turn-off is easy to miss, so stay alert when the road becomes rocky.

The trail turns left again, at mile 1.9, just before the forest road crosses a saddle with drop-offs on both sides. If you continue across this saddle, the bulldozed path will dead-end at mile 2.0. From there you have a spectacular view of Cave Run Lake **[6]**, looking like a crystalline hourglass glistening in the sun.

Return to the saddle and rejoin the trail. Although the land slopes off steeply on both sides of you, the trail itself descends almost imperceptibly. At mile 2.8 you'll junction with the Buckskin Trail **[7]**. Turn sharply right, following the yellow diamond blazes.

The terrain becomes more rolling than hilly, with lots of downed timber. Drains, which were almost

absent above, are common. The woods are thicker and younger, and the flora reflect the damper environment of the lake. At mile 3.3 you'll reach the shore of Cave Run Lake **[8]**. Cave Run is one of the cleanest and wildest lakes in the Bluegrass state. You might even see an angler land a musky. Those giant members of the pike family thrive in the cool waters of the lake.

The trail stays level for the next 1.25 miles as it plays leapfrog with the lake. Then, at mile 4.57 it turns right and climbs steadily away from the lake, steepening as you ascend. About halfway up the hill a tent caterpillar nest forms a sunlit umbrella across several tree limbs—a party canopy for the elven folk.

The one serious climb is in front of you as you ascend out of the lake valley. There will be several doglegs, and the trail gets steeper, then flattens several times, until mile 4.9, where you hit the gangplank **[9]**. This is a flat, almost graded ridgeline with sharp drop-offs on each side, which passes through mature second-growth oaks and hickories. You'll finally top out at a wildlife clearing at mile 5.23 **[10]**. Approach stealthily, because there are usually wild turkey feeding in the clearing. Across the clearing you'll pick up Hog Pen Trail, which is FS-1225 at this point. Follow it back to the trailhead.

1. Trailhead
2. Old wagon road
3. Wildlife clearing
4. Cave Run Trail
5. View of lake
6. Spectacular view of lake
7. Buckskin Trail junction
8. Lakeshore
9. Gangplank
10. Wildlife clearing

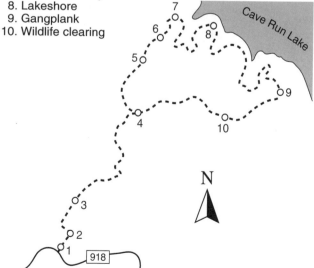

Tater Knob Trail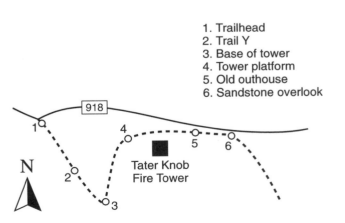

Distance Round-Trip: .9 miles

Estimated Hiking Time: 60 to 90 minutes

Cautions: Be careful of high cliffs, exposed roots and rocks, and exposed stairways.

Trail Directions: A short, easy trail leads to, then up, Tater Knob Fire Tower, the last remaining fire tower in the Daniel Boone National Forest.

The trailhead **[1]** is at a small parking area off Zilpo Road, 4 miles from FS 129. Note the fire tower interpretive sign on the opposite end of the parking lot from the trail. The trail enters a young, second-growth hardwood forest, following a ridgeline that parallels the fire tower access road.

At mile .25 you'll enter a wildlife clearing. The trail continues straight, but take the side trail on the left instead. This leads to the fire tower access trail. Cross a small parking lot, where the trail forms a Y at mile .28 **[2]**. The right-hand trail leads to a spring in the cliffs; take the left-hand trail and start climbing the 137 wooden steps.

These stairs climb the base of Tater Knob, ending at a bench at mile .33. From the bench, during the

leafless months, you can see into Buck Creek Valley and the far ridges framing the valley. The rest of the year you see the ridges covered with greenery and sense the great bowl of the valley.

Above the stairs you have to rock hop about 47 feet to the bottom of the first metal staircase leading to the fire tower. This consists of 62 steep steps, followed quickly by a 7-step ladder, and, after a short hike, a third ladder—this one with 16 steps. The trail crosses rough sandstone slabs until reaching the base of the tower at mile .4 **[3]**. Two long, steep metal stairways, with a total of 42 steps, lead to the tower platform **[4]** at mile .41.

Fire towers once were the first line of defense against forest fires. Aircraft and other modern techniques made them obsolete. Built of wood in 1934, the Tater Knob Lookout Tower was replaced in 1959 with a 10-foot-by-10-foot metal building. It operated until the late 70s and was restored in 1993.

From the tower you have a 360-degree view of the ridge and valley topography of the region, along with Cave Run Lake. During the fall color season, this is a spectacular view.

Return to the base of the tower, and take the side trail at the northeast corner. At mile .43 are the remains of the two-hole outhouse that served the fire lookouts **[5]**. A little farther, at mile .44, is a natural sandstone overlook **[6]**. Before the fire tower was built, local people used to picnic here. Return to the base of the knob, and follow the trail to the left. At mile .63 you'll reach a spring at the base of the cliffs. This spring has been in use for at least 10,000 years and served the fire crews as drinking water until the 1970s. Unfortunately, it is no longer considered safe to drink untreated.

Return to the wildlife clearing. If you haven't had enough climbing, follow the trail left. It descends 450 feet in about a half mile and terminates at the Buck Creek Trail. If, as is likely, you've had your fill of climbing, return to the trailhead the way you came.

1. Trailhead
2. Trail Y
3. Base of tower
4. Tower platform
5. Old outhouse
6. Sandstone overlook

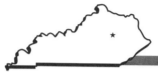

9. Clear Creek Recreation Area

- Explore one of the best-preserved early-1800s iron furnaces left in Kentucky.
- Watch nesting Canada geese at the site used to build a resident flock on nearby Cave Run Lake.
- Walk part of the Sheltowee Trace (a 254-mile-long trail) to an overlook used by Civil War soldiers, to natural arches and other geologic formations.

Park Information

Clear Creek Recreation Area is part of the Daniel Boone National Forest, which stretches in a northeast/southwest line almost the entire width of the state. The namesake Clear Creek Lake is a small, man-made lake formed by the damming of Clear Creek. The lake was used as a protected nesting area to create a resident flock of Canada geese on nearby Cave Run Lake, a major impoundment with 8,200 surface acres. Several of these geese still use the lake as a resting and nesting area, and you can almost always see them there.

In the Clear Creek picnic area are the remains of the 1839 Clear Creek iron furnace. Iron making was an important industry in Kentucky, and the state is dotted with the remains of these open-hearth furnaces that produced wrought iron. The Clear Creek furnace is one of the best preserved of these furnaces, and an interpretive plaque describes what you are looking at.

The terrain is mountainous, but the area has few of the escarpments (hills that climb gradually on one side, then suddenly drop off on the other) that typify the national forest further south. Thus, the cliffs and natural overlooks you do come across are that much more dramatic.

As you explore the area, you'll be surrounded by typical second-growth Appalachian hardwood forests, primarily oak and hickory, with some maple and tulip poplar as well. The entire region can best be described as rugged.

One general caution: Clear Creek abuts the Pioneer Weapons Hunting Area, a special area set aside for the use of primitive weapons (bows and arrows, muzzle-loading firearms, and crossbows). Clear Creek is open to hunting, and during the open seasons you may run into some overflow from the Pioneer Weapons Hunting Area.

Directions: From I-64 exit 123, go east 6 miles on US-60 to Salt Lick. Turn right on KY-211. Go 4 miles to FS-129 (Leatherwood Road); this road has no street sign, but there is a billboard directing you to the Zilpo Recreation Area. Two miles on FS-129 takes you to the parking area at Clear Creek Lake.

Hours Open: Open year-round; but the picnic ground is for day use only, closing at dark.

Facilities: Picnic ground, campground.

Permits and Rules: No primitive camping within 300 feet of roads or trails.

Further Information: Contact District Ranger, Morehead Ranger District, 2375 KY-801S, Morehead, KY 40351; 606-784-5624.

Other Points of Interest

The Pioneer Weapons Hunting Area (see park #8) abuts and surrounds Clear Creek, with several trails of its own and one of the last fire towers in the state.

Cave Run Lake, an 8,200-acre impoundment formed by the damming of the Licking River, offers fishing, swimming, and recreational boating opportunities. Information is available from the Resource Manager, U.S. Army Corps of Engineers, Cave Run Lake, Route 4, Box 223, Morehead, KY 40351 (606-784-9709); or from Scott Creek Marina (606-784-9666), where you can rent boats.

Park Trails

There are only two trails at Clear Creek, but you can connect to trails in the Pioneer Weapons Hunting Area from the lake or picnic ground.

Clear Creek Recreation Area

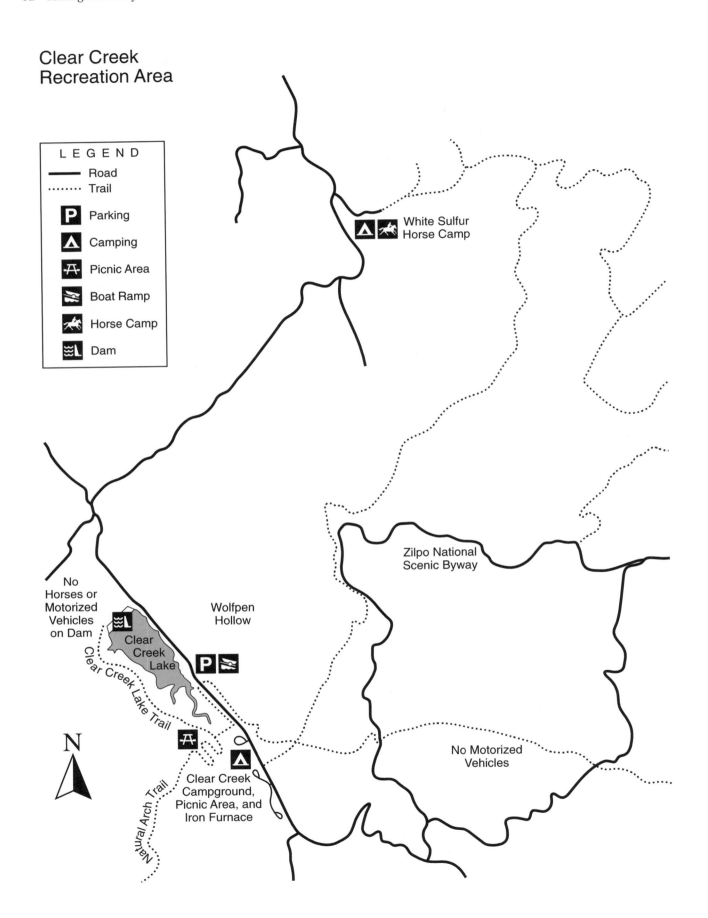

LEGEND

—— Road

······ Trail

P Parking

▲ Camping

⊼ Picnic Area

≋ Boat Ramp

🐎 Horse Camp

≋ Dam

White Sulfur Horse Camp

Zilpo National Scenic Byway

No Horses or Motorized Vehicles on Dam

Wolfpen Hollow

Clear Creek Lake

Clear Creek Lake Trail

No Motorized Vehicles

N

Natural Arch Trail

Clear Creek Campground, Picnic Area, and Iron Furnace

Natural Arch Trail

Distance Round-Trip: 7.75 miles

Estimated Hiking Time: 5 to 6 hours

Cautions: Be aware of exposed rocks and roots, high cliffs, boggy areas, unbridged stream crossings, and flowing water on the trail.

Trail Directions: Natural Arch is a very rugged trail, with lots of steep climbing. The trailhead **[1]** is just south of the entrance to the lake parking lot. The trail is a section of the Sheltowee Trace Trail. Although a sign says "Natural Arch 2.5 miles," the arch is about 1 mile further than that.

The trail starts out firm, level, and sandy. But at mile .06, you'll come to a boggy area where the trail seems to disappear into mud **[2]**. Complicating things further, there are several blowdowns (uprooted and wind-blown trees) across the trail. About 200 feet after refinding the trail, you'll T into a gravel road. Go right.

Almost immediately you'll wade Clear Creek. The trail stays on the gravel road for 500 feet; it then turns left at a sign for the Sheltowee Trace Trail, ascending gradually. At mile .94 you'll rejoin Clear Creek **[3]**—literally. A 20-foot section of the trail has washed out into the creek. You have to bushwhack around it. In another 350 feet, a bridge on your left takes you to the picnic ground and the Clear Creek furnace.

You'll now climb steeply and steadily, ascending 700 feet in a lung-busting .75 miles, with about a dozen switchbacks.

As you reach the first switchback, at mile 1.07, pause and look left. Clear Creek has carved a gorge **[4]**, which the trail is circling. The mountains of eastern Kentucky were all formed by the same action that created this mini-chasm.

At mile 1.6, during the leafless months, there's a panoramic view on your right **[5]**. You'll peer into the valley cut by Clear Creek, with the lake just visible below and Salt Lick off in the distance.

Following the trail another 750 feet, you'll reach the final switchback, and in another 600 feet you'll top out on a ridge at mile 1.75 **[6]**. You'll be on a high cliff. At your feet is the Pioneer Weapons Hunting Area, and behind that, the ridges edging Cave Run Lake. A large amphitheater-like overhang to the left is a natural arch in the early stages. The end of this

ridge is Carrington Rock, which was used by Native Americans and Civil War soldiers as a lookout.

The trail now follows the ridge through open woods, periodically joining an old logging road. Keep an eye out for wildlife here, as there are deer, wild turkey, and even bobcat up on the ridgetop. At mile 2.21 you'll reenter the woods, cross a gravel road, and climb gradually. The trail meanders up and down for another mile or so, with a generally upward direction. You'll top out at a large, eroded rock formation and then follow a rock face, passing over, around, and through some rather large boulders. At mile 3.49 there's a panoramic view of mountains on the right. But 350 feet further is a short side trail leading to a narrow limestone ridge at mile 3.54 **[7]**, so flat and level you'd swear it had been hewn with power tools. You are on the roof of Natural Arch. Below you is a spectacular view, resembling the basin and range country of the Rocky Mountains.

Return to the trail, which now descends steeply. You'll bottom out along a cliff face. Follow it 150 feet to Natural Arch, a medium-sized finished arch—that is, one that is no longer ragged around the edges—at mile 3.66 **[8]**.

About .33 miles further you'll reach a gravel road. The trail technically ends here. Instead of backtracking, go left and follow it, through hardwoods, for 3.2 miles to the intersection with FS-129. Turn left again and return to the trailhead .9 miles further.

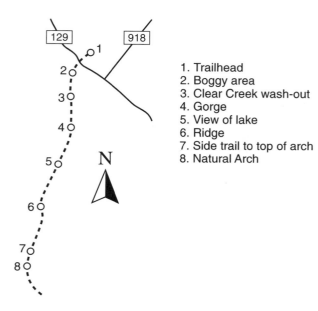

1. Trailhead
2. Boggy area
3. Clear Creek wash-out
4. Gorge
5. View of lake
6. Ridge
7. Side trail to top of arch
8. Natural Arch

Clear Creek Lake Trail 👢👢

Distance Round-Trip: 1.8 miles

Estimated Hiking Time: 45 to 60 minutes

Cautions: Be aware of one large boggy area and some unbridged creek crossings.

Trail Directions: This is a fairly easy trail, across rolling countryside, that follows the shore of Clear Creek Lake. It is one of the best wildlife-viewing trails in the region, and you are likely to see a diversity of critters, from songbirds of the forest canopy to Canada geese, deer, wild turkeys, and raccoons.

The trailhead **[1]** is 50 feet south of the lake parking lot entrance. It starts out firm, level, and sandy. However, at mile .06 you enter a boggy area where the trail seems to disappear into mud. Several blowdowns (uprooted and wind-blown trees) complicate trail finding further. You'll rejoin the trail after about 500 feet. A couple of hundred feet further on, the trail Ts into a gravel road.

If you want to avoid the boggy stretch, an alternate trailhead is this road. Pick it up 600 feet south of the parking lot entrance road.

At this point, from either trailhead, you'll immediately cross Clear Creek. During low water you may be able to rock hop. But most times, expect to get your feet wet. Follow the gravel road until mile .22, where you'll cross a second creek **[2]**, this time on a bed of cut-up and flattened car tires. A short distance further, the road turns left. The trail enters the woods on the right, following an overgrown forest road. (Caution: It may be muddy here, because you'll pass through a creek bottom.) Stay particularly alert for deer, which graze the road and the water in the creek.

At .4 miles you'll get your first glimpse of the lake **[3]**, a flat mirror reflecting the surrounding forest and sky. From here on you'll follow the shoreline. In another 500 feet you will see a goose nesting platform, built by the Forest Service to create favorable nesting conditions. Time it right, and you'll see the adults towing strings of dirty yellow fuzzballs behind them. The youngsters, until their feathers come in, are covered by hair and look like balls of stiff yarn rolling across the surface.

Continue through the second-growth hardwoods to mile .69, where the trail turns inland to avoid a large drain **[4]** whose mouth forms a lagoon or hollow, depending on how wet the conditions are. You'll return to the lakeshore and follow it another 1,000 feet to mile .87, where the trail ends at the earthen dam forming the lake **[5]**. Because of the ecosystem changes found here, this corner is particularly good for wildlife watching, so you might want to hunker down in the brush and spend some quality time observing the critters going about their lawful occupations.

Cross the dam, using the mowed path along its top, and note how the wildflowers have changed from forest types to those of the open fields. The dam is straight for about 900 feet. It then bends to the left. At any convenient point, you should descend toward the lake, angling in the direction of the highway above you. On your left you'll pick up a fisherman's path, which junctions with FS-129 at mile 1.07. Follow it about .75 miles back to the trailhead.

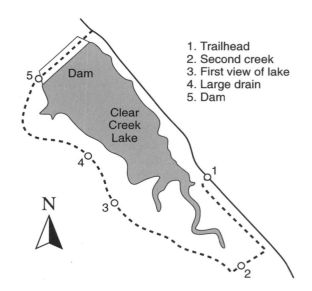

1. Trailhead
2. Second creek
3. First view of lake
4. Large drain
5. Dam

10. Red River Gorge Geologic Area

- Explore the largest concentration of known natural bridges and arches in the country.
- Join the search for Jonathan Swift's lost silver mines.
- See the story of geologic time told in the weathered and eroded cliffs.

Park Information

Red River Gorge is a 28,000-acre wilderness area known for the number, size, and variety of natural stone arches found inside its borders. Sculpted by 70 million years of wind and water, the gorge offers eye-filling topography with spectacular views of heavily forested land, ridges, and cliffs, in addition to the more than 100 known natural arches.

The area is rich in human history as well. Prehistoric people, as well as modern Native Americans, hunted through the region and used many of the rock houses (cavelike openings in the cliffs) as campgrounds and dwelling places.

In the 1700s, long hunters (residents of late-18th-century settlements who spent long periods hunting in the mountains of Tennessee and Kentucky) and settlers passed through on their way to the Bluegrass country to the west. Later, much of the land was mined for coal and was timbered heavily.

The story of Jonathan Swift and his lost silver mines is told throughout eastern Kentucky. On the basis of descriptions left in his many journals, treasure hunters believe the mines may have been located in what is now the Geologic Area.

Topographically, the gorge is a series of escarpments that slope on one side and then drop off suddenly on the other. Because the vegetation is very thick, off-trail hiking is discouraged unless you are very experienced traveling through this kind of country. Lacking such experience, you might find yourself slogging through a "rhody hell" that ends, unexpectedly, with a 300-foot drop.

Directions: Take I-64 east from Lexington or west from Ashland to the Mountain Parkway. Go east to the Slade interchange (exit 33) and connect with KY-15. Alternative access points are off KY-15: 3 miles west to KY-77; 3 miles east to Tunnel Ridge Road; 4.5 miles east to Koomer Ridge Road; and 8 miles east to KY-715. Each take you to a different trailhead.

Hours Open: Open year-round.

Facilities: Picnic areas with rest rooms; campgrounds; Gladie Information Center.

Permits and Rules: No motorized or mechanical vehicles on trails (this includes mountain bikes); no camping within 300 feet of roads or trails; no disturbing archeological sites or collecting artifacts.

Further Information: Contact Stanton District Office, Daniel Boone National Forest, 705 West College Avenue, Stanton, KY 40380; 606-663-2852.

Other Points of Interest

The Clifty Wilderness (606-663-2852) abuts Red River Gorge and is open to wilderness pursuits.

Four miles west on KY-11 is **Natural Bridge State Park** (see park #13), which offers a lodge, camping, and other resort activities in addition to hiking trails of its own.

Further west is **Torrent Falls** (606-668-6441), which drops 160 feet into a natural stone grotto. It is the heart of one of the premier rock-climbing areas in the East.

Nada Tunnel (no phone), 3 miles east on KY-77, is a 900-foot-long, one-lane tunnel, hand dug through a ridge. It was built around 1900 for steam locomotives.

Park Trails

There are more than 60 miles of hiking trails in the Red River Gorge, spread across 18 maintained trails. Most of these are strenuous, with large gains and losses of altitude in short stretches. The majority of trails are not loops. But because they crisscross each other, you can easily combine them into loop hikes of your own design. Here we list several typical hikes.

Silvermine Arch Trail 🥾🥾🥾—2 miles round-trip—is an easy trail except for the last .25 miles, which gets somewhat steep. Silvermine Arch is believed to mark one of Swift's lost mines.

Rough Trail 🥾🥾🥾🥾🥾—8.5 miles—is the longest continuous trail in the gorge, and one of the most strenuous. At one point, you gain (or lose) 600 feet in only .125 miles.

Hidden Arch Trail 🥾🥾—2 miles—is an easy trail that takes you to a diminutive arch measuring only four feet high and six feet long.

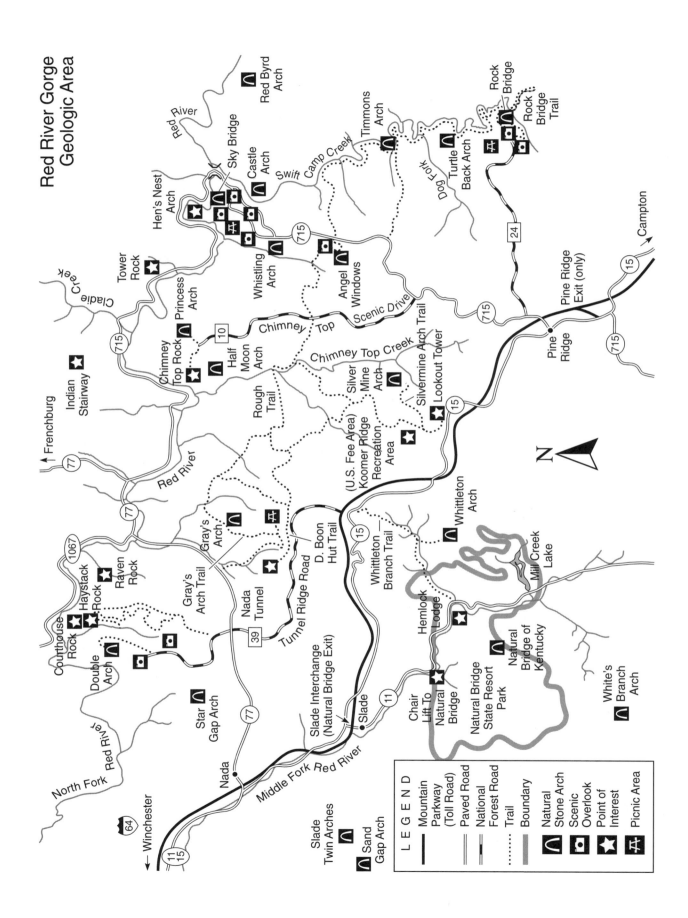

Red River Gorge
Geologic Area

Red River

Red Byrd Arch

Rock Bridge

Rock Bridge

Sky Bridge

Timmons Arch

Rock Bridge Trail

Castle Arch

Hen's Nest Arch

Swift Camp Creek

Turtle Back Arch

Camp Creek

Dog Fork

Tower Rock

Cradle Creek

715

24

Campton

Princess Arch

Whistling Arch

715

Angel Windows

Scenic Drive

Pine Ridge Exit (only)

15

Chimney Top

Indian Stairway

Frenchburg

715

10

Half Moon Arch

Chimney Top Creek

Silvermine Arch Trail

715

Pine Ridge

Chimney Top Rock

Rough Trail

Silver Mine Arch

Lookout Tower

15

Red River

77

(U.S. Fee Area)
Koomer Ridge
Recreation
Area

N

77

Whittleton Arch

Gray's Arch

D. Boon Hut Trail

15

Whittleton Branch Trail

Mill Creek Lake

1067

Raven Rock

Gray's Arch Trail

Nada Tunnel

Tunnel Ridge Road

Hemlock Lodge

Haystack Rock

Courthouse Rock

39

Natural Bridge of Kentucky

White's Branch Arch

Double Arch

Slade Interchange (Natural Bridge Exit)

Slade

Chair Lift To Natural Bridge

Natural Bridge State Resort Park

Star Gap Arch

77

11

North Fork

Red River

Nada

Middle Fork Red River

Winchester

64

11
15

Slade Twin Arches

Sand Gap Arch

LEGEND

Mountain Parkway (Toll Road)	
Paved Road	
National Forest Road	
Trail	
Boundary	
Natural Stone Arch	
Scenic Overlook	
Point of Interest	
Picnic Area	

Rock Bridge Loop Trail 👢👢👢

Distance Round-Trip: 1.35 miles

Estimated Hiking Time: 45 to 60 minutes

Cautions: Watch for drop-offs.

Trail Directions: From KY-715, take Rock Bridge Road right 3 miles to the picnic area and parking lot. The trailhead **[1]** is at an interpretive sign across from the parking lot. The trail starts through open hardwoods lined with laurel. It was once paved its entire length for easy walking and drainage, but there are now gaps and missing sections. At mile .05 the pavement ends at a set of 26 stone steps **[2]**, which dogleg to the right. In all, there will be four sets of stairs taking you down into the gorge cut by Swift Camp Creek.

Following the remaining pavement through a tunnel of laurel, you'll cross a small run at mile .13, over a plank bridge. On the right is a rock house (a cavelike opening in the cliff) with evidence of use by Native Americans **[3]**. Look for the black smoke stains on the ceiling.

You'll continue descending through a hardwood forest that includes broadleaf magnolias. If they're in bloom you'll know it by the large white blossoms, that can be as much as a foot across. The similar, smaller blooms are tulip poplars. At mile .34 the trail bottoms out, and you'll see Swift Camp Creek on your right **[4]**. The bottom is smooth and sandy here, making it a good place to cool off by wading in the creek. The trail climbs away from the creek, but generally follows it. Here you'll be shaded by magnolias and hemlocks that line the trail for about 500 feet. The blacktop ends, for now, except for one large patch.

At mile .62, you'll rejoin Swift Camp Creek at a small waterfall **[5]**. Only about 12 feet high, it usually doesn't have a heavy flow. If you can see behind the fall, you'll notice an arch in formation. It's a miniature version of Rock Bridge itself. Come back in about 20,000 years, and it might be completed.

You'll be tempted to cross the creek for a better view of the waterfall from downstream. This isn't necessary. Only a few feet further on the trail is a side trail taking you 35 feet to a stone-enclosed overlook that provides the best view.

A little further, at mile .66, you'll actually reach Rock Bridge **[6]**. This is the only arch in the Red River

Gorge that has water flowing under it. You can scramble up the arch and cross the creek here if you like.

Rock Bridge is noteworthy because many of Swift's journals seem to describe it as a landmark. Swift Camp Creek was, indeed, so named because Swift supposedly camped on it. You may notice some man-made defacing of the bridge. This was not done by treasure hunters. Back in the 1930s, when the area was logged, an effort was made to blow up the bridge so it wouldn't cause logjams.

The trail continues through a notch cut in the base of the bridge. From here on, it's paved all the way. There are several false trails around the bridge, so be sure to stay on the blacktop.

The trail climbs 750 feet, following the creek, to a trail junction. Dogleg sharply to the left to stay on the trail. You'll then climb 300 feet or so very steeply. There's a bench at the top of this stretch if you are weak of knee and short of lung. Use it! You'll be climbing some more.

At mile .97, you'll top out at an overlook **[7]**. The trail disappears in some exposed boulders. Just follow them generally upward and to the left until you reach a stone retaining wall. If the foliage isn't too thick, you can see back down into the Swift Camp gorge. Otherwise, you'll just see a bowl of trees.

The worst of the climb is over. You'll continue upward about 140 feet. The trail then levels out. In another .33 miles you'll reach the picnic area, east of the parking lot.

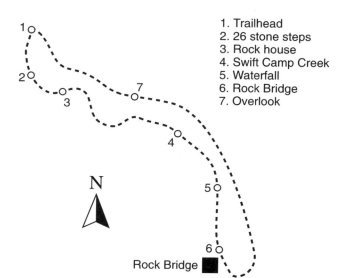

1. Trailhead
2. 26 stone steps
3. Rock house
4. Swift Camp Creek
5. Waterfall
6. Rock Bridge
7. Overlook

N

Rock Bridge

Gray's Arch Trail 👢👢👢👢

Distance Round-Trip: 2.24 miles

Estimated Hiking Time: 60 to 90 minutes

Cautions: Look out for high cliffs, hidden drop-offs, and slippery sections.

Trail Directions: From KY-15, take Tunnel Ridge Road 1 mile to Gray's Arch Recreation Area. The trailhead is near the rest rooms **[1]**. Start on trail #205, which is smooth, level, and sandy as it passes through a hardwood forest. At mile .25 it dead-ends into Rough Trail (#221) **[2]**, which you should follow to the right. The trail follows a ridgeline, with a valley on your left, and then a parallel ridge that shows interesting rock formations and cliff faces.

You'll come to a meadow at .45 miles that was a homestead until it was absorbed by the National Forest. The foundations of a cabin used to be visible, but now they are pretty well covered by vegetation. The trail narrows to footpath size as it passes the meadow, then widens again when it reenters the woods.

As you follow the trail through the forest, you'll come to a large hollow on the right at mile .70 **[3]**. This is one of the microhabitats these mountains are known for. When we visited, for instance, the magnolias, which were barely budding in most of the area, were in full bloom here. This was at least three weeks before they bloomed anywhere else. And there are so many of them in the hollow you'd think you had stumbled onto a patch of rain forest.

Shortly after passing the hollow, the trail is redirected. Stay to the left. The trail will narrow and start descending on a long, gradual grade.

At mile .95, Gray's Arch suddenly comes into view on the right **[4]**. Do not cross the safety rail. There's a hidden drop-off just a few feet off the trail. And that first step is a doozy—dropping about 200 feet into a rocky hollow. Unfortunately, the edge is not visible until you've stepped over it.

Gray's Arch is a "buttress arch," so called because it forms in the very end of a ridge and seems to support it. From the trail it looks like a huge elephant's trunk reaching down into the valley. You're standing on the elephant's head, just over his eye.

If you turned around here, the trail would rank as a moderate two-boot or three-boot hike. The rough part is in front of you.

About 200 feet along the trail, at mile .99, is a large rock-shelter (a cavelike opening in the cliff) that is very popular as a rest stop **[5]**. A sheer cliff drops off in front of it, so watch your footing and hang on to your children. Shortly after the rock-shelter is the head of a steep staircase with 50 steps. You dogleg right at the bottom and then face 13 more steps. The trail then turns sharply left and goes steeply downhill. This section is almost always slippery and can be especially slick after a rain.

You'll bottom out in a fern garden at mile 1.0 **[6]**. Rough Trail turns left; you want to go straight on the trail leading to the arch. On your right is a view of the drop-off from the elephant's head position and the hanging garden that hides it. You can see why it's not a good idea to cross the safety rail.

About 100 feet further is a set of rock-shelters eroded into the base of Gray's Arch. This is a popular party spot, especially with young people, so don't be surprised if you find lots of trash left here. Volunteers and Forest Service staff do their best to keep it clear, but sadly, this is a never ending battle. The trail continues through some loose rock to the far base of Gray's Arch (where the elephant's trunk touches the ground) at mile 1.12 **[7]**.

Return to the trailhead by backtracking.

1. Trailhead
2. Rough Trail
3. Magnolia hollow
4. Gray's Arch overlook
5. Rock-shelter
6. Fern garden
7. Base of Gray's Arch

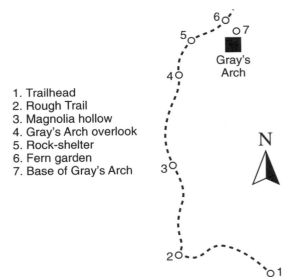

D. Boon Hut Trail 👢👢👢👢

Distance Round-Trip: 1 or 1.5 miles with extension

Estimated Hiking Time: 1 to 2 hours

Cautions: Be aware of exposed rocks and roots and possible water on the trail. Use caution if you are rock hopping, and watch for steep drop-offs.

Trail Directions: D. Boon Hut Trail is a moderate hike, with some climbing and rock hopping, that takes you to a massive rock-shelter (a cavelike opening in the ridge) containing the remains of an old niter mine. A side trail takes you to Indian petroglyphs.

The trailhead **[1]** is off the east driveway from the Gray's Arch parking area on Tunnel Ridge Road. The trail descends, gradually, parallel to Tunnel Ridge Road, with a deep hardwood hollow on the right, until mile .08, where you'll reach a wooden stairway descending 43 steep steps **[2]**. Turn left at the bottom of the stairs until reaching the eroded cliffs and rock-shelter at mile .13 **[3]**. A well-defined trail doglegs right here. This turn is a side trail leading to the Indian petroglyphs. The direct route goes straight, but the .25-mile side trail is worth taking.

It descends into a second large hollow that contains many large-leafed magnolias. These are more brushy than treelike and make up most of the understory.

A large eroded and undercut cliff comes into view at mile .19 **[4]**. This cliff contains several large, round openings, looking like nesting holes for giant swallows. In fact, they are caused by imbedded shale "pipes," which erode more slowly than the surrounding matrix. The trail climbs up to the cliff, which you'll reach at mile .21 **[5]**, entering a large rock-shelter.

On the right end of the rock-shelter is a sandstone rock enclosed by a chain-link fence. Lots of luck reading the petroglyphs incised in that rock. Archeologists have no idea what they mean. Return to the trail junction **[3]** and turn right. At the end of the rock-shelter is a second set of stairs, not as steep.

As you follow the trail, note the rock-shelters in the cliffs across a deep valley on your right. The area around this trail contains more recessed caves than anywhere else in the region. You'll see many of them, in fact, that are duplexes, that is, stacked one above the other.

The trail is level here. Note, at mile .43, the laurel overhanging the cliffs on your left **[6]**. You can clearly see the danger of bushwhacking through rhody hells, as the edge of the cliff is totally obscured by the greenery. From the top, that first step is a killer—literally. At mile .49, you'll cross a small creek on a footbridge. Look to your left, where there's a duplex rock-shelter **[7]**. The creek issues from the lower one. Both, however, were cut by that creek eroding headward.

You'll come to a fern garden at mile .52 **[8]**. Although the ferns and laurel form a dark green tunnel, we were more impressed with the cushion of fallen magnolia leaves that made a floral carpet beneath our soles. The green tunnel continues to mile .66, where the Martins Fork Trail junctures from the right **[9]**. Go left, ascending to the cliff face, and follow it to the large, fenced rock-shelter at mile .75 **[10]**.

Behind the chain-link fence (which the Forest Service erected to prevent vandalism) are artifacts from a niter mine dating to the War of 1812. The boards scattered about used to be a hut. On one of the boards the inscription "D. Boon" was discovered, but nobody is sure whether the great pioneer visited this site. Signs interpret both the mine and the hut.

When you're finished opining whether the name was carved by Boone or not, retrace your steps to the trailhead.

1. Trailhead
2. Wooden stairs
3. Rock-shelter
4. Undercut cliff
5. Petroglyphs
6. Overhanging laurel
7. Duplex rock-shelter
8. Fern garden
9. Trail junction
10. D. Boon Hut rock-shelter

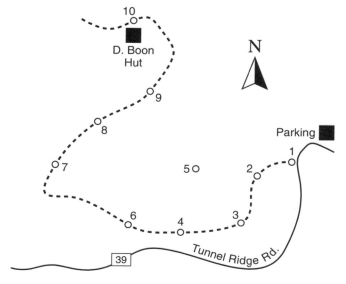

Whittleton Branch Trail

👢👢👢👢

Distance Round-Trip: 2.3 miles

Estimated Hiking Time: 1.5 to 2 hours

Cautions: The area includes high banks, washouts, and exposed rocks and roots. The trail is covered by creek rock, so be careful if you are hopping.

Trail Directions: Although offering some technical challenges, Whittleton Branch is the prettiest trail in Kentucky. In addition, it provides insights into the geology of eastern Kentucky.

The trailhead **[1]** is at the intersection of KY-15 and Tunnel Ridge Road. The trail ends at the Whittleton Campground, by Natural Bridge State Park. If you have two vehicles, do the whole trail. If not, hike only to Whittleton Arch and return the same way.

The trail is part of the 254-mile Sheltowee Trace and is marked by white diamonds and white turtles. Although starting level, it quickly descends, with a couple switchbacks, fairly steeply. You'll bottom out at a T at mile .1 **[2]**. The trail right leads to a layered rock-shelter. Go left, following Whittleton Branch. The trail is level and smooth, passing through laurel, hemlock, and second-growth hardwoods dating from the 1930s, when the area was extensively logged.

At mile .39 you'll cross the creek on the first of several footbridges **[3]**. The old Mountain Central Railroad, whose bed you are following, actually crossed 26 times. You have fewer crossings than that, but about half will require wading when the creek is high.

At mile .44 you enter the creek bed **[4]** and share it in a minicanyon, for the next 200 feet, before it flows to the right. The trail is rough after leaving the creek, until mile .48 where the creek plunges about 8 feet over a stone lip **[5]**, then cascades downward another 20 feet or so. A few feet farther, at mile .5, there is a rock-shelter below you on the left **[6]**. It, and several like it, are lower than the trail because the railbed was raised to maintain an even grade. There are still rail ties imbedded in the trail in this section.

At mile .72 watch for the undercut cliff on the left **[7]**. The swirls and twists of the folded and faulted imbedded shales covering the rock face form a surrealistic relief map. However, the roads on the map lead only to your imagination.

You'll cross the creek several times over the next .2 miles, sometimes on footbridges and sometimes by wading or rock hopping. Just before wading across at

mile 1.0, note the small cave mouth low on the right-hand cliff **[8]**. You can hear an underground stream flowing in the cave. Entering this cave without proper equipment can be dangerous, so don't do it!

The Whittleton Arch Trail **[9]** enters left at mile 1.12, starting on a footbridge high over Whittleton Branch Trail. The trail is a steep, steady climb along the banks of a feeder creek. You'll cross that creek on a footbridge, then, a few feet farther, at mile 1.33, is the arch itself **[10]**.

Known as a waterfall step arch, you'll enter a massive, wide opening that looks more like a giant rock-shelter than an arch. High above you is a much smaller opening, through which water once flowed, eroding and enlarging the opening on the downhill side.

Return to the trail junction **[9]**. If you are returning to KY-15, retrace your steps. If not, turn left. The trail continues, level, with several bridge crossings, for .8 mile until reaching Whittleton Campground **[11]**. Frankly, this section is not as scenic as the trail, and you won't miss anything by returning to the trailhead on Tunnel Ridge Road.

1. Trailhead
2. T
3. Footbridge
4. Minicanyon
5. Waterfall
6. Depressed rock-shelter
7. Undercut cliff
8. Cave
9. Whittleton Arch Trail junction
10. Whittleton Arch
11. Whittleton Campground

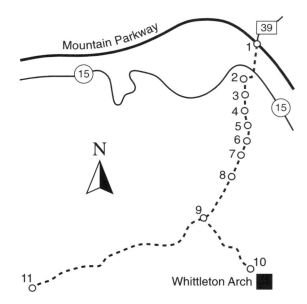

11. Cumberland Gap National Historical Park

- Travel the route taken by more than 400,000 settlers as well as innumerable Native Americans before them.
- Stand at the Pinnacle, where three states—Kentucky, Tennessee, and Virginia—come together.
- Visit Hensley Settlement—site of an isolated, turn-of-the-century mountain farm community that is being restored by the National Park Service.

Park Information

Cumberland Gap, the only pass in the Cumberland Mountains for more than 100 miles, made the lands west of the Allegheny Mountains accessible. Long before Dr. Thomas Walker "discovered" the 900-foot-deep gap in 1750, the Warrior's Path passed through it, carrying prehistoric and modern Indians back and forth through the mountains.

Cumberland Gap was once thought to be a wind gap (an opening in a ridge carved by wind and dust), but such is not the case. Yellow Creek once flowed here, but it was diverted northward by land movements into the Cumberland River. Yellow Creek Valley, however, leads to the Narrows, a gap crossing Pine Mountain. This opened the Bluegrass region to exploration and settlement.

Daniel Boone and his party of long hunters first crossed the gap in 1769. Then, in 1775, he was in charge of the tree cutters who blazed a road for Richard Henderson and the first group of settlers that included women.

By 1800, the Wilderness Road was the major route through the mountains, carrying settlers west and livestock and other goods east. Later on, Federal and Confederate forces jockeyed for control of Cumberland Gap, as it was the key to the middle South.

Rich in human as well as natural history, Cumberland Gap is being restored to its pre-1800 condition. US-25E, which once carried vehicular traffic through the gap, has been closed. Traffic now passes under the mountain through a new set of tunnels. The roadbed will be removed and the topography restored to its original contours. The Wilderness Road, which once carried pioneers into Kentucky, will also be restored. Plans are to have the restoration completed by the year 2010. Right now you can see the process going on, but because of the construction and restoration work in progress, the official brochure is out of date. Be sure to ask for clear directions at the Visitor Center.

Directions: From Middlesboro, Kentucky, go south on US-25E 1 mile to the Visitor Center. Trailheads are at various locations in the 20,000-acre park that sprawls over Kentucky, Virginia, and Tennessee.

Hours Open: Open year-round. The Visitor Center is open from 8:00 A.M. to 5:00 P.M. Day trails close at dark.

Facilities: Campground, picnic areas, Visitor Center.

Permits and Rules: Camping and fires in authorized locations only, with free backcountry-use permit.

Further Information: Contact Cumberland Gap National Historical Park, P.O. Box 1848, Middlesboro, KY 40965; 606-248-2617.

Other Points of Interest

Pine Mountain State Resort Park (see park #12) is half an hour north.

Wilderness Road Tours (606-248-2626) conducts interpreted van tours of historical sites in and near Cumberland Gap and along the Wilderness Road and Boone's Trace.

Park Trails

There are about 50 miles of hiking trails in the park, ranging from self-guided nature walks to overnight treks. Few of these trails are loops, but you can, with some planning, create your own loop hikes. Most of the trails at Cumberland Gap lend themselves more to overnight backpack trips. If you plan on backpacking, don't forget to obtain a backcountry permit at the Visitor Center.

Tri-State Peak 🥾🥾🥾🥾—2.6 miles round-trip—takes you from the iron furnace in Cumberland Gap to the highest point in the park.

Sugar Run Trail/Ridge Trail/Pinnacle 🥾🥾🥾🥾—3.9 miles each way—is a strenuous 7.8 miles with much climbing.

Chadwell Gap Trail 🥾🥾🥾🥾🥾—6.2 miles round-trip—is a steep climb from the trailhead above Caylor, Virginia, to Hensley Settlement and back.

Cumberland Gap
National Historical Park

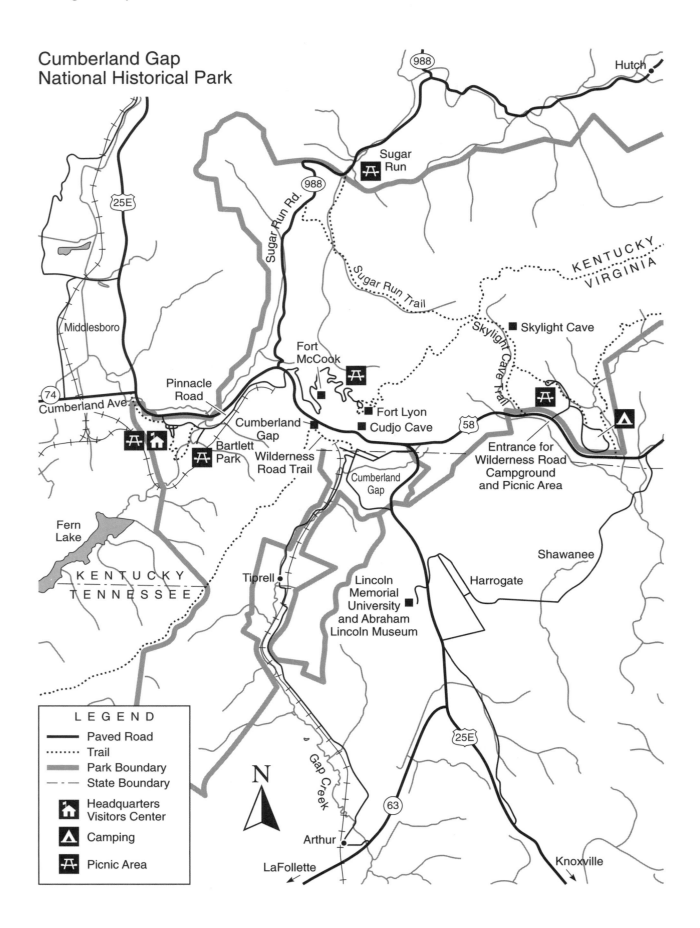

Skylight Cave Trail 👢👢👢👢

Distance Round-Trip: 1.2 miles

Estimated Hiking Time: 60 to 90 minutes

Cautions: Watch for exposed rock. You will need a flashlight in order to explore the cave fully.

Trail Directions: It's a steep, steady climb to Skylight Cave. But the rewards are worth the effort, because this is a wild cave you can safely explore with no more equipment than a flashlight.

The trailhead **[1]** is in the Wilderness Road Picnic Area, off US-58 in Virginia. Use the campground entrance. You'll start on the Lewis Hollow Trail, through a hardwood forest. The trail is paved as it passes through the campground, but the blacktop ends fairly quickly.

At mile .24 you'll T into Skylight Cave Trail **[2].** Turn right. The trail steepens as it passes through open hickory/oak woods. There are several false trails along the way, but the main trail is very obvious—it's broad, fairly level, and well maintained.

Limestone Cliffs will appear on the right at mile .47. Shortly afterward, at mile .49, a side trail on the right leads very steeply to a small, gated cave **[3].** Shine your light into it and you'll see that it resembles a rough-hewn tunnel. This is not a safe passageway; that's why the mouth is sealed. Return to the main trail.

In about 500 feet you'll come on a set of stairs leading to Skylight Cave, which you'll reach at mile .61 **[4].**

The mouth of the cave is low, and the word "mouth" fits it well. Passing through this, you'll enter a high-ceilinged chamber. On your right is the lighthouse (or skylight) that gives the cave its name.

The skylight is a small, round opening into the cave, maybe six feet in diameter. It opens onto a ridge about 15 feet above you. The opening allows ample light into the front half of the cave; that's why you can enter this part without a flashlight.

Under the skylight, a thin crack tunnels down into the limestone making up the ridge. The back of the chamber seems to be blocked by a pile of fallen boulders, but it isn't. You can climb over, or around, the rock pile.

If you haven't brought a light, you can easily explore up to this point anyway. But do not enter the tunnel under the skylight without a flashlight. Do not explore it if you are alone—if something goes wrong, nobody will know you are in there. Be cautious as you examine the cave. The floor is slick and muddy, and you could easily slip.

Behind the rock pile, the chamber continues. The floor there is covered with edge-stone walls, looking like the Great Wall of China done in miniature. These walls are formed when minerals collect at the edges of standing water. When the water evaporates, the walls—or edges—are left behind. Each time water puddles in that spot, the walls grow higher and thicker.

The chamber narrows down into a natural tunnel, about 30 feet long. It's here, at the rear of the chamber, that you'll find cave formations. There are young stalactites and stalagmites forming everywhere, measuring from about one-half inch to four inches. Especially interesting are the lines of them, forming in thin ceiling cracks. Left alone, in about a quarter-million years they will form a set of bars across the tunnel.

Do not touch them! If you do, oils from your fingers will prevent further growth. Nature has already spent several thousand years getting them to this size, and you don't want to stop the process.

When you've had your fill of the cave, return the way you came. Or, for a longer hike, you can continue to the Ridge Trail and then take it to the Pinnacle—a total of 2.8 strenuous miles.

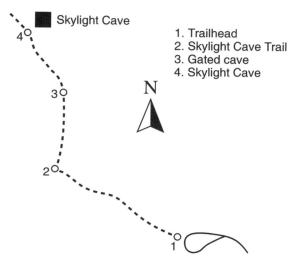

1. Trailhead
2. Skylight Cave Trail
3. Gated cave
4. Skylight Cave

Wilderness Road Trail 👢👢👢👢

Distance Round-Trip: 1.25 miles

Estimated Hiking Time: 45 to 60 minutes

Cautions: Watch for exposed rocks and wash-outs.

Trail Directions: The Wilderness Road Trail takes you to Cumberland Gap Pass, partially overlying the original Wilderness Road. You'll literally be walking in the footsteps of the pioneers who explored and settled the "dark and bloody land" of Kentucky.

The trailhead [1] is east of the iron furnace in Cumberland Gap, Tennessee. This was a cold-blast furnace that used charcoal as fuel to produce wrought-iron pigs. It dates to 1820.

The trail climbs through an oak/hickory forest, with some maples and tulip poplars, until mile .26, where you'll reach the site of an old homestead [2]. Stone retaining walls and brick walkways are all that remain in a clearing that's being reclaimed by the forest. Ignore the steep trail climbing above the homestead. It's easier climbing on the main trail.

The trail doglegs to the left as it rises. Just above the site of the old homestead, a seasonal waterfall has formed a multi-tiered wash-out above and below the trail at mile .34 [3]. During wet periods, water stair-steps down these tiers in a bridal veil of spindrift.

A thousand or so feet further is a small rock covered with orange, green, red, and white lichen, at mile .54 [4]. It's easy to bypass, but when you spot it you'll think you're gazing at a small Jackson Pollock painting.

The trail continues climbing until mile .6, where you'll face a set of steep stone stairs [5]. Climb them 150 feet until you top out in Cumberland Gap Pass—the highest point in the gap itself. Between 1750 and the early 1800s, more than 400,000 explorers and settlers passed through the gap on their way to the western wilderness.

To your left is old US-25E, which is now bypassed by the new tunnels. If there is anything in the world as lonely as an abandoned highway, we don't know what it is. The blacktop is there, awaiting the load of traffic it never will carry again. Stand on the white line and listen as the wind whistles through the pass. You'll think you've somehow fallen into a postapocalypse movie.

Examine the low hills on either side of the pass. They were originally much higher, but were dynamited out when the road was built. The original contour will be reestablished as part of the park's restoration program. Just down the slope, on the southwestern side of the highway, was the original Wilderness Road. It too is slated for restoration to the way it looked in 1800.

A few feet to the south, historical markers explain some of the Civil War actions that took place in the gap area. Because it controlled access to the southern states, Cumberland Gap was a strategically important site during the Civil War. Both regular troops and guerrilla units raided back and forth through it, yet no major battles actually occurred in the area.

Return to the trail and continue another 115 feet to mile .63, where you'll come upon the Tri-State Monument [6]. Erected in 1915, it is a four-sided truncated pyramid; the sides were sponsored by Daughters of the American Revolution chapters in Kentucky, Virginia, Tennessee, and North Carolina. The North Carolina plaque is unfortunately missing. Ironically, each of the states uses a different date for when Daniel Boone made his trek.

The monument sits on the original Wilderness Road and will remain in place. Park officials say it may be restored as well.

Return to the trailhead by retracing your steps. If you prefer a longer hike, continue past the monument to Tri-State Peak, the highest point in the park. This will add .8 miles to the hike, each way.

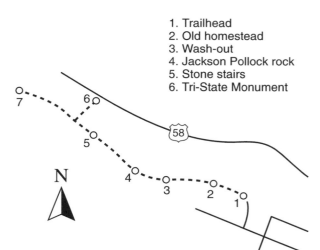

1. Trailhead
2. Old homestead
3. Wash-out
4. Jackson Pollock rock
5. Stone stairs
6. Tri-State Monument

12. Pine Mountain State Resort Park

- See a huge boulder chained to a cliff, supposedly to prevent the rock from sliding down into the town of Pineville.
- Explore a remnant old-growth forest of massive hemlock, beech, and tulip poplar trees.
- Search out the pale corydalis—a pink and yellow wildflower with delicately divided grayish-green leaves that grows nowhere else in Kentucky—and other rare plants.

Park Information

Pine Mountain, like all mountains making up the Cumberland Range, is a massive ridgelike structure, stretching 125 miles from Pineville almost to the Virginia border.

Pine Mountain State Resort Park, the oldest of Kentucky's state parks and to many the most beautiful, sprawls across the southeastern slopes of the mountain. Here some of the prettiest native flowering plants flourish, including mountain laurel, red azalea, pink lady's slipper, and great rhododendron. Pale corydalis can be found nowhere else in the Bluegrass state, and the rare showy gentian also grows in the dry woods on the upper slopes.

Laurel Cove is a natural forest cove that has been transformed into an amphitheater with seating for 2,000. Each May the Mountain Laurel Festival is held there.

The park is best known for the chained rock. In 1933, as a practical joke, local teenagers attached a large chain to a huge boulder and anchored the chain to the cliffside. The legend soon grew that the chain keeps the boulder in place, protecting the town of Pineville.

Pine Mountain is rich in human as well as natural history. The Narrows, one of the few passes through the mountain, lies just outside the park borders. This allowed access to the interior Bluegrass country, and the Wilderness Road passed just beyond the park gates. About 400,000 pioneers traveled the road between 1775 and the early 1800s.

Directions: From Pineville, follow US-25E south 1 mile to the second park entrance. Turn right and follow the park access road 4 miles to the lodge. The first entrance also leads to the lodge, but the distance is 3 miles longer this way.

Hours Open: Open year-round; the campground is open from April 1 to October 31. Trails close at dusk.

Facilities: Lodge, cottages, campground, convention center, golf course, swimming pool, picnic grounds.

Permits and Rules: Only foot travel on trails.

Further Information: Contact Pine Mountain State Resort Park, 1050 State Park Road, Pineville, KY 40977; 606-337-3066.

Other Points of Interest

Cumberland Gap National Historical Park (see park #11) is a half hour south on US-25E.

Dr. Thomas Walker State Historic Site (606-546-4400), 31 miles northwest, has a replica of Kentucky's first log cabin, built shortly after Dr. Walker "discovered" Cumberland Gap in 1750.

Wilderness Road Tours (606-248-2626) in Middlesboro conducts interpreted van tours of historical sites in and near Cumberland Gap and along the Wilderness Road and Boone's Trace.

Park Trails

Nine trails ranging in length from .5 to 1.75 miles provide access to the varied ecosystems found in the park. Most of the trails are hilly, some very hilly. In one case, you literally climb from the bottom of the mountain to the crest, with an 1,100-foot change in elevation in less than 2 miles.

Hemlock Garden Trail 🥾🥾🥾🥾—a .63-mile loop—takes you through a section of old-growth hemlocks, oaks, and tulip poplars, some of them more than 200 years old.

Chained Rock Trail 🥾🥾🥾—.5 miles each way—is a short, downhill walk to the famous

chained rock. The hike back is strenuous, with a 300-foot change in altitude.

Laurel Cove Trail 🥾🥾🥾🥾—1.75 miles each way—is the longest and most difficult trail in the park.

Lost Trail 🥾🥾🥾🥾—this .5-mile loop is a short but difficult trail through some of the prettiest sections of the park.

Rock Hotel Trail 🥾🥾🥾🥾—1 mile each way—is a strenuous hike to a large sandstone rock-shelter (a cavelike opening in the cliff, usually the start of a natural arch).

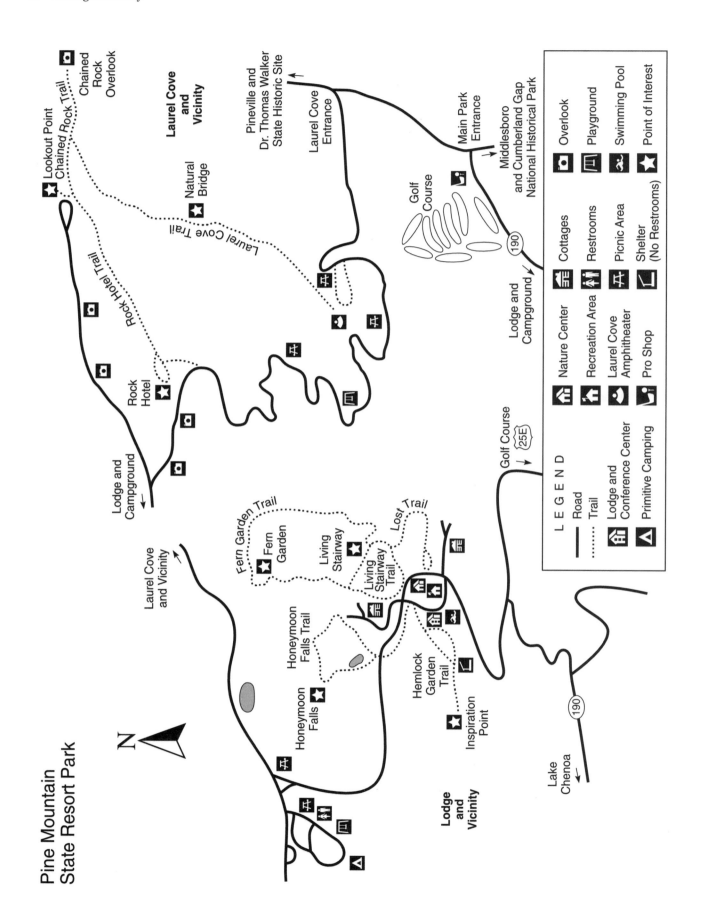

Pine Mountain
State Resort Park

Living Stairway/Fern Garden Double Loop

Distance Round-Trip: 1.3 miles

Estimated Hiking Time: 45 to 60 minutes

Cautions: Look out for drop-offs, exposed rock and roots, and loose rock.

Trail Directions: To reach the trailhead **[1]**, follow the path from the lodge past the fossil tree and Nature Center to the road. Make two rights to the trail, a total of about 300 feet. You can also reach the trailhead by following the park road, but the distance is then more than 1,000 feet.

From the trailhead, the trail climbs gradually through mixed pines and hardwoods until reaching a crack in a rock outcrop. A short set of stairs takes you up and over these rocks, where at mile .11, you cross a sandstone outcrop **[2]** whose unusual shape has given it the name "turtleback rocks." From here you can see part of the Log Mountains south of Pine Mountain.

The trail climbs steadily until mile .21, where you'll come to a sharp cliff dropping off into a laurel-filled hollow **[3]**. Time it right, and the hollow will be a blaze of bright white flowers. Otherwise, a painting of this hollow would have to be called "a study in green"—green lacquered laurel and rhododendron leaves, lighter shades of fern, still lighter mosses, and the dark greens of hemlock needles. The trail turns left and follows the edge of the hollow.

At mile .25, a side trail on the right leads down to the metal stairway that parallels the living stairway **[4]**. The living stairway is a large tulip poplar that for many years connected a mountain bluff with a laurel bottom. Despite the damage created when it had stairs cut into it, the tree survived. With the living stairway no longer in use, the metal stairway now serves the purpose. At the bottom, you can cross the creek for an up-close look at the 90-foot-long tulip poplar that for many years served as the only way up and down the sandstone cliff. Note the steps cut into the wood and the stone stairs held in place with spikes. It seems like a miracle that the tree survived this abuse.

Turning right at the bottom of the stairs brings you to the Fern Garden Trail.

You'll soon pass through the hollow you saw from above. Indeed, the cliffs supporting the Living Stairway Trail are now on your right, with hanging gardens of ferns and moss cascading down their face. At mile .4 you'll start climbing out of the hollow through a green tunnel of laurel **[5]**, much of which overhangs the trail.

The trail climbs steadily until, at mile .46, you'll climb through a crack in the rocks into a T. On the right is a false trail. Go left, noting the scale lichen on the rocks as you make the turn. It looks as though the sandstone has received a bad sunburn and now is peeling **[6]**.

About 500 feet further, you'll top out and then immediately descend steeply into another hollow. The overhanging ledge at the bottom of the trail, at mile .55 **[7]**, is a good place to stop and catch your breath.

A thousand feet further, ferns start appearing. You'll descend gradually into yet another hollow, where it's much cooler. Ferns, in big patches, increase until at mile .74 you come to the Fern Garden **[8]**—several acres of cinnamon and royal ferns, some of which tower chest high. Because of the moist environment, sweet gum trees can be found here as well. The air feels icy and has a greenish cast, reflected off these giant ferns.

The trail climbs out of the fern bottom until reaching an unmarked Y. Go left, and descend steeply into another hollow. Climbing out of it, you'll rejoin the Living Stairway Trail. Turn right until you reach a Y. The left trail descends to the trailhead.

1. Trailhead
2. Turtleback rocks
3. Study-in-green hollow
4. Living stairway
5. Laurel tunnel
6. Peeling rocks
7. Overhanging ledge
8. Fern Garden

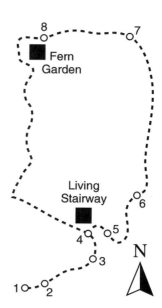

Honeymoon Falls Trail

🥾🥾🥾🥾🥾

Distance Round-Trip: 1.46 miles

Estimated Hiking Time: 60 to 90 minutes

Cautions: Watch out for high banks, eroded sections, exposed roots and rocks, and loose rocks.

Trail Directions: Honeymoon Falls is the largest waterfall in the park. Visible all year, it may be a mere trickle during long dry spells but is spectacular during the wet seasons. The section from the trailhead to the falls is lush with thick growths of rhododendron and old-growth hemlock.

More than any other trail in the park, Honeymoon Falls Trail is a delight to all your senses. You'll hear, smell, feel, and even taste as much as you see.

To reach the trailhead [1], follow the path from the lodge past the fossil tree and Nature Center. Ignore the arrowed sign saying "hiking trails." Cross the park road to the trail, a total of about 280 feet. A stone cairn marks the trailhead, which starts uphill through mixed hardwoods. In just a few feet you'll pass several slump blocks (large rock chunks, broken off the cliffs, that have migrated), each wearing a crown of ferns.

The trail follows a stream hidden below you in laurel and rhody thickets. You'll hear its laughter more than you see it. Then, at mile .16, you'll feel a blast of cold air [2]. Low down on the right is a small entrance to a cave, and the frigid air is issuing from the cave.

You'll start climbing fairly steeply from here until topping out at the park access road across from a picnic area at mile .22 [3]. Turn left, following the road until you pick up the trail at mile .26. There is limited parking here, and you can use this spot as an alternate trailhead [4].

Here you'll start on an old dirt road that becomes the top of a cement retaining wall. This is the remains of a dam that formed a pond, now overgrown and filled with rotting vegetation. On hot, still days you can taste the fetid sweet-and-sour aroma of the land reclaiming its own.

In just over 300 feet you'll cross the creek that fed the dam. The trail follows this creek through a tunnel of laurel and rhododendron, crossing it several times (sometimes on footbridges; at other times you'll have to wade). Then, at mile .55, you'll reach a natural amphitheater. Honeymoon Falls [5] drops 25 feet

from the semicircular cliff edge above you. Depending on water flow, it can be a miniature Niagara—or a mistlike blanket of water droplets you're not quite sure you're seeing.

The trail moves left, away from the falls, until reaching an undercut cliff at mile .56 [6]. There's an intermittent waterfall on the right side of the cliff. Because it's often obscured by trees, you are as likely to hear it as see it. From here the trail climbs very steeply, following the edge of a laurel-choked gorge. You'll crest out at mile .67 and then immediately descend until mile .71, where you'll pass through a slump-block tunnel [7]. Rock slabs, leaning against each other, created this natural passageway. Two hundred feet further, you'll squeeze through a crack in a moss-covered boulder and then climb steeply again.

At mile .8, you'll top out in a mixed upland forest of hardwoods and pines [8]. Listen here for the sound of pileated woodpeckers hammering for grubs. During leafless months, the Log Mountains are visible through the trees on your right.

The trail follows the ridge for 1,000 feet and then descends steeply right at the 1-mile mark. At mile 1.2, you'll pass through the picnic area [3] to the park access road. Descend from there to the trailhead.

1. Trailhead
2. Cold-air outlet
3. Picnic area
4. Alternate trailhead
5. Honeymoon Falls
6. Undercut cliff
7. Slump-block tunnel
8. Upland forest

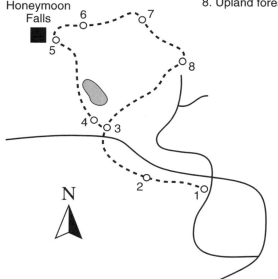

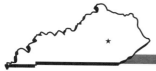

13. Natural Bridge State Resort Park

- Visit the most famous natural stone arch in the Southeast.
- Discover rare and endangered species, such as the Virginia big-eared bat and the small yellow lady's slipper.
- Explore the flora, fauna, and geography of this preserved Cumberland Plateau forest landscape.

Park Information

Contrary to popular belief, Kentucky's Natural Bridge is not the largest of the natural carved arches and bridges in the state. In fact, there are at least 105 natural stone arches within 5 miles of the park, and two of those are larger. But the 65-foot-tall, 78-foot-long sandstone span is the most famous such formation in the Southeast. It's been a tourist attraction since the early 1800s.

But there's a lot more to this area than Natural Bridge. About half the park—994 acres—has been set aside to protect and preserve the unique Cumberland Plateau landscape, typified by carved and eroded sandstone and limestone cliffs and rhododendron thickets (called "rhody hells" throughout the Plateau region).

For an overview of the park, ride the sky lift to Laurel Ridge. From the end of the sky lift, it is a short walk to the top of Natural Bridge.

Directions: Take I-64 east from Lexington or west from Ashland to the Mountain Parkway. Follow that east to the Slade interchange (Route 11). Take Route 11 east about 2 miles to the park entrance.

Hours Open: Open year-round.

Facilities: Hiking is the only activity allowed in the preserve section. The rest of the park has facilities for camping, fishing, picnicking, bicycling, and boating.

Permits and Rules: There is no fee for use of the park. Rock climbing is not permitted in the park; no backcountry camping or fires. Pets, even on leashes, are prohibited in the backcountry. Only hiking is permitted on the trails. There is a moderate fee for use of the sky lift.

Further Information: Contact Natural Bridge State Resort Park, 2135 Natural Bridge Road, Slade, KY 40376; 606-663-2214.

Other Points of Interest

About 5 miles east of the park are the **Daniel Boone National Forest** and the **Red River Gorge Geologic Area** (see park #10). Known as "the Land of Arches," the Red River Gorge is a 53,000-acre wilderness area containing more than 80 known natural arches. The region is crisscrossed with a network of hiking trails. In addition, a 45-mile drive tour, starting and stopping at Natural Bridge State Resort Park, provides a good overview of the area. The drive takes you right to, or within a short hike of, some of the arches, including Sky Bridge, Moonshiner's Arch, and Castle Arch.

A mile east of the park is **Jim Harrison's Kentucky Reptile Zoo** (606-663-9160). This is not one of those typical side-of-the-road animal parks. Rather, it's a serious educational facility with more than 70 reptiles on display and ongoing presentations. Harrison also runs a large venom lab nearby and is considered the man to call for information about treating snake bites.

Several miles to the west is **Torrent Falls** (606-668-6441), where a waterfall drops 70 feet off a cliff. The cliffs in the Torrent Falls gorge are very popular with climbers, who consider them the finest in Kentucky. A new bed-and-breakfast sits at the mouth of the gorge. An immense rock-shelter has been formed behind the falls, and you can make arrangements at the bed-and-breakfast to camp there.

Park Trails

There are more than 18 miles of trails in Natural Bridge State Resort Park, all of which either start or stop at the arch. Most of them are straight runs, but it's easy to construct loops from several trails for longer hikes.

Sand Gap 👢👢👢👢—8.5 miles—is the longest, and one of the most strenuous, trails in the park; it climbs several steep ridges.

Lakeside 👢—.5 miles—is a fairly flat walk along the shore of the Hoedown Island lake.

Henson's Arch 👢👢👢—.3 miles—is a short but steep trail to a small arch on the hillside overlooking Whittleton Campground.

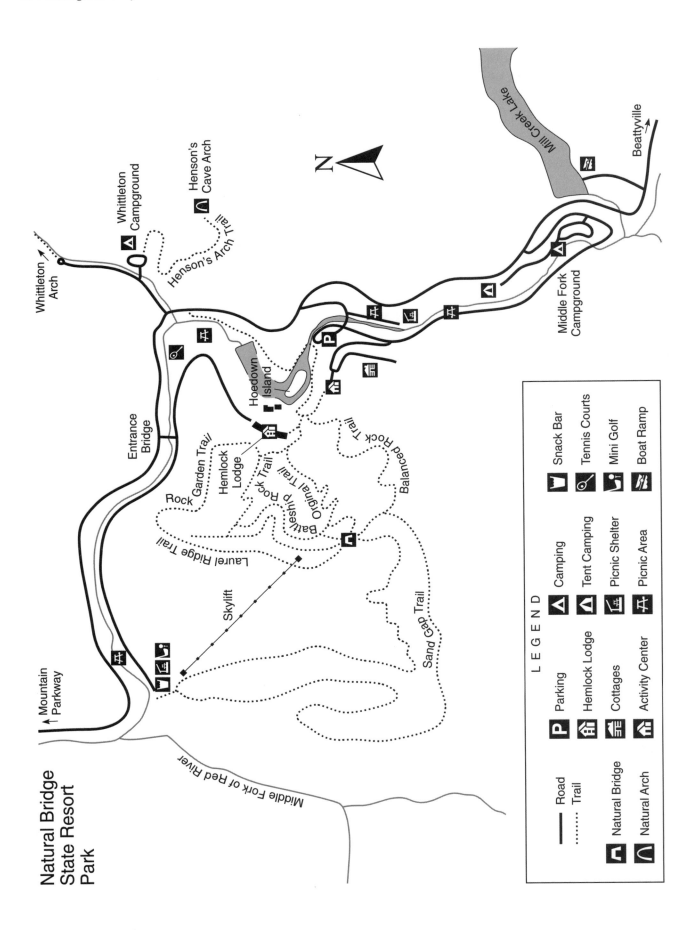

Natural Bridge State Resort Park

Rock Garden Trail/Balanced Rock Trail Loop 👢👢👢👢

Distance Round-Trip: 2.2 miles

Estimated Hiking Time: 1.5 to 2 hours

Cautions: Watch out for rocks and roots on the trail. Be aware that there are cliffs and drop-offs.

Trail Directions: The trailhead is behind Hemlock Lodge. Start on Original Trail **[1]**. There's an immediate steep climb as you ascend a bare sidehill. Included are two sets of steep stone stairs. A little further on, at mile .06, Battleship Trail comes in on the right. Take the nine steep steps down to it **[2]** and follow Battleship Trail 250 feet to a Y. In the spring, a large patch of trillium blooms in this stretch. At 0.1 miles, take Rock Garden Trail on the right **[3]**. The trail climbs steeply 630 linear feet, then levels out and follows a ridgeline. On the right is a drop-off into a large hollow. The trail passes through open hardwoods, laurel, and rhody thickets for 1,000 feet, where it turns left and climbs.

Shortly you'll ascend 31 stone steps in only 43 linear feet and, at mile .38, come to a set of 62 very steep steps carved into the native sandstone **[4]**, followed by 15 more steps. Then, in just a few steps, you'll top out on another ridge.

About .2 miles further on you'll come to a shallow rock house on the left. Rock houses, or rock-shelters, are cavelike openings, usually the start of an arch. You may be tempted to take a break here, but hold off. Just 90 feet further, at mile .63, is an eroded and colored cliff face **[5]**. The rock, stained yellow, white, and red, along with the naturally formed seats, makes this a prettier rest stop.

The trail now parallels a cliff face. In 400 feet it turns toward the cliff and seems to disappear in a rock garden. Just keep angling right as you move toward the cliff; the trail reappears at mile .70 **[6]** and passes through a thick rhody patch. In a couple of hundred feet more it enters the second set of overhanging cliffs.

Shortly afterward, at mile .90, the trail passes under a low-hanging rock **[7]**. This is a potentially dangerous spot. You only have four feet of headspace, and there's a sudden drop-off on the right.

A little further on, you'll pass under the sky lift. Then, in another .25 miles, you'll reach Natural Bridge, coming into it below the arch **[8]** at 1.25 miles. Climb up Fat Man's Misery (a crack where the rock has broken off the arch) and take some time to walk out on the bridge. There are some incredible

panoramic views of the surrounding mountains and rock formations.

From the top of Natural Bridge, pick up the trailhead sign for Balanced Rock Trail. From there you cross 150 feet of slab sandstone before actually reaching the trail. The trail climbs steeply about 400 linear feet; then, at mile 1.31, you reach the first of 28 staircases taking you down off the ridge **[9]**. You'll face a total of 450 stairs on this trail.

After several more staircases, at mile 1.7, you'll see two enclosed ladders on the cliff to the right. These are used for mountain rescue training. No other climbing is allowed in the park.

After going down several more staircases you'll come, at mile 1.85, to the longest staircase on the trail **[10]**, consisting of 85 wood and 30 stone steps. Almost immediately after you come to the bottom is Balanced Rock, on the right. There are some benches here as well.

Seven hundred feet and several staircases later, at mile 1.98, you'll come to a large rock-shelter on the left **[11]**. A few steps further is the top of the last staircase—98 stone steps—leading to the bottom of the hill; the end of the trail is 200 feet further **[12]**.

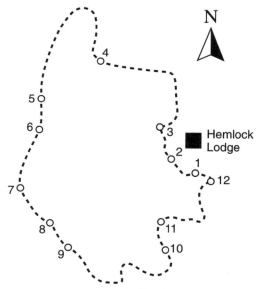

1. Trailhead
2. Battleship Trail junction
3. Rock Garden Trail junction
4. 62 carved steps
5. Eroded cliff
6. Trail disappears in rock garden
7. Low-hanging rock
8. Natural Bridge
9. First of 28 staircases
10. Long staircase and Balanced Rock
11. Rock-shelter
12. End of trail

Original Trail/Battleship Trail Loop 👢👢👢

Distance Round-Trip: 1.25 miles

Estimated Hiking Time: 60 to 90 minutes

Cautions: Look out for exposed rocks and roots on trails.

Trail Directions: The trailhead is behind Hemlock Lodge **[1]**. Start with a steep climb including 6 stone steps, followed by a second staircase of 49 stone steps, as you ascend a bare sidehill. About 250 feet further, at mile .08, a sinkhole appears on the left **[2]**. At the bottom is a cave that passes through the ridge and connects to Balanced Rock Trail. If you want to explore, you'll need a flashlight. (Caution: The cave usually is wet and slippery, and sometimes contains standing water.) From the cave the trail climbs gently through laurel and hemlock groves.

The trail turns left and steepens, following a cliff face on the right. You can see a very small rock house forming in the cliff at mile .32 **[3]**. This cavelike opening will, in several centuries, itself become an arch. You'll pass a trail junction shortly and get your first view of Natural Bridge at mile .325 **[4]**. The cliff face suddenly sweeps skyward, with a large opening underneath it. From this angle, the bridge looks man-made.

Follow the trail left, climbing toward what looks like an eroded cliff face; this is actually the base of Natural Bridge. The trail turns sharply right there, then goes up several small sets of stairs to the bottom of the arch at .49 miles **[5]**.

After exploring the arch (be sure to climb Fat Man's Misery to the top of the arch), pick up Battleship Trail where you first reached the bridge. The trail follows the arch base for several hundred feet, then turns right, down 76 wooden steps, and then turns left again. At mile .59 you'll see a shallow cave on the left **[6]**.

The trail is level and smooth for the next 2,000 feet as it follows the edge of a deep hollow on the right. It then junctions with trails to Devil's Gulch and Needle's Eye **[7]** at mile .97.

Needle's Eye is a lighthouse you can sit in. A lighthouse is formed when two opposing rock houses erode through the ridge and start to form an arch. It's well worth a side trip, but to get to it you need to climb a stone staircase that is ladderlike in its steepness. Devil's Gulch is a different set of steep stairs climbing through a notch in the ridge. It can be a rough climb.

Go right on Battleship Trail and descend into the hollow on 14 erosion control steps. A little further, the trail doglegs to the left. On your right, at mile 1.01, is a tree whose roots encircle a large boulder **[8]**. You have to wonder what keeps the tree upright!

Battleship Trail then goes steadily downward for .2 miles, to the junction with Rock Garden Trail. The next 250 feet can be marshy at times. Ascend nine steps to the trail's end at the junction with Original Trail **[9]** at mile 2.2. Go left to return.

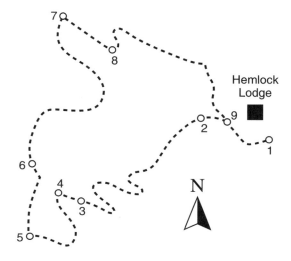

1. Trailhead
2. Sinkhole and cave
3. Rock house in formation
4. First view of Natural Bridge
5. Natural Bridge
6. Cave
7. Trails junction
8. Rock-hugging tree
9. End of trail

14. Pilot Knob State Nature Preserve

- Stand on a natural sandstone overlook where Daniel Boone first saw the land of Kan-Tu-Kee that he would later settle.
- Visit rare old quarry sites where the special conglomerate sandstone used in millstones was mined.
- As you ascend, note the differences in tree size and type due to changes in environment. Red maple and tulip poplar predominate low down, blackjack oak and Virginia pine on top.

Park Information

Pilot Knob State Nature Preserve is the site of Pilot Knob, a sandstone outcropping where Daniel Boone and his party first viewed "the beautiful level of Kentucky," on June 7, 1769.

Standing 1,400 feet above sea level, the knob itself is 730 feet higher than the surrounding landscape. It commands a 270-degree view of the Cumberland Plateau, knobs, and the Bluegrass country.

Originally purchased by the Nature Conservancy, the 308-acre preserve now belongs to the Kentucky State Nature Preserves Commission and is managed for the commission by a division of Eastern Kentucky University.

The preserve features a second-growth forest broadly classified as oak/hickory. But within that category are several different environmental conditions that determine the actual ecostructure, such as elevation, soil type, bedrock, soil moisture, and exposure to sunlight. For instance, blackjack oak and Virginia pine, common on the summit, are not found at the lower, moister elevations. In the same way, tulip poplar and red maple are not seen at the summit.

The predominant rock is conglomerate sandstone, with a mixture of sands and gravels of various sizes. A particularly hard stone, it was mined here in the early 1800s for use as millstones. Several unfinished millstones are located at the quarry sites within the preserve.

Directions: From Clay City, Kentucky, take KY-15 north 3 miles to a historic marker. Turn right until the road dead-ends at a loop.

Hours Open: Open year-round; trails are open sunrise to sunset.

Facilities: None.

Permits and Rules: Only foot travel on trails; no camping or fires allowed.

Further Information: Contact Kentucky State Nature Preserves Commission, 801 Schenkel Lane, Frankfort, KY 40601; 502-573-2886.

Other Points of Interest

Natural Bridge State Park (see park #13), **Red River Gorge Geologic Area** (see park #10), **Clear Creek Recreation Area** (see park #9), and the **Pioneer Weapons Hunting Area** (see park #8) are all within one hour of Pilot Knob State Nature Preserve.

Pilot Knob State Nature Preserve

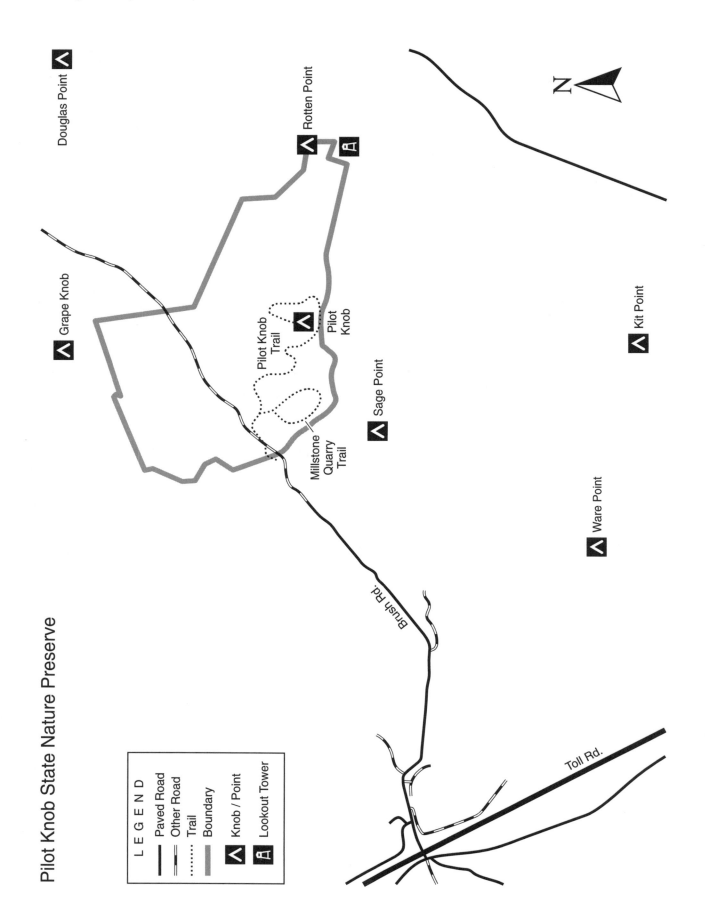

L E G E N D
Paved Road
Other Road
Trail
Boundary
Knob / Point
Lookout Tower

Douglas Point

Rotten Point

Grape Knob

Pilot Knob Trail

Pilot Knob

Millstone Quarry Trail

Sage Point

Kit Point

Ware Point

Brush Rd.

Toll Rd.

N

Pilot Knob Trail 👢👢👢👢👢

Distance Round-Trip: 2.3 miles

Estimated Hiking Time: 1.5 to 2 hours

Cautions: Be aware of high cliffs and some exposed rocks and roots. While not common, copperhead do inhabit the preserve.

Trail Directions: The trail is a fairly steep climb (more than 700-foot elevation change in just over a mile) to the site where Daniel Boone first viewed the land he would forever be associated with. The trip up is a lung- and knee-buster. But the view is worth the hike. However, because of the steepness of the trail and the many exposed high cliff edges, it is recommended that only experienced hikers, without small children, attempt the climb.

From the parking area, follow an old dirt road along Brush Creek for about 500 feet. Wade the creek to the steel-pipe water gate, and go up six wood steps. Turn left to the actual trailhead **[1]**.

You'll pass a registration box 850 feet further; then, at mile .17, the Millstone Quarry Trail **[2]** enters on the right. The moderate slope now steepens, and you'll face numerous erosion-control steps. You'll curse them now but bless them when you descend because they act as brakes. At mile .56 you'll top out at the base of the cliff that has the overlook **[3]**. You might want to take a breather here.

The trail now runs fairly level as it circles the knob. There's a steep cliff on your right; during leafless months, it presents a moving-picture show of the Cumberland Plateau, knobs, and the Bluegrass country. But the best view will be from the overlook.

Soon enough you'll start climbing again, although not as steeply. Then, at mile .7, you'll come to a natural spring that seeps out of the sandstone **[4]**. There's something appealing about drinking from the same source as the long hunters, the eastern settlers who spent long periods of time hunting in the mountains of Tennessee and Kentucky. But the spring is not potable by modern standards, so treat this water if you use it. A neckerchief soaked in the always-cold water can, however, be used to cool the sweat that's probably pouring off your brow.

As you climb, an exposed cliffside reveals the conglomerate sandstone favored for millstones, which were quarried in the area for many years in the early 1800s. From this point, the changing flora are particularly noticeable.

At 1.1 miles you'll reach Boone's Overlook **[5]**, perhaps the most awesome scenic climax in the state. As you stand on the same limestone outcrop Boone did, all of Kentucky's terrains are visible. On the left are the Cumberland Mountains.

The Cumberland Plateau is not shaped like regular, conical mountains. Instead it consists of ridgelike structures, stretching for many miles with few passes. Cumberland Gap, the nearest of these, is not visible from the overlook, so the plateau presents a solid wall, seemingly impregnable.

In front of you are the Knobs, a row of rounded hills stretching about 80 miles. Often mistaken for western foothills, they actually are a separate geologic formation.

The view to the right is the Bluegrass. When Boone looked at this scene, he saw canebrakes, meadows, and a future. You'll see towns, farms, and highways—the future realized. But the Knobs and the Cumberlands look much as they did when Boone first viewed "the beautiful level of Kentucky."

After gazing your fill, return the same way.

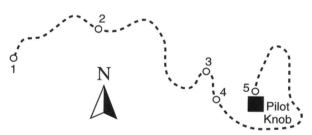

1. Trailhead
2. Millstone Quarry Trail
3. Base of Pilot Knob overlook
4. Natural spring
5. Boone's Overlook

Millstone Quarry Trail

Distance Round-Trip: .87 miles

Estimated Hiking Time: 40 to 60 minutes

Cautions: Watch for exposed rocks and roots.

Trail Directions: Millstone Quarry is a moderate trail that takes you to the site of several quarry sites used to produce millstones in the early 1800s.

From the parking area, follow an old dirt road along Brush Creek for about 500 feet. Wade the creek to the steel-pipe water gate, and go up six wood steps. Turn left to the actual trailhead **[1]**.

You'll pass a registration box 850 feet further; then, at mile .17, Millstone Quarry Trail **[2]** turns right. The trail moves through young second-growth hardwoods and pines, crosses a deep drain on a plank footbridge (which, interestingly, has nonskid strips glued to each plank), and reaches a trail junction at mile .31 **[3]**. This is the start of the loop section.

You can go in either direction. If you prefer climbing down, go right. The trail to the left climbs, immediately and steadily. It's also the route of the newly installed interpretive trail (for which the

brochure was not yet available at press time). Our suggestion is that you take that left trail.

After a steady but not particularly strenuous climb, you'll top out near the site of the first quarry **[4]** at mile .4. This is a square depression in the hillside, with obviously worked bits of conglomerate sandstone lying about. There are better sites down the trail.

After remaining level, the trail turns right and goes gently downhill. Just as you start down, at mile .46, you can see the remains of a wagon road **[5]** being reclaimed by the forest. Finished millstones were hauled away using this road and mule-drawn wagons.

A little further downhill, at mile .49, is a partially carved millstone **[6]** on your right. The stones were actually shaped and carved in place, cut from the substrate, and hauled away on the wagon road just above this site.

Note the twisted, partially burned tree directly behind the millstone—an interesting graphic in black and tan. Just a few feet further are yet other partially carved stones, as well as pieces of conglomerate showing tool marks.

The trail levels out until it merges with the main trail at mile .56 **[2]**. Turn left and retrace your bootsteps to the trailhead.

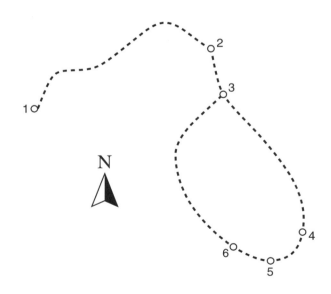

1. Trailhead
2. Millstone Quarry Trail turn-off
3. Start of quarry loop
4. First quarry site
5. Old wagon road
6. Partially carved millstone

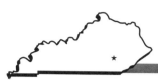

15. Levi Jackson Wilderness Road State Park

- Experience the human history of an area justifiably known as "the dark and bloody ground," including the site of the worst Indian massacre in the state's history.
- See a restored, operating gristmill that dates to the early 1800s, where you can purchase stone-ground cornmeal.
- Explore a recreated pioneer settlement, built around authentic log cabins and artifacts from the 19th century.

Park Information

Levi Jackson Wilderness Road State Park commemorates an early pioneer family, whose descendants donated the land for the park, and the Wilderness Road, which passes through it. This road and Boone's Trace, which also goes through the park, were the two most important trails leading to westward settlement.

Early explorers and settlers followed what had been the Warrior's Path, a trail through Cumberland Gap. With European settlement, the path was broadened and extended, and it came to be called the Wilderness Road. Boone's Trace followed it until Crab Orchard, where the two roads diverged—Boone's Trace heading north to Boonesboro and the Wilderness Road continuing northwest to Fort Harrod, and eventually, Louisville.

Both trails pass though the park property, and the park's hiking trails use parts of the original paths.

Levi Jackson, Laurel County's first judge, was the son of Reuben Jackson and Rebecca Freeman Jackson, whose people had claimed land using Revolutionary War land patents. Levi's children donated the land for the park in 1937.

McHargue's Mill is a restored gristmill that dates back to about 1817. Surrounding the mill is part of the associated millstone collection (which is actually called a "library"), the largest in the country.

Just down the road is the Defeated Camp Cemetery, site of the worst Indian-led massacre in Kentucky's history. Here a party of settlers were attacked in their sleep by a group of Shawnee and Chicamauga who felt that their sacred ground was being defamed.

Also found here is the Mountain Life Museum, which uses original log structures and artifacts to pay tribute to life in 19th-century Laurel County and southeastern Kentucky.

Directions: From I-75 exit 38 (London), go east on KY-192 2.5 miles to US-25W, then south 1.8 miles to KY-1006. Make a left to the park entrance, .5 miles further on.

Hours Open: Open year-round; museum sites are open from April through October.

Facilities: Campground, picnic areas, pool, playground.

Permits and Rules: None.

Further Information: Contact Manager, Levi Jackson Wilderness Road State Park, 998 Levi Jackson Mill Road, London, KY 40741; 606-878-8000.

Other Points of Interest

Mays Log Cabin Craft Village and Museum (606-878-7498), 4 miles south of the park, is a collection of Appalachian memorabilia housed in original log cabins.

Big South Fork National River and Recreation Area (see park #20), **Cumberland Gap National Historical Park** (see park #11), and **Pine Mountain State Resort Park** (see park #12) are all within one hour of the park.

Colonel Harland Sanders Cafe and Museum (606-528-2163) in Corbin is the place where the Kentucky Fried Chicken king got his start in the restaurant business.

Park Trails

There are 9 miles of trail at Levi Jackson Wilderness Road State Park. They may, however, be the least maintained and poorly marked trails in the state park system. Signs are missing, or they face the wrong way and point in the wrong direction; trails tend to be overgrown and cluttered with debris. But because of

their historical value they are worth the trouble. According to a park spokesperson, they were slated for renovation in the fall of 1997.

Frazier Knob Trail 👢👢👢—2.2 miles—is the official horse trail in the park. It leads through second-growth forest to an overlook.

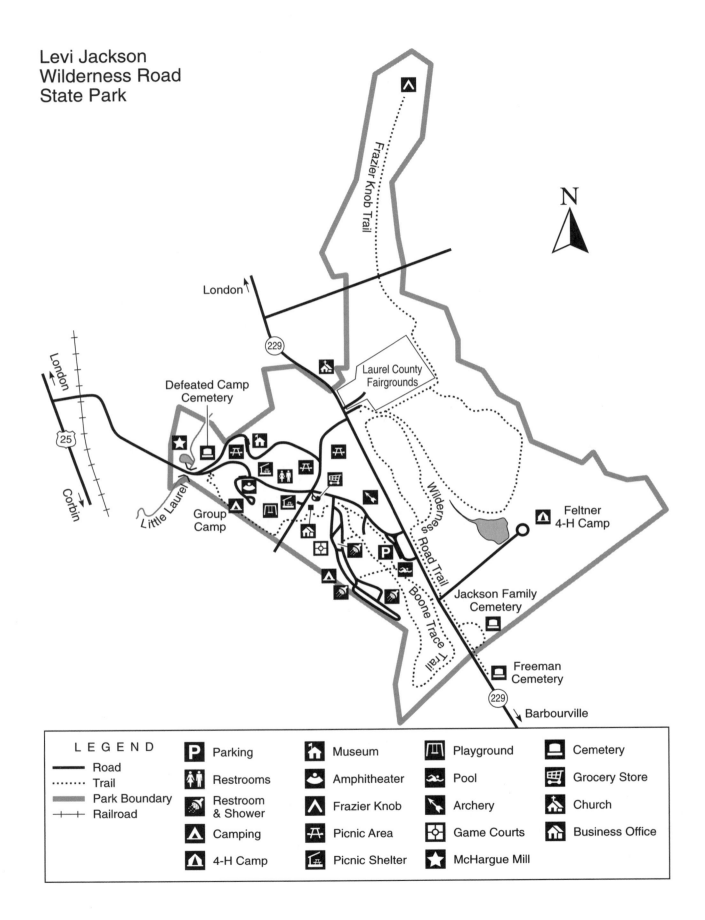

Levi Jackson Wilderness Road State Park

London

229

London

US 25

Corbin

Little Laurel

Defeated Camp Cemetery

Group Camp

Laurel County Fairgrounds

Wilderness Road Trail

Boone Trace Trail

P

Feltner 4-H Camp

Jackson Family Cemetery

Freeman Cemetery

229

Barbourville

N

Frazier Knob Trail

LEGEND

— Road
···· Trail
— Park Boundary
—+—+— Railroad

P Parking
Restrooms
Restroom & Shower
Camping
4-H Camp

Museum
Amphitheater
Frazier Knob
Picnic Area
Picnic Shelter

Playground
Pool
Archery
Game Courts
McHargue Mill

Cemetery
Grocery Store
Church
Business Office

Boone Trace Trail 👢👢👢

Distance Round-Trip: 2.9 miles

Estimated Hiking Time: 1.5 to 2 hours

Cautions: Be aware that trail junctions are unmarked or incorrectly marked. Watch out for muddy patches, overgrown sections, and some exposed roots.

Trail Directions: Several poorly marked and unmarked trail junctures and turns make hiking Boone Trace an exercise in trail finding. But the trail partially follows the route of Boone's Trace and the Wilderness Road. Walking in the footprints of explorers makes it appealing, despite the problems.

Park on the north side of the bridge near McHargue's Mill. The trailhead [1] is 300 feet south. A memorial marker and sign clearly indicate the trail's start. You'll climb a short set of steps, pass the marker, and then climb a longer staircase. Then, at mile .04, you'll reach a very confusing trail junction [2]. Four or five trails converge here, and none of them are marked. Take the second left, and then continue straight.

At mile .11, you'll see a circular stone wall on your left [3]. During the Defeated Camp massacre, a pregnant woman took refuge in a hollow stump here and bore her child. Unfortunately, nothing remains of the stump itself. But you can easily imagine her fear and uncertainty.

The trail turns right here and descends gently until it Ts. Go left, following the park property line, past the group camp. At the far side of the camp, at mile .3, is a historical marker [4] that looks like a headstone. Although this shows Boone's Trace going in both directions, it is incorrect. You actually left the Trace at the trailhead.

Reenter the woods at the left-hand trail (there are two, one of which goes nowhere). Follow it until the playground comes into sight. The trail appears to go there. Instead, follow what seems to be a false trail to the highway, cross the blacktop, and reenter the woods. When the trail Ys, go left until you emerge at the campground [5] at mile .6. Turn left until you reach the woodshed. Cross the campground toward the mini-golf course, and circle it on the right-hand side until you pick up the trail again. The trail parallels the highway, almost to the maintenance area driveway. If you reach the drive, you've gone too far.

Just before reaching the maintenance access road, the trail turns right. It's easy to miss, especially since a trail sign points the wrong way and the trailhead is obscured by a fallen tree. Watch across the highway until you are even with a picnic pavilion with a sign

pointing straight ahead. That's where you want to turn right. At mile .94 the trail turns right. But an old road joins it from the left, and there is no marker. Continue onward until you reach a crossroads behind the pool at the 1-mile point [6]. Go straight. There will be a trail below you, and you'll soon notice a short path joining that lower trail with the one you are on. Stay on the upper path, which circles the pool and then runs parallel to State Highway 229—which overlies the Wilderness Road.

This section tends to be overgrown with grasses, forbs, and "gotcha" bushes. If you time it right, they'll be loaded with blackberries—a sweet treat while you are fighting your way through. Along this section, at mile 1.1, you'll start seeing Virginia pines [7]. These were planted by the Civilian Conservation Corps in the 1930s and are not native.

The trail turns downhill, leaving the overgrown section behind. You are now on the lower trail of the loop, which rejoins the trail from the pool at mile 1.9, a few feet lower down. Then, 150 feet further on, you T into the main trail. Turn left and follow it back to the trailhead.

Before returning to your car, continue downhill across two roads and slightly to your right, where you'll find the Defeated Camp Cemetery [8], which is on Boone's Trace.

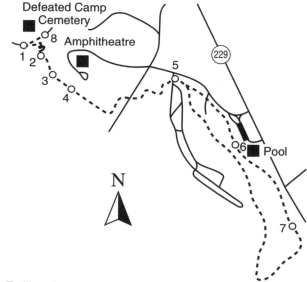

1. Trailhead
2. Confusing trail junction
3. Pregnant woman's stump
4. Boone's Trace marker
5. Campground
6. Pool
7. Virginia pines
8. Defeated Camp Cemetery

Wilderness Road Trail

Distance Round-Trip: 1.4 miles

Estimated Hiking Time: 45 to 60 minutes

Cautions: Be aware that the route is poorly marked, and watch for exposed rocks and roots. Parts of the trail have been torn up with Caterpillar tracks.

Trail Directions: Wilderness Road Trail is a loop and stem. Part of the stem overlies the Wilderness Road; the loop section parallels the Wilderness Road, but does not overlie it.

Trail maintenance is at best spotty. The loop section is especially bad. The "stem" is the interesting part of the trail.

Park by the pool and walk to the trailhead [1], located by the entrance to the 4-H camp. You can either follow State Highway 229 or follow part of Boone Trace Trail. A walk in the woods always being better than a stroll on blacktop, we opted for the trail when we were there. You can find it behind the pool.

For the loop, turn left at the camp gate. The trail here is still part of the stem, and is in good shape. In about 1,400 feet, at mile .27, you'll T into an unmarked trail [2]. Follow it to the right. This puts you on the loop. This is nothing more than a bulldozed slash through the new second growth. But along the way, you can observe how life develops along edges—either man-made or natural.

Although Frazier Knob Trail is the official bridle trail, horse riders use the Wilderness Road Trail, too. So be leery of droppings.

At mile .6 you'll enter a large fern garden [3]. The cool green fronds make an otherwise boring walk worthwhile. And they are such a refreshing break that you might be tempted to roll around in them. A little further, at mile .69, you'll intersect the horse trail at an unmarked crossroads. Go left.

You'll return to the 4-H gates at mile 1.3. Cross the access road and pick up the trail again. You are now following the original Wilderness Road, joining the 400,000 pioneers who came west on it.

You'll come to an unmarked Y. Ignore it, as it is the return loop from the Jackson cemetery. Continue on the lower road. At mile 1.5 the trail actually turns left and climbs. Before following it, continue straight another 90 yards to the Freeman cemetery [4].

The Freemans were among the earliest settlers in Laurel County. Within the graveyard are headstones of several Revolutionary War veterans and their family members. A little further on is the site of the Wilderness Road Inn, which the Freeman family started in 1804. The inn and tavern burned in 1962.

Return to the trail and follow it up to the Jackson cemetery at mile 1.6 [5]. The Jacksons were another early pioneer family whose descendants donated the land for the park.

Note the small stones in the cemetery. They are not, as is commonly believed, the graves of children. Rather they are footstones, marking the end of the grave site— a practice we've not seen anywhere except in Kentucky and West Virginia. The cemetery dates to 1816.

The trail turns left just before the cemetery and goes downhill, where it forms a T with the main trail. Turn right and return first to the trailhead, then to the pool by either trail or road.

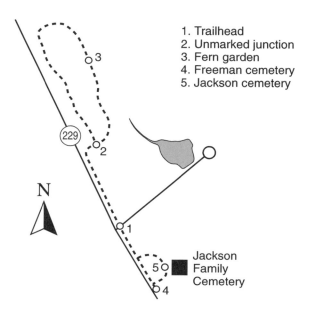

1. Trailhead
2. Unmarked junction
3. Fern garden
4. Freeman cemetery
5. Jackson cemetery

N

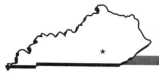

16. Bee Rock Recreation Area

- Walk through a natural tunnel and under a waterfall.
- Watch ospreys dive for fish.
- See one of the heaviest rapids in the Bluegrass state up close and personal.

Park Information

Sprawling along both banks of the Rockcastle River, Bee Rock Recreation Area sits about halfway up the 16-mile section classified as a Kentucky Wild and Scenic River. The designation is rather arbitrary, because the entire Rockcastle River is thought by many to be the most scenic river in the state.

Because water levels are controlled by downstream dams, the area never looks the same. One time, the Rockcastle may be out of its banks. The next visit sees it flowing low and placid. On one day, the streams and drains feeding the river are all but impassable. A week or so later they are mere trickles, or even nonexistent.

Upstream from the park is the Narrows. Here, high banks and palisades squeeze the river to about a third of its normal width. The result: A set of rapids unequaled in the state. Roaring like an uninterrupted thunderstorm, the river boils and rumbles through this rocky gorge, throwing water and spindrift in all directions.

The Narrows is a favorite site for white-water enthusiasts. But running these rapids is not for the inexperienced. On the six-point scale used to rank white water, the Narrows scores a five or six most of the time.

Surrounding the river are forested hills and cliffs, most of them undeveloped. Indeed, once away from the campgrounds, Bee Rock is as close to wilderness as you are likely to get anywhere in the eastern United States. The two campgrounds appeal more to people who fish than to hikers, so you usually have the trails to yourself. Just you and the wildlife and birds that inhabit the woods.

You'll almost always see deer, as well as myriad forms of birdlife, including white-eyed vireos and prairie warblers. Spring and fall are wildflower times, and the area boasts several waterfalls as well.

The best time to explore Bee Rock is during the leafless months. Once the foliage is out, many of the better views are blocked, including all but the barest glimpse of the Narrows.

Directions: Take KY-192 west from London 18 miles to the Rockcastle River. Bee Rock is located on both sides of the river.

Hours Open: Open year-round.

Facilities: Campgrounds with rest rooms but no water; boat launch on the east side. Stay off the abandoned bridge that used to join the two campgrounds; it isn't safe.

Permits and Rules: Only foot travel on trails; 14-day maximum campground stay.

Further Information: Contact London Ranger District, Daniel Boone National Forest, P.O. Box 907, London, KY 40743 (606-864-4163); or Somerset Ranger District, Daniel Boone National Forest, 156 Realty Lane, Somerset, KY 42501 (606-679-2018).

Other Points of Interest

Several parks lie within a short distance of Bee Rock, including **Natural Arch Scenic Area** (see park #19), **Cumberland Falls State Resort Park** (see park #18), and the **Big South Fork National River and Recreation Area** (see park #20).

Nearby, **Laurel Lake** provides fishing, boating, and water sports. There is almost no development on the 5,600-acre lake except for Holly Bay Marina (606-864-6542), where fishing boats, sport boats, and houseboats can be rented.

Park Trails

Rockcastle Narrows East 👢👢👢—3.8 miles each way—provides a view of the Narrows. It involves crossing Cane Creek, but you have to bushwhack upstream until you find a safe crossing spot—which varies with water levels—and then head back down to the trail.

Winding Stair Gap 👢👢👢—1.2 miles each way—descends from an old logging road to the river. There's a 350-foot elevation loss in less than a mile.

Bee Rock
Recreation Area

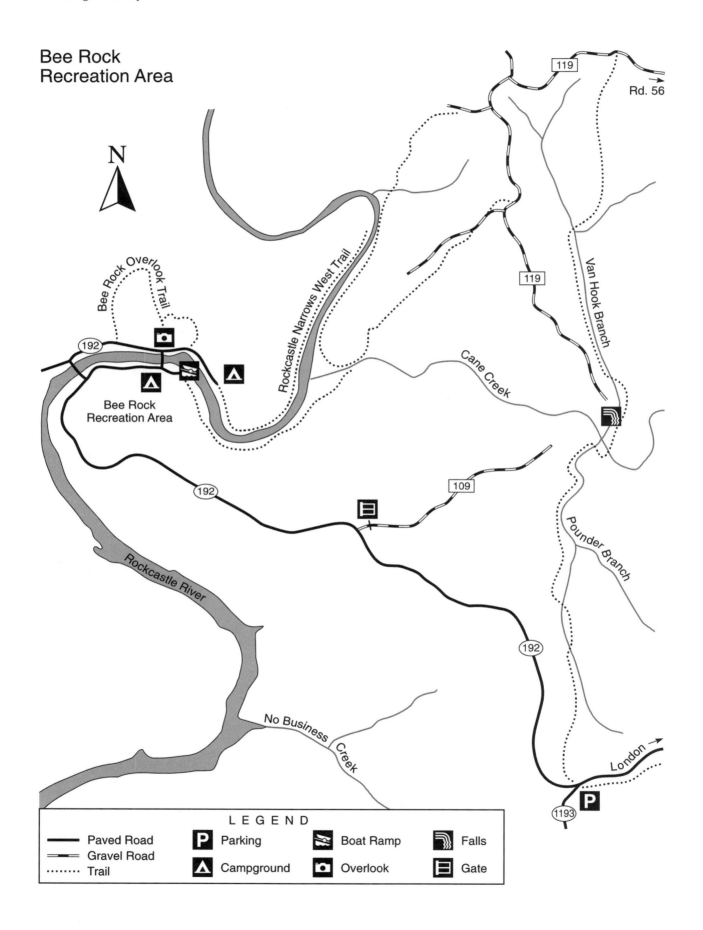

L E G E N D

—— Paved Road		**P** Parking		Boat Ramp	Falls
—= Gravel Road					
···· Trail		**⛺** Campground		**◉** Overlook	**⊟** Gate

Rockcastle Narrows West 👢👢👢

Distance Round-Trip: 4.62 miles

Estimated Hiking Time: 2.5 to 3 hours

Cautions: Watch for possible mud, for water that may be flowing on the trail, for exposed roots, and for large rock cairns blocking the trail.

Trail Directions: Rockcastle Narrows West is the easiest way to view the Narrows, one of the most dramatic rapids found anywhere in the Bluegrass state. The best time, however, is when there is no foliage to block the view.

The trail follows the river upstream until passing the Narrows; it then turns inland to eventually dead-end in the forest. You can extend the hike by taking FS-807 back to Bee Rock Overlook and connecting with the Bee Rock Overlook trail (see description later in this chapter).

The trailhead **[1]** is found in a gravel parking area at the north end of the west campground. It is obvious from the wooden gateway, but was otherwise unmarked when we visited. White diamond trail markers are few and far between, but the trail is well trodden. It passes through a hardwood forest of poplar, maple, and tulip gum while following the river. At 500 feet, a false trail leads down to the river, and a second one is straight. This false trail actually rejoins the main trail later on, but passes through some very muddy low places. Avoid it and others like it. Go left. A second such false trail is 300 feet further. Go left again.

At .3 miles there will be a seasonal waterfall **[2]** cascading down the rocks to your left. Although narrow, it can be dramatic. (Caution: When the fall is running, it actually flows across the trail.) Passing the waterfall, you'll rock hop as the trail squeezes between large boulders for the next 170 feet.

There's a boulder **[3]** you'll want to study at mile .44. Its face is covered with moss, which, growing in the natural striations, resembles ripples on a pond—a green, growing waterfall. You'll start ascending very gently here until reaching the Thunderbird rock at mile .64 **[4]**. This is a slump block—a section of rock that has fallen from a cliff and migrated—whose downhill side looks like the bird of Indian legend. Check out the small rock house (an eroded opening in a cliff face) under the Thunderbird's beak. The trail descends from here to a drain 250 feet further, which you'll cross on a plank bridge.

If you have any doubts about the power of flowing water, look below you to the right as you cross the bridge. You'll see the remains of a footbridge that was washed out by water moving down the drain.

You'll come to another false trail on the right, 500 feet further. The trail now levels out and follows the river for 300 feet, at which point you'll cross another footbridge and then climb again. The forest changes here, and you'll enter hemlocks. You'll cross another cascade flowing across the trail two hundred feet further. About 600 feet after this, you'll enter a glade. By now you should hear the thunder of the rapids and might be able to see them if the leaves are off the trees.

At mile 1.24 there are several maples and poplars blocking the trail **[5]**; you'll have to thread your way through these. They block about 60 feet of trail, and you may think the trail ends here. But it continues on.

Once you've refound the trail, follow it for 550 feet. A side trail enters on the right; it leads down to the rapids at mile 1.35 **[6]**. This side trail is very steep and potentially dangerous, so use caution, especially if the trail is wet and muddy. Hang on to children!

Back on the main trail you'll parallel the rapids for about 1,200 feet, but you won't be able to see them unless the leaves have fallen. At mile 1.57, some of the palisades that form the Narrows come into view across the river **[7]**. A thousand feet further the trail turns left, away from the river, and in another 500 feet it reenters a mixed forest on an old logging road. The rock cairns and fences you occasionally cross were put there to prevent travel by motorized vehicles and mountain bikes. White diamond trail markers are much more prominent along this section of trail.

You'll move through the woods another 1,880 feet until the trail joins FS-807 at mile 2.21 **[8]**. The trail itself dead-ends in the woods .1 miles further at mile 2.31.

Return to the trailhead by retracing your steps. Or, for a longer hike, follow FS-807 back to Bee Rock Overlook.

1. Trailhead
2. Seasonal waterfall
3. Mossy boulder
4. Thunderbird rock
5. Fallen trees
6. Side trail
7. Palisades
8. FS-807

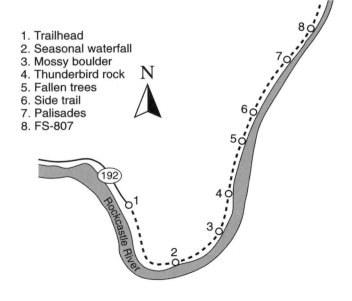

Bee Rock Overlook Loop

Distance Round-Trip: 2.25 miles

Estimated Hiking Time: 1.5 to 2 hours

Cautions: Look for flowing water on the trail, exposed rocks, and steep drop-offs. Bug spray is a must on this trail.

Trail Directions: Although this trail is just over 2 miles long, you'll see more cascading water on this hike than along any comparable 2 miles in the state. Three waterfalls and several streams with sharp gradients flowing through laurel thickets lend the aura of a rain forest.

The trailhead **[1]** is .2 miles from the entrance to the west campground. You'll start climbing immediately, through hardwoods, up 29 erosion steps in 85 feet. The trail then climbs steadily through oak, beech, and hickory woods, with laurel thickets above and below the path. You can hear, but probably not see, a stream bouncing through rocks below on the left.

At mile .25, the forest changes to hemlocks and pines. A bit further, the stream flows under the trail and runs along it on the right. Cliffs first appear on your left 200 feet further. Then, at mile .43, you'll come to a rock house (a cavelike opening in the cliff) and the first of the waterfalls **[2]**. The rock house looks like a cave wearing a top hat, because the opening is capped with what seems to be a hewn rock beam, covered with an overhanging slab. On the extreme left, the waterfall stair-steps down the side of the cliff.

Four hundred feet further, at mile .5, you'll first hear, and then see, the second waterfall **[3]**. A sheer cliff runs perpendicular to and above the trail. The stream flows through a gap in this wall and falls about 25 feet before dashing itself to spray on the loose boulders below.

About 500 feet further, the trail turns right over a wooden footbridge. You've finished the long climb. The trail levels out and reenters hardwoods, with lots of sassafras lining the edges.

You'll T into FS-807 at mile .75. When we visited, someone had broken the trail marker. The trail, and the overlook, are to the right at mile 1.2 **[4]**.

From the overlook, you'll be viewing a wilderness-like setting. To the right, the KY-192 bridge and part of the road are visible through the thick trees. Directly below you is the abandoned bridge in the campground. Upstream, only time and the river are flowing! Thick forest leads to the river's edge and a short stretch of the palisades that form the Narrows. Buzzards may be visible riding the thermals, and you might see an osprey dive for its dinner.

When you're ready, backtrack 250 feet and take the second trail on the right. You'll descend rather steeply, with several switchbacks and staircases, until bottoming out at mile 1.35 beside a sheer cliff on your left **[5]**. Check out the thin lines in the rock that look like stone roots, or maybe sinews. Just 350 feet further, the trail seems to disappear after crossing a plank footbridge. Enter the cave on your left, and you'll find yourself in a naturally carved tunnel that doglegs to the right **[6]**. On the far end, a waterfall showers across the mouth of the tunnel at mile 1.41. Walk through the waterfall. Emerging from this natural shower, you'll find a steep drop-off on your right, and in front of you some boulders to hop for 150 feet. Twice that distance further, the trail turns right. A bit further still, at mile 1.57, you'll cross a rushing torrent, with a 16-foot cataract below you. The trail turns right here and roughly follows the stream for about 500 feet, where you'll come to an unmarked Y. The right fork is an unauthorized trail. The trail goes left, reaching the campground at mile 1.86 **[7]**. Turn right and return to the trailhead along the campground road.

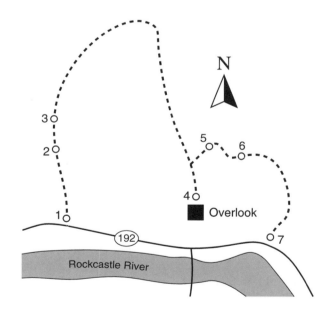

1. Trailhead
2. First waterfall
3. Second waterfall
4. Trail to overlook
5. Sheer cliff
6. Dogleg tunnel and third waterfall
7. Campground

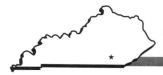

17. Rockcastle Recreation Area

- Explore the woods and springs that made this area a popular 19th-century resort destination.
- Descend 100 feet through a crevice forming the only break in the surrounding cliffs.
- See an unusual two-room rock-shelter (a cavelike opening in the cliff face) divided by a natural limestone wall.

Park Information

The cool forests and mineral springs found along the Rockcastle River made this area a popular resort destination during the early 1800s. In 1835, Rockcastle Springs Resort opened upstream from the mouth of the river, and it remained in operation until after the turn of the century. The resort was frequented by local residents and southern travelers who came north to escape epidemics of malaria and yellow fever. Newspapers described the resort as an Eden for children, a sanitarium for invalids, a paradise for lovers, and a haven of rest for the tired.

Unfortunately, no remains of the hotel are accessible to hikers. But as the U.S. Forest Service notes, the resorts may be gone but the restorative power of the forest remains.

Although some area trails merely follow the shorelines of the Rockcastle River and Lake Cumberland, many of them rank among the most strenuous in eastern Kentucky. The trails themselves aren't particularly rough, but the country they pass through is.

You'll pass through undeveloped second-growth forests interspersed with rock formations and cliffs. Rock-shelters (cavelike openings in the cliff face) abound, but surprisingly there are no natural arches in the area. There are several waterfalls and cascades, however, more than making up for the lack of natural bridges. Spring wildflowers are particularly abundant along the trails here.

Spring is the best time to visit the Rockcastle Recreation Area because wildflowers and flowing water contribute so much to its appeal.

Directions: From London, Kentucky, take KY-192 west 12 miles to KY-1193, which comes in on the left. Take that .6 miles to KY-3497 and follow it 5.3 miles to the Scuttle Hole trailhead; or follow it 6.9 miles to the Dutch Branch trailhead, which you'll find on the far side of the campground.

Hours Open: Open year-round.

Facilities: Boat dock and marina, campground. Until 1997 there was a picnic area, but it was replaced with additional camping pads. A primitive campground is located off Twin Branch Trail, and two Adirondack shelters with tables can be found just west of there on the Lakeside South Trail.

Permits and Rules: Only foot travel on trails.

Further Information: Contact District Ranger, London Ranger District, P.O. Box 907, London, KY 40743; 606-784-5624.

Other Points of Interest

Bee Rock Recreation Area (see park #16), **Cumberland Falls State Resort Park** (see park #18), **Natural Arch Scenic Area** (see park #19), and the **Big South Fork National River and Recreation Area** (see park #20) are all within one hour of Rockcastle Recreation Area.

Levi Jackson Wilderness Road State Park (see park #15) in London provides a view of the human history of the region. The Wilderness Road and Boone's Trace diverge here. The Mountain Life Museum is a recreated mountain settlement. McHargue's Mill is a working gristmill that includes the largest collection (called a "library") of millstones in the country.

Park Trails

Ned Branch Trail 🥾🥾🥾—1.9 miles each way—is downhill 300 feet through a gorge carved by the trail's namesake. There are several stream crossings along the way.

Lakeside South Trail 🥾🥾—4.2 miles each way—follows the shoreline of Lake Cumberland, with little change in elevation.

Twin Branch Trail 🥾🥾🥾🥾—1.1 miles each way—descends 300 feet following Twin Branch. It connects the Ned Branch Trail with the Lakeside South Trail to create a loop trail more than 7 miles long.

Rockcastle Recreation Area

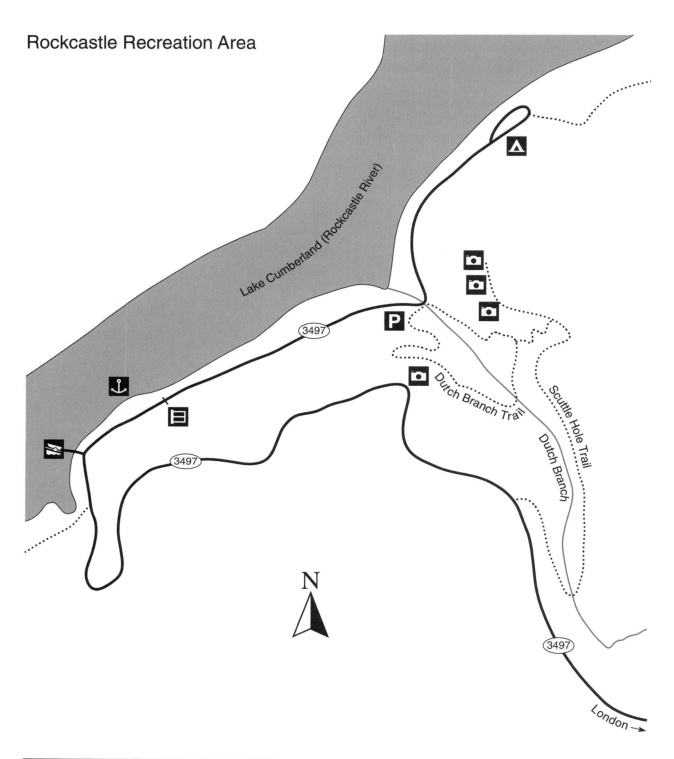

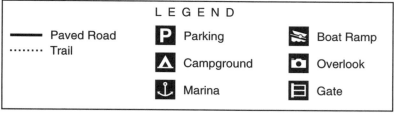

L E G E N D

— Paved Road

P Parking

Boat Ramp

····· Trail

Campground

Overlook

Marina

Gate

Scuttle Hole Trail 👢👢👢👢

Distance Round-Trip: 1.9 miles

Estimated Hiking Time: 1.5 to 2 hours

Cautions: Be careful on high cliffs. Watch for some exposed rocks and roots and for possible flowing water on the trail.

Trail Directions: An easy to moderate hike for most of its length, the trail turns into a strenuous hike on the trip down and back through the scuttle hole. Before making the descent, the trail leads to three overlooks that provide exceptional views of the Rockcastle River and the head of Lake Cumberland. The trailhead **[1]** is at a gravel parking area off KY-3497. It's a well-trodden path as it moves through hardwoods with pines and hemlocks mixed in. About 350 feet from the trailhead, a fallen tree blocks the trail and lies semiparallel to it. The tree does not obscure the trail, so merely step over it at any convenient point. Then, at mile .17, you'll descend three large natural steps into a fern garden **[2]**. Caution: The steps may be slick and the fern garden boggy.

Low cliffs on your left form a wall from 8 to 20 feet high. The cliffs were cut by the seasonal creek flowing at their base. At mile .33, the creek flows over a high cliff **[3]** and drops to the valley below. A seasonal waterfall, when the water is high, makes a spectacular leap over this cliff. The trail jogs right to avoid the drop-off, then follows the cliff edge. At mile .6, the trail splits. The left-hand fork leads to the scuttle hole. The right-hand fork, which you should take, leads to a set of three overlooks, the furthest of which is 800 feet away at mile .77 **[4]**. The first overlook provides a view into the valley. You'll see high cliffs laid out at your feet, and if the foliage is off the trees, you'll have a view of the waterfall you passed on the way in. From the second overlook you can just make out the Rockcastle River 300 feet below. And from the third, you see the river as it forms the head of Lake Cumberland, the park marina,

and—upstream—only wild country, much as it may have looked to early settlers.

Return to the trail split, 859 feet from the last overlook, and proceed to the head of the scuttle hole at mile .9 **[5]**. Here you'll descend 113 wooden steps through a natural crack in the cliff. The crevice is five to six feet wide, but the high, sheer walls make it seem thinner. Not the place for anyone who is claustrophobic, by any means.

At the base of the scuttle hole, there's a large rock-shelter (a cavelike opening in the cliff face) at mile 1.15 **[6]** that looks like the prow of a ship, riding a wave cast in stone. Several square boulders make great natural chairs, just where you need to take a rest.

Once you've caught your breath, follow the rest of the trail, which descends sharply. About 150 feet below the rock-shelter is a wooden footbridge with a seasonal waterfall below it. When conditions are right, the fall plunges 12 feet, kicking up spray and spindrift. Ninety feet further, the trail ends at Dutch Branch Trail, at mile 1.22 **[7]**. Climb back through the scuttle hole and return to the trailhead the way you came.

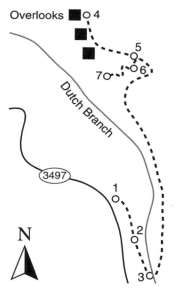

Overlooks

1. Trailhead
2. Fern garden
3. High cliff
4. Three overlooks
5. Head of scuttle hole
6. Ship's prow rock-shelter
7. Dutch Branch Trail

Dutch Branch Trail 👢👢👢👢👢

Distance Round-Trip: .75 miles

Estimated Hiking Time: 60 to 90 minutes

Cautions: Pay attention to steep drop-offs, exposed rocks and roots, and flowing water on the trail.

Trail Directions: Dutch Branch Trail is a short but strenuous hike that climbs about 300 feet in a relatively short distance. You'll climb to the cliffs above the Rockcastle River and descend again, but you won't see the river itself from the trail. Along the way are some special rock formations you'll not likely see anywhere else.

The trailhead [1] is just south of a small parking area on the far side of the campground. Cross the road toward a Forest Service billboard. Go past the first trail (which leads to the scuttle hole) and take the second one to the left. You'll start climbing immediately. The trail is very steep and includes several switchbacks as you climb above Dutch Branch.

At mile .15, a large poplar has fallen; its head is using the trail as a pillow [2]. You'll have to bushwhack through this crown, which covers about 70 feet of trail. A bit further, the trail steepens even more until leveling out at the base of the cliffs at mile .25.

From a distance, these cliffs seem to be vertical. From their base, however, you can see that they curve gently outward, like the face of a hydroelectric dam. Right where you first join them is a twin rock-shelter (a cavelike opening in the cliff) [3]. Two rooms are separated by a low limestone wall that should have eroded, but didn't. Note the yellow and green lichen in the wall, as well as the individual layers of limestone sediment. A block of this same limestone at the end of the second room makes a convenient seat as you catch your breath from the climb.

Follow the base of the cliffs. A hundred feet further, at mile .34, is a smaller rock-shelter with a chimney stretching to the cliff top [4]. Rock climbers do not seem to have discovered this site, so it remains pristine.

As you follow the cliffs, note that they are not solid. Instead, you are looking at a row of giant children's blocks, some of which have their alphabets chipped and scraped, others of which are broken and cracked. You'll follow a fairly level path along these broken blocks for slightly more than 1,000 feet. At mile .55, a side trail straight ahead leads to a giant amphitheater [5]. The water you hear gurgling in the "pit" is the headwaters of Dutch Creek. When we visited, a single bullfrog sang solo, his voice deepened and mellowed by the resonance of the rock walls. Return to the main trail and turn right, downhill.

You are about to lose the elevation you gained climbing up, dropping almost 200 feet in only 528 linear feet. You'll bottom out at Dutch Branch and then pass up and through a natural split in a slump block (a large rock chunk that has fallen and migrated) [6] at mile .56. Four steps have been carved in the rock to carry you through the crack.

A short distance from the slump block, you'll cross a wooden footbridge over Dutch Branch. Pause in the middle and look upstream. A series of natural stone steps—called ledge rock—forms a row of cascades during high-water periods. Another 150 feet takes you to the junction of Scuttle Hole Trail at mile .61 [7]. If the climb isn't too daunting, you might want to explore the scuttle hole—a natural crevice that forms the only opening in the cliffs on that side. There are 113 wooden steps up (and back down) the scuttle hole, and if you make the climb you'll add a half mile to the trip.

From the junction, the trail descends gradually to the trailhead at mile .75.

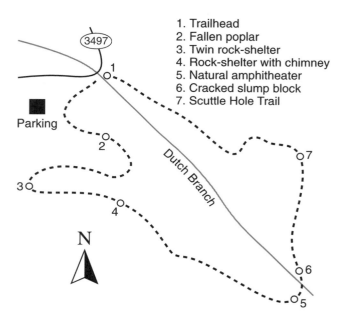

1. Trailhead
2. Fallen poplar
3. Twin rock-shelter
4. Rock-shelter with chimney
5. Natural amphitheater
6. Cracked slump block
7. Scuttle Hole Trail

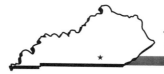

18. Cumberland Falls State Resort Park

- Watch the unique moonbow—a rainbow that appears in the mist of Cumberland Falls during the full moon. This is the only place in the Western Hemisphere where a moonbow can be seen.
- See the whirlpool created by the falls as it eroded itself upstream. Catfish weighing more than 200 pounds are said to inhabit the whirlpool area.
- Compare the awesome power of Cumberland Falls with the delicacy of other waterfalls in the area, like Eagle Falls and Dog Slaughter Falls.

Park Information

Cumberland Falls State Resort Park offers all the amenities of a resort as well as the bountiful outdoor recreation opportunities of the park and surrounding national forest. Park lands on the west side of the river are a nature preserve.

Best known for the falls from which it gets its name, and for the moonbow produced there, the site has been popular with visitors for more than 100 years.

Cumberland Falls, one of the largest waterfalls in the state, is 125 feet wide and plunges 68 feet into a gorge that it cut over time. Awesome in its power, water flows over the falls at the rate of 59,600 cubic feet per second.

During the three-day full moon period each month, a rainbow can be seen in the foam and spray thrown up by the falls. This is one of only two known places in the world where a moonbow can be seen (the other is at Victoria Falls, in Africa). The best time to view the moonbow is during the winter months, because it shows some color then. During the rest of the year, it's merely a silvery-bright arc.

The park was originally constructed in the early 1930s by the Civilian Conservation Corps. Little was available in the way of power equipment, so the lodge (since replaced) and trails were built with picks, shovels, and sweat. Much of the work of the Civilian Conservation Corps can still be seen throughout the park, especially along the trails.

Canoeing and rafting are very popular below the falls, and at least one outfitter (Sheltowee Trace Outfitters, 800-541-RAFT) books such trips.

Directions: The park is 16 miles west of Corbin, Kentucky. Take US-25 west until it forks at KY-90. Take that west to the entrance.

Hours Open: The park and lodge are open year-round. Some activities are seasonal. The area around the falls closes at midnight for safety reasons.

Facilities: Lodge, cottages, camping, dining, canoeing, swimming, horseback riding, and similar resort amenities.

Permits and Rules: Camping is allowed in established campground only; the falls area is closed after midnight. Only foot travel is allowed on unpaved trails.

Further Information: Contact Cumberland Falls State Resort Park, 7351 Highway 90, Corbin, KY 40701; 606-528-4121.

Other Points of Interest

Big South Fork National River and Recreation Area (see park #20) is south of the park. **Natural Arch Scenic Area** (see park #19) lies 10 miles to the southwest.

Colonel Harland Sanders' Original Restaurant (606-528-2163), an authentic restoration of the first Kentucky Fried Chicken restaurant, is in Corbin.

Park Trails

There are 13 trails in the park, ranging from .25 to 10.8 miles in length and classed from easy to very strenuous. Here we list five of them.

Moonbow Trail 🥾🥾🥾—10.8 miles—follows the Cumberland River downstream from the falls to the junction with Laurel River.

Cumberland River Trail 🥾🥾🥾—5 miles—follows the Cumberland River, then turns inland and connects with the Moonbow Trail.

Anvil Branch Trail 🥾🥾🥾🥾—2.5 miles—has some very steep sections and is noted for its abundance of spring wildflowers.

Blue Bend Loop 🥾🥾🥾—4.5-mile loop—gradually climbs to the ridge over the river and then descends back down, joining the Sheltowee Trace Trail at the river 4.5 miles from the trailhead.

Wildflower Loop Trail 🥾🥾🥾—1.25 miles—follows the sandstone cliffs.

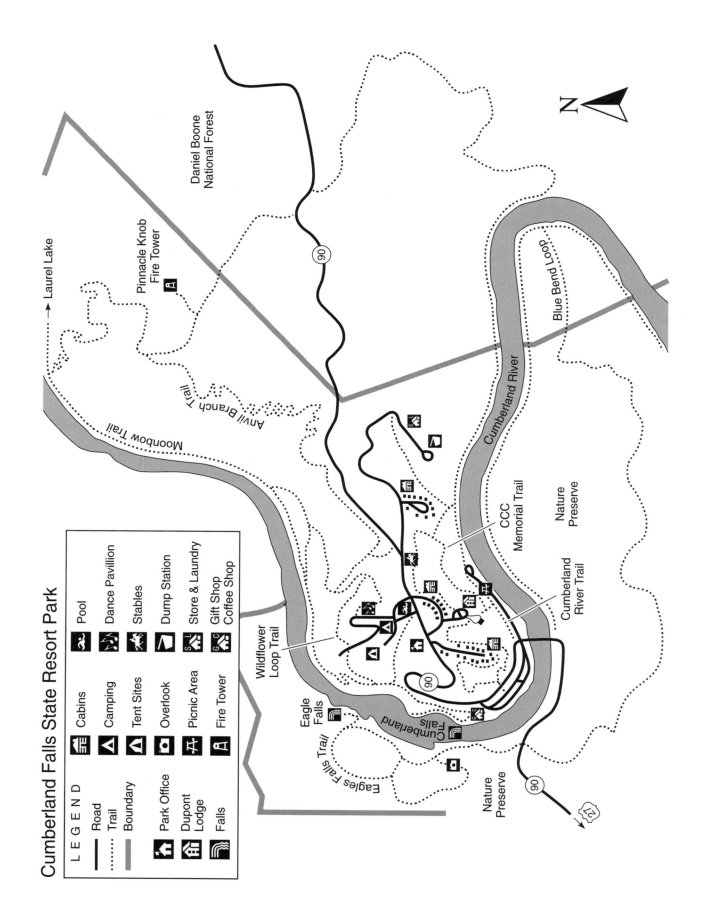

Cumberland Falls State Resort Park

L E G E N D
- —— Road
- ••••• Trail
- ▬▬ Boundary

Park Office
Dupont Lodge
Falls

Cabins
Camping
Tent Sites
Overlook
Picnic Area
Fire Tower

Pool
Dance Pavillion
Stables
Dump Station
Store & Laundry
Gift Shop Coffee Shop

Daniel Boone National Forest

N

Laurel Lake

Pinnacle Knob Fire Tower

Anvil Branch Trail

Moonbow Trail

Cumberland River

Blue Bend Loop

CCC Memorial Trail

Nature Preserve

Cumberland River Trail

Wildflower Loop Trail

Eagle Falls

Cumberland Falls

Eagles Falls Trail

Nature Preserve

90

Eagle Falls (Trail #9) 👢👢👢👢👢

Distance Round-Trip: 2.1 miles

Estimated Hiking Time: 2 to 2.5 hours

Cautions: Be careful on high cliffs. Watch for exposed roots and rocks. In some spots you will be crossing water.

Trail Directions: The trail is a very strenuous one that sometimes all but disappears; it takes you to Eagle Falls, a lesser-known waterfall tucked away in a rock grotto edging the Cumberland River. The trailhead [1] is on KY-90, .3 miles west of the Gatliff Bridge, on the west side of the river. Park in the gravel pull-off on the river side of the highway.

You'll start walking toward the river but almost immediately turn downstream and follow the river through hardwoods. Four hundred feet further you'll come abreast of Cumberland Falls and start climbing. In another 200 feet you'll pass overhanging ledges on the left. These were actually carved by the falls in past eons.

You'll pass under a rock ledge, climb four stairs, and at .14 miles reach a house-sized boulder on the right [2]. There is a good view of Cumberland Falls from atop this rock.

There will be some stiff up-and-down climbing for the next .2 miles, including stairs and switchbacks. Then, at mile .32, you'll reach a hemlock and rhododendron thicket surrounding a small creek [3]. The whole thing is very much like a tropical forest.

In a few feet you'll cross the creek and go up a short staircase to the second junction with trail #10. Go right. In less than 300 feet you'll reach a rock ledge with safety rail at mile .33 [4]. From here there's an unobstructed view of Cumberland Falls and of a stretch of river up- and downstream. You won't get a better view of the falls.

Continue following the trail, which is fairly level, for about 1,000 feet, to the side trail leading to Eagle Falls. Follow the side trail, which descends 250 feet to a wooden platform and stairs, then drops steeply another 270 feet to the river. The last hundred feet or so has a cable handrail to assist you.

Reaching the shoreline, turn downstream. You'll have to rock hop (there is no defined trail) about 200 feet to Eagle Falls [5], at mile .63. About 44 feet high,

and that wide, Eagle Falls drops like a bridal train off an exposed rock lip.

Retrace your steps back to the main trail. Turn right. The trail appears to end. But take three or four steps toward the fallen log in front of you and you'll see the trail, turning sharply to the right again. Follow it for 335 feet, down several switchbacks, to Eagle Creek. You are now at the top of the falls. Turn left and follow the creek. Caution: The trail edge is eroded and undercut by Eagle Creek for the next 350 feet, where it literally disappears in a small waterfall that flows over a large rounded rock at mile .89 [6]. Stay on the left bank, and rock hop (or wade) past the waterfall. You'll pick up the trail just upstream. The trail leaves the stream 300 feet further, turns left, and climbs steeply. Much of the path is ungroomed in this section and obscured by foliage. After 500 feet, you'll top out at a large overhanging ledge. Take a breather, because the trail starts climbing again and will do so for another 1,065 feet before topping out in open woods at mile 1.24. The trail is level for about 400 feet and then starts descending until, 700 feet later, it ends at trail #10.

Here you have a choice. If you turn right, you'll follow a very strenuous loop that extends the hike by 1 mile. Turning left, you'll follow a smooth, fairly level trail for 1,000 feet; at this point the path rejoins the Eagle Falls trail. Turn right, and retrace your steps back to the trailhead.

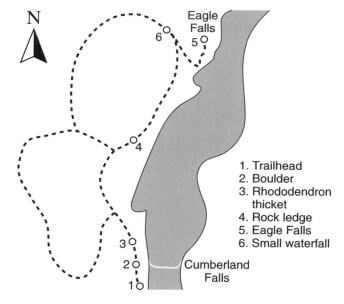

1. Trailhead
2. Boulder
3. Rhododendron thicket
4. Rock ledge
5. Eagle Falls
6. Small waterfall

CCC Memorial Trail 👢👢👢

Distance Round-Trip: .87 miles

Estimated Hiking Time: 40 to 60 minutes

Cautions: There are drop-offs and steep stairs.

Trail Directions: This is a moderate trail with some hills and one bad set of steps. If it were not for this long stairway, the trail would rate only two boots in difficulty.

Built by the Civilian Conservation Corps in the early 1930s, the CCC Memorial Trail has, along its path, 20 markers that interpret the flora, fauna, and human history of the area. Although you could merely walk this trail in 25 minutes, take the time to read the markers and examine the world they describe. There are several false trails along the way, so pay attention to where you are going.

The trailhead **[1]** is off the main parking lot, northwest of the lodge. You'll descend gradually for 133 feet through a hardwood forest. There are a few steps along the way. Then the trail levels out and reaches a bench. There will be some low cliffs on your left.

At mile .06 you'll come to a Civilian Conservation Corps storage bin in the cliff **[2]**. A natural opening in the rock was trued up with mortar and small stones. Then a set of doors were cut out of sandstone slabs and attached to the native rock with wrought-iron strap hinges. Explosives were stored in cubicles like this wherever the Civilian Conservation Corps did blasting work.

There's a false trail going downhill about 200 feet to the right. You want to follow the trail left. Then, 350 feet further, another false trail comes in on the right. Take the five stairs on the left.

A second bench comes up 1,000 feet further at mile .28 **[3]**. This is a good place to contemplate the restorative power of the woods despite their being surrounded by the hoopla of a major resort park. The trail descends from here until you cross a gravel road, and then a spur from that road, before climbing again. Twelve hundred feet further, at mile .52, a large concrete structure is visible on your right. This is a pumping station that serves the sanitary needs of the lodge.

As you ascend slightly from the pump house, a false trail comes in on the left. This leads to an unauthorized falls overlook when the foliage is thin. However, safer views are coming up along the trail, which turns right here and then follows a ridge along the Cumberland River, for 500 feet, where it Ts into a set of stone stairs. The trail markers are a little confusing here. If you turn left, you'll descend to a picnic area near the falls. The trail actually turns right, and climbs. A short distance further is yet another bench, at the foot of the long stairs at mile .62 **[4]**.

In front of you are 130 stone steps in 16 uneven groups. This stairway was built by Civilian Conservation Corps workers in 1932. The stones were set and mortared in place completely by hand labor—an incredible demonstration of the kind of construction work possible without power equipment. It's a long, steep climb, so take your time.

After topping out, the trail ascends gradually another 338 feet, to end at the parking lot on the right side of the lodge at mile .87.

1. Trailhead
2. Civilian Conservation Corps storage bin
3. Bench
4. Long stairs

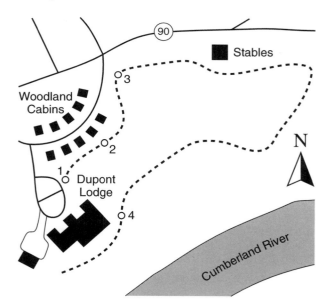

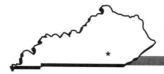

19. Natural Arch Scenic Area

- Observe the erosional process that produces natural arches, bridges, and rock-shelters (cavelike openings that may in time become arches).
- See an optical illusion that makes a natural stone arch look like a fireplace chimney.
- Walk through a deep canyon, surrounded by sandstone bluffs and cliffs.

Park Information

The Natural Arch Scenic Area, in the Somerset Ranger District of the Daniel Boone National Forest, is a 945-acre wild area at the headwaters of Cooper Creek. The namesake arch is a large sandstone bridge with a 60- by 100-foot opening. A .5-mile nature trail surrounds the arch. Because the trails intersect, the Great Gulf Recreational Area, 1 mile to the west, is included in this park.

Although the region is primarily southern hardwoods, the picnic area contains many shortleaf pines, planted there by the Daughters of the Confederacy in 1943 in memory of the soldiers who gave their lives in the Civil War. Unfortunately, many of those trees were severely damaged in 1994, when the worst ice storm in memory devastated the forests of eastern Kentucky. You can still see much of the damage.

This part of the national forest is characterized by rimrock cliffs and deep canyons, so you can see spectacular sandstone formations just about anywhere.

Trails were cut in this region by the Civilian Conservation Corps in the 1930s, and some of these work projects are still visible. You can, for instance, see the original pump house from the trail leading to the overlook.

Directions: From Somerset, Kentucky, go south on US-27 for 22 miles, to KY-927. Take KY-927 west 1.8 miles to Natural Arch parking lot. Trailheads are at the far end of the lot. Alternatively, continue on KY-927 an additional 1.2 miles to the Great Gulf parking lot. Trails from the two areas intersect in Great Gulf, a canyon carved by Spruce Creek and Gulf Fork.

Hours Open: Open year-round. Natural Arch is a day-use area; the picnic area and parking lot close at 10:00 P.M.

Facilities: Picnic area with barrier-free pit toilets; water is not available.

Permits and Rules: Vandalism has been a problem in this area, so be sure to keep all valuables with you or lock them securely out of sight.

Further Information: Contact Somerset District Office, Daniel Boone National Forest, 156 Realty Lane, Somerset, KY 42501; 606-679-2018.

Other Points of Interest

A few miles east lies the **Beaver Creek Wilderness** (see park #21), a 4,791-acre wilderness area nestled within four sandstone cliff lines. The human history of the region is well preserved in this natural area.

About 10 miles from Beaver Creek is **Cumberland Falls State Resort Park** (see park #18), where you can see the only moonbow in the Western Hemisphere. Under the light of the full moon, a rainbow appears in the mist thrown up by the waterfall.

South of Natural Arch is the **Big South Fork National River and Recreation Area** (see park #20) a 105,000-acre natural area straddling the Kentucky/Tennessee border. Virtually every outdoor activity is available in the Big South Fork, as well as a specially preserved old mining village at Blue Heron.

Park Trails

Despite being located above and through canyons, the trails in Natural Arch and adjacent Great Gulf are not particularly strenuous. Each of them has steep stretches as you climb into and out of the gorges. But once you get down, the trails are fairly level and would rank as one or two boots in difficulty.

Buffalo Canyon Trail 👢👢👢—5.1 miles—is sometimes called the "five-mile-loop trail"; it picks up at Natural Arch and loops through the Great Gulf.

Gulf Bottom Trail 👢👢—1.7 miles—meanders along the top of a cliff line, passes through a gap in the cliff, and then drops down a steep metal stairway into the Great Gulf.

Panoramic View Trail 👢—.5 miles—is an easy walk along an old roadway to the ridgeline overlooking Great Gulf.

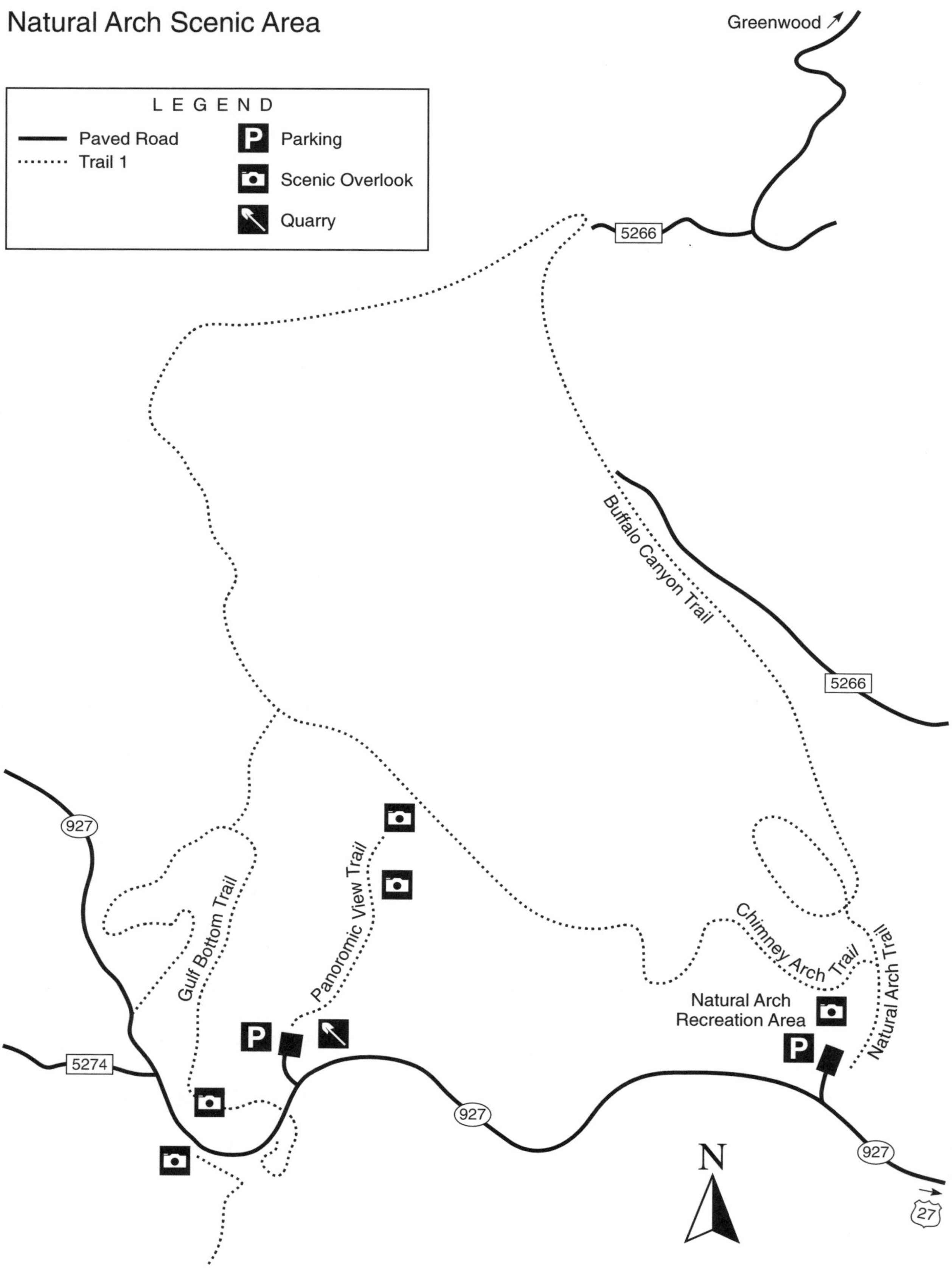

Natural Arch Scenic Area

Greenwood ↗

LEGEND

──── Paved Road
········ Trail 1

P Parking

[📷] Scenic Overlook

[◣] Quarry

5266

Buffalo Canyon Trail

5266

927

Gulf Bottom Trail

Panoromic View Trail

Chimney Arch Trail/

Natural Arch Trail

Natural Arch
Recreation Area

P

5274

927

927

N

27

Natural Arch Trail and Shawnee Nature Path 🥾🥾🥾

Distance Round-Trip: 1.27 miles

Estimated Hiking Time: 60 to 75 minutes

Cautions: Watch for steep stairs, high cliffs, and exposed rocks and roots.

Trail Directions: Natural Arch Trail is paved its entire length. The trail starts in the Natural Arch picnic area **[1]** and moves through mixed hardwoods and Virginia pines. You can still see damage done to these pines by the great ice storm of 1994—the worst in memory.

After .1 mile there's a panoramic view on the right, into one of the gorges. There is a much better view coming up shortly. At mile .15, the trail junctions **[2]**. On the right are trail #508 and an overlook into the same valley. On the left is a vista into a second valley, with Natural Arch clearly visible. The arch, from this view, is so perfectly formed you'd think it was man-made in a factory and then set down in the woods. Straight ahead the trail continues down a flight of shallow stairs, and 300 feet further, you hit a second set of stairs. These are steep, and there's a metal handrail. There's a second set of steps with handrailing 100 feet further, then a third set 100 feet after that, and a fourth (and last) set 130 feet from there.

The trail to Great Gulf and Chimney Arch Trail junctions at the bottom of the stairs, at mile .29 **[3]**, on the left. Continue straight. In .2 miles you'll come to the base of Natural Arch, at mile .48 **[4]**. An interpretive sign describes the 50-foot-high, 90-foot-wide opening in the cliff, which was a camping ground for Shawnee and Cherokee hunting parties.

Take the sandy side trail up to the arch itself. The base rock here can be slippery if it has rained recently, so be careful. Pass through the arch opening and turn left on the path. For about 200 feet, you'll pass what at first seems to be merely an overhanging cliff. Then it appears as a giant rock-shelter (a cavelike opening). And then you realize what you are looking at: Natural Arch extending itself. Come back in about a half-million years; the opening will be half again its current size.

One hundred feet further is the Buffalo Canyon trailhead. The Shawnee Nature Trail, a .5-mile trail that circles the ridge containing Natural Arch, climbs to the left. Along the way you'll see exactly how wind, water, and time erode the sandstone to form arches, rock-shelters, and lighthouses (small openings formed when rock-shelters on either side of a ridge meet—this is the way many arches start).

At mile .10 you'll pass through a natural split in the rock **[5]**. Heavy moss grows on both sides as you pass through this small gap. From here on, the cliff walls are filled with numerous tiny rock houses and mini-arches in formation. Also watch for the domed layers of sandstone. All this region was once the bottom of a sea. As the Cincinnati Arch rose, the layers were bent and twisted to form these swirling patterns.

At mile .26, stop and look up to the cliff top on your left **[6]**. There are several balanced rocks, yet another result of erosion and time. If and when they fall, they'll be known as slump blocks—pieces of the cliff that fall and migrate into the bottoms.

A little further, at mile .265, there's an arch in formation at the very base of the cliff, on the left **[7]**. Superficially it looks like a deep, low cave. But it is working its way through the cliff. From here on, the trail roughens, with lots of exposed roots and rocks, until you rejoin the paved trail at mile .46 for the return hike.

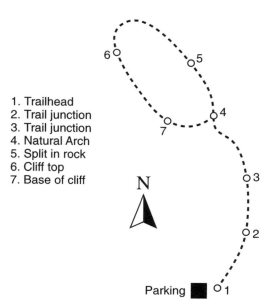

1. Trailhead
2. Trail junction
3. Trail junction
4. Natural Arch
5. Split in rock
6. Cliff top
7. Base of cliff

N

Chimney Arch Trail 👢👢

Distance Round-Trip: 2.44 miles

Estimated Hiking Time: 60 to 75 minutes

Cautions: Be careful in boggy areas and near drop-offs. Watch for falling rock and exposed roots and rocks.

Trail Directions: Chimney Arch Trail is accessed from Natural Arch Trail. Take that paved trail (described in the first part of this chapter) to the bottom of the last set of stairs. There's a trail sign pointing to the left **[1]** that says "Great Gulf 2, Chimney Arch 1."

Much of Chimney Arch Trail was cut in the sidehill, so there are drop-offs along most of its length. These are not dangerous, but you should mind children here. You'll also find stretches with many exposed rocks and roots, especially near the start of the trail.

The trail runs fairly level until mile .10, where a spearhead-shaped rock slab has fallen and lies propped against the cliff face **[2]**, forming a fern- and rhododendron-enclosed grotto. If dry, this is a pleasant rest stop. The trail turns right and in 300 feet comes to a large, deep, but low rock house (a cavelike opening) on the left. The trail seems to continue straight here, but actually switchbacks to the right.

The trail continues across rolling terrain until mile .63, where you'll pass a large slump block on the left **[3]**. A slump block is a section of cliff that has fallen and has usually migrated as well. A hundred feet further you'll cross a creek junction, where two small streams come together right on the trail. An unauthorized path, beaten by hikers, detours to the left to avoid the boggy area created by the streams.

In another 200 feet, the trail doglegs to the left. (Caution: Two false trails merge here. Stay on the extreme left.) The trail starts to climb—recrossing one of the false trails along the way—and then tops out at mile .82. In another .2 miles, you'll reach Chimney Arch **[4]** at mile 1.02.

Staring at the arch, you'll see what resembles a giant fireplace, with a rock-strewn hearth sloping down toward where you stand. From any angle, you'll think that there's an opening in the top of the cliff, with the arch forming the firebox. Not so!

Hike into the arch, and you'll see it was all an optical illusion. There's a cliff face about 12 feet behind what is a true arch, which forms the back of the fireplace. But there is a gap between it and the arch.

Return the way you came, or turn left at the trailhead to visit Natural Arch.

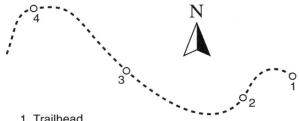

1. Trailhead
2. Rock slab
3. Slump block
4. Chimney Arch

Scenic Wonderlands

Topography

The Scenic Wonderlands are bordered by Tennessee to the south, the Eastern Highlands to the east, and an imaginary line running roughly from Crab Orchard west to Logansport, then south to the Tennessee line.

The entire region is classed within the Interior Low Plateaus. About 40 million years ago a twisting of the earth's surface caused an uplifting called the Cincinnati Arch. This anticline extends on a north-south line. Over time, the soft beds of Pennsylvanian limestone, coal, and sandstone eroded, removing the center of the dome to form the central plateaus.

Geologically, the Scenic Wonderlands are known as the Highland Rim, a region of gently rolling landscape. However, the Pottsville Escarpment extends into the region on the southeast, providing some steep, rugged country and the Shawnee Hills, including part of the Muldraugh's Hill Escarpment, dip down from the north.

The western section includes the great karst plain, limestone cave country with few surface streams and numerous sinkholes. Commonly thought of as well-like holes, sinkholes actually are surface depressions formed when caves and tunnels in the limestone substrate collapse. Many sinkholes are so large they support agriculture.

Crowning jewel of the karst plain is Mammoth Cave, the world's largest cave. It has more than 300 known miles of passages, tunnels, and caverns—all interconnected. The National Park Service, custodian of Mammoth Cave, runs seven different tours of the underground caverns. Hundreds of other caves underlie the surface. Many have been explored, and several run commercial tours.

The portion of the Highland Rim south and southwest of Bowling Green is known as the Penny-royal Plain, but, locally, it is simply called the Pennyrile.

Major Rivers and Lakes

The Scenic Wonderlands are home to some of the largest impounds in the state, created for flood control and hydrogeneration purposes by damming the many rivers of the region. Among the lakes thus formed are Lake Cumberland, Dale Hollow Lake, Barren River Lake, Nolin River Lake, and Green River Lake.

These impoundments are huge. Lake Cumberland, for instance, is 101 miles long, with 1,255 miles of shoreline, and more than 50,000 surface acres. At one time it was the largest man-made lake east of the Mississippi River. Even Nolin River Lake, the smallest of the region's impounds, is 39 miles long, has 179 miles of shoreline, and more than 2,000 surface acres. The lakes constitute one of Kentucky's greatest recreational resources, providing fishing, boating, and water sports to millions of visitors each year.

The Cumberland River and its tributaries (notably the Big South Fork) comprise the major drainage in the region. Originating in the Eastern Highlands and Tennessee, the Cumberland flows westerly and northerly, dipping into Tennessee, then up into Kentucky, before emptying in the Ohio River. It is not navigable in the Scenic Wonderlands region but becomes so farther west.

The Green River and its tributaries—including Nolin River and Barren River—are the only major rivers in Kentucky that rise and flow completely within the state. As the Green River flows through the karst plain, it is fed from many underground streams emanating from the caves and caverns.

Common Plant Life

Because this is primarily farm country, you won't find the vast, unbroken forests typical of the Eastern Highlands. Instead, dense hardwood forests are found in each park and surrounding the large impoundments. Some are extensive. There are, for instance, 50,000 surface acres at Mammoth Cave National Park, most of them wooded.

Several forest communities can be found in the diverse habitats of the Scenic Wonderlands, with oak/hickory and beech/maple the most common dominant communities. However, most of the 84 tree species found in Kentucky can be seen in this region. Among other common trees are tulip poplar, hack-berry, black walnut, and sycamore.

The understory is more diverse than the canopy. Typical of the small trees are redbud, flowering dogwood, sassafras, and several varieties of magnolia—including the umbrella magnolia, whose leaves can stretch to three feet long and two feet wide.

Young American chestnut are common. Unfortunately, they rarely grow more than 20 feet before succumbing to the blight that wiped out the vast chestnut forests that once thrived here. Similarly, American elms that survived Dutch elm disease can be found in majestic solitude here and there.

Both red and white cedar are common native conifers. Pines, planted primarily by the Civilian Conservation Corps in the 1930s, also can be seen frequently.

Kudzu, itself a blight on the landscape, has been encroaching steadily from the south, and there are large areas—sometimes several hundred acres—in which everything is blanketed by the persistent vine.

Kentucky hosts nearly 400 varieties of wildflowers. Most are found in the Scenic Wonderlands. During spring and fall especially, parti-colored blankets cover the ground, as one wildflower variety succeeds another. Just about anywhere, during the peak March through May period, you'll see at least 30 kinds of wildflowers in bloom.

Agriculture changes east to west in the Scenic Wonderlands. In the east you'll more likely see tobacco growing, changing to corn and beans as you move west. Many farmers are turning to alternative

crops too, so there are a growing number of apple and peach orchards and numerous berry farms.

Common Birds and Mammals

Due to the almost perfect mix of habitat types, the Scenic Wonderlands are also a wonderland of birds and other animals.

White-tailed deer, which had once been eradicated from the state, now are common. In fact, it's rare that a hiker does not see deer along the trails, often in good-sized herds.

Other frequently seen mammals include raccoon, squirrel, beaver, muskrat, and skunk.

Bats are notable, especially in the cave country. At least four species of bat are native to Kentucky, and the endangered Indiana bat winters here.

Wild turkey, another great conservation story, are also common but are spotted less frequently.

About 250 species of birds can be counted in the region, including bald eagles and ospreys, which, thanks to enlightened management practices, are making a strong comeback. You'll most likely find them around the lakes.

Climate

Climate, the old saw has it, is what you want. Weather is what you get. This is nowhere truer than in the Scenic Wonderlands.

Climate is temperate here. Winter lows, although occasionally reaching into the teens, are more likely to be in the 20s at night, then reach into the 30s and 40s during the day. Don't be surprised to find sudden dips into single digits, or, conversely, warm sunny days in the 60s.

Summers are hot and muggy, but the temperature rarely breaks the 100-degree mark. More typical are high 80s to mid-90s, but the humidity is usually high. A typical August day might have 94-degree temperature and 97-percent humidity—which is why most hikers prefer walking in the spring and fall.

Best Features

- Mammoth Cave and its 300 miles of passages, chambers, tunnels, underground rivers, and human history.
- Big South Fork National River and Recreation Area is a 105,000-acre outdoor paradise offering hiking, backpacking, horseback riding, whitewater rafting and canoeing, rock climbing, hunting, fishing, and exploring.
- Any major impoundment.

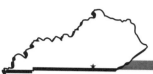

20. Big South Fork National River and Recreation Area

- Explore the ghost structures that interpret life in an isolated mining community, 600 feet down a river gorge.
- See the site of the first commercial oil well in the United States and the river rapids where the devil jumped up to reclaim his oil.
- Hike to overlooks, rapids, waterfalls, and reclaimed strip mines in the wildness of the Cumberland Plateau.

Park Information

It wasn't until late last century, and the early part of this century, that significant development took place on the Cumberland Plateau west of the Appalachian Mountains. However, it did so with a vengeance. Loggers all but denuded many parts of it, and coal mines stripped the land.

As early as the 1930s there were plans to dam the Big South Fork and flood what is now the canyon of the Big South Fork National River and Recreation Area.

Conservationists and river enthusiasts led the battle to prevent such a dam and to preserve the natural beauty of the river corridor. In 1974 Congress created the Big South Fork National River and Recreation Area, a 105,000-acre wilderness area that sprawls across the Kentucky and Tennessee border. With minor exceptions, there are only two sites where development is allowed—Blue Heron, in Kentucky, and the Bandy Creek Campground, in Tennessee. The rest is a vast wilderness preserved for outdoor recreation, including hiking, river running, hunting, and fishing.

The heart of the region is the Big South Fork of the Cumberland River, formed by the confluence of Clear Creek and the New River. Popular with river runners, it contains two Class IV rapids— Angel's Falls and Devils Jump. Legends of the region are typified by how the last got its name.

Oil was shipped from the first oil well in the United States upstream along the river. Few modern uses of oil were known then. The smell of the crude oil, and the fact that it ignited easily and burned readily, led people to believe it came right from hell.

A gentleman who'd been hired to raft the barrels of oil downstream lost a shipment in these rapids. Returning to the well site, he told the owner that the devil had jumped up from the rocks and had taken back his oil.

Directions: The Kentucky side of the recreation area is accessed from US-27. Go south from Whitley City 6.8 miles to KY-92 and take that west 1.2 miles to Stearns. From Stearns access Blue Heron via KY-1651, Yamacraw Bridge via KY-92, and Yahoo (pronounced Yeah-Hoe) Falls via KY-700.

For Blue Heron, take KY-1651 for 1.2 miles to KY-742. Go right 8.6 miles to the parking lot at Blue Heron.

Hours Open: Open year-round.

Facilities: Visitors centers, campgrounds, picnic areas.

Permits and Rules: Free permit needed for overnight parking at Blue Heron.

Further Information: Big South Fork National River and Recreation Area, P.O. Drawer 630, Oneida, TN 37841, 615-879-4890.

Other Points of Interest

Natural Arch Scenic Area (see park #19), **Cumberland Falls State Resort Park** (see park #18), **Beaver Creek Wilderness** (see park #21), and **Alpine Recreation Area** (see park #22) are within 45 minutes of the Big South Fork National River and Recreation Area.

Historic Rugby (615-628-2441), near Oneida, Tennessee, is a Victorian English village, first built in the late 1880s, restored to its original appearance.

Park Trails

There are more than 200 miles of trails in the park, most of which are on the Tennessee side. Among those in Kentucky are the following:

Yahoo Falls 👢👢👢—about 2 miles—is actually two trails, the Yahoo Falls Loop and the Yahoo Arch Trail. Several overlooks and a 113-foot waterfall highlight this walk.

Nancy Grave School Site 👢👢👢👢—2.8 miles each way—takes you past remains of the tram railway that pulled coal cars to the tipple.

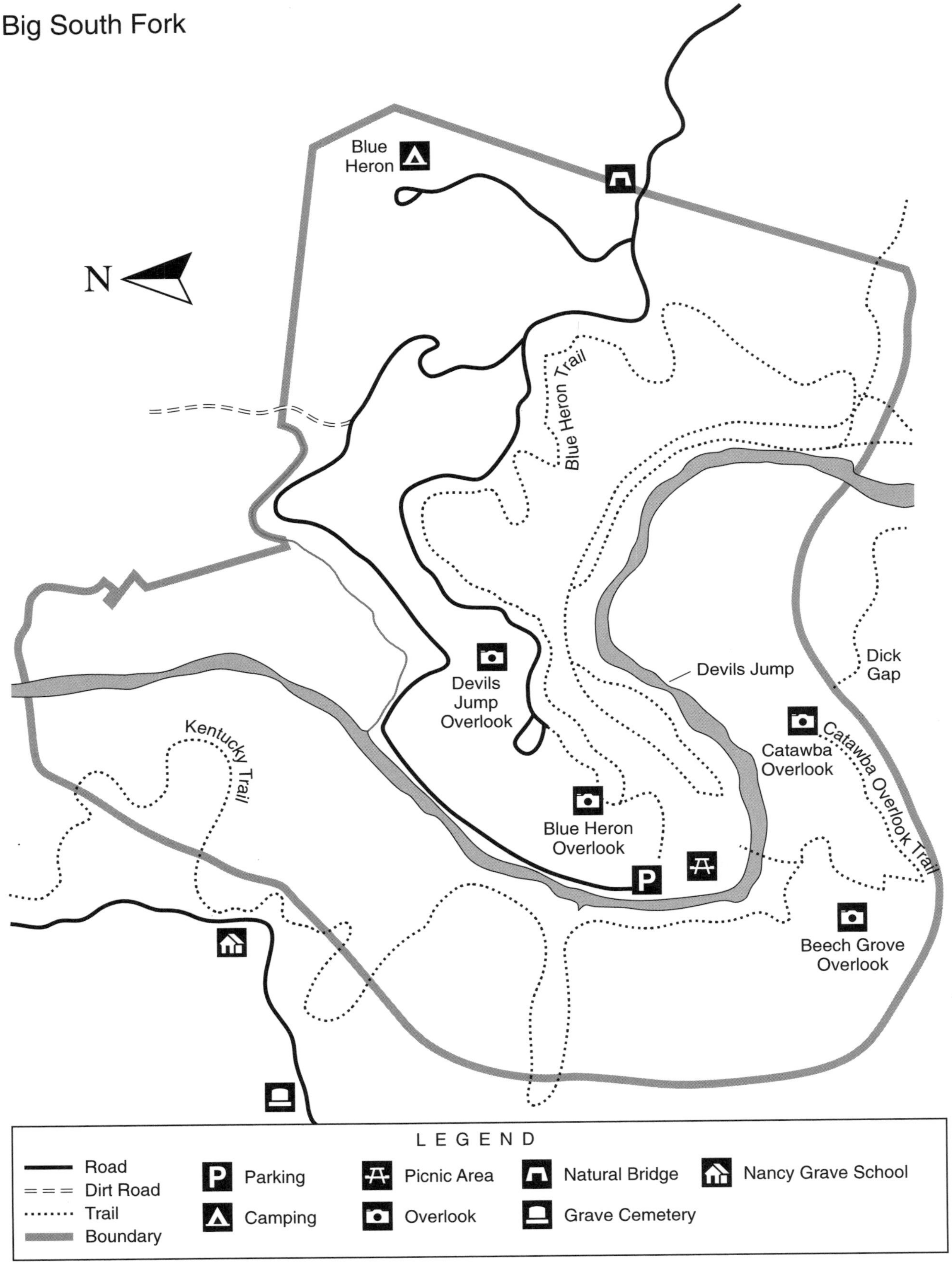

Big South Fork

N

Blue Heron

Blue Heron Trail

Devils Jump

Dick Gap

Devils Jump Overlook

Catawba Overlook

Catawba Overlook Trail

Kentucky Trail

Blue Heron Overlook

P

Beech Grove Overlook

LEGEND

—— Road	P Parking	⊼ Picnic Area	Natural Bridge	Nancy Grave School
= = = Dirt Road	△ Camping	Overlook	Grave Cemetery	
·········· Trail				
—— Boundary				

Blue Heron Loop 👢👢👢

Distance Round-Trip: 6.4 miles

Estimated Hiking Time: 3.5 to 4 hours

Cautions: Watch out for steep cliffs, exposed rocks and roots, and some steep stairs.

Trail Directions: Although the Blue Heron Loop climbs 600 feet from the gorge to the cliff top, then back down, it is so well engineered that there is little steep climbing.

The trailhead **[1]** is at the top of a short stairway from the parking lot. Turn left on the paved trail. You'll reach the head of the coal tipple at mile .08. The tramway once crossed the river, on the footbridge to your left, hauling as many as 50 ore cars at once.

Stay on the pavement until reaching the mine portal **[2]** at mile .11. Then, at mile .19 the pavement ends **[3]**. The trail starts climbing gradually through second-growth hardwoods mixed with hemlocks.

The trail switches back several times until reaching Cracks In the Rock at mile .59 **[4]**. Here, several large, stone blocks have broken off the cliff and tumbled together, with a thin, natural tunnel leading through them. About 450 feet farther, at mile .68, you'll reach a set of steep wooden stairs **[5]**. This is the only seriously steep walking you will encounter on the whole trail. Shortly after the top of the stairs a side trail leads to the Blue Heron Overlook. Note how the vegetation changes, as you are now in a dry upland forest. Blueberries and holly appear, and the hemlock and laurel almost disappear, except in damp patches, such as the wet and mossy rock-shelter at mile .83 **[6]**.

Following the cliff line, the trail becomes paved at mile 1.27. This leads to Devils Jump Overlook at mile 1.39 **[7]**. Do not take the false trail leading downslope, even though you can clearly see the overlook!

From the overlook the river does a long, lazy S, with the rapids of Devils Jump visible to your right. A hundred feet from the overlook the trail splits off and enters the woods, staying level the next couple miles as it plays leapfrog with Mine 18 Road until mile 3.37. There it turns right across planks below the highway and ascends gradually **[8]**.

At mile 4.0 the trail doglegs through a slump block garden **[9]**. Slump blocks are large hunks of rock that break off the cliffs, then migrate. As you walk through this garden of house-sized rocks you'll pass under the edge of one at mile 4.1 that forms a giant overhang—it's almost like walking through a cave for 180 feet **[10]**.

Continue descending gradually until, after going down a short flight of stairs at mile 4.3, the trail Ts **[11]**. On the right is an unmarked Y. The hiking trail goes down to the left. Coal is still plentiful, and you'll be crunching it underfoot as well as seeing it on the hillsides.

At mile 5.3 you'll pass an undamaged coal seam at the base of the cliffs, on the right **[12]**. This whole area is honeycombed with horizontal seams like this, many of them considerably larger.

A set of stairs at mile 5.5 leads down to a meadow **[13]** with the only confusing section of trail. Posts have small arrows pointing the way, but they're sometimes ambiguous. Merely follow the most beaten down path toward the river.

Follow the river to Devils Jump at mile 5.7 **[14]**. The water boils and thunders so hard through the rocks here, that river guides make their clients walk around the rapids.

After viewing Devils Jump, continue on to the trailhead.

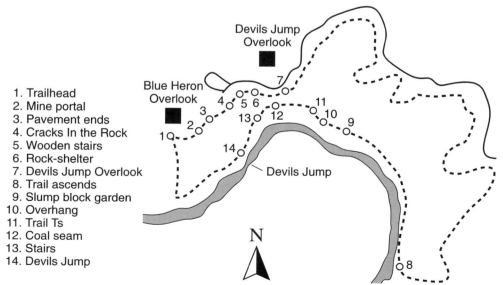

1. Trailhead
2. Mine portal
3. Pavement ends
4. Cracks In the Rock
5. Wooden stairs
6. Rock-shelter
7. Devils Jump Overlook
8. Trail ascends
9. Slump block garden
10. Overhang
11. Trail Ts
12. Coal seam
13. Stairs
14. Devils Jump

Catawba Overlook 👢👢👢

Distance Round-Trip: 3.5 miles

Estimated Hiking Time: 2 to 2.5 hours

Cautions: This area has high cliffs and loose and exposed rocks.

Trail Directions: Catawba Overlook is a moderate trail that leads to a spectacular overlook. Although the view of the Big South Fork and Devils Jump is incredible at any time, it is especially worthwhile during the fall color season.

The trailhead **[1]** is at the head of the tramway/footbridge over the coal tipple. Before crossing, examine the sand house—a concrete building that held sand. This was spread on the tramway tracks, during icy weather, to provide extra traction.

Cross the tramway. The section over the tipple is covered, and a sign—half serious, half humorous—says, "Caution: Wasp Zone Ahead."

Halfway across is a coal car and interpretive data about how the tramway was used. There are, naturally enough, great views of the river as well. From here, the bottom, seen through the crystal clear water, looks to be only inches deep. It's actually a deep pool. At the end of the footbridge turn left, following the bed of the tram route. At mile .21 you'll pass several old, rusting ore cars **[2]** that the Park Service pushed out of the way when the trail was built. Each dump-bottom car held up to three tons of coal.

Continue on the old tram bed until mile .6, where you'll cross the creek on a plank footbridge **[3]**. The slope increases somewhat on the other side of the creek and climbs through laurel-choked drains.

Watch ahead as you approach the .75 mile mark for the large slump block (a chunk of rock fallen from the cliff that has migrated) on the left **[4]**. As you approach, its rounded edge looks like a giant millstone. As you pass it, however, it looks like a cresting whitecap, with ferns forming the feathery, foam edge of the wave.

You'll continue climbing, moderately, until mile 1.1 where a large overhanging cliff appears on your right. Preserved in the sandstone are ripple marks, left there by an ancient sea **[5]**. A few steps farther, at mile 1.19, is a set of 27 steep, wooden stairs **[6]**, the only steep part of the trail.

At mile 1.27 you'll join the horse trail for a short distance, then turn left away from it **[7]**, following the cliff line. The coal tipple comes into view **[8]** through the woods on your left at mile 1.39 as the trail turns right, following the river. At mile 1.75 a short side trail leads to the overlook **[9]**.

From Catawba Overlook you can see downstream to the Blue Heron Community and the coal tipple. Directly across is the Blue Heron Overlook. To the right and across are the cliffs supporting Devils Jump Overlook, and, during the leafless months, Devils Jump itself. This is one of the greatest views in the park.

One cautionary note. When we visited, a fallen tree had broken much of the safety rail around the overlook. Nobody at the park could tell us when it was slated for repair, so be careful— especially if you have youngsters with you.

When you've gazed enough, return the way you came.

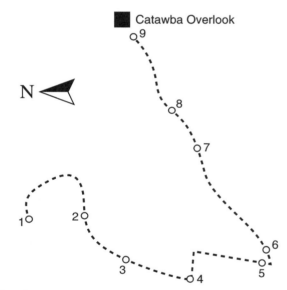

1. Trailhead
2. Rusted ore cars
3. Plank footbridge
4. Cresting wave slump block
5. Ripple marks in cliff
6. Wooden stairs
7. Horse trail junction
8. View of coal tipple
9. Overlook

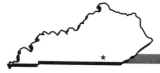

21. Beaver Creek Wilderness

- Experience a true wilderness, with trails little more visible than those found by the first white explorers.
- Visit the best overlook in Kentucky for viewing fall foliage.
- Explore vestiges of early human history, from the age of prehistoric Indians to the days of coal mining settlements in the early 1900s.
- See stands of old-growth hemlock towering more than 100 feet.

Park Information

Although not designated a "pocket wilderness," the 4,791 acres of the Beaver Creek Wilderness are more deserving of the name than most that carry it. For starters, the wilderness is totally enclosed within four walls of sandstone cliff line. In addition, the wilderness is nestled in the Beaver Creek Wildlife Management Area. Thus, it is pocketed within a pocket.

Although Beaver Creek has been under U.S. Forest Service management since the 1930s, it was not given wilderness status until 1975. Thus there are many indications of man's habitation and use. Prehistoric Indians sought shelter in caves and rock houses (cavelike openings in the cliffs), and signs of that occupancy remain. Remains of stone fencing, exotic shrubs, and old grave sites provide evidence of white use, as do the remains of the Bauer Coal Mining settlement of the early 1900s.

Nature is slowly erasing these signs, and Beaver Creek is as close to true wilderness as it is possible to get. This includes the trails, many of which are mere traces, all but unmarked by signs and blazes. This is so

by intent, to provide visitors a feel for what it was like for Indians and early explorers who first trod this land.

Preservation of the naturalness of the wilderness is the major management goal. Related to this is the idea of providing opportunities for solitude, primitive recreation, and scientific and historical study.

Access to the Beaver Creek Wilderness is limited to a few forest roads. Travel into the wilderness itself is recommended only for experienced hikers with trail-finding skills.

Directions: From Somerset, Kentucky, take US-27 south 17 miles to FS-50, on the left. A sign points to Hammond's Camp and Jasper Bend. Take FS-50 for 2.3 miles to Bowman Ridge W (FS-51) and follow it .7 miles to the Three Forks Loop trailhead, or 1.7 miles to the Bowman Ridge trailhead.

Hours Open: Open year-round.

Facilities: None.

Permits and Rules: No mechanized vehicles (including bicycles); primitive camping no closer than 100 feet to a trail, road, or water source.

Further Information: Contact Somerset Ranger District, Daniel Boone National Forest, 156 Realty Lane, Somerset, KY 42501; 606-679-2018.

Other Points of Interest

Big South Fork National River and Recreation Area (see park #20), **Alpine Recreation Area** (see park #22), **Natural Arch Scenic Area** (see park #19), **Cumberland Falls State Resort Park** (see park #18), **Rockcastle Recreation Area** (see park #17), and **Bee Rock Recreation Area** (see park #16) are all within an hour of the Beaver Creek Wilderness.

Park Trails

Only 12.3 miles of formal trails can be found within Beaver Creek Wilderness, with only three primary access points (Three Forks of Beaver Overlook, Bowman Ridge, and Swain Ridge). Register boxes mark the wilderness boundary on all trails. Once past the registration boxes, many of the trails are, by intent, poorly marked in order to provide a true

wilderness experience. There's only one formal loop, but you can construct your own loops by combining trails. We recommend that approach, along with carrying plenty of water (or a filtration device), trail snacks, and a map and compass. And allow more time for these trails than you might otherwise for similar distances, as trail finding can sometimes eat up the hours.

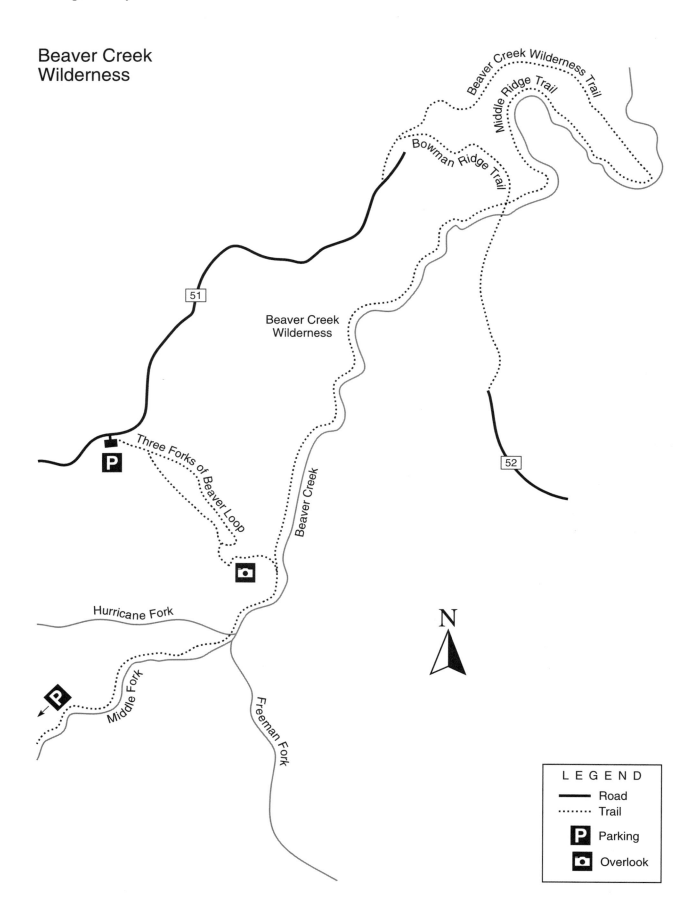

Beaver Creek
Wilderness

Beaver Creek Wilderness Trail

Middle Ridge Trail

Bowman Ridge Trail

51

Beaver Creek
Wilderness

52

Three Forks of Beaver Loop

P

Beaver Creek

Hurricane Fork

Middle Fork

P

Freeman Fork

N

L E G E N D
——— Road
.... Trail
P Parking
◘ Overlook

Three Forks of Beaver Loop

👢👢👢

Distance Round-Trip: 1.9 miles

Estimated Hiking Time: 60 to 90 minutes

Cautions: Be careful on high cliffs. Watch for loose and exposed rock.

Trail Directions: A moderate hike along the top of the cliff line surrounding Beaver Creek Valley takes you to one of the most scenic overlooks in the Bluegrass state. The trailhead **[1]** is at the east end of the parking lot, to the left of FS-51. About 500 feet further, the trail starts descending, following the edge of a hollow on the left filled with very young second-growth hardwoods. There's more understory than there are trees surrounding you.

Beaver Creek Wilderness is enclosed on all sides by high cliffs. At mile .35, you can see the far ridges edging the valley **[2]**. The slope increases, and the trail roughens until you bottom out in a fern garden **[3]** at mile .41. The trail then climbs through mixed hardwoods and hemlocks. Ferns and wildflowers line the trail, with laurel below you in the hollow.

You'll come to a natural overlook at mile .5 that looks into the Beaver Creek drainage from a high, sheer cliff **[4]**. Note the thickness and height of the old-growth hemlocks, which climb straight up from the valley floor until they tower over you. These trees were here when Daniel Boone first crossed Cumberland Gap and will be here when your grandchildren walk these trails; so it's more than their size that makes you feel small.

You'll T into an old road at mile .8, with a Y immediately to the left **[5]**. Take the right fork toward the overlook **[6]**, which you'll reach at mile 1.0.

From where you stand, humpbacked overlapping domes surround you on all sides, marching off into infinity. Below you, during the leafless months you can see the three forks that join to form Beaver Creek. Little Hurricane Fork will be on your right, followed by Middle Fork and Freeman Fork.

For those in the know, Three Forks of Beaver Overlook is the place to be during fall color displays. There is no finer foliage view available in Kentucky.

Nor will it be your imagination if you see naked nymphs cavorting in the sylvan glades and forest glens of the valley. When the Rainbow People visit the Daniel Boone National Forest, Beaver Creek is one of their favorite playgrounds.

When you've had your fill, return to the trail junction **[5]**, but stay on the road, which is FS-51. It ascends gradually to your left. This section of the loop is a designated watchable-wildlife area, with interpretive signs along the trail to explain features. Parts of the road will be overgrown with grasses, and wildflowers line the sides. At mile 1.6 you'll emerge at a native-plants meadow **[7]**. Take the side trail 150 feet to a small woodland pond, where interpretive signs explain the importance of such small watering holes.

As you circle the meadow, other signs discuss the importance of native plants. Unfortunately, many of the signs have been vandalized. At mile 1.7 you reenter the woods by a very small interpreted pond **[8]**. From here on, the trail is graveled to facilitate travel for those with disabilities. Follow the gravel back to the trailhead.

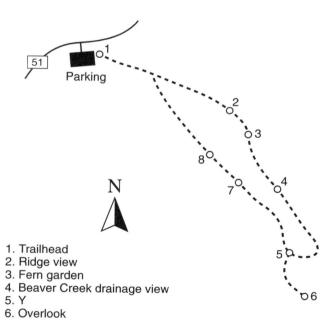

1. Trailhead
2. Ridge view
3. Fern garden
4. Beaver Creek drainage view
5. Y
6. Overlook
7. Native-plants meadow
8. Small pond

Bowman Ridge/Middle Ridge/ Beaver Creek Wilderness Loop 👢👢👢👢

Distance Round-Trip: 4.06 miles

Estimated Hiking Time: 2 to 2.5 hours

Cautions: Be aware that there are high banks, overgrown trails, unmarked trails, loose rock, and washouts.

Trail Directions: The Middle Ridge Trail is almost unmarked, designed to provide hikers with a wilderness challenge comparable to what it was like for Native Americans and early explorers who first entered this area. It lies within one of the richest wildflower environments in the state.

From the parking lot, pick up the old road in front of you and follow it to the right through a pine forest for 240 feet to a gate. The trailhead **[1]** is 275 feet further. Turn right onto it, and descend into hardwoods.

At mile .2, the trail divides. Take #514 to the right. About 500 feet further, at mile .3, examine the tall, weathered hollow stump **[2]**. About 12 feet tall, it looks like a modern sculpture, the sort you'd expect to see in front of the entrance to a bank. The trail continues until mile .35, where it junctions with an old road, now covered with grass. Turn left and continue to the trail register at mile .38 **[3]**. These register boxes actually mark the wilderness area. Be sure to sign in.

The grassy road continues downward on a steady, but not steep, descent, following the ridge above a hollow filled with maples, oaks, hickory, and other trees. This is a great fall-foliage walk. Eventually, at mile .84, the road is sandwiched between creek-carved hollows on both sides **[4]** before dropping down to Beaver Creek.

Just before a concrete bridge over the creek, turn right down a short flight of stairs **[5]**. A trail sign points to trail #532, and a few feet further, a marker tells you that you are on trail #518. These are the last markers you'll see almost until you return to the trailhead.

Trail #518—Middle Ridge Trail—becomes narrow and overgrown as it plays leapfrog with Beaver Creek. Much of the pathway here is overgrown, and in some areas it is washed out. It will challenge your trail-finding ability. Indeed, you might talk yourself into the idea that you're in the wrong place. But hang in there. The profusion of wildflowers and the picturesque pools and flats of the creek make the hike worthwhile.

Stay alert at mile 1.7, where there are beaver cuttings in some rather large trees **[6]** quite some distance from the creek. Chances are these were made during high-water periods. The trail gets rougher after this point, with several areas that are nothing more than sidehills of loose rock. Keep at it until mile 2.3, where you'll cross through an overgrown meadow **[7]** and pick up an old road that climbs steeply to the left **[8]**. You are now on Beaver Creek Wilderness Trail, and here you face the only steep climb on the route.

The trail roller-coasters as it climbs back to the ridge until mile 3.3, where it Ys at a grassy road, which turns right. A trail marker **[9]** points straight. This is the first marker or blaze since you left the concrete bridge.

The trail plays hide-and-seek with the grassy road. At mile 3.7 there's another Y, with an arrow pointing straight ahead **[10]**. The arrow is ambiguous, however. Bear left for the trail, and follow it back to the trailhead.

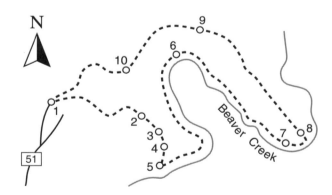

1. Trailhead
2. Hollow stump
3. Trail register
4. Hollows
5. Stairs
6. Beaver cuttings
7. Overgrown meadow
8. Beaver Creek Wilderness Trail junction
9. Trail marker
10 Ambiguous trail marker

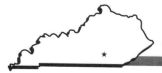

22. Alpine Recreation Area

- Explore a wild area recaptured from an old railroad town.
- Look for remnants of old coal mines that dotted the area.
- Find nearly perfect examples of forest fungi, such as chocolate lenzites and sulphur polypore.

Park Information

Alpine was once a thriving railroad town that shipped coal and timber from this rugged area of the Cumberland Plateau. The town migrated from the railroad in the late 1920s, at which time the land was purchased by the federal government.

An old farmhouse in what is now the picnic area was used as a rental property for many years, and the Civilian Conservation Corps actually replaced the chimney on that house. All that remains of the home is the chimney, which now stands alongside the picnic shelter. The shelter itself was built in the late 1960s, and the recreation area and trails were put in by the Accelerated Project Works at about the same time.

As you explore the nearby second-growth hardwood forests, you'll find evidence of old closed-up coal mines and the remains of logging operations.

Directions: From Somerset, Kentucky, go south on US-27 for 15 miles. The Alpine Picnic Area is on the right. The trailhead is at the first parking area within the picnic grounds.

Hours Open: Open year-round during daylight hours.

Facilities: Picnic sites, pit toilets.

Permits and Rules: Only foot travel on trails.

Further Information: Contact Somerset Ranger District, Daniel Boone National Forest, 156 Realty Lane, Somerset, KY 42501; 606-679-2018.

Other Points of Interest

Beaver Creek Wilderness (see park #21), **Rockcastle Recreation Area** (see park #17), **Bee Rock Recreation Area** (see park #16), **Natural Arch Scenic Area** (see park #19), and **Big South Fork National River and Recreation Area** (see park #20) are all within one hour of Alpine Recreation Area.

Alpine Recreation Area

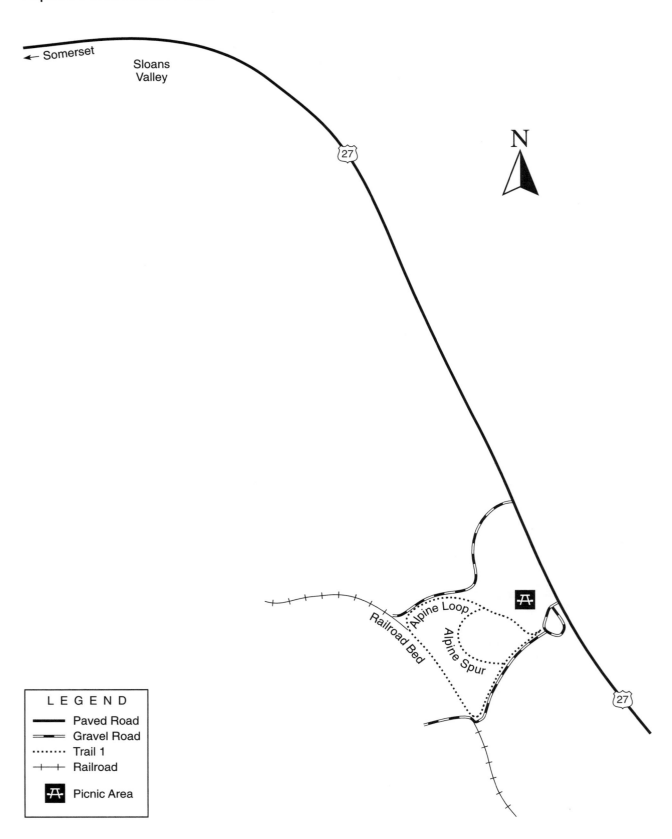

Alpine Loop 👢👢👢

Distance Round-Trip: 1.1 miles

Estimated Hiking Time: 30 to 45 minutes

Cautions: Be aware of blind trail junctions, which do not indicate which direction to take.

Trail Directions: The Alpine Loop is a relatively easy trail that uses old roads and railbeds to take you through a new second-growth hardwood forest replete with human history. Look sharp and you'll see signs of logging operations and old, closed-up coal mines.

The trailhead **[1]** is at the first parking area within the picnic grounds, near the pit toilets. The trail descends gradually, initially on gravel, until mile .07, where the Alpine Spur Trail comes in on the left **[2]**. When we visited, the trail marker had been knocked down by vandals, but the junction is obvious. Continue straight.

At mile .09, an old block building **[3]** appears on the right, about 15 yards into the woods. This was the pump house that served the area when it was used as a vacation rental property by the Forest Service. A little further, after a short stairway, you'll T into a road that goes to the pump house. Turn left to follow the trail, which is lined with ferns and wildflowers.

The trail continues downward until mile .23, where you seem to face an unmarked Y **[4]**. In actuality, the trail divides around a foliage-covered triangle—almost as if a buffalo herd had split to avoid an obstruction. Take either fork. The trail turns right after circling the triangle, following the gorge cut by a seasonal creek.

As you descend, you'll pass under a living arch at mile .42 **[5]**. Here, fallen oaks and poplars, which are still alive, form a rainbow over the trail. Eventually these trees will fall and block the path. But for now they are a natural gateway to the rest of the walk.

You'll reach a grown-over clearing at mile .46 and an unmarked T **[6]**. This is the bed of the old railroad that carried coal and timber off to market. Turn left, and follow the railroad grade upward. As you walk, there will be deep hollows filled with second-growth timber on both sides. Pines join the oaks and hickories as part of the dominant canopy.

Soon enough you'll reach an exposed sandstone outcrop at mile .56 **[7]**, where you can clearly see how slump blocks form. A slump block is a large chunk of rock that breaks off a cliff and migrates. This one has moved just a few feet from its source. Come back in several thousand years, however, and it will have continued its slow march across the trail, finally coming to rest near the creek below.

At mile .65 there's a deep rock house (a cavelike opening in the cliff) **[8]** partially obscured by hanging gardens of laurel and ground cedar that overhang the lip and trail down over the opening like a bead curtain.

A couple hundred feet further you'll reach a blind intersection. The railroad bed turns right. Take the trail straight; it steepens as it climbs back out of the valley. You'll pass the end of the Alpine Spur at mile .92 and then reach the picnic area road at mile 1.09 **[9]**. Turn left and return to the trailhead.

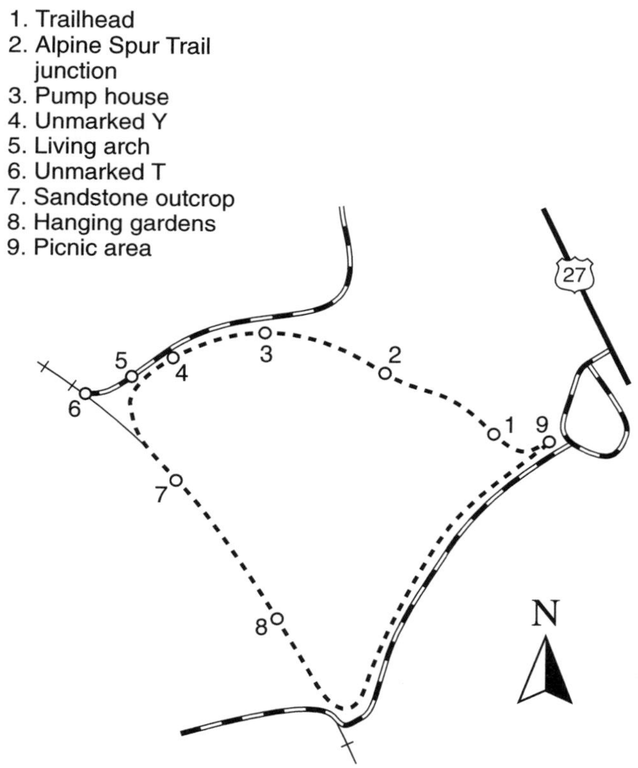

1. Trailhead
2. Alpine Spur Trail junction
3. Pump house
4. Unmarked Y
5. Living arch
6. Unmarked T
7. Sandstone outcrop
8. Hanging gardens
9. Picnic area

Alpine Spur 👢👢👢

Distance Round-Trip: .69 miles

Estimated Hiking Time: 20 to 30 minutes

Cautions: You will encounter some exposed roots.

Trail Directions: The Alpine Spur is a short loop within the larger Alpine Loop Trail. A relatively easy trail, it passes through the drier uplands instead of descending into the valley as the Alpine Loop does. As a result, there are some differences in the flora, fauna, and geology you'll see.

The trailhead **[1]** is at the second parking area within the picnic grounds. To start, you'll actually be on the Alpine Loop Trail, which descends gradually through second-growth hardwoods. This area was seriously logged in the 1920s, so these are fairly young trees. At mile .07 you'll reach the Alpine Spur, which comes in on the left **[2]**. When we were there the trail marker had been knocked over by vandals, but the turn is very obvious. Go left.

The trail ascends steadily, but gradually. Unlike what happens on the main loop, where pines are all but absent, you'll pass under many towering pines mixed in with the hardwoods. These were planted in the 1930s by the Civilian Conservation Corps.

At mile .08 there is a fungus-covered erosion step **[3]**. These are chocolate lenzites, a thin, bright rusty-brown shelving fungus with white, yellow, and orange edges. Because the trail gets little use, the lenzites have been able to spread across the entire step, undisturbed by any footfalls. Rarely do you find so much of it, arranged so perfectly, remaining unbroken by the passage of people and animals.

At mile .29 the trail starts descending very gradually until mile .36, where you'll drop steeply into a large, open drain and then immediately climb back out **[4]**. Then, at mile .43, you'll junction with the Alpine Loop **[5]**. Turn left.

The trail climbs more steeply now, through mixed hardwoods and mature pines. You'll reach the picnic area road at mile .62 **[6]**. Turn left and return to the trailhead.

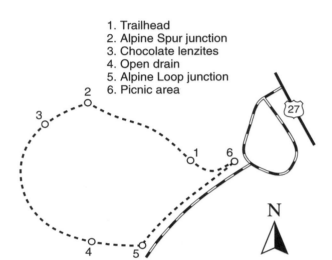

1. Trailhead
2. Alpine Spur junction
3. Chocolate lenzites
4. Open drain
5. Alpine Loop junction
6. Picnic area

23. Lake Cumberland State Resort Park

- Share the park with the large herds of deer and the huge raccoon population found there. You're likely to see these and other wildlife species at any time.
- Explore the fjordlike, cliff-lined bays of the largest lake in Kentucky.
- Try your hand at the striped bass, largemouth bass, and smallmouth bass fishing that has made Lake Cumberland world famous.

Park Information

At 50,000 surface acres, and with 1,255 miles of shoreline, 101-mile-long Lake Cumberland is the largest lake in Kentucky.

This deep, clear mountain lake—created in 1952 when the U.S. Army Corps of Engineers dammed the Cumberland River at Wolf Creek—winds a serpentine path across the Cumberland Plateau, with numerous cliff-lined bays and inlets that resemble fjords. The grandeur of these fjordlike embayments can be enjoyed from many locations in the park.

A mecca for fishing enthusiasts, Lake Cumberland is especially known for its striped bass fishery. In fact, many authorities expect the next world-record striper to come from Lake Cumberland's waters. Largemouth and smallmouth bass fishing is also very popular, and there is growing interest in the walleye fishery that has developed over the last few years.

Because of the availability of protected space and suitable habitat, the park is a haven for many animal species. Large deer herds call the park home, and you can see them almost any time, although early morning and late afternoon are best. The huge raccoon population makes its presence felt continually. Indeed, the masked bandits frequently visit the patio area of Lure Lodge during the evening, and you are just about guaranteed to see them in the cottage areas.

Other animals commonly spotted in the park include red fox, skunk, wild turkey, and squirrels.

Caution: Because of their protected status in the park and the fact that they are used to being around people, many of these animals appear tame. This is not the case! They are wild, and should be treated as such. Feeding of wildlife is strictly prohibited!

Directions: Take US-127 south from Jamestown, Kentucky, 15 miles to the park entrance. Lure Lodge and the Activities Center are 5 miles from the gate.

Hours Open: Open year-round, but some facilities are seasonal.

Facilities: Two lodges, cottages, campground, marina, picnic areas, golf. Lake Cumberland State Resort Park has the only indoor pool complex in the state park system.

Permits and Rules: Only foot travel on trails.

Further Information: Contact Lake Cumberland State Resort Park, 5465 State Park Road, Jamestown, KY 42629; 502-343-3111.

Other Points of Interest

Alpine Recreation Area (see park #22), **Beaver Creek Wilderness** (see park #21), **Natural Arch Scenic Area** (see park #19), and the **Big South Fork National River and Recreation Area** (see park #20) are within one hour east. **Barren River Lake State Resort Park** (see park #24) is the same distance west.

Mill Springs Battlefield (606-679-5725) in Nancy has been identified by the Civil War Trust as the model for battlefield preservation. A five-site tour is available.

Eight miles from the park are the **Wolf Creek Dam** (no phone available), forming Lake Cumberland, and the **Wolf Creek Federal Fish Hatchery** (no phone available). Both are open to visitors.

Park Trails

Because the 4-mile-long Lake Bluff Nature Trail frequently crosses park roads, various loops can be constructed. The trail is marked with white blazes. Secondary trails (there are two) are marked with yellow blazes.

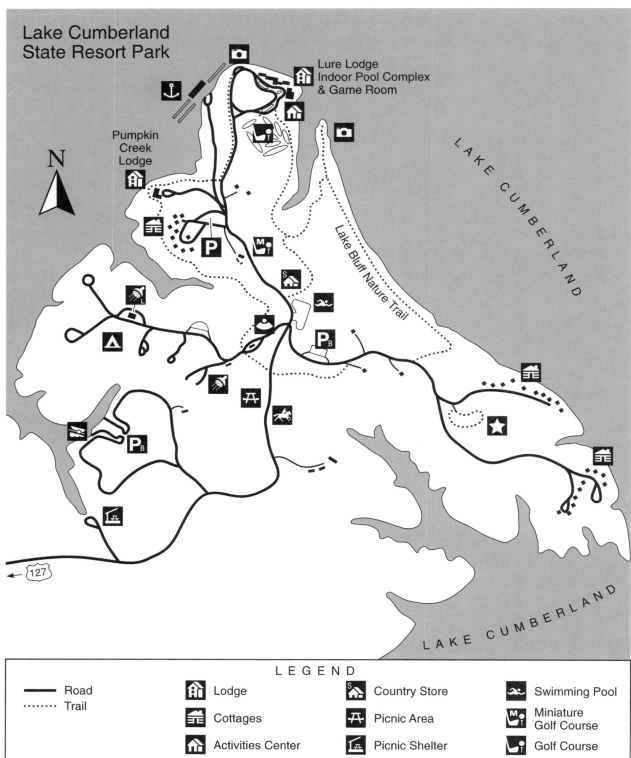

Lake Cumberland
State Resort Park

Lure Lodge
Indoor Pool Complex
& Game Room

Pumpkin
Creek
Lodge

N

Lake Bluff Nature Trail

LAKE CUMBERLAND

LAKE CUMBERLAND

127

L E G E N D

— Road

···· Trail

Lodge

Cottages

Activities Center

Campground

P Parking

P_B Boat & Trailer Parking

Restrooms, Showers & Laundry

Restrooms & Showers

Country Store

Picnic Area

Picnic Shelter

Overlook

Amphitheater

Wildlife Viewing Area

Swimming Pool

Miniature Golf Course

Golf Course

Boat Launch

State Dock

Stables

Lake Bluff Nature Trail (Short Loop) 👢👢👢

Distance Round-Trip: 2.1 miles

Estimated Hiking Time: 1.5 hours

Cautions: Be aware that there are high cliffs and possible slick sections; watch for exposed roots and exposed rocks.

Trail Directions: By utilizing the Country Store spur you can walk about half the Lake Bluff Trail, with spectacular views of the main lake, including a view from an overlook that juts out into the lake itself. Watch for the many interpretive markers, which are tamperproof.

The trailhead **[1]** is on the southeast corner of the Country Store, approximately 1 mile from Lure Lodge, on an old dirt road that passes below the pool and then crosses a small field behind the pool. At mile .1, you'll enter second-growth hardwoods **[2]**. The trail descends gradually, with deep hollows on both sides. Then, at mile .23, it doglegs right and

steepens. Toward the bottom of this slope you may encounter slick spots just before joining the main trail **[3]** at mile .27. Turn right.

The trail follows the contour of a fjordlike embayment. You can clearly see the layers of sandstone composing the sheer cliffs above it. These bays are formed by feeder streams and are backed by "V-valleys." As the streams cut into the underlying rock, erosion causes their banks to widen far from the water. In cross section, these form *V*s, giving the valleys their name.

At mile .55 you'll enter a climax beech forest **[4]**. Few other trees have taken hold in the shade of these towering old-growth trees, but there are some tulip poplar mixed in. The small, low, broad-leaved trees are umbrella magnolias. The trail climbs to the ridgeline, and at mile .7 forms a T with the overlook trail, which you should take to the left, reaching the scenic overlook **[5]** at mile .74.

The overlook is a rocky sandstone point extending into the lake itself. Several windswept cedars make you feel as though you've fallen into a Japanese minimalist painting. From here you can see one of the widest sections of the lake, with the blue waters broken by several tree-covered islands, and the cliffs and hills of the far shore asserting their presence.

Return to the main trail, which climbs along high cliffs. You are very likely to see deer along here, feeding on the acorns and beechnuts that have fallen. Here the trail has several fairly steep ascents and descents. Finally, after one fairly long (but not particularly steep) pitch, you'll reach the cottage area road at mile 1.6 **[6]**. Turn right and follow it back to the trailhead.

1. Trailhead
2. Hardwoods
3. Junction with main trail
4. Climax beech forest
5. Scenic overlook
6. Cottage area road

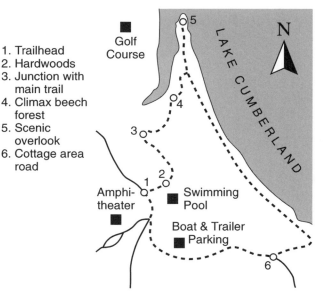

Lake Bluff Nature Trail (Long Loop) 👢👢👢👢

Distance Round-Trip: 3.8 miles

Estimated Hiking Time: 2.5 to 3 hours

Cautions: There are high cliffs, loose and exposed rocks, exposed roots, and confusing trail junctions.

Trail Directions: Lake Bluff Nature Trail meanders along the cliffs overlooking Lake Cumberland. A self-guiding nature trail, it offers numerous tamper-resistant interpretive plaques explaining the natural history and geology of the area. Theoretically the trail is accessible to people with disabilities, but there are some rather steep pitches.

The trailhead **[1]** starts down a set of stairs by the Activities Center, just south of Lure Lodge. The trail descends through an oak/hickory forest, crosses a footbridge, and then follows the lakeshore. At mile .06 you'll get your first good view of the lake **[2]**. What you are looking at is a cliff-lined inlet, formed when the lake flooded the mouth of a major inlet. The trail continues around the inlet, crossing several wooden footbridges, until mile .34; here a seasonal waterfall at the head of the inlet **[3]** clearly shows how V-valleys are formed. Small creeks, eroding downward, cut channels in the underlying rock. Erosion widens the banks of these channels, which in cross section look like *V*s.

The side trail from the Country Store comes in on your right at mile .46 **[4]**. Shortly after that you'll cross the inlet on a plank footbridge and then follow the inlet back toward the lake. At mile .75 you'll enter a climax beech forest **[5]**. Few other trees have taken hold in the shade of these towering old-growth trees. The low, broad-leaved trees are umbrella magnolias, whose leaves can reach two feet or more in length. The trail climbs to the ridgeline and at mile .91 forms a T with the overlook trail, which you should take to the left to reach the scenic overlook **[6]** at mile .95.

The overlook is a rocky sandstone point extending into the lake itself. Several windswept cedars make you feel as though you've fallen into a Japanese minimalist painting. From here you can see one of the widest sections of the lake, with the blue waters broken by several tree-covered islands.

Return to the main trail, which climbs along high cliffs. You are very likely to see deer along here, feeding on the acorns and beechnuts that have fallen. Finally, after one fairly long (but not particularly steep) pitch, you'll reach the cottage area access road at mile 1.76 **[7]**. Turn right, following the road. At mile 2.0 you'll pick up the trail again after crossing the

road. The trail descends gradually, through open woods, parallel to the road. It then climbs back to the road, crosses it, and climbs toward the control station.

You'll reach the campground gate at mile 2.3 **[8]**. Cross the campground road and descend, through cedars, until you come to very young second-growth hardwoods. To your left the land drops off into a hollow with a creek at the bottom. After a short, steep climb you'll T into an unmarked path. Go left, passing below the cottages.

The lake becomes visible again at mile 2.9. The trail turns rocky as it descends toward an unmarked Y at mile 3.1 **[9]**. Below you is a spectacular view of a fjordlike embayment, with shelving cliffs lining its shores. Take the right fork. At mile 3.1 you'll reach another Y. Go left. Then, 300 feet further you'll T at a footbridge. Take the right-hand trail, over the footbridge, and follow it to mile 3.2, where a rocky bluff forms a natural overlook into the main body of the lake **[10]**. The trail switches back to the right here and climbs, topping out at Pumpkin Creek Lodge at mile 3.4 **[11]**.

The trail parallels park roads until mile 3.8, where it joins the Lure Lodge entry road.

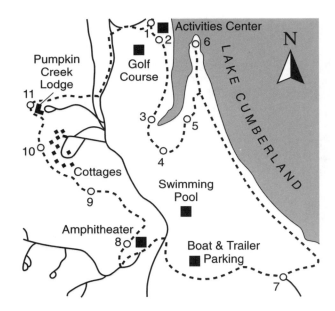

1. Trailhead
2. First view of lake
3. Seasonal waterfall
4. Country Store side trail
5. Climax beech forest
6. Scenic overlook
7. Cottage area road
8. Campground
9. Unmarked Y
10. Rocky bluff overlook
11. Pumpkin Creek Lodge

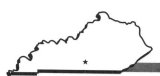

24. Barren River Lake State Resort Park

- Hike some of the least used trails in the state park system.
- Observe wildlife in a virtually undisturbed state.
- Walk through a second-growth forest thriving on land once thought too barren (hence the name of the area) to grow anything.

Park Information

The area surrounding Barren River Lake State Resort Park was nothing but grassland when the pioneers first began settling it. Because they thought it was too barren to grow anything, they named it "the Barrens." They were later surprised to find out how rich the land was.

In fact, Native Americans had burned off the land for centuries. The prairies thus created were more attractive to game, including deer, elk, and bison, making hunting easier. This was an important consideration for hunter-gatherer cultures. Because of the burning, there were no trees when the white settlers came—which is what misled them into thinking the land was barren.

Instead they found a land so rich that, as one of them put it, "If you plant a nail at night, by morning it will have grown into a spike."

In 1964, Barren River Lake was formed when the Corps of Engineers dammed the Barren River (the major tributary to the Green), creating a 10,000-acre impoundment surrounded by forested, rolling hills. Stretching along the east shore are the 2,100 acres of Barren River Lake State Resort Park.

Water sports are, naturally, a big draw, with recreational boaters and fishing enthusiasts flocking to this flood-control reservoir that contains large-mouth bass, hybrid striped bass, catfish, and panfish in abundance.

It's also an ideal place to study the effects of such impoundments, because among all such lakes, this has one of the most severe drawdowns. With more than 10,000 acres at summer pool, the lake retains less than 4,400 acres at winter-pool levels.

Directions: From Glasgow, Kentucky, take US-31E 12 miles south to KY-87. Turn right into the park. The Louie B. Nunn Lodge is 1.2 miles farther.

Hours Open: Open year-round, but some facilities are seasonal. Trails close at dusk.

Facilities: Two lodges, cottages, campground, golf, swimming pool, picnic areas, horse stables.

Permits and Rules: Only foot travel on trails.

Further Information: Contact Barren River Lake State Resort Park, 1149 State Park Road, Lucas, KY 42156; 502-646-2151.

Other Points of Interest

Mammoth Cave National Park (see park #25) and **Lost River Valley and Cave** (see park #26) are a half hour west; **Logan County Glade State Nature Preserve** (see park #27) is a half hour further west.

Nearby **Bowling Green** contains numerous cultural and historical sites, including Riverview at Hobson's Grove, the National Corvette Museum, and the Kentucky Museum. Contact Bowling Green-Warren County Tourist Commission (502-782-0800) for details.

Park Trails

Two of the three trails at Barren River Lake State Resort Park rank among the least used in the state park system. As such, they are ideal for wildlife viewing.

Bike Trail 👢👢—2.5-mile loop—is a paved trail that circles the golf course and passes through wooded meadows and stretches of hardwood forest.

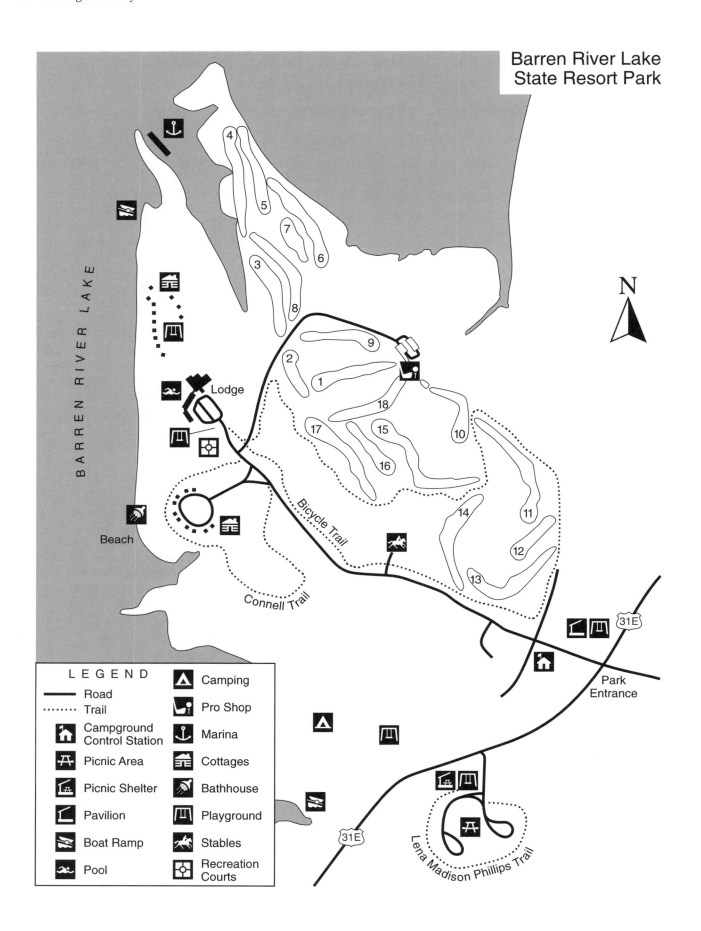

Barren River Lake
State Resort Park

BARREN RIVER LAKE

Lodge

Beach

Bicycle Trail

Connell Trail

Park
Entrance

31E

31E

Lena Madison Phillips Trail

N

L E G E N D

— Road

······ Trail

Campground
Control Station

Picnic Area

Picnic Shelter

Pavilion

Boat Ramp

Pool

Camping

Pro Shop

Marina

Cottages

Bathhouse

Playground

Stables

Recreation
Courts

Lena Madison Phillips Trail

Distance Round-Trip: .6 miles

Estimated Hiking Time: 30 to 45 minutes

Cautions: Watch for exposed roots and for blowdowns across the trail.

Trail Directions: The Lena Madison (spelled "Madesin" on the trailhead sign) Phillips Trail is found further south on US-27 than the park gates. Continue past the park gates about .2 miles. A sign and road lead to the picnic pavilion. The trailhead [1] is behind the pavilion.

Because of vandalism, the gate to the picnic area is often locked if the pavilion isn't booked. If this is the case when you visit, park by the gate (trying not to block it) and walk in.

The trail is little used and poorly maintained. But the tamper-resistant markers do a good job of interpreting the ecology of the Cumberland Plateau. That, and the wildlife you are likely to see, make the trail a worthwhile hike even though the exposed roots, blowdowns across the trail, and eroded patches make the hike rougher than it needs to be.

You'll descend from the trailhead through a mature beech/hickory forest. Split hulls, discarded by squirrels feeding in the trees, crunch under your feet. Occasionally you'll kick a whole nut that the rodents have missed, in a woodsy version of kick-the-can.

During the peak color time—about the third week in October—you'll find yourself walking down a parti-colored tunnel as the trail descends through the beech, hickory, oaks, and other trees. Try to walk softly, though, because you'll likely spook deer and wild turkey feeding on the nut crop, as well as small mammals.

At mile .17 you'll cross a wet-weather stream [2]. Note the layered rock formations where the stream stair-steps down the hillside. Normally common, these are the only such formations you will pass on this trail. The Cumberland Plateau was once the bottom of a sea. The rock you are looking at is

successive layers of sediment that was fossilized in the dim past.

The stream path itself is a narrow V-valley. These form when the banks of steep-gradient streams erode and the distance between the banks becomes much wider than the stream that cut them. In cross section they describe the letter **V**.

Continue downward until bottoming out at mile .3, by a cane thicket [3] in a large V-valley. Cane, used by pioneers for many purposes from livestock forage to pipe stems to torches, once covered much of Kentucky. Now there are only scattered patches of it. The interpretive sign says that this patch is contained by a fence, but there was no indication of it when we were there.

Leaving the cane patch, you'll start climbing out of the creek bottom, gradually. The trail climbs more steeply 1,000 feet further, with several interpretive signs along the way. You may want to pause at each of them to learn what they say and to catch your breath. Then, at mile .52, you'll reach the picnic area [4]. Angle right as you cross it to reach the pavilion.

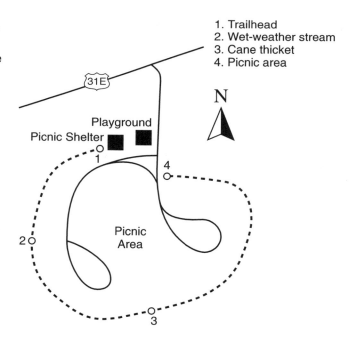

1. Trailhead
2. Wet-weather stream
3. Cane thicket
4. Picnic area

31E

N

Playground
Picnic Shelter
1
4
Picnic Area
2
3

Lewis Hill (Connell) Nature Trail 👢👢👢👢

Distance Round-Trip: 1.29 miles

Estimated Hiking Time: 60 to 90 minutes

Cautions: Hazards are broken stairs, exposed roots, blowdowns across the trail, overgrown patches, and possible flowing water across the trail.

Trail Directions: Lewis Hill is a longer version of the Lena Madison Phillips Trail but lacks the interpretive signs found there. To fully appreciate it, walk the shorter trail first, so you can understand what you are looking at by reading the interpretive markers. Then when you hike on Lewis Hill, apply what you've learned.

Called "Lewis Hill Trail" on park maps, this walk is identified as "Connell Nature Trail" on the trailhead sign. The trailhead [1] is on the park access road where it junctions with the beach road shortly before you reach the lodge. The trail actually starts on a set of steep wooden stairs through second-growth hickories. Some of the steps are cracked, broken, and rotted, so be careful. At mile .03, you'll bottom out by an old brick water tank [2] just before a plank footbridge. The trail follows the edge of a large V-valley (a creek-eroded valley that is wider at the top than the stream is). At mile .12 you'll cross the creek again, on a plank footbridge, and follow the V-valley back to the left. A trail marker at the bridge [3] had been vandalized when we visited, but the trail is obvious, so you shouldn't have any trouble even if the sign has not been repaired.

The trail ascends and switches back, parallel to the creek until mile .29, where there are cottages on a bluff above you [4]; you can just make out the lake through a meadow on the right. Then, at mile .35, you'll enter a clearing that overlooks the lake and the park beach [5].

From here, your view belies the actual size of the lake. It appears more like a small, natural lake, with water plants and gently sloping shoreline. During the winter drawdown period, vast mud flats are exposed along with bluffs of rotted, layered rock. The trail follows the lakeshore for a while, then turns away from it until mile .51, where it reaches an unmarked trail junction [6]. The right-hand trail provides beach access to the cottages above you. If you feel the need for a cooling dip, it's worth the

side trip. Otherwise, there's not much to see at beach level, so continue straight.

You'll cross several wet-weather creeks, which you may have to wade, as the trail climbs, sometimes steeply. You'll top out at mile .87 with beech/hickory hollows falling away on both sides [7]. During fall-foliage time, the colors in these hollows can only be described as spectacular. And as a bonus, you're also likely to see deer and wild turkey in these hollows.

After a scant 150 feet of level trail, you'll descend. Note the two old-growth beech trees (one dead) to the left at mile .92 [8]. There will be another climax beech, this one hollow but alive, right on the trail at mile .96 [9]. The trail will bottom out shortly, in a wet-weather creek at mile .97 [10], and then climb again.

At mile 1.14 you'll intersect the park access road [11], across from the golf course. During early-morning and late-afternoon hikes, it's practically guaranteed that you'll see deer grazing there—especially during the fall months. So approach stealthily.

Turn left at the road and return to the trailhead.

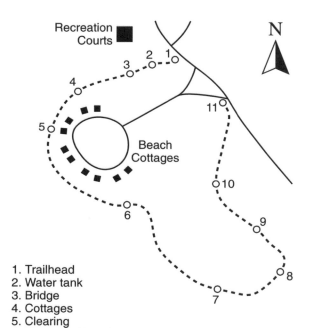

1. Trailhead
2. Water tank
3. Bridge
4. Cottages
5. Clearing
6. Unmarked junction
7. Beech/hickory hollows
8. Old-growth beech trees
9. Hollow climax beech
10. Wet-weather creek
11. Park road

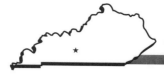

25. Mammoth Cave National Park

- Explore the world's largest known cave network.
- Ramble through the water-carved world unique to karst typography.
- Ride a riverboat through the Palisades country of the Green River for a different view of the karst.

Park Information

Mammoth Cave National Park contains the largest cave network in the world, with more than 350 known passages. Geologists estimate that there could be as many as 600 more miles of undiscovered passageways. This vast underground system also holds the world's most diverse cave ecosystem, with about 130 life-forms found there.

The human history of the cave goes back 10,000 years, when Paleo-Indians hunted game in the Green River Valley. Late Archaic and early Woodland Indians actually explored and mined minerals from Mammoth Cave. Artifacts left by these earliest explorers are found even today in the drier passageways.

The modern "discovery" of Mammoth Cave dates to 1811, and the site has had international renown since 1816. It's been in continuous use as a mine, TB hospital, and tourist attraction ever since.

Fourteen formal tours let visitors explore the natural and human history of this underground world. Not all tours are given every day, so it's best to check availability with the park. Reservations are always recommended and are all but essential during the peak summer visiting hours.

Less well known than the cave system are the 50,000 surface acres encompassed by the park. The trails, roads, and cave entrances found here allow you to discover and explore the unique topography of a karst formation.

Karsts consist of landforms with insoluble sandstone caps covering permeable and soluble limestone. Typified by caves, sinkholes (some of them large enough to support agriculture), and underground rivers, the region surrounding Mammoth Cave is one of the largest karsts in the world.

Covered by an eastern hardwood forest, the karst is home to dozens of animal species, ranging from white-tailed deer and wild turkey to small mammals, amphibians and reptiles, and innumerable birds.

Directions: From exit 48 off I-65 at Park City, take KY-255 west .5 miles to the park entrance, then 7.5 miles to the Visitor Center.

Hours Open: Open year-round; some facilities and cave tours are available seasonally.

Facilities: Lodge, cottages, restaurant, campground, cave tours, scenic boat ride.

Permits and Rules: On some trails, only foot travel is allowed. A backcountry permit is necessary for overnight camping. No fishing license is required for waters inside the park, but all other state regulations apply.

Further Information: Contact National Park Service, Mammoth Cave National Park, Mammoth Cave, KY 42259; 502-758-2328.

Other Points of Interest

Lost River Valley and Cave (see park #26), **Logan County Glade State Nature Preserve** (see park # 27), and **Barren River Lake State Resort Park** (see park #24) are all within an hour of Mammoth Cave.

There are tours of several privately owned caves in the **Cave City** and **Park City** area. For information, contact Cave City Tourist and Convention Commission, P.O. Box 518, Cave City, KY 42127; 502-773-3131.

Park Trails

Although there are nearly 70 miles of trails within the park, many of the backcountry trails are difficult to find and follow. While researching his book, *Guide to the Surface Trails of Mammoth Cave National Park,* Stanley Sides carried an altimeter, two digital pedometers, a pocket transit, and topographic maps, and he still managed to get lost a couple of times. So unless you are an experienced hiker, well versed in trail finding, it's best that you stick to trails around the Visitor Center.

Echo River Spring Trail —2.2 miles each way—follows the Green River floodplain from Echo Spring to River Styx Spring, both of which are exits of underground rivers.

Heritage Trail —.67-mile loop—is a handicapped-accessible boardwalk overlooking the Green River Valley.

Mammoth Dome Sink Trail —2 miles each way—descends from the Heritage Trail to Echo Spring.

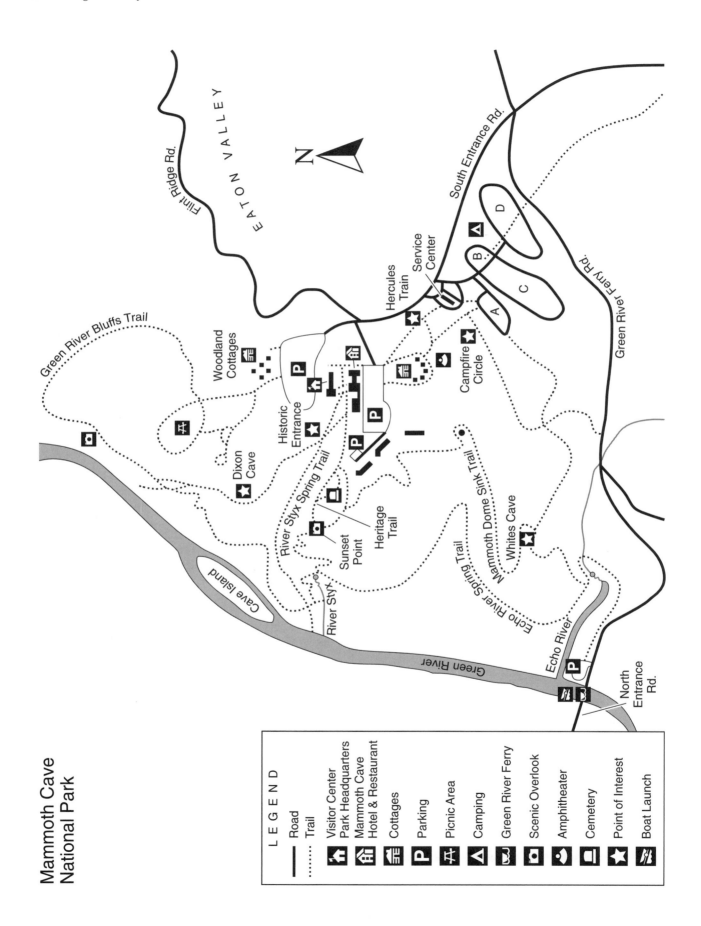

Mammoth Cave
National Park

EATON VALLEY

Flint Ridge Rd.

N

South Entrance Rd.

Green River Ferry Rd.

Hercules
Train

Service
Center

D

A

B

C

Green River Bluffs Trail

Woodland
Cottages

Historic
Entrance

Dixon
Cave

River Styx Spring Trail

Sunset
Point

Heritage
Trail

Campfire
Circle

Mammoth Dome Sink Trail

Echo River Spring Trail

Whites Cave

Cave Island

River Styx

Green River

Echo River

North
Entrance
Rd.

LEGEND

——	Road
······	Trail
	Visitor Center
	Park Headquarters
	Mammoth Cave
	Hotel & Restaurant
	Cottages
P	Parking
	Picnic Area
	Camping
	Green River Ferry
	Scenic Overlook
	Amphitheater
	Cemetery
★	Point of Interest
	Boat Launch

Green River Bluffs Trail 👢👢👢

Distance Round-Trip: 1.8 miles

Estimated Hiking Time: 1.5 to 2 hours

Cautions: There are high cliffs, exposed rocks, and exposed roots.

Trail Directions: Green River Bluffs is a relatively easy trail that lets you explore all facets of karst topography, from the sandstone capstone, to sinkholes (that let water enter the limestone substrate), to cave mouths (that let water escape), to the Green River, which dominates it all. A karst consists of insoluble sandstone covering soluble and eroded limestone. The numbered posts you see along the way correspond to a trail guide available for 25 cents at the Visitor Center.

The trailhead **[1]** is in the picnic area near the Visitor Center. As you enter, it is broad, level, and graveled as it moves through second-growth hardwoods. The trail, which roller-coasters somewhat, actually descends down a long, gentle grade as it follows the cliff line.

At mile .3 there's a moss-covered rock ledge on the left **[2]**. This is a sandstone outcrop. Most of the surface rock is sandstone, which protects the softer, water-soluble limestone below from totally eroding.

A greenbelt separates you from the cliff edge most of the way. But at mile .48 you can just make out the river **[3]** through the trees. Better views are coming up.

At mile .57 you'll drop into a depression carved by a wet-weather stream **[4]**. On the far side is a large beech tree whose exposed roots stand in the streambed. Check here for the beechdrop—a nongreen flowering plant that resembles a dried floral arrangement. The beechdrops take their nourishment parasitically from the tree roots.

A couple of hundred feet later, at mile .6, you'll reach the first railed overlook **[5]**. From here the river flows straight toward you, with exposed islands and wild woods on all sides. The river doesn't look like much from here—just another slow-flowing stream, running past wild hillsides. But in fact, the Green River has shaped, and defines, the entire karst country. Water on its ever downward path carved the caves, and it forms the underground rivers flowing toward the Green.

The trail follows the edge of the bluff above the river from here, with steep drop-offs. At mile .79 the trail junctions **[6]**. Bear right to the second scenic overlook—a sandstone point projecting over the river. The overlook spur rejoins the main trail, at the official end of the trail. In front of you is the Dixon Cave Trail, which you should follow a short way.

Right at the trail junction, at mile .81, is a large, amphitheater-like depression **[7]**. This is a sinkhole. Water flowing into it drops down, and through, the limestone underlayers, eroding the limestone and helping form and define the caves typical of a karst.

Dixon Cave is only 300 feet further, at mile .86 **[8]**. It's totally enclosed by a chain-link fence, for two reasons. During the winter, the endangered Indiana bat hibernates in this cave. And during the summer, turkey vultures nest in the area and raise their young at the cave mouth. You can often see them there. And despite the fence, you can clearly see what a wild cave entrance looks like in comparison to the manicured entrances typical of commercial caves.

Return to the trailhead the way you came. Or, if you'd like a longer hike, continue on Dixon Cave Trail .2 miles to the original entrance of Mammoth Cave. From there it's an additional .2 miles to the Visitor Center.

1. Trailhead
2. Moss-covered rock ledge
3. View to Green River
4. Wet-weather stream
5. Overlook
6. Trail junction
7. Sinkhole
8. Dixon Cave

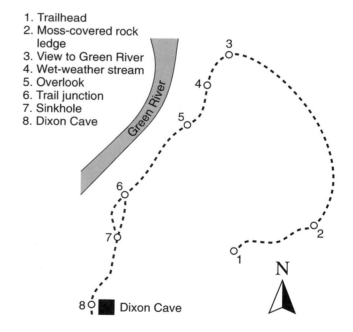

River Styx Spring Trail

Distance Round-Trip: 1.4 miles

Estimated Hiking Time: 60 to 90 minutes

Cautions: Be aware of exposed rocks, loose rocks, and exposed roots. Be careful on high cliffs.

Trail Directions: The River Styx Spring Trail descends from the sandstone-capped bluffs above the Green River to the river itself. Along the way you'll walk through or past every geological formation found in a karst. A karst is a formation consisting of an impermeable sandstone cap covering soluble and eroded limestone.

The trailhead [1] is next to the hotel, actually starting as part of the Heritage Trail (which is a barrier-free boardwalk). At mile .04, a side trail leads to the historic cave entrance [2]. Ignore it for now. Follow the boardwalk to mile .21, where a dirt side trail on the left leads to the Old Guides Cemetery, which you'll reach at mile .23 [3].

Buried here, along with unknown tubercular patients, is Steven Bishop. While still a slave, this self-educated black man was the first to explore many of the cave's major passages. He also discovered many of the connections between major portions of the cave. Continue past the cemetery until you rejoin the boardwalk. Turn left.

At mile .33 you'll reach Sunset Point, at the apex of the Heritage Trail loop [4]. In this spot, named for its spectacular sunset views, you can also see down into the Green River Valley during leafless months. The trail going right is the River Styx Spring Trail, which you should take.

Although you'll be descending several hundred feet down the cliff, the trail switches back often in order to prevent the grade from getting too steep. But while the grade is gentle, the trail is covered with exposed rocks and roots, as well as quite a bit of loose rock that has eroded off the hillsides. So take your time, and be careful.

At mile .67 you'll T into Echo River Spring Trail [5], an almost flat, level trail joining Echo River Spring to the left and River Styx Spring to the right. At mile .72 a large, deep valley appears below you, cut by a

stream that seems far too small to have done that work. The stream is the River Styx. River Styx Spring is directly under your feet, but you can't see it yet.

Shortly after passing over the spring, the trail descends gently. At mile .81 there's a flood gauge that seems to be embedded in a tree [6]. Actually, it was planted in the ground years ago, and the tree has since grown into and partially absorbed it. Floods reaching 60 feet have been recorded on that gauge. Yet in late summer, the River Styx can be a mere trickle.

A bit past the gauge, at mile .82, you'll reach a multi-trail junction [7]. Go left to the River Styx Spring, at mile .86 [8]. What you are looking at is a cavelike opening from which the River Styx issues. The cave mouth is at water level. That is, it is at this point that the underground stream and Green River are at the same elevation. The underground river can then achieve its goal of merging with the Green a few yards away.

Return to the trail junction [7], but bypass the trails leading uphill. Continue to the river, where there is an interpretive sign discussing steamboats and ferries and their effects on life in the area. A ferry used to operate between the landing at your feet and Cave Island, out in the river.

Backtrack 200 feet to the trail junction, taking the second left. The first goes to Dixon Cave, and the third is the one you entered from. After a moderate but steady climb, you'll come to the historic entrance to Mammoth Cave at mile 1.27 [9]. From here back to the Visitor Center, the trail is paved.

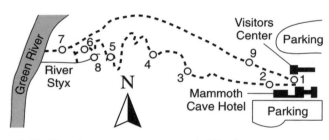

1. Trailhead
2. Trail to historic entrance
3. Old Guides Cemetery
4. Sunset Point
5. Echo River Spring Trail
6. Flood gauge
7. Multi-trail junction
8. River Styx Spring
9. Historic entrance to Mammoth Cave

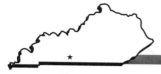

26. Lost River Valley and Cave

- Marvel at the world's shortest, deepest river, which flows only 300 feet before disappearing.
- Explore the special topography of a sunken valley.
- Visit the Butterfly House, where plantings and native butterflies provide a living painting.

Park Information

The Lost River Valley and Cave are geologically two different formations.

The valley itself was created when a subterranean cave system collapsed. A thin band of the surface, corresponding to the width of the cavern, sank with it. This produced a narrow valley with high flanking bluffs. Despite its similarity to other narrow valleys, Lost River Valley was not carved by a stream.

But there is a stream. Lost River, which may have flowed through the original cave system, rises in the valley. The headwaters are at the Blue Hole, a "bottomless" pit (railroad engineers measured almost 500 feet without striking bottom) from which the waters emerge. The river flows about 300 feet, then disappears into a cave mouth said to be the largest cave entrance in the eastern United States.

Human use of the valley dates back to the Paleo-Indians, who camped and hunted here, continuing through the years when there was a mill inside the cave and a night club in the cave entrance. Both Federal and Confederate troops used the valley, and Jesse James and his gang hid in the cave after robbing the bank in Russellville. Evidence of all these uses remains, along with numerous interpretive monuments.

Vandalism was a problem in the past, and many of those markers were broken. But the Friends of Lost River have restored most of them and are now working hard to restore and develop the valley and cave as the great natural wonder that it is. You can help by contacting Friends of Lost River, 1928 Grider Pond Road, Bowling Green, KY 42104.

Directions: From exit 22 off I-65 in Bowling Green, take Scottsville Road north 1.3 miles to Cave Mill Road (third traffic light). Turn left and follow Cave Mill Road 3.2 miles to Nashville Road. Turn left again, then immediately left into the park entrance.

Hours Open: Saturday and Sunday, 1:00 to 5:00 P.M.

Facilities: None.

Permits and Rules: Do not enter cave without a tour guide.

Further Information: Contact Bowling Green-Warren County Tourist Commission, 352 Three Springs Road, Bowling Green, KY 42104; 502-782-0800.

Other Points of Interest

Mammoth Cave National Park (see park #25) is a half hour north; **Logan County Glade State Nature Preserve** (see park #27) is a half hour west; and **Barren River Lake State Resort Park** (see park #24) is 45 minutes east.

Bowling Green contains numerous cultural and historical sites, including Riverview at Hobson's Grove, the National Corvette Museum, and the Kentucky Museum. Contact Bowling Green-Warren County Tourist Commission (502-782-0800) for details.

Park Trails

Existing trails in the park are easy and well interpreted. Currently, there are only two (with some side trails), but Friends of Lost River has others planned.

Lost River Valley and Cave

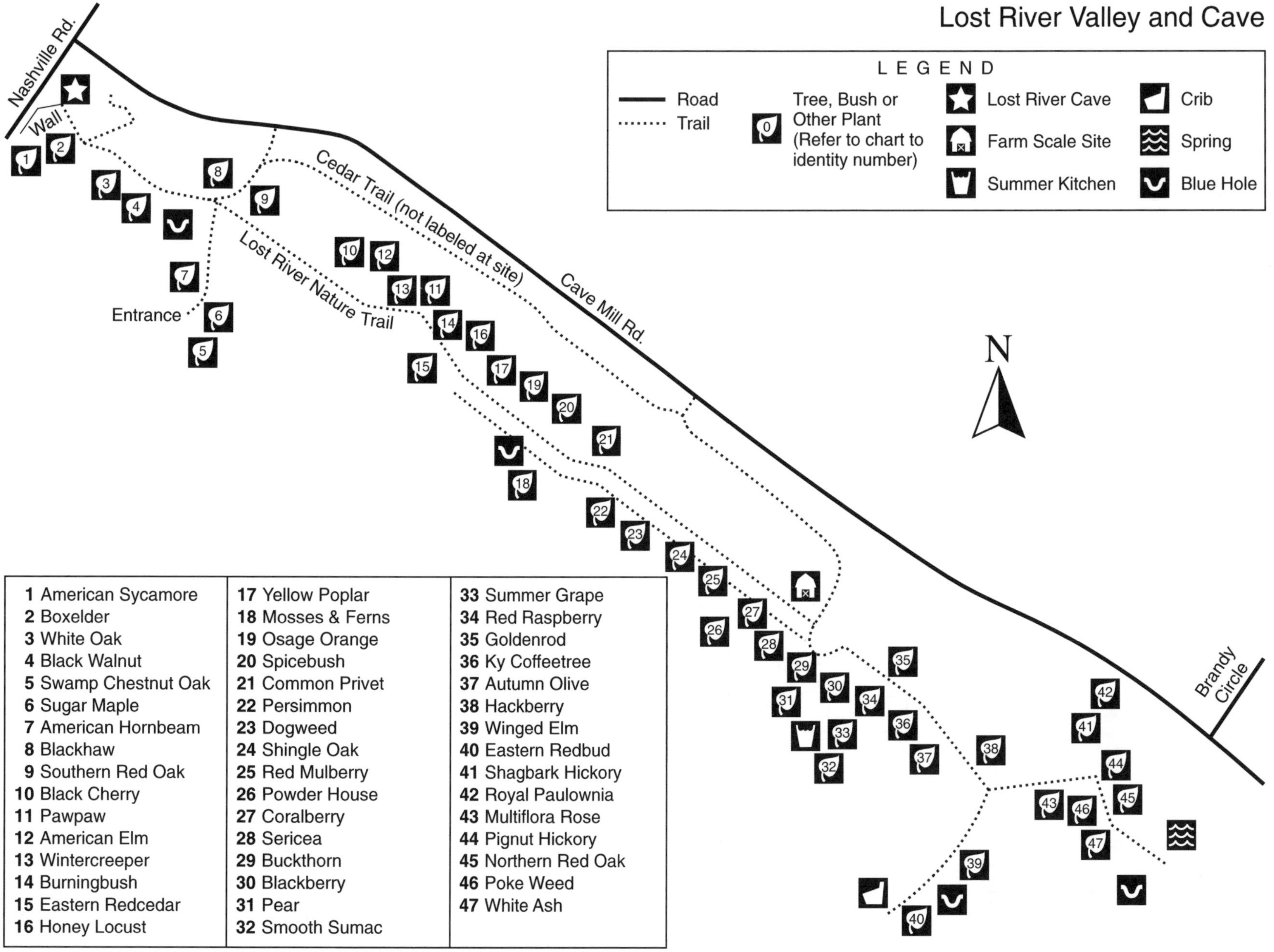

LEGEND

— Road
······ Trail

Tree, Bush or
Other Plant
(Refer to chart to
identify number)

★ Lost River Cave
🄌 Farm Scale Site
Summer Kitchen
Crib
Spring
Blue Hole

Brandy Circle

N

Cave Mill Rd.

Cedar Trail (not labeled at site)

Lost River Nature Trail

Nashville Rd.

Well

Entrance

1 American Sycamore
2 Boxelder
3 White Oak
4 Black Walnut
5 Swamp Chestnut Oak
6 Sugar Maple
7 American Hornbeam
8 Blackhaw
9 Southern Red Oak
10 Black Cherry
11 Pawpaw
12 American Elm
13 Wintercreeper
14 Burningbush
15 Eastern Redcedar
16 Honey Locust

17 Yellow Poplar
18 Mosses & Ferns
19 Osage Orange
20 Spicebush
21 Common Privet
22 Persimmon
23 Dogweed
24 Shingle Oak
25 Red Mulberry
26 Powder House
27 Coralberry
28 Sericea
29 Buckthorn
30 Blackberry
31 Pear
32 Smooth Sumac

33 Summer Grape
34 Red Raspberry
35 Goldenrod
36 Ky Coffeetree
37 Autumn Olive
38 Hackberry
39 Winged Elm
40 Eastern Redbud
41 Shagbark Hickory
42 Royal Paulownia
43 Multiflora Rose
44 Pignut Hickory
45 Northern Red Oak
46 Poke Weed
47 White Ash

Lost River Nature Trail 👢👢👢

Distance Round-Trip: 1.8 miles

Estimated Hiking Time: 60 to 90 minutes

Cautions: None.

Trail Directions: With the exception of a short, steep descent from the parking lot, Lost River Nature Trail is level and easy to follow.

Developed with the help of the Warren County 4-H, there are 55 marked sites with flora and natural features identified. In addition, the area immediately surrounding the cave entrance has several interpretive headstones explaining some of the human history of the valley.

The trailhead **[1]** is at the rear of the parking lot, between the portable toilets and ticket booth. The trail descends steeply until reaching the main trail at mile .04 **[2]**.

At the junction are part of the old dam pumping station, pieces of the turbine that provided electricity for the night club that operated in the cave until the 1960s, and markers explaining use of the valley during the Civil War. Turn left.

Immediately on your left is the Blue Hole **[3]**. This is the headwaters of Lost River, which flows only 300 feet before disappearing into the cave. The Blue Hole is said to be bottomless.

Follow the trail to the dam site in front of the cave at mile .15 **[4]**. The dam was built in the early 1800s to drive a gristmill. Later it helped focus the river's force on a turbine that provided electricity to a night club in the cave. Just inside are the remains of the dance floor constructed for the night club. After that is a gated entrance into the wild parts of the cave. Do not enter there without a tour guide!

Return to the Blue Hole via the Riverwalk, a side trail that follows closer to the water. From here you can see the entire length of Lost River and ponder the geologic mechanics that produce it. Just past the trail juncture, at mile .26, are interpretive markers **[5]** that discuss the three additional blue holes and the more than 50 varieties of native trees and wildflowers found in the 23-acre park.

The other blue holes, which are spots where Lost River bubbles to the surface, are all smaller. For instance, the first of them, at mile .34 **[6]**, is thin and narrow; it is topped by a bowl-shaped cliff. It looks like a shallow woodland pond. Across the trail from this blue hole is a picnic clearing.

Continue on the trail to mile .50, where Cedar Ridge Trail enters from the left. This is the location of the Charles Miller Butterfly House **[7]**, a mesh Quonset hut with plantings, an artificial pond, and native butterflies inside. When we visited, a young woodchuck had burrowed inside and couldn't find his way out. Don't be shocked if he's still in there.

The trail branches at an old stone building just beyond the Butterfly House. Take the left branch. The trail here is broad and grassy. At mile .6 it Ys again. Follow the side trail right, then left 200 feet further to the second blue hole **[8]** at mile .64. This one is called the Water Hole. The trail ends above it, at the mouth of a small cave entrance. The "cave" seems more like an eroded well as it drops steeply down into the earth. Do not enter the cave—that first step is a dilly! Instead, return to the main trail and turn right.

At mile .82, the trail Ys yet again. Go right, over a metal-grate footbridge, to the final blue hole at mile .85 **[9]**. This one is shaped like an hourglass laid on its side, and the bluff above it is seriously undercut. Return to the main trail and follow it to mile .9, where it dead-ends at a spring below Cave Mill Road.

Return the way you came.

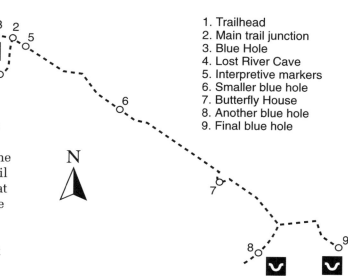

1. Trailhead
2. Main trail junction
3. Blue Hole
4. Lost River Cave
5. Interpretive markers
6. Smaller blue hole
7. Butterfly House
8. Another blue hole
9. Final blue hole

Nature Trail/Cedar Trail Loop

Distance Round-Trip: .96 miles

Estimated Hiking Time: 1 hour

Cautions: None.

Trail Directions: Using part of the Nature Trail and the Upper or Cedar Trail for a return, you can create a loop through the park that lets you experience the entire ecosystem of this sunken valley.

The trailhead **[1]** is at the left rear of the parking lot, by the ticket booth. It descends steeply, joining the main trail at mile .04. Turn left, and on your immediate left is the Blue Hole **[2]**, from which Lost River flows. The Blue Hole, said to be bottomless, taps the vast underground waterways common to the region. From here, the river flows only 300 feet before disappearing into the cave. Follow the river to the cave, at mile .15 **[3]**.

The dam in front of you was built to operate a gristmill in the early 1800s. Later it worked a turbine to generate electricity for the night club that operated in the cave. The flat paving stones just inside the cave mouth are all that remain of the club's dance floor. Do not go beyond the entrance unless accompanied by a tour guide.

Return to the trail junction **[2]**. Just beyond it at mile .26 is a set of interpretive markers **[4]** discussing

the three additional blue holes found in the 23-acre park, as well as the more than 50 native trees and wildflowers you can find there.

At mile .34 you'll pass the second blue hole **[5]**; this one is thin and narrow. The bluff forms a bowl around the hole, all but enclosing it. Across the trail is a picnic clearing.

Follow the trail, past numerous identified trees, to mile .5 and the Charles Miller Butterfly House **[6]**. Opened in 1997 it's a mesh Quonset hut; inside are floral plantings, a small artificial pond, and various butterflies native to Kentucky.

When we visited, a young woodchuck had burrowed into it and couldn't find his way out. Don't panic if he's still in there. But don't go chasing him, either.

When leaving the Butterfly House, take the gravel road in front of you instead of turning right on the trail. The road climbs very gradually through increasingly thicker cedars until it forms a T with a vehicle entrance gate at mile .63 **[7]**. The trail, which is now covered with bark chips, follows the top of the bluff through a cedar forest. You'll likely see different wildflowers here because of the difference in elevation and soil structure.

At mile .78 you'll reach a second gated road. Take it to the right, and in a few steps you'll reach Cave Mill Road. **[8]**. Turn left along the road. At mile .9 you'll reach Nashville Road. Turn left again, and return to the parking lot.

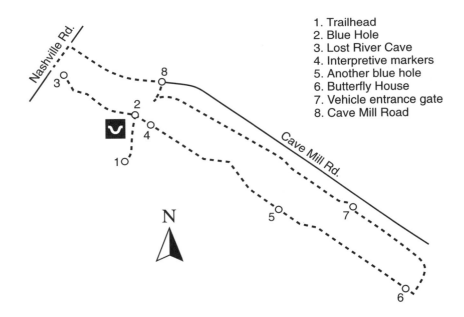

1. Trailhead
2. Blue Hole
3. Lost River Cave
4. Interpretive markers
5. Another blue hole
6. Butterfly House
7. Vehicle entrance gate
8. Cave Mill Road

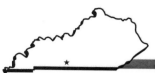

27. Logan County Glade State Nature Preserve

- Examine remnants of the prairie that once covered most of this area.
- Hike through the topography of a high-quality limestone glade.
- See several species of rare plants found only in this ecostructure.

Park Information

Before European contact, prehistoric and modern Indians regularly burned the land in south-central Kentucky. The prairies thus attracted grazing animals such as deer, elk, and bison, making them easier to hunt—an important consideration for hunter-gatherer cultures.

Because there were no trees here, early white settlers thought the land would not grow anything, and called it barren. They were pleasantly surprised to find the land very fertile. As one of them put it, "If you plant a nail at night, by morning it will have grown into a spike."

Over time, trees have grown, and much of the nonagricultural land in the area is forested. At Logan County Glade State Nature Preserve, however, a wide band of limestone slopes has hindered the advancement of trees and shrubs into the natural grass-dominated openings that characterize a glade. The native plants found here are remnants of the original prairie vegetation that grew in the "Big Barrens" region located to the south of Russellville.

Prairie grasses found here such as indian grass, big bluestem, and little bluestem were once widespread in the lush, nearly treeless plains encountered by early settlers. They're now found only in small, protected patches.

Directions: From the traffic circle in Russellville, Kentucky, take US-68 east .6 miles to the county health center. Enter the driveway there and go .1 miles to the back parking lot. The trailhead is just north of the lot.

Hours Open: Open year-round from sunrise to sunset.

Facilities: None.

Permits and Rules: Only foot travel is allowed; no camping and no open fires.

Further Information: Contact Kentucky State Nature Preserves Commission, 801 Schenkel Lane, Frankfort, KY 40601; 502-573-2886.

Other Points of Interest

Lost River Valley and Cave (see park #26), **Mammoth Cave National Park** (see park #25), and **Barren River Lake State Resort Park** (see park #24) are within 45 minutes east.

Bowling Green, half an hour east, offers numerous cultural and historic attractions, including Riverview at Hobson's Grove, the National Corvette Museum, and the Kentucky Museum. Contact Bowling Green-Warren County Tourist Commission (502-782-0800) for details.

Gander Park (no phone) in Hopkinsville honors soldiers who died in a plane crash at Gander, Newfoundland, as they were returning from a United Nations peacekeeping mission.

Logan Glade Nature Trail 👢👢👢

Distance Round-Trip: .53 miles

Estimated Hiking Time: 30 to 45 minutes

Cautions: Watch for exposed rock and loose rock.

Trail Directions: After reading the interpretive sign at the trailhead **[1]**, enter the glade through very young second-growth hardwoods. At mile .02 is an old wire fence **[2]**. Right after the wire fence the trail follows an old stone fence. Universally called "slave fences," they were actually built by Irish immigrants after the Civil War.

At mile .05 you'll reach a side trail on the left, and a glade **[3]**. Stay on the main trail as you explore what is the largest remnant glade in the 41-acre park. Note the redbud and cedars that are slowly invading the glade. Common pioneers in forest clearings, they will eventually turn the glade into a hardwood forest if left undisturbed.

Beyond the glade, at mile .09, the trail reenters the woods. A limestone outcrop **[4]** on the left looks man-made because it's so squared and trued up by ero-sional forces. This is the sort of outcrop that hinders the trees. About 500 feet further, at mile .17, you'll enter a heavy growth of cedars—showing that the forest, given enough time, will take over.

The trail turns left and climbs steadily, and in some spots steeply, over exposed and loose limestone. At mile .35 you'll top out by a wall of large limestone blocks **[5]**. These rocks are covered by various lichens, presently a patchwork quilt of colors and textures.

A little further, at mile .43, there's a small sinkhole on the right **[6]**. One of the hallmarks of karst topography (soluble limestone laden with impermeable sandstone), sinkholes allow water to enter the permeable limestone. Eventually it reaches, and helps shape, a cave.

You'll return to the glade **[3]** from above at mile .50. Pause and note the profusion of wildflowers there. While some are the same ones you've seen on forest paths, there are many common only to grass-lands such as this.

At the corner of the glade you'll rejoin the main trail. Turn right and return to the trailhead.

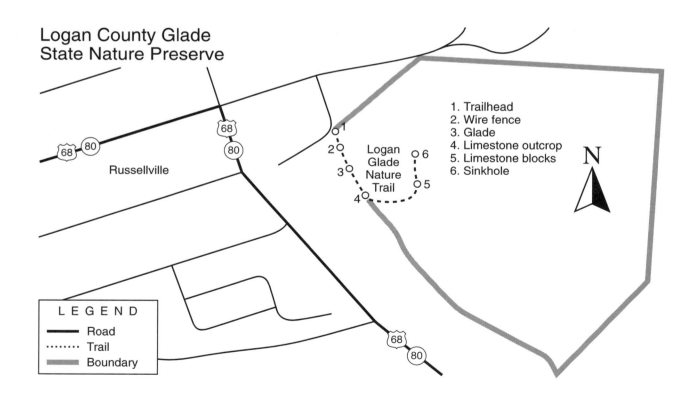

Logan County Glade
State Nature Preserve

Russellville

Logan
Glade
Nature
Trail

1. Trailhead
2. Wire fence
3. Glade
4. Limestone outcrop
5. Limestone blocks
6. Sinkhole

N

LEGEND
— Road
······· Trail
— Boundary

Bluegrass Heartlands

Physically the largest region of Kentucky, the Bluegrass Heartlands are also the most geologically diverse.

Bordered on the north by the Ohio River, on the east by the Eastern Highlands, on the south by the Scenic Wonderlands, and on the west by an imaginary line drawn from Hawesville south to Logansport, the Bluegrass Heartlands are classed as part of the Interior Low Plateaus. However, the area is broken into several other geological provinces.

For instance, the region extends into the Pottsville Escarpment on the east, where the high ridges are fronted by the Knob Belt—a series of individual, rounded hills separated from the Escarpment by a long valley. Superficially, the Knobs appear to be part of the eastern mountains, but are actually a different formation, extending 75 miles northwest from Berea.

Topography

The Lexington Peneplain, known as the Bluegrass region, is a gently rolling landscape filled with the most famous horse farms in the world. Exposed rock here is middle Ordovician limestone, which has eroded to form rich soils ideal for growing grasses and other forage crops. The cane fields that once thrived here were said to provide the most nourishing feed available for livestock and wildlife. The oldest exposed bedrock in Kentucky is found in the Bluegrass.

The extreme northern tip of the Lexington Peneplain is the only area in Kentucky that was affected by the ice age, albeit indirectly. The area south of Cincinnati is a glacial outwash, and the hills there are composed of cemented gravels released by the ice, rather than the marine sediments that make up the rest of the state. Some of these gravels traveled from northern Canada before coming to rest here.

To the west is the Muldraugh's Hill Escarpment, part of the Highland Rim, which rises as much as 600 feet above the Peneplain. Appearing as a mountain range, Muldraugh is actually a single mountain. Backing that up is the Shawnee Hills Province, which includes the Dripping Springs Escarpment, a low uplift of exposed sandstone, pointing like an arrow into the karst plain and cave country. The escarpment runs northeast to southwest, extending into the Pennyrile.

Major Rivers and Lakes

The Ohio River borders the Bluegrass Heartlands its entire length. When it was a wild river, the Falls of Ohio, near Louisville, marked the head of navigation. When the various locks and dams were constructed this century, navigation was extended to Pittsburgh.

The locks and dams have not, however, fully tamed the river. As recently as spring of 1997, major flooding of river towns occurred. The flooding extended along the banks of all the river's tributaries to the Ohio. Included in this number are the Licking River, which has maximum historic importance to the settlement of Kentucky; the Kentucky River itself; the Salt River; and Green River.

By and large, the Bluegrass Heartlands lack the large impoundments found farther south. The few larger lakes in this region were created by damming tributaries to the major flows, rather than blocking those rivers. Thus, Herrington Lake was formed by damming the Dix River before it meets the Kentucky River. Similarly, Rough River Lake was formed in the Rough River, rather than in the Green. Taylorsville Lake, with 3,050 surface acres, is the one exception. It was impounded by damming the Salt River.

Making up for this lack are the myriad small lakes created in streams and creeks of the region. There are, for instance, more than a dozen lakes smaller than 200 acres in the Bluegrass section alone. These small lakes provide a kicked-back recreational resource, more appealing to fishing, canoeing, and low-powered recreational boating.

Common Plant Life

Most of the Bluegrass Heartlands is in agriculture, notably thoroughbred horses. The world-famous bluegrass meadows are the primary plant life found through the region, along with numerous wildflowers. In fact, more than 300 of the nearly 400 wildflower species found in Kentucky can be seen in the Bluegrass Heartlands.

Vast forested tracts are absent. However, hikers can walk through all four of the forest communities found in the region, often in the same parklands.

Oak/hickory forests predominate in the higher elevations of the Knobs, Pottsville Escarpment, and Shawnee Hills. Maple/beech woods are the dominant canopy in the glacial outwash hills of northern Kentucky, and bottomland hardwoods, such as sycamore, slippery elm, and water maple, are found along the streams and rivers.

Red and white cedar are common, especially as pioneer trees reclaiming old farm fields and meadows.

Surprisingly, in the most populated region of the state, there are still patches of old-growth forest, especially in the glacial outwash area along the Ohio River.

Common Birds and Mammals

The Bluegrass Heartlands are synonymous with horses, and you'll see plenty of them—thoroughbreds primarily, but also saddlebreds, Rocky Mountains, quarter horses, and other breeds. Anywhere you drive you'll pass horse farms, paddocks, and those million-dollar barns.

You'll also see cows. Beef is the number two cash crop in Kentucky, just after tobacco, and many farmers raise both.

This does not mean there is little wildlife. White-tailed deer are plentiful, as are wild turkey. Small mammals abound, including foxes, coyotes, rabbits, raccoon, squirrel, skunks, and opossum.

Kentucky boasts more than 250 species of birds, and all of them can be found in the Bluegrass Heartlands. Cardinals—the state bird—are ubiquitous, and hummingbirds, it sometimes seems, are the most common summertime bird around.

Increasingly, shorebirds have been making their presence felt in the wetlands and around ponds and streams. Great blue herons have become noteworthy, along with green herons, bitterns, and egrets.

Raptors can be seen on every fence post and telephone pole. Among them are red-shouldered and red-tailed hawks; osprey; and, thanks to an ongoing hacking program, peregrine falcons.

Climate

If you don't like the weather in the Bluegrass Heartlands, just wait an hour. It likely will change.

The Bluegrass Heartlands follow the same temperature gradients as the rest of central Kentucky. Summers are hot and muggy, with typical temperatures in the high 80s and 90s, with occasional days topping the century mark. Humidity is always high.

Winter temperatures typically drop into the teens at night, then bounce into the 30s and 40s during the day. Snow and bitter days are infrequent, but there's always a dampness in the air. Fog is common.

Weather systems sweeping up the Ohio Valley affect the Bluegrass. As a result, you might find more snow here than usual during Kentucky winters and more rain during the summer—including dramatic summer thunderstorms.

There are two wet seasons, spring and fall. Rains typically begin in April, then start again in October.

Best Features

- Horse farms, especially in Bourbon, Fayette, and Woodford Counties; many stud farms offer tours.
- Distillery tours; Kentucky is the home of bourbon and most of it is still produced here.
- Living history sites abound. Check out Fort Boonesborough and Old Fort Harrod, the William Whitley House, Ashland (home of Henry Clay), Lincoln's Birthplace, and Locust Grove (home of George Rodgers Clark).

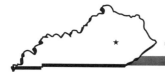

28. Berea College Forest

- See the Bluegrass country from some of the highest points in the state.
- Explore the special topography of the Knobs—a geologic formation unique to the western Appalachians.
- Examine the fantasy world created by wind, dust, and water as they carve sedimentary rock into fanciful forms.

Park Information

The Berea College Forest covers about 7,800 acres of the Knobs—a row of rounded hills forming an 80-mile-long barrier on the western side of the Appalachians.

A multiple-use Mixed Mesophytic Forest, it is primarily used by the College's forest department for educational and scientific purposes. About 1,800 acres (north of KY-21 to Blue Lick) are open to passive recreation, including hiking, nature study, picnicking, outdoor drama, and mountain climbing. This partially fills the demand placed on the school by its charter for the social benefits of recreation, wild areas, wildlife habitat, and forest use.

Subsistence agriculture in the last century caused most of the land now in the forest to be cleared by a "slash and burn" method. Then, when the soil was too depleted of nutrients to produce crops, the land was abandoned.

In 1887, under the advice of Professor Silas Mason, the original plots were purchased for two reasons: first, to provide a source of lumber and fuel wood for the college, and second, as a resource to aid in teaching a general forestry class.

All the forest is now in second-growth hardwoods, with species diversity naturally following the land's contours. White oak, ash, hickory, sugar maple, and walnut predominate in the limestone uplands, while in the lowlands and stream valleys, sycamore, red maple, and various oaks, along with red cedar and Virginia pine, are the dominant species.

Wildlife is equally mixed, ranging from small mammals to white-tailed deer and wild turkey.

Although we disagree with those who claim that the prettiest views in Kentucky are seen from the Berea College Forest's natural overlooks, we wouldn't want to argue the point too strongly. The fact is, the views are spectacular, especially during peak fall color, about the third week in October.

Directions: From downtown Berea, Kentucky, take KY-21 east 3 miles to Indian Fort Theater. Access to all trails is at the north end of the parking lot.

Hours Open: Open year-round during daylight hours.

Facilities: Picnic area, outdoor theater, bathrooms.

Permits and Rules: Only foot travel is allowed on trails. No off-trail travel; no fires, firearms, or alcoholic beverages.

Further Information: Contact Berea College Forest, CPO 605, Berea, KY 40404; 606-986-9341.

Other Points of Interest

Berea College (606-986-9341) is a tuition-free college dedicated to the less affluent students of Appalachia. Tours of the historic campus are given daily.

The town of **Berea** bills itself as the crafts capital of Kentucky. Numerous stores and workshops offer handicrafts ranging from hand-loomed fabrics to furniture. For details, contact Berea Tourist and Convention Commission, 201 North Broadway, Berea, KY 40403; 606-986-2540.

Park Trails

There are about 19 miles of trails in the park, but many of them suffer from a serious lack of maintenance.

Buzzard Roost/Eagle Nest 👢👢👢👢—4.5 miles round-trip—takes you to the Buzzard Roost and Eagle Nest overlooks along the northeast edge of a major ridge.

Robe Mountain 👢👢👢👢👢—6.4 miles round-trip—is the longest hike in the park, taking you to a little-visited knob and overlooks.

East Pinnacle 👢👢👢—3.5 miles round-trip—leads you to the most visited point in the park.

Berea College Forest

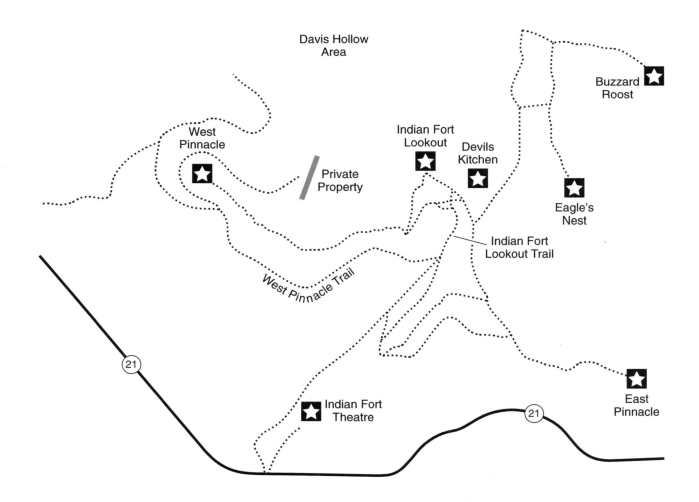

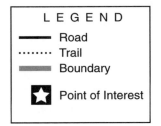

West Pinnacle Trail 👢👢👢👢👢

Distance Round-Trip: 2.9 miles

Estimated Hiking Time: 2 to 2.5 hours

Cautions: There are high cliffs, loose rock, and exposed rocks and roots. Some rock hopping is required. Trail intersections can be confusing because of missing signs.

Trail Directions: At more than 1,400 feet, the West Pinnacle is one of the highest points in the region. It is a very popular destination, especially with college students from nearby Berea and Richmond.

From the trailhead **[1]**, follow the paved path through second-growth oaks and hickories. Crows are likely to sing you along as you climb slightly uphill, through the picnic area. At mile .14 the pavement ends at the drama amphitheater, and the actual trails begin **[2]**. An interpretive sign identifies Indian Fort Mountain as a place sacred to the prehistoric Hopewell culture from 100 B.C. to 400 A.D.

The trail climbs up a ridge among several hardwood hollows that are particularly beautiful during fall-foliage periods. There are numerous erosion steps made out of old logs, which you'll have to climb over, until leveling out at mile .37 **[3]**; here you'll overlook a large, deep hollow. Shortly afterward, at mile .48, an unmarked trail joins from the right **[4]**. This is one of the spurs you could take if you were going to the East Pinnacle. There's a long, moderate climb ahead. As you climb, notice the size and straightness of the trees that tower over you in the open woods on both sides of the trail. A hundred years of management has allowed those trees to take their ship's mast configuration.

Continue along the edge of the hollow until reaching the Indian Fort Lookout Trail junction at mile .6 **[5]**. Switchback to the left, following the hollow on the other lip. On all sides, sheer limestone walls enclose the area. All the lookouts are on top of those cliffs.

The trail is basically level as it proceeds along the hollow, and there are numerous wildflowers along the way. The trail remains unbroken until mile 1.05, where a natural spring bubbles up from the base of the hill and flows across the trail. Like all surface water in Kentucky, this is not considered potable.

At mile 1.25 there's a trail junction that may or may not be marked. Go right and climb gradually to the second junction at mile 1.28. Go right again on a steep, rough trail **[6]** that carries you to the limestone wall 900 feet away.

You'll enter that wall at mile 1.35 alongside an undercut cliff that's almost a rock house (a cavelike opening in a ledge) **[7]**, and climb over it to mile 1.37, where a natural cut through the wall provides views into the Bluegrass country and toward other knobs. Don't worry if foliage blocks your view, as this is essentially the panorama you'll be seeing from the pinnacle.

You'll reach the base of West Pinnacle at mile 1.42 **[8]**. This is a pyramidal pile of rocks forming an outcrop above the ridgeline. Note the rounded indention with the beehive cross-hatching. You're looking at what was once the floor of a cave. The raised miniwalls are edge-stone, formed when dissolved minerals were left behind by evaporating puddles. The yellow and orange colors that spread out like an artist's palette are from oxides leaching out of the rock.

After a bit of rock hopping, you'll reach the top of the pinnacle at mile 1.45 **[9]**. Spread out at your feet is a 270-degree view of the valley between the Knobs and the mountains, of the Bluegrass country, and of other knobs marching in a row.

According to its motto, Madison County is "where the Bluegrass meets the mountains." You can see why from up here.

Return to the trailhead the way you came.

1. Trailhead
2. Amphitheater
3. Deep hollow
4. Unmarked trail junction
5. Junction with Indian Fort Lookout Trail
6. Rough trail ahead
7. Undercut cliff
8. Base of West Pinnacle
9. Top of West Pinnacle

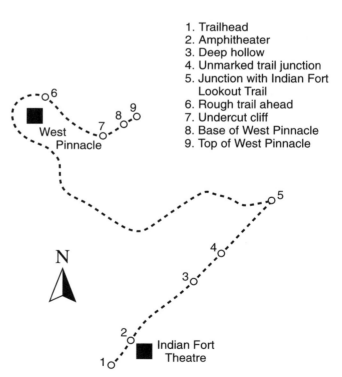

Indian Fort Lookout Trail

👢👢👢👢

Distance Round-Trip: 1.84 miles

Estimated Hiking Time: 1.5 to 2 hours

Cautions: You will come to high cliffs and also encounter unexpected cracks and crevasses, loose and exposed rocks, and wash-outs.

Trail Directions: The Indian Fort Lookout Trail takes you, via an extremely rough trail, to one of the most spectacular overlooks in the Knobs. From here, it is said, Native Americans and early explorers looked out over the Bluegrass country to see if any enemies were moving about.

From the trailhead **[1]**, follow the paved path through the picnic area. Crows, upset by your passage, may sing you along, albeit off-key. At mile .14 the pavement ends at the drama amphitheater, and the actual trails begin **[2]**.

The trail climbs up a ridge between several hardwood hollows that are particularly appealing during fall color displays. The color usually peaks about the third week in October. Continue up the trail until mile .48, where an unmarked trail joins from the right **[3]**. This is one of the spurs to the East Pinnacle. There's a long, moderate climb ahead. Old second-growth hardwoods, unusual in both their size and their straightness, line the trail like so many ships' masts springing from a moss-covered deck.

You'll follow the edge of a large hollow containing those mastlike trees until mile .6, where the West Pinnacle Trail junctions on the left **[4]**. Continue straight.

The most challenging part of the trail is in front of you, as you climb steadily and steeply up a path that is eroded and full of loose rock and gravel. We'd advise that you take frequent rests and proceed slowly. At mile .65, a natural spring burbles out of the rocks on your right, then flows down the trail **[5]**. Note the small, almost tropical grotto surrounding the springhead—wet-loving plants that have found a sanctuary in these otherwise dry uplands.

Another good resting point comes at mile .76, where a tulip poplar reminiscent of Siamese twins grows on the left **[6]**. At some time the tree branched, low down. But instead of spreading, both halves grew straight up. The net effect is of two trees joined at the base and roots.

At mile .78, a side trail on the left **[7]** leads to the West Pinnacle, but continue straight. You immediately climb over a sandstone slab that clearly shows ripple marks left by an ancient tide. A few steps later a deep crack appears suddenly at your feet, at mile .789 **[8]**. Stay alert, as it is just wide enough for you to fall into, assuring severe bodily damage. Turn left sharply. The trail climbs over the roots of a tree, then tops out at another trail junction. Going right takes you to the East Pinnacle; the left path brings you to the West Pinnacle. Go straight, following the sign toward Devils Kitchen and the lookout.

In only 100 feet you'll T at a natural overlook. After gazing into the valley and to the Knobs beyond, turn left, following the cliff line. You'll soon see, and then cross, the top of a large rock-shelter (a cavelike opening in the cliff) **[9]** at mile .85. It looks like a man-made arch, as its walls and roof are worn so smooth. This is the Devils Kitchen. There's a hole in the roof, safely grated, that lets you peer down into the rock-shelter. The old trail that used to go into it has been closed in order to protect this unique geologic structure.

Continue along the ridgetop to the overlook **[10]**, at mile .92.

The overlook is a double sandstone point projecting out from the cliff. On your left is the main body of the Knobs. In front, and to the right, is the Bluegrass country. On the extreme right are additional knobs, including Robe Mountain—the second of the twin knobs anchoring the row.

Return by backtracking to the trailhead.

1. Trailhead
2. Amphitheater
3. Unmarked trail
   junction
4. West Pinnacle Trail
   junction
5. Natural spring
6. Siamese twins tree
7. Trail to West
   Pinnacle
8. Deep crack
9. Devils Kitchen
10. Overlook

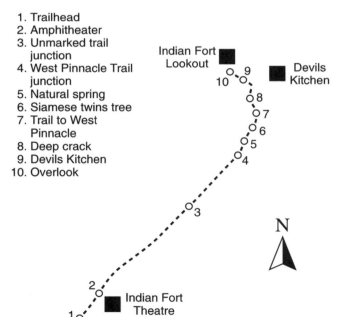

29. Quiet Trails State Nature Preserve

- See the various emergent plant communities as they reclaim the land of what was once a heavily used farm.
- Walk in quiet solitude, far from the madding crowds of towns and cities.
- Explore the floodplain of the Licking River, historically one of Kentucky's most important waterways.

Park Information

The area now known as Quiet Trails State Nature Preserve was once a thriving, active farm. Signs of such usage are readily evident in the old barns, rusted fences, and stock ponds that yet remain.

Far from the hustle and bustle of cities and major highways, the park now offers a peaceful retreat for those needing the rejuvenating powers found only in the green world. A series of habitats, ranging from cedar thickets to open prairie to second-growth hardwoods and riverine bottoms, meets each visitor.

The preserve amply lives up to its name. As this is one of the most infrequently used nature preserves in the state, you are unlikely to see anyone else here, except perhaps on a spring weekend when the wildflowers are at their showy finest.

When we visited during the fall color season, not one other person was on the aptly named quiet trails.

Directions: From Cynthiana, Kentucky, take US-27 north 11 miles to KY-1284. Make a right and go 2.7 miles to the T. Go straight across the intersection to a narrow blacktop road alongside the Sunrise General Store. That's Pughs Mill Road. Follow it 1.8 miles to the preserve entrance on the right.

Hours Open: Open year-round during daylight hours.

Facilities: None.

Permits and Rules: Only foot travel is allowed. No fires, no camping, no firearms or alcoholic beverages.

Further Information: Contact Kentucky State Nature Preserves Commission, 801 Schenkel Lane, Frankfort, KY 40601; 502-573-2886.

Other Points of Interest

Kincaid Lake State Park (see park #30) is a half hour north, near Falmouth, Kentucky.

Half an hour southeast, **Blue Licks Battlefield State Park** (606-289-5507) is the site of the last battle of the American Revolution. A reenactment of the battle is held here on the third weekend in August each year.

Park Trails

There are eight trails in the park, ranging in length from .25 miles to just over 1 mile. All trails connect with the trail called The Challenger, the longest and steepest of them, so it's easy to create long loops from several shorter trails. The trails are all broad, fairly level, and well maintained, so they should not present difficulties to most walkers.

The Challenger 👢👢👢—1 mile each way— descends 300 feet to the Licking River floodplain.

Whitetail Rest Trail 👢👢—.5 miles each way— parallels Pughs Mill Road through a series of small loops. An old barn on the trail can be used as a photo blind for wildlife photography.

River's Edge 👢👢—.8 miles each way—runs along the bank of the Licking River, above the floodplain. Wildflowers are particularly abundant here.

Cliff Hanger 👢👢👢—.5 miles each way—runs along a level of a steep cliff above the Licking River. The cliff itself is a paradise for wildflower watchers. Bring a guidebook!

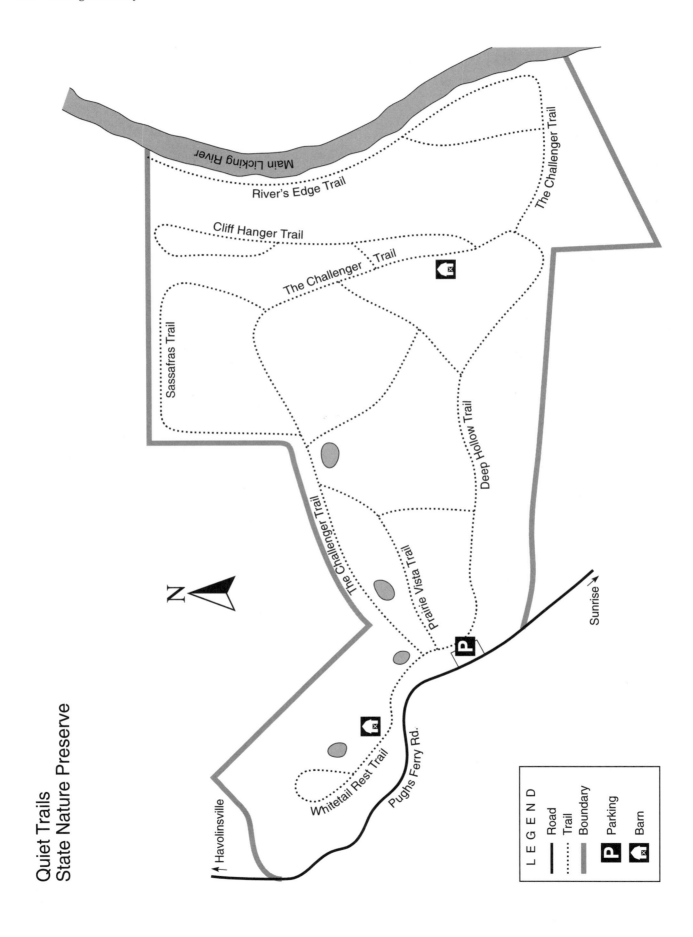

Quiet Trails
State Nature Preserve

Main Licking River

River's Edge Trail

The Challenger Trail

Cliff Hanger Trail

The Challenger Trail

Sassafras Trail

Deep Hollow Trail

The Challenger Trail

Prairie Vista Trail

N

Sunrise

Whitetail Rest Trail

Pughs Ferry Rd.

Havolinsville

L E G E N D
Road
Trail
Boundary
Parking
Barn

Challenger/Sassafras/Prairie Vista Loop 👢👢 or 👢👢👢

Distance Round-Trip: 1.15 miles

Estimated Hiking Time: 1 hour

Cautions: None.

Trail Directions: This loop takes you through most of the ecosystems found in the preserve. As such, it is a good introduction to the way nature recovers its own from an abandoned farmstead.

The trailhead **[1]** is to the right of the stile gate at the parking lot. There you'll find a large mailbox serving as a registration post. A trails map billboard is supposed to stand next to it, but was missing when we visited.

The Challenger Trail is an old tractor road that follows a ridge though young hardwood trees. On your right is a tree break with an overgrown meadow on the far side. During leafless months you can see the mountains framing the Licking River through those trees.

At mile .13 you'll come to an old stock watering pond **[2]**. Now it is home to frogs, turtles, and dragonflies in their iridescent coats of many colors. Mornings and evenings you might see white-tailed deer drinking here. The trail descends gently, with several trails connecting to it (some of them unmarked), until mile .25, where the Sassafras Trail enters on the left **[3]**. This is the path you should take.

Although the trail was named for a large patch of sassafras that once grew at the entrance, few of these interesting plants with the mitten-shaped leaves remain. And most of what still grows is all but obscured by a group of cedars. Still, you want to look for them. Pick up a leaf or twig and rub it in your hands. You'll smell the aroma of root beer—one of the many culinary and medicinal uses of sassafras.

Almost immediately after you enter the trail, a mowed path goes right. Follow it. There will be very young woods—more understory than canopy—on your left, and a strip of prairie on the right. At the blind T, go left. Going straight would put you back on The Challenger Trail. Go left again to the next T. Here, if you are opting for a shorter walk (and a two-boot hike), go left. For the full-length trail, turn right, and descend through a mixed oak/hickory forest.

At mile .58 you'll cross a creek on an old, moss-covered bridge **[4]**. You may not think it would support your weight, but the bridge probably could still handle the tractors that once crossed it on their way to and from the farm fields. The trail climbs from here until it tops out at mile .65, where during leafless months you can see the mountains flanking the Licking River **[5]**. Shortly afterward you'll again join The Challenger Trail. Turn right, and follow it back toward the trailhead.

The first cutoff to the Prairie Vista Trail comes in at mile .91 from the left **[6]**. Take the cutoff, and follow the trail along the edge of a meadow that has been reclaimed by native plants. In addition to seeing the various wildflowers spread out like an artist's palette, you'll have unobstructed views into the Licking River Valley and the mountains beyond.

Remain on the Prairie Vista Trail to its common trailhead with The Challenger Trail near the preserve gate.

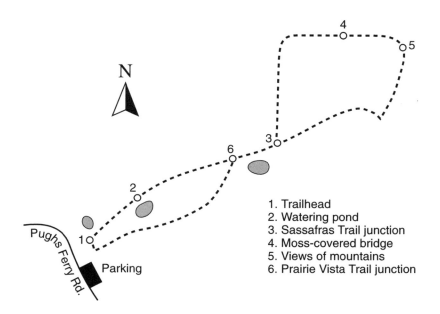

N

1. Trailhead
2. Watering pond
3. Sassafras Trail junction
4. Moss-covered bridge
5. Views of mountains
6. Prairie Vista Trail junction

Pughs Ferry Rd.

Parking

Deep Hollow/Challenger Loop

Distance Round-Trip: 1.2 miles

Estimated Hiking Time: 30 to 45 minutes

Cautions: None.

Trail Directions: This loop also takes you through several of the park's ecosystems, including a ravine and wet-weather creek, which you do not see from the other trails. Wildflower watchers will find this trail particularly rewarding, even during the hot summer months.

The trailhead **[1]** is at the gate from the parking lot. Turn right, and cross the head of the prairie. On the far side of this old meadow, the trail enters the woods and descends through mixed cedar and young second-growth hardwoods. The ravine **[2]** that gives the trail its name appears on your right at mile .05.

The trail is a grassy path. The swishing of the grass on your boots beats a gentle cadence to your footsteps until you bottom out at a seasonal creek at mile .15 **[3]**. After crossing the creek on rocks (you may have to wade during wet weather), the trail ascends. In the fall, leaves rain down like multicolored snow as you climb back up to the prairie, which you'll rejoin at mile .18 **[4]** before descending again, following the ravine.

At mile .27 you'll see an iron footbridge crossing the ravine **[5]**. This is another mute reminder that people once worked this farm. Today it leads nowhere. Continue downhill, bypassing the connector trail at mile .3, which leads back to the Prairie Vista Trail.

You'll cross a creek at mile .4, on a rock-covered culvert, and then encounter a short, fairly steep climb. Then, at mile .49, another prairie patch comes into view on your right **[6]**. This is a good spot to see wildlife, especially early in the morning and evening. Deer and wild turkey are likely visitors. Indeed, from here on, the distinctive droppings left by wild turkey all but covers the trail.

You'll T into The Challenger Trail at mile .5 **[7]**. Go left and start the long, moderate climb back toward the trailhead. Along the way you'll pass much evidence of the preserve's human history, starting with the remains of a rock fence shortly after you turn onto the trail. Universally called "slave" fences, they were actually built by Irish immigrants after the Civil War.

At mile .56 you'll come to a weathered old barn **[8]**. Inside are the remains of two flatbed wagons used to haul tobacco. A rickety ladder leads to the loft area of the barn, but there is no loft as such. This was a tobacco barn, so it has no stalls, loft floors, or other such dividers. Sticks of tobacco were hung from the exposed beams to cure. You can still see this being done at area farms. Photographers and wildlife watchers are welcome to use the barn as an observation blind.

You'll climb steadily from the barn, passing several trailheads along the way, until mile 1.07, where a small pond lies next to the trail **[9]**. Once a watering tank for cattle, it is now overgrown, providing refuge for frogs, turtles, and dragonflies, whose jewel-like bodies and wings glint in the sun.

Continue past the pond and return to the trailhead.

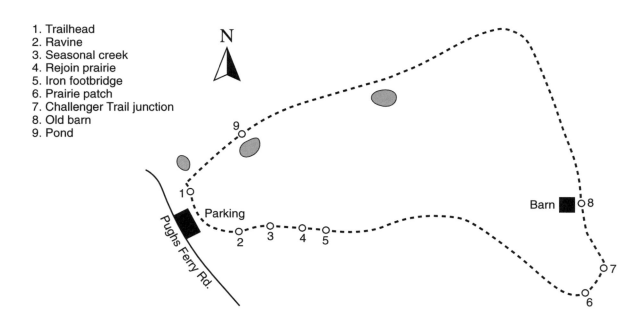

1. Trailhead
2. Ravine
3. Seasonal creek
4. Rejoin prairie
5. Iron footbridge
6. Prairie patch
7. Challenger Trail junction
8. Old barn
9. Pond

30. Kincaid Lake State Park

- Cross a feeder stream over a wooden suspension bridge that reminds you of the giant cable-suspension bridges in New York and San Francisco.
- Explore the varied habitats, ranging from wetlands to dry uplands, and their associated flora.
- Examine the natural history exhibits displayed in a trail shelter away from the madding crowds.

Park Information

Kincaid Lake is one of a dozen or so small lakes found in the Bluegrass region, nestled in the hill country of northern Kentucky. Designed for flood control, the 183-acre impoundment is sheltered in a bowl of second-growth hardwoods. The state park takes up much of the south side of the lake, providing a wilderness setting.

Although close to the population centers of northern Kentucky, Kincaid Lake State Park is far enough off the beaten path that it is less used than you might think. The big draws are fishing and camping. The campground, open year-round, has 84 sites, many of them with electric and water hookups.

The park is a semiresort, in that there are many amenities, but no lodging. Local residents, especially, use the pool and other recreation facilities. However, the trails are virtually untrod most of the time.

There is a trailside shelter and interpretive center, with numerous four-color photos explaining the flora and fauna of the park. Many visitors will walk down

to it, but that's as far as they go. As a result, you usually have the trails to yourself.

A highlight of the trail system is the wooden suspension bridge that crosses a major tributary to Kincaid Lake. It is larger, sturdier, and engineered far beyond anything you'd expect for that purpose.

Directions: From Falmouth, Kentucky, take KY-22 across the Licking River bridge to KY-159. Go left 3.5 miles to the park entrance, then 1.5 miles to the recreation area, where you'll find the trailhead behind the basketball courts.

Hours Open: Open year-round, but some facilities are seasonal.

Facilities: Camping, boating, pool, miniature golf, paddle tennis, picnic grounds, multipurpose activities building.

Permits and Rules: Foot travel only on trails.

Further Information: Kincaid Lake State Park, Route 1, Box 33, Falmouth, KY 41040; 606-654-3531.

Other Points of Interest

Quiet Trails State Nature Preserve (see park #29) is a half hour to the southeast. **Fort Thomas Landmark Tree Trail** (see park #31), **Boone County Cliffs State Nature Preserve** (see park #35), and **Big Bone Lick State Park** (see park #34) are within one hour of Kincaid Lake.

Blue Licks Battlefield State Park (606-289-5507), 45 miles southeast, is the site of the last battle of the American Revolution. The battle is reenacted the third weekend in August each year.

Park Trails

Trails in the park consist of a double-loop system that traverses all the varied habitats in the park. Because they are little used (and maintained commensurate with their usage), you'll feel as though you are on wilderness trails.

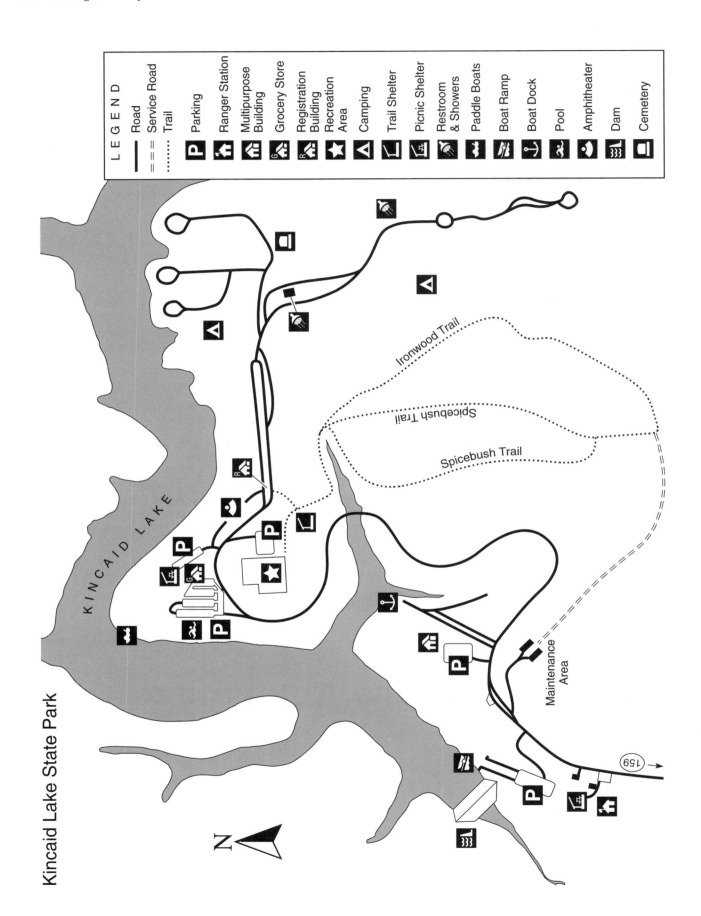

Kincaid Lake State Park

Ironwood Trail

Distance Round-Trip: 2.2 miles

Estimated Hiking Time: 1.5 to 2 hours

Cautions: The area has loose rock, exposed rocks and roots, eroded sections, and water flowing across the trail.

Trail Directions: Ironwood Trail, named for the ironwood plants that grow in the area, descends from the park ridge, overlooking Kincaid Lake into a valley carved by a tributary of the lake. It then climbs to a second ridge, following a route you can convince yourself is wilderness.

From the trailhead **[1]** behind the basketball courts, you'll descend over exposed rocks and roots through a mixed cedar and second-growth hardwood forest. The trail quickly levels out, however, until you reach the trail shelter **[2]** at mile .10. Pause here to admire the full-color photos of native flora and fauna and to read the interpretive plaques that line the walls of the shelter. They'll help you understand the natural history of the Cumberland Plateau.

Leaving the trail shelter, you'll face a steep, rough descent, until bottoming out at mile .16. In front of you is a marshy meadow **[3]**. At this site, an intermittent tributary stream meets a backwater of the lake, to create a secession bog. You can see the progression from open water, to marsh, to upland forest. The trail turns left and follows the creek, running smoothly and levelly.

At mile .28 you'll come to a wooden suspension bridge **[4]**, looking as out of place as blue jeans at a formal tea party. A sign tells you to continue straight for the Ironwood Trail, but a few steps farther, at mile .3, what appears to be a side trail **[5]** comes in on the right. That is actually the trail. If you go straight from this unmarked junction, you'll wind up confused in the campground.

The trail roller-coasters along the creek, leaving it to climb a knoll, then rejoining it several times. During the fall color season, leaves rain down on your shoulders like parti-colored confetti.

The creek bed, by the way, is chock-a-block with marine fossils, dating from the days this country was a shallow sea. Admire them, but remember this is a state park. Collecting them is against the rules.

Because the trail is little used, it is great for wildlife watching. Small mammals and birds are especially plentiful, but you can see deer and turkey too. At mile .67, for instance, there's a small clearing by the creek **[6]** that usually has deer beds. In the early morning and late afternoon, you are likely to see the deer themselves.

You'll cross the creek on rocks at mile .86 and start climbing seriously until mile .9, where you'll enter a cedar thicket **[7]**. Cedars are among the pioneering trees when forests reclaim the land from farm fields and clear-cuts. From the size of these, it's obvious that the land here is well on its way to recovery.

At mile 1.1 the trail ends at a T with a park maintenance road **[8]**, which is itself a dirt trail. Return the way you came, or, you can pick up the Spicebush Trail .2 miles to the right.

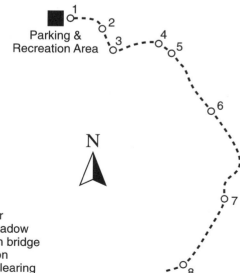

1. Trailhead
2. Trail shelter
3. Marshy meadow
4. Suspension bridge
5. Trail junction
6. Deer-bed clearing
7. Cedar thicket
8. Park maintenance road

Spicebush Trail 👢👢👢👢

Distance Round-Trip: 1.76 miles

Estimated Hiking Time: 1.5 to 2 hours

Cautions: Be aware of loose and exposed rocks and exposed roots.

Trail Directions: Spicebush Trail, like Ironwood Trail, is named for the plants that grow in the area. From the trailhead [1] behind the basketball courts, you'll descend over exposed rocks and roots through a mixed cedar and second-growth hardwood forest. The trail levels out soon, though, until you reach the trail shelter [2] at mile .10. You'll want to pause here to study the full-color photos of native flora and fauna and to read the interpretive signs, so you'll be able to recognize the plants and animals you'll see along the way—all of which are typical of the Cumberland Plateau.

Leaving the trail shelter, you'll face a steep, rough descent, until bottoming out at mile .16. In front of you is a marshy meadow [3]. You can trace the natural progression from open water, to marsh, to upland forest here, because it is all visible at once. The earth's land and water masses are in a continual adversarial relationship. At bogs and marshes like this are the sharp points of the spears in that ongoing battle. Turn left and follow the creek. The trail will be level.

At mile .28 you'll come to a wooden suspension bridge [4]. As you cross it, you can't help but reflect on the bureaucratic mind that would overengineer a creek crossing on trails so poorly maintained. This massive bridge is as out of place as a mouse at a cat picnic. The trail turns right and follows the creek along the far bank, back to the marsh. The trail turns left and climbs steeply above the marsh through open, mature second-growth hardwoods until mile .5 [5], where it turns left. The trail steepens considerably here and merges with a drain coming off the ridge. During wet weather you will have soggy toes as the muddy water swirls around your feet.

Continue climbing to mile .56, where you'll reach a stand of mature Virginia pines, whose regular symmetry indicates they were planted, then cross a small clearing [6]. When we were there during the early fall it suddenly sounded like rain, although the sky was clear and the sun bright. Turns out a plague of grasshoppers—well, 50 of them anyway—were spooking through the dried understory, creating the sound of a rainstorm.

On the other side of the grasshopper clearing you'll pass through cedars. Cedars are pioneer trees, starting the process of forest reclamation. Shortly afterward you top out on the park maintenance trail, at mile .78 [7]. Turn left and start descending on a rough trail. You'll continue downward until reaching the creek [8] at mile 1.0. Note the old-growth maple on the far shore, which somehow escaped the loggers' axes when this land was cleared in the 1930s. The trail follows the creek, level and smooth, until reaching the suspension bridge [4] at mile 1.1. Cross the bridge and retrace your steps to the trailhead.

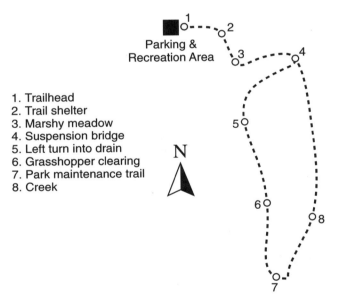

1. Trailhead
2. Trail shelter
3. Marshy meadow
4. Suspension bridge
5. Left turn into drain
6. Grasshopper clearing
7. Park maintenance trail
8. Creek

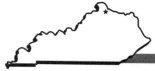

Handwritten: 12/27/05

31. Fort Thomas Landmark Tree Trail

- Visit more than a dozen old-growth hardwood trees, some dating back to the 1600s.
- Explore the environment of a glacial outwash.
- See numerous wildflowers indigenous to a maple/buckeye forest.

Park Information

The Fort Thomas Landmark Tree Trail was built in 1993 to preserve some of the last old-growth trees found by early pioneers in northern Kentucky. Fifteen of these trees have been identified. Fourteen of them are more than 125 years old, and at least one of them is more than 350 years old.

The trail, built by volunteers, is entirely on private property belonging to the Carmel Manor Nursing Home and Mr. Ed Wilbers, who have given their permission for people to use the trail.

The hill country of extreme northern Kentucky is a glacial outwash area. The ice reached equilibrium here; that is, the face of the glacier melted at the same rate the ice advanced. As a result, ground rock picked up by the ice's travel was deposited in a ridgelike formation, called a glacial till, composed of conglomerate rock. Later erosion exposed outcrops of this conglomerate and carved the hills and hollows of this unique geologic structure.

Directions: Take I-471 south from Cincinnati to exit 3, which is Grand Avenue (KY-1892). Go east 1.7 miles, where Grand merges with South Fort Thomas Avenue. Continue past Tower Park two blocks to Carmel Manor Drive. Turn left. Park in the Army Reserve Center lot or by the athletic fields. Do not park at Carmel Manor itself.

Hours Open: Open year-round.

Facilities: None.

Permits and Rules: Foot travel only; no collecting plants.

Further Information: Stephanie Howard, City of Fort Thomas, 130 North Fort Thomas Avenue, Fort Thomas, KY 41075; 606-441-1055.

Other Points of Interest

Quiet Trails State Nature Preserve (see park #29), **Kincaid Lake State Park** (see park #30), **Boone County Cliffs State Nature Preserve** (see park #35), and **Big Bone Lick State Park** (see park #34) are all within one hour of Fort Thomas.

There are numerous cultural and historic sites in northern Kentucky and the greater Cincinnati area. For details, contact Northern Kentucky Convention and Visitors Bureau, 605 Philadelphia Street, Covington, KY 41011; 606-261-4677.

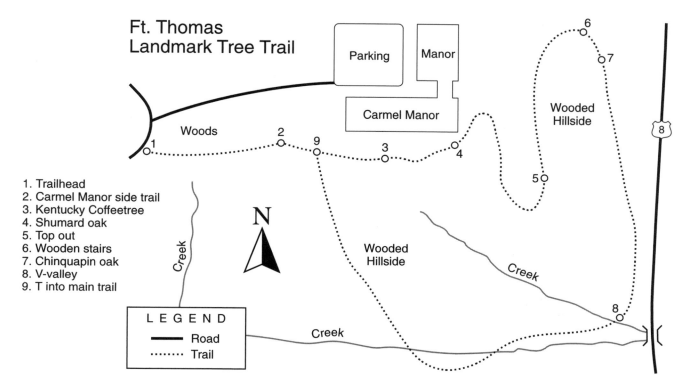

Ft. Thomas Landmark Tree Trail

1. Trailhead
2. Carmel Manor side trail
3. Kentucky Coffeetree
4. Shumard oak
5. Top out
6. Wooden stairs
7. Chinquapin oak
8. V-valley
9. T into main trail

LEGEND
—— Road
······ Trail

Fort Thomas Landmark Tree Trail 👢👢👢

Distance Round-Trip: .82 miles

Estimated Hiking Time: 40 to 60 minutes

Cautions: Be on the lookout for steep drop-offs and exposed rocks.

Trail Directions: The Fort Thomas Landmark Tree Trail is a moderate hike through the most secluded and best preserved wooded area in the Fort Thomas region. Within it are nearly a score of old-growth trees more than 100 years old. Fifteen of them are identified.

The trailhead [1] is on the east side of the Army Reserve Center, .15 miles from the parking lot. The trail enters a northern hardwood forest composed primarily of oaks, maples, and buckeyes that provide spectacular fall foliage displays. Shortly after entering the woods, at mile .02 a side trail [2] from the lawns of Carmel Manor joins the main trail at a trail information sign.

The first identified tree—a Kentucky Coffeetree—overlooks the trail at mile .1 [3]. The youngest, and smallest, of the 15 trees on the hike is only 40 years old, 45 feet high, and has a 2.5-foot circumference.

The trail descends gradually until mile .15, where it turns left at the site of a 175-year-old Shumard oak [4] and steepens. The trail turns left again, following a small seasonal creek. You'll cross this creek at mile .2, dogleg back along the far bank, then climb gently, topping out at mile .24 [5]. Below you, especially during the leafless months, is a fine view of the Ohio River and the hill country of southern Ohio across the waters. This is a confusing spot, as the trail seems to continue upward to the left. If you follow that trail,

you'll wind up on the back lawn of Carmel Manor. Instead, turn right. Although you are about to lose 200 feet in elevation, the trail switches back gradually, so there are no steep sections. During the fall color season, you'll find yourself walking through woods ablaze with reds, oranges, and yellows while you trod a Technicolor carpet of fallen leaves.

You'll descend a short wooden staircase at mile .29 [6], then continue downhill. At mile .31 you'll see a large Chinquapin oak [7]. This is site 7 on the trail, but the number was missing when we visited. However, it's hard to miss. The oldest (and largest) tree on the trail, it is more than 350 years old. The Chinquapin towers 90 feet above you and has a circumference of almost 14 feet.

It's not the size that makes you feel insignificant, so much as the age. This tree was already old when Simon Kenton and Daniel Boone first came to this land. It saw the Shawnee abandon this "dark and bloody ground" long before that, and it watched industrial man erect buildings taller than itself. When those buildings are dust, will it still be here?

After moving parallel to the Ohio River for a while, the trail crosses a wet-weather creek on a wooden footbridge (there's a 200-year-old red oak on the far side), then climbs moderately along the edge of a hollow until reaching the creek that forms it at mile .50 [8]. Look up the rocky bed of this creek and you'll understand why they are called V-valleys. Wind and water have eroded the banks much wider than the stream itself. In cross section, a letter V is formed.

You'll cross a second seasonal creek a couple of times, passing several more old shumard and chinquapin oaks along the way, until reaching an unmarked T at mile .73 [9]. This is the main trail. Turn left and follow it back to the trailhead.

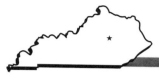

32. Raven Run Nature Sanctuary

- See one of the few undeveloped limestone gorges in the state.
- Stand atop the Kentucky River Palisades on a rock pinnacle.
- Hike past more than 300 varieties of wildflowers.

Park Information

This 374-acre nature sanctuary is a special natural area dedicated to the preservation of the flora and fauna of the Kentucky River Palisades region. Located less than 12 miles from downtown Lexington, Kentucky, Raven Run offers several hiking trails (including a barrier-free trail accessible to those in wheelchairs and people who are visually impaired), a Nature Center, and a wildlife-viewing blind.

This is a fragile area, so only hiking and nature observation are allowed. Visitors are asked to hike only on marked trails. Collecting, destroying, or defacing anything, living or nonliving, is prohibited. This includes picking wildflowers!

Several animal species normally considered rare in Kentucky can be found here, including the least weasel and the nine-banded armadillo, along with more common species ranging from bats to white-tailed deer. Nearly 200 bird species have been sighted in the park, many of them from the bird blind located between the parking lot and the Nature Center.

Raven Run is rich in human as well as natural history. As you hike, you'll see signs of previous human use, such as stone "slave" fences (actually built by Irish immigrants) and the remains of a lime kiln. The former sites of other human uses are marked.

Being so close to Lexington, the area gets fairly heavy use, especially on weekends. April and May are the peak months for wildflower viewing.

Directions: From downtown Lexington, take Richmond Road to Jacobson Park. Turn right on US-25/421. In about 3 miles you come to Jakes Mill Road. Follow that to the park. The Nature Center is .25 miles from the parking lot. All trails, except the barrier-free Freedom Trail, start at the Nature Center.

Hours Open: Open year-round, but hours vary seasonally.

Facilities: Picnic area, Nature Center.

Permits and Rules: There is no fee for use of the park. Only foot travel is permitted, on marked trails. There are picnic tables near the parking lot; no other picnicking is allowed, and camping and fires are prohibited. Pets are prohibited.

Further Information: Contact Lexington-Fayette Urban County Division of Parks and Recreation, 545 North Upper Street, Lexington, KY 40508; 606-288-2900. Raven Run's phone number is 606-272-7105.

Other Points of Interest

Several parks and museums can be found within 15 miles of Raven Run. Of special note are **Fort Boonesborough State Park** (606-527-3131), which includes a replica of the refuge fort first constructed near that site on the Kentucky River; the **Kentucky Horse Park** (800-678-8813), the only state park in the country dedicated to horses and equine activities; and **White Hall State Historic Shrine** (606-623-9178), home of Cassius Clay.

In nearby Richmond, Kentucky, is the **Valley View Ferry** (no phone), the oldest continuously operated business west of the Alleghenies. Until just a few years ago, the ferry fee was only 10 cents. Unfortunately, budget constraints have changed that.

Park Trails

There are more than 8 miles of marked trails making up the Raven Run trails system. The trails are generally well groomed and well marked, but unfortunately the marking system can sometimes be confusing. Two systems are used: (1) posts showing a letter keyed to the trail map, an icon of a ranger and tent, and a mileage figure indicating remaining distance to the Nature Center; and (2) metal disks, supposedly color coded to the trail, with an icon of a hiker. These markers are not always clear, especially where trails junction.

Meadow Trail—1 mile—is a level trail that passes through a meadow environment rich in native grasses and wildflowers. The trailhead is the same as that for the Red Trail. This trail is popular with joggers.

Yellow Trail—.25 miles—is accessible only from several points on the Red Trail; this is a hilly and confusing trail that follows the route of a pioneer road.

Raven Run
Nature Sanctuary

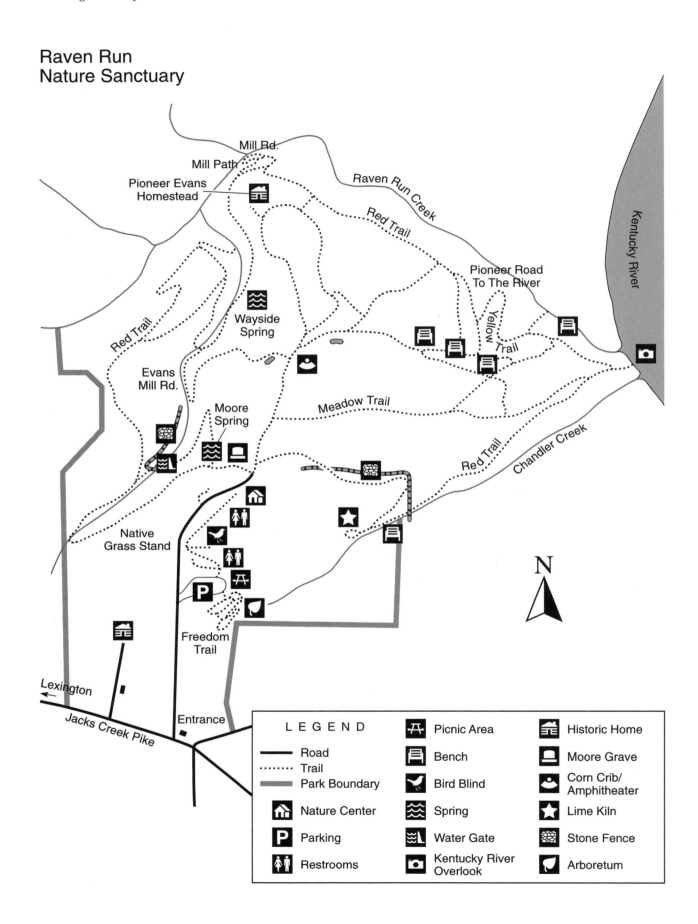

Mill Rd.

Mill Path

Pioneer Evans
Homestead

Raven Run Creek

Red Trail

Kentucky River

Red Trail

Pioneer Road
To The River

Wayside
Spring

Yellow Trail

Evans
Mill Rd.

Meadow Trail

Moore
Spring

Red Trail

Chandler Creek

Native
Grass Stand

N

Freedom
Trail

Lexington

Jacks Creek Pike

Entrance

L E G E N D

— Road
····· Trail
▬ Park Boundary

🏠 Nature Center
🅿 Parking
🚺 Restrooms

🔼 Picnic Area
🪑 Bench
🐦 Bird Blind
〰 Spring
〰 Water Gate
📷 Kentucky River Overlook

🏛 Historic Home
⬜ Moore Grave
Corn Crib/ Amphitheater
★ Lime Kiln
Stone Fence
Arboretum

Red Trail 🥾🥾🥾

Distance Round-Trip: 4.2 miles

Estimated Hiking Time: 2 to 2.5 hours

Cautions: Rocks and roots are exposed on some parts of the trail. There are several steep cliffs and drop-offs; mind children. Insect repellent is a must.

Trail Directions: This loop trail starts and ends at the rail gate northeast of the Nature Center. You can run the trail in either direction. The trail will take you through several ecosystems, and you are likely to spot wildlife.

Pass by the left-hand trailhead and continue to the trailhead on the right **[1]** marked with an arrow saying "overlook." Going straight puts you on the Meadow Trail. The Red Trail initially passes through meadow and open woods.

After .2 miles you'll walk through a gate in a dry-laid stone fence **[2]**. Called "slave fences" throughout the region, these actually were built by Irish immigrants during the last century. You'll enter open woods here, with the slave fence on the left. Starting out smooth and level, the trail soon becomes rough, with exposed rocks and roots, and descends. At .75 miles **[3]**, the trail divides. On the right is a side trail leading to an old lime kiln site. Straight ahead is an unofficial trail. The Red Trail doglegs 180 degrees to the left, following a creek on the right.

The trail remains fairly level, with some climbing, for 1 mile, where it Ts. Follow the "overlook" sign to the right. The trail descends 13 steps, then Ts again at mile 1.9 **[4]**. There's a drop-off into a large hardwood hollow straight in front of you, leading to the river. Go to the right about 200 feet to the overlook **[5]**.

You'll be atop a pinnacle that's part of the Kentucky River Palisades. There is little development along this stretch of river, so the view you see of unbroken forest, cut only by the river, is about the same as that seen by early settlers. Note particularly the exposed limestone palisades upstream on the left bank.

Retrace your path to the T, but continue straight. The trail will shortly turn left and climb steeply to a junction with a side trail on the left. Continue straight. At 2.4 miles, you'll reach a Y that is not marked clearly **[6]**. The left trail has a blue flash. On the right is a faded yellow flash. Bear to the right, and you'll pick up the red flashes. The trail descends and narrows to shoulder width. In 600 feet, it Ys again. Stay to the left. In .5 miles you will cross under power lines for the first of several times. The trail descends 500 linear feet to a T. Bear right. The limestone gorge and creek for which the park is known will be on your right. In 500 feet it Ts yet again, at 2.7 miles.

To the right, the trail leads to the site of the Evans Grist Mill **[7]**, to the creek, and to a seasonal waterfall. Mr. Evans, a pioneer who settled here in the 1820s, built his mill where the creek cascades down some boulders, forming the falls. Only the foundation remains. The Red Trail goes left, climbing steeply for 450 rocky feet. You'll pass under the wires again, and then go by a spring on the left at 2.8 miles **[8]**. This was the site of the Evans homestead. Only the rock-lined spring remains. In .2 miles, the trail Ys yet again. Go right. In a short time, you'll cross the creek on rocks. The trail then climbs to the right. In .2 miles, you'll come to the power lines again, and then switch back and forth through the power line right-of-way. You'll come to a stone wall on the left, and then, at mile 3.6, reach a red cedar thicket—the first significant group of conifers on the trail **[9]**.

The trail now passes through a different environment. Following a creek, you'll be in the bottom of it, instead of above it, until you cross it on a wooden bridge at mile 3.8 **[10]**. The trail climbs gradually but steadily from the bridge for .25 miles and then Ts. Go right here. At mile 4.15, there will be two gravestones on your right **[11]**. This is the burial site of Archibald Moore, who homesteaded 12 acres here. He was buried in the front yard of his log cabin in February 1871. The smaller stone indicates the position of his feet.

A few steps further are the trailhead and gate at mile 4.2.

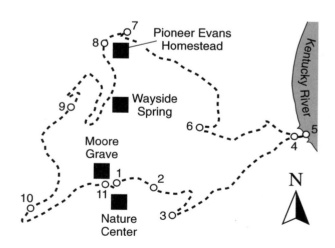

1. Trailhead
2. Slave fence
3. Trail doglegs left
4. Trail Ts at hollow
5. Overlook
6. Trail junction unclear
7. Evans Grist Mill
8. Evans homestead spring
9. Red cedar thicket
10. Wooden bridge
11. Archibald Moore grave

Freedom Trail 🥾

Distance Round-Trip: .62 or .45 miles

Estimated Hiking Time: 30 minutes walking; 45 to 60 minutes in wheelchair

Cautions: One section is too steep for wheelchair use; those in wheelchairs should use the secondary loop instead.

Trail Directions: Freedom Trail is a barrier-free interpretive trail designed specifically for people in wheelchairs and strollers and for people who are visually impaired. It features four distinct ecosystems—meadow, cedar thicket, stream, and woodland edge. Although theoretically barrier free, it has challenging hills approaching 8 percent grade and one section that is not barrier free at all. There are numerous paved pull-outs for wheelchair resting. A solid white line is painted along the right-hand edge of the pavement. It's suggested that hikers who are visually impaired use that line as a guide.

From the parking lot, a short section takes you to the trailhead and interpretive billboard **[1]**. Turn right here. The trail passes through the meadow ecosystem for 300 feet or so. Along the way you are likely to see meadowlarks, bluebirds, and other birds; black and honey locust trees; and various grasses and other meadow plants such as Queen Anne's lace. Very occasionally an eastern hognose snake is spotted, and deer may be seen sometimes.

The trail then turns left and enters the woods. If you use the non-barrier-free section, you come to a bridge and the stream ecosystem **[2]** in .1 miles. If you take the barrier-free path, the distance will be almost .2 miles longer.

The stream ecosystem consists of a meandering creek and its associated edge. Walnut, hackberry, and wild cherry are the predominant trees, with dogwood, redbud, and spicebush forming the understory. Rabbits, deer, and wild turkey are frequently spotted, and barred owls live in the nearby trees.

A short way further you'll cross a second bridge over the same creek, and in a few hundred feet you will come to the woodland edge ecosystem **[3]** at mile .23.

The woodland edge consists of a hardwood forest and pond/wetland environment. Sycamores, river birch, and bald cypress overlook the marshy wetland and small, limestone-bottomed pond. Green-backed herons and raccoons feed on the crayfish, frogs, and salamanders living in the water. And you'll likely see turtles sunning themselves.

At mile .30 you'll come to the cedar thicket **[4]**. Fallen cedars provide shelter for bobwhite quail and other ground birds while songbirds flitter about the standing trees. Ground cover consisting of mosses, ferns, and ground ivy grows profusely under the trees, and you are likely to see lily-leafed twayblade orchids along with other wildflowers.

In many respects, the four ecosystem areas are artificially designated. To be sure, they represent the major environmental type found at each spot. But you are just as likely to see examples of those systems along the whole trail. So take your time along the remaining 700 feet or so as you walk back to the parking lot. You'll see an amazing diversity of flora and fauna along the way.

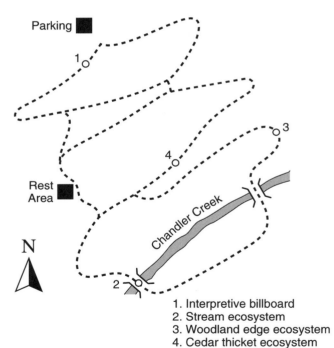

1. Interpretive billboard
2. Stream ecosystem
3. Woodland edge ecosystem
4. Cedar thicket ecosystem

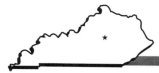

33. City of Lexington

- Explore the cultural and historic sites of Kentucky's second largest city.
- See the tree collection in a cemetery that's also an arboretum, among other things.
- Make a wish in any of the numerous fountains throughout the downtown area.
- Capture the spirit of horse racing with the life-size bronzes at Thoroughbred Park.

Park Information

In 1775 a group of settlers had just established a station at McConnel Springs when news was brought to them of the first battle of the American Revolution. They decided to name their settlement after that battle. So, Lexington was born.

Ironically, Bryan Station, which is now part of Lexington, was intimately involved in the last battle of the American Revolution. After the siege of Bryan Station, militiamen, pursuing the invading British and Indian force, were ambushed at Blue Licks. Although a defeat for the Kentuckians, it was the last major battle of the war, and the last major Indian incursion into Kentucky.

Lexington is the second largest city in Kentucky. Located in the geographic center of the Bluegrass Region, there is nothing second rate about its cultural, social, and historical sites and attractions, many of which can be seen from its walk tour—inarguably the finest city walk in the state.

Lexington, too, is the heart of Kentucky's horse industry. Two tracks within the city (Keeneland and the Red Mile) offer months-long flats and harness meets. You can watch morning workouts at either famous track, as well as attend races and sales. Keeneland, itself, is a National Historic Landmark. The Red Mile, established the same year as the Kentucky Derby, has seen more world-record harness events than any other track.

Thoroughbred Park, at the corner of Main and Vine, contains life-size bronze sculptures of race horses in action. The 2.5-acre park is a popular lunch-break area.

The Lexington Cemetery holds a unique spot in the hearts of Lexingtonians. Since its establishment in 1848, residents have thought of it more as a public park than a burial ground. Until the Board of Directors stopped the practice, folks held picnics there. There are still requests to allow weddings in this garden cemetery.

Directions: Lexington sits at the intersection of I-75 and I-64. Numerous exits put you on roads leading downtown.

Hours Open: Open year-round.

Facilities: Anything needed.

Permits and Rules: None.

Further Information: Lexington Convention and Visitors Bureau, 301 East Vine Street, Lexington, KY 40507; 800-845-3959.

Other Points of Interest

Raven Run Nature Sanctuary (see park #32) is just a few miles from downtown. **Clyde E. Buckley Wildlife Sanctuary** (see park #36), **Berea College Forest** (see park #28), and the **Central Kentucky Wildlife Refuge** (see park #37) are less than an hour away.

The Kentucky Horse Park (800-678-8813), off I-75 exit 120, is the only state park in the country dedicated to horses. Included on the grounds is the American Saddle Horse Museum (606-259-2746), a contemporary museum that celebrates the only horse breed that originated in Kentucky.

Fort Boonesborough State Park (606-527-3131) is a replica of the first settlement in Kentucky, built near the original site.

The City of Lexington

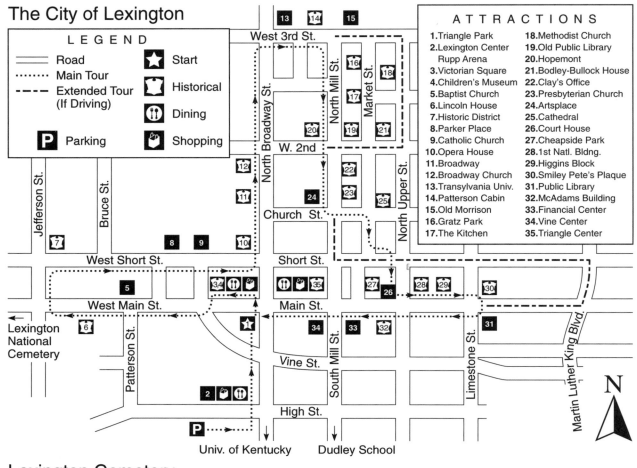

LEGEND

Road	★ Start
Main Tour	Historical
Extended Tour (If Driving)	Dining
P Parking	Shopping

ATTRACTIONS

1. Triangle Park
2. Lexington Center Rupp Arena
3. Victorian Square
4. Children's Museum
5. Baptist Church
6. Lincoln House
7. Historic District
8. Parker Place
9. Catholic Church
10. Opera House
11. Broadway
12. Broadway Church
13. Transylvania Univ.
14. Patterson Cabin
15. Old Morrison
16. Gratz Park
17. The Kitchen
18. Methodist Church
19. Old Public Library
20. Hopemont
21. Bodley-Bullock House
22. Clay's Office
23. Presbyterian Church
24. Artsplace
25. Cathedral
26. Court House
27. Cheapside Park
28. 1st Natl. Bldg.
29. Higgins Block
30. Smiley Pete's Plaque
31. Public Library
32. McAdams Building
33. Financial Center
34. Vine Center
35. Triangle Center

Lexington Cemetery

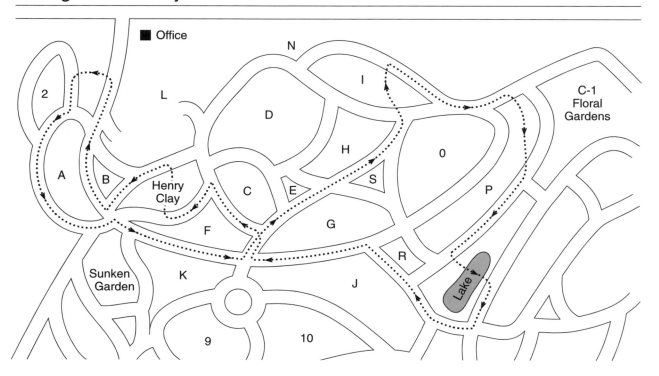

Lexington Walk Tour 👢👢

Distance Round-Trip: 1.77 miles

Estimated Hiking Time: 2 hours to 2 days

Cautions: None.

Trail Directions: The Lexington Walk takes you to many cultural and historical sites the city is known for. Although it takes barely two hours to cover the whole route, this leaves little time for exploring the sites and attractions. A better bet is to make a weekend of it, staying at the Brand House at Rose Hill (606-226-9464), an award-winning bed-and-breakfast, itself an historical building, only a couple blocks off the route.

The walk starts at Triangle Park **[1]**, on the corner of North Broadway and West Main streets. Designed by internationally famed landscape architect Robert Zion, it contains 100 stepped fountains and flowering pear trees, fronting Rupp Arena, home court of the University of Kentucky Wildcats.

After exploring the park, return to Main Street, cross over, and turn left. You'll be walking along Victorian Square **[2]**, a solid block of 19th-century buildings converted to a downtown mall.

Continue west on Main to mile .25 and the First Baptist Church **[3]**, a large, collegiate Gothic-style church, built in 1913. A block or so farther, at mile .33, is the Mary Todd Lincoln House **[4]**. The 16th First Lady was raised in this 22-room house. There are guided tours of the fully restored home. Turn right on Jefferson Street, go one block to West Short, and turn right again. You are now in the Western Suburb Historic District. At mile .6 you'll rejoin Victorian Square and the entrance to the Lexington Children's Museum **[5]**, where children of all ages interact with the hands-on displays that make learning and play indistinguishable.

Continue to North Broadway and the Lexington Opera House at mile .65 **[6]**. Shortly after opening in 1887, the opera house gained a reputation as "the best one-night stand in America." Restored in 1975, it is the home of the Lexington Ballet Company. Turn left on Broadway and follow it to West Third and the campus of Transylvania University at mile .94 **[7]**.

Established in 1780, Transy is the oldest college west of the Alleghenies. Its graduates include 50 U.S. senators, 36 governors, 34 ambassadors, and the only president of the Confederate States of America. As you stroll its border you'll pass the Patterson Cabin, a log house built by one of Lexington's founders, and Old Morrison, Transy's haunted administration building.

Cross West Third to Gratz Park and its famed children's fountain at mile 1.0 **[8]**. Then continue down North Mill, past the old public library, to mile 1.16 and the Hunt-Morgan House **[9]**, where, legend has it, John Hunt Morgan—Thunderbolt of the Confederacy—once rode his horse through the front steps, paused in the hall to kiss his mother, then galloped out the back door, with Union troops in hot pursuit. Continue down North Mill to Church, make a left to Market, then a right to Short.

In front of you is the Romanesque-style county courthouse and Cheapside Park at mile 1.35 **[10]**. Cheapside Park used to be a through street that, among other things, housed Lexington's slave market.

Across from the courthouse, on the corner of North Upper and East Main is the First National Building at mile 1.42 **[11]**. When erected in 1914 it was the tallest building between Cincinnati and Atlanta.

Follow Main east, passing the Higgins Block and its partial cast iron facade, to the corner of Limestone. Cross Main there to Phoenix Park at mile 1.5 **[12]**. The nomad and camel statue you see there was Lexington's zero milestone, until it was moved.

To complete the walk, go west on Broadway back to Triangle Park.

N

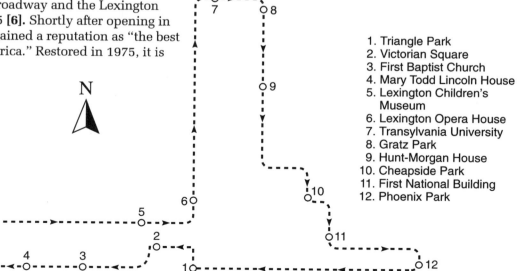

1. Triangle Park
2. Victorian Square
3. First Baptist Church
4. Mary Todd Lincoln House
5. Lexington Children's Museum
6. Lexington Opera House
7. Transylvania University
8. Gratz Park
9. Hunt-Morgan House
10. Cheapside Park
11. First National Building
12. Phoenix Park

Lexington Cemetery Tree Walk 🥾

Distance Round-Trip: 1.22 miles

Estimated Hiking Time: 1.5 hours

Cautions: None.

Trail Directions: Long thought of as a public park by area residents, the Lexington Cemetery is an archtypical garden cemetery of the mid-1800s. More than a burial ground, it is also an arboretum where the trees are allowed to grow naturally, with no insecticides or fertilizers. In most cases, the 41 trees on the walk are the best specimens of their species growing in the area, and some are the largest of their kind. None of the trees—each marked with a metal identification plate—has ever been pruned or trimmed into an artificial shape.

The walk follows cemetery roads, but there is some cross-country travel required. As you look at the trees and historical gravesites, stay alert for birdlife. More than 170 species have been identified in the cemetery. You can get a bird checklist at the office. At the same time, pick up a copy of the tree walk brochure, to help you identify the trees you'll be seeing.

Do not try and see the trees in numerical order. You'll spend too much effort backtracking if you do. Instead, start at the Henry Clay site **[1]**, in front of which is an American basswood (tree 21), the largest of its kind in the United States. More than 18 feet in circumference, it stands 101 feet tall, with a crown spreading nearly 83 feet.

Cross the Henry Clay plot to the right of the building and turn left at the road. Following it you'll pass four identified species, until reaching an intersection at mile .05. Follow the road between sections B and A, toward the office, looking at the European hornbeam, eastern redbud, osage orange, and common hackberry, in that order. At mile .12 is a large yellowwood **[2]**. The marker is missing from this Appalachian native, from which pioneer women made a yellow dye.

Swing around section A, passing the weeping mulberry, panicle hydrangea, and eastern red cedar to the next intersection at mile .24, where you'll find a sweet gum and common sassafras in the sunken garden section, and a grouping in section K **[3]** of an American holly, white pine, and black gum.

Follow the road between sections F and K, then swing left past C, E, and H, to section I. At the intersection, there's a European larch. Directly across section I, at mile .44 is a Kentucky coffeetree **[4]**. The official state tree, coffeetrees have long leaves that are the last to appear in the spring and the first to drop in the fall. The trees' long seedpods, hanging from bare branches, present a special appearance all their own.

From section I continue toward section P, passing a shellbark hickory and Amur corktree along the way. Go halfway across the edge of section P, then cross-country, following the arc of the Prewitt family head-stones at mile .75, to the bloodleaf Japanese maple and northern white cedar **[5]**. The formal gardens can be found just across the road from here and are well worth visiting. There's also a northern catalpa in the garden.

Follow the road between section P and the gardens to the lake at mile .92 **[6]**. There are several trees worth seeing there, especially the bald cypress and European black alder growing together, and a short distance farther, the royal paulownia.

Turn right at the main road, and follow it between sections J and P, G and J, and, finally, F and C, and return to the Henry Clay site. For a special treat, make a side trip to section L where you can see a cucumber tree, another Appalachian native little known outside the region.

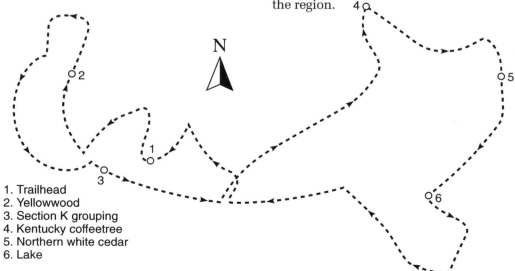

1. Trailhead
2. Yellowwood
3. Section K grouping
4. Kentucky coffeetree
5. Northern white cedar
6. Lake

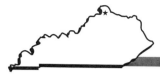

34. Big Bone Lick State Park

- Walk in the footsteps of mastodons, hairy mammoths, and giant ground sloths.
- See a herd of bison, restored to their native land.
- Explore the world of Kentucky in the Pleistocene era at the park museum.

Park Information

Big Bone Lick State Park preserves an area early explorers found covered with large bones.

Sulfur and saline springs dotted the meadows of the region during the ice age. Large mammals—including mastodons, mammoths, ground sloths, and bison—migrating in front of the ice were attracted to the salt-laden ground, or licks. Many were trapped in the bogs and marshes, and their bones mineralized.

Early explorers, starting with the French soldier Charles Le Moyne, in 1739, found these bones lying on the surface. Mary Draper Ingles, who had been captured by Shawnee, was taken here on a salt-making expedition by her captors—making her the first white woman in Kentucky. When she escaped, in 1756, a Frenchman in the party was reportedly "sitting on a giant bone, cracking walnuts."

Early notables such as Thomas Jefferson and Ben Franklin collected and studied bones from Big Bone Lick. The first organized paleontological expedition in the United States was conducted here in the early 1800s.

Salt making was an ongoing process in the area. Before white settlement, Native Americans journeyed to the licks to evaporate salt from the saline springs. White settlers improved on the process, and the first commercial salt-making operation was started in the 1790s, with a fort built on an island in Big Bone Creek to protect the workers from Indian attack.

The prehistoric meadows have dried up, as have most of the salt springs. At least one major spring still flows, however. The saline content is so high that the water, itself, is white.

From time to time, bones and fragments are still found along Big Bone Creek. All the large bones have been collected. You can explore their history in the park museum.

Near the museum is a small herd of bison. Bison once were common to Kentucky and roamed this region. In fact, the first leg of Mary Ingles' escape was along a so-called buffalo trace—a trail made by migrating bison.

Directions: Take exit 171 off I-75 in Walton, Kentucky. At the off-ramp pick up KY-1292 and take it north 4.8 miles until you cross KY-42/127, where it becomes KY-338. Continue north 2.9 miles to the park entrance, then .7 miles to the museum.

Hours Open: Open year-round during daylight hours; some facilities seasonal.

Facilities: Campground, museum and gift shop, grocery store, picnic areas, fishing lake, swimming pool, miniature golf, athletic fields.

Permits and Rules: Only foot travel allowed on trails.

Further Information: Big Bone Lick State Park, 3380 Beaver Road, Union, KY 41091; 606-384-3522.

Other Points of Interest

Boone County Cliffs State Nature Preserve (see park #35), **Fort Thomas Landmark Tree Trail** (see park #31), **Kincaid Lake State Park** (see park #30), and **Quiet Trails State Nature Preserve** (see park #29) are all within one hour of Big Bone Lick State Park.

Park Trails

Coralberry Trail 👢👢👢—2 miles round-trip—circles the fishing lake through young hardwood forests.

Gobbler's Trace 👢👢👢—.5 miles each way—connects the museum and campground.

Big Bone Lick State Park

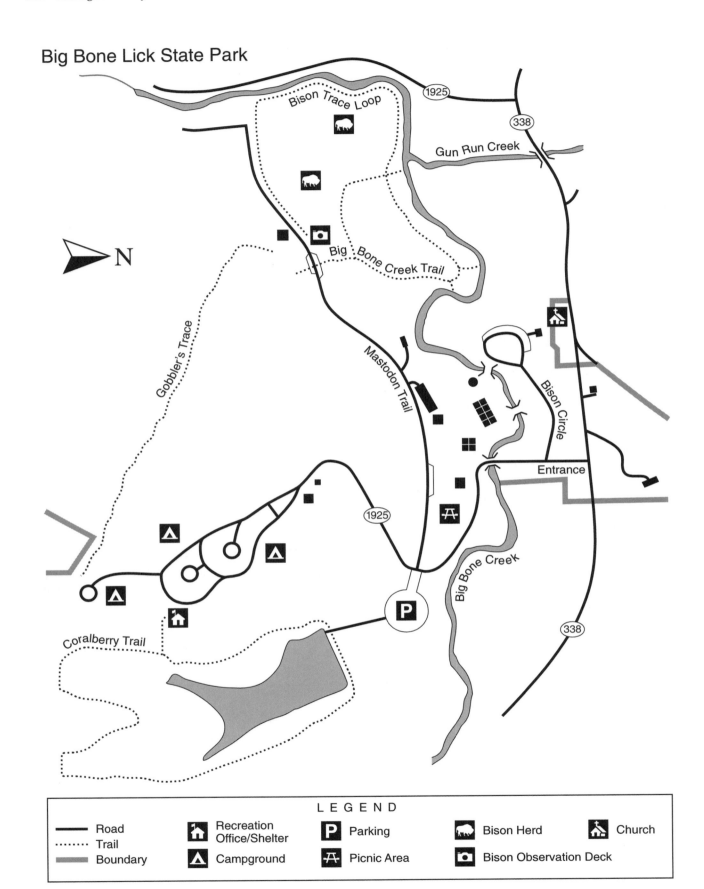

LEGEND

— Road
······ Trail
━━ Boundary

Recreation Office/Shelter
Campground

P Parking
Picnic Area

Bison Herd
Bison Observation Deck

Church

Big Bone Creek (Diorama) Trail 👢👢

Distance Round-Trip: .8 miles

Estimated Hiking Time: 1 to 1.5 hours

Cautions: None.

Trail Directions: The Big Bone Creek Trail (which park officials refer to as the Diorama Trail because of the full-sized statue of a woolly mammoth that forms its centerpiece) is a paved, barrier-free post and loop that interprets the natural history of the area. The post runs downhill, however, and wheelchairs might need assistance on it. The loop is basically flat.

The trailhead [1] is at a set of white poles east of the museum. You'll descend toward the life-sized statue of a mammoth, whose 15-foot tusks point benignly at your hiking boots. At mile .06 you'll T into the loop section of the trail [2]. Turn left.

Almost immediately, at mile .1, is an interpretive sign explaining invertebrate fossils and how they help geologists and paleontologists date things [3]. The sign sits at the eastern most point of the bison meadow, and you may see some of the huge beasts.

Bison, the largest land mammals in North America, were common here until the late 1700s. This is one of several herds that restore them to their natural habitat.

The trail follows the edge of the bison meadow to mile .24 and a sign that interprets ice-age rivers and how they shaped the land. The Bison Trace Trail comes in on the left. The Diorama Trail turns right and leads to the statue of a mammoth at mile .34 [4]. Prehistoric animals such as the hairy mammoth, mastodons, giant ground sloths, and bison were drawn here by the salt-laden ground. Many were trapped in the bogs and marshes and their bones subsequently mineralized. Those bones gave the park its name.

At mile .42 is an interpretation of the geology of Big Bone Lick [5], explaining how the marshes were formed more than 18,000 years ago. Note how the double terraces that gave the land its shape and

flavor still exist (you're on the higher one), albeit in reduced form.

You'll reach a side trail at mile .47 leading first to a sign discussing salt making, then to Big Spring, which you reach at mile .53 [6]. A decked walkway circles one of the few remaining sulfur and saline springs typical of those found in the valley. The water in the spring and its runoff flow white with salt, and you can almost see the prehistoric mammals in the meadow across the creek. Return to the main trail, and turn left.

At mile .64 a sign interprets the use of this area by Shawnee Indians [7]. Mary Draper Ingles escaped from their captivity near this spot in 1756, and walked more than 1,000 miles back to her home in what is now West Virginia—one of the great captivity stories of all time.

A few feet farther you'll rejoin the post section of the trail. Follow it back to the trailhead.

1. Trailhead
2. Loop section
3. Invertebrate fossils sign
4. Woolly mammoth statue
5. Big Bone Lick geology
6 Big Spring
7. Shawnee Indians sign

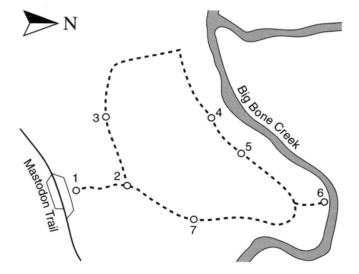

Bison Trace Loop 👢👢

Distance Round-Trip: 1.1 miles

Estimated Hiking Time: 30 to 35 minutes

Cautions: Do not touch the fence enclosing the buffalo herd.

Trail Directions: The Bison Trace Loop combines part of the Diorama Trail with a walk around the Bison Meadows. Although there are no barriers, wheelchairs might need assistance at the trailhead and along the Bison Trace itself, which, though flat and level, is not paved.

The trailhead **[1]** is at a set of white poles east of the museum. Follow the paved trail downhill, toward the tusks of the woolly mammoth statue in the field below. At mile .06 you'll **T** into the Diorama Loop. Go right.

At mile .14 is an interpretive sign explaining how the Shawnee Indians used the region **[2]**.

At mile .2 a side trail leads to the right. Take it first to the salt-making interpretive sign, then to Big Spring, which you'll reach at mile .26 **[3]**. Big Spring is one of the last sulfur and saline springs that created the area and trapped the prehistoric animals. Notice that the salt content is so high the water flows white.

You'll reach the mammoth statue at mile .42 **[4]**, with a sign explaining why the giant mammals were attracted to the area. The statue is life-size. Imagine how many piano keys could be made from just one set of tusks, which are about 15 feet long.

The trail reaches an intersection at mile .52 **[5]**. To your right is an explanation of pre-ice age rivers and how they shaped the land we see today. The paved Diorama Trail turns left. The Bison Trace is straight ahead. Follow it.

You'll be walking along the banks of Big Bone Creek. From time to time, bones and bone fragments are still found there, so you want to watch sharply for them. It's hard, though, to tear your eyes away from the bison in the fenced meadows on your left. About a dozen animals live there year-round.

The trail turns left, still following the creek, until mile .76 **[6]**, where there's a corral and interpretive signs that discuss the history of bison in Kentucky and the importance of the herd in the meadow.

Continue on the trail to mile .85 and the blacktop park road, which makes a 90-degree turn here. Go straight uphill, following the fence enclosing the bison meadow. At mile 1.05 you'll come to an observation deck **[7]**, a raised wooden platform overlooking the bison meadow. Interpretive signs repeat the information at the corral.

Bison, by the way, are the largest land mammals found in North America. Bulls can reach 11 feet in length and 6 feet in height, weighing 2,000 pounds.

After watching the buffalo from the deck, return to the trail and follow it to the trailhead.

1. Trailhead
2. Shawnee Indians sign
3. Big Spring
4. Woolly mammoth statue
5. Trail intersection
6. Corral
7. Observation deck

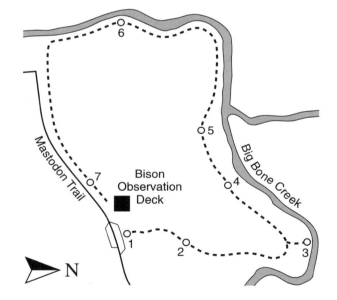

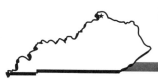

35. Boone County Cliffs State Nature Preserve

- Explore four different forest communities.
- Examine the geology of a glacial till in the only region of Kentucky affected by the ice ages.
- See rare animals and plants, such as the redback salamander and yellow corydalis.

Park Information

Boone County Cliffs is named for the 20- to 40-foot high conglomerate cliffs that outcrop on the valley slopes. These cliffs, rare examples of glacial effects in the Bluegrass state, are composed of well-cemented, coarse gravels deposited as glacial outwash about 700,000 years ago.

The glaciers reached equilibrium near here; that is, the ice melted at the same rate as the glaciers advanced. Gravels and ground rock trapped in the ice were deposited in a formation called a glacial till. Later, wind and water eroded the till, exposing and shaping the conglomerate. How far were the rocks carried? Some gravels have been identified as originating in Canada.

This 75-acre state nature preserve protects an example of old-growth forest and habitat for several species of plants and animals uncommon in Kentucky, such as the redback salamander, yellow corydalis, and several species of nesting and migrating warblers. Other wildflowers found here include bright yellow celandine poppies, blue phlox, squirrel corn, Dutchman's breeches, bloodroot, wild ginger, and early saxifrage.

Mature examples of four forest communities are found on the various slopes of the park. Although sugar maple dominates all the communities, there are red and chinquapin oaks, basswood, beech, and slippery elm that codominate on their respective slopes. In addition, you'll see white ash, tulip poplar, and black locust, as well as redbud and dogwood in the understory.

A spring-fed tributary to Middle Creek flows through the preserve, providing a moist stream valley environment in counterpoint to the forested slopes. The cutting action of this creek helps expose and shape the conglomerate cliffs.

Boone County Cliffs is said to be the most visited preserve in the state. When we were there, midweek during the height of fall color, however, there was nobody else in the preserve.

Because of the fragile nature of the cliffs, it is impera-tive that you stay on established trails while in the park, and do not cross any "Fragile Environment" gates.

Directions: From exit 181 off I-75 at Florence, Kentucky, take KY-18 west 10.2 miles to Middle Creek Road. Go left 2 miles to a small gravel parking lot on the left.

Hours Open: Open year-round during daylight hours.

Facilities: None.

Permits and Rules: Foot travel only; stay on trails; no cliff climbing or rappelling; no fires, camping, or firearms permitted.

Further Information: Kentucky State Nature Preserves Commission, 801 Schenkel Lane, Frankfort, KY 40601; 502-573-2886.

Other Points of Interest

Quiet Trails State Nature Preserve (see park #29), **Kincaid Lake State Park** (see park #30), **Fort Thomas Landmark Tree Trail** (see park #31), and **Big Bone Lick State Park** (see park #34) are all within one hour of Boone County Cliffs.

There are numerous cultural and historic sites in northern Kentucky and the greater Cincinnati area. For details, contact Northern Kentucky Convention and Visitors Bureau, 605 Philadelphia Street, Covington, KY 41011; 606-261-4677.

Boone County Cliffs
State Nature Preserve

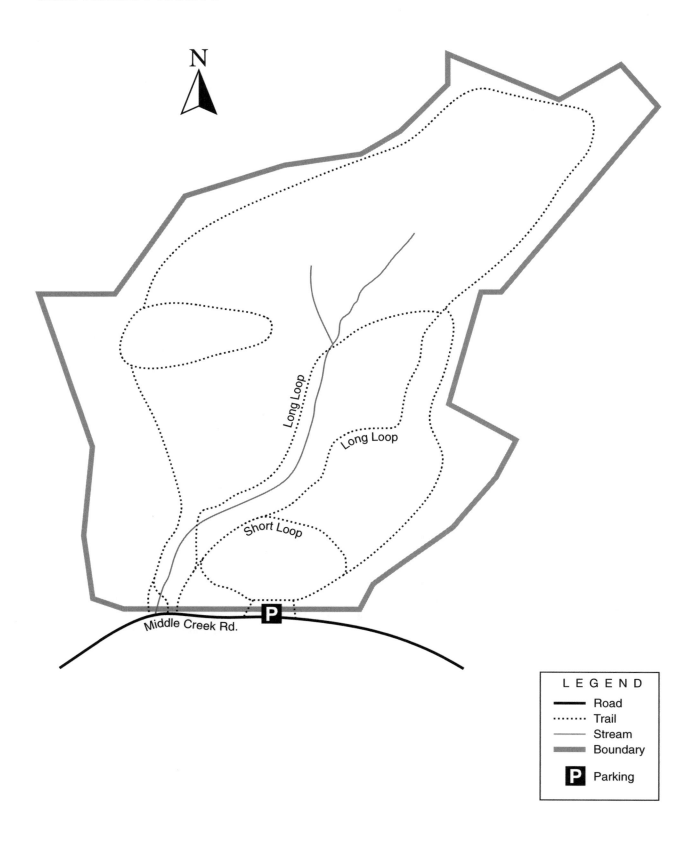

Long Loop Trail 👢👢👢👢

Distance Round-Trip: 1.69 miles

Estimated Hiking Time: 60 to 90 minutes

Cautions: Watch out for high cliffs and exposed rocks and roots.

Trail Directions: The Long Loop Trail takes you up and around several exposed conglomerate cliffs that are the hallmark of this park. As you follow the trail, you'll pass through all four forest communities found in the region.

The trailhead **[1]** is to the left of the parking area. There's an interpretive billboard at the trailhead, along with a registration box. The trail ascends gradually through second-growth hardwoods, until mile .05, where you'll reach the banks of the permanent creek that helped shape the region **[2]**. Turn right, following the V-valley formed by the creek. A V-valley forms when the banks of a down-cutting stream erode outward, wider than the creek itself. In cross section, it resembles a letter V.

At mile .1 the trail is blocked by a fragile habitat gate **[3]**. Turn right, here, and climb steeply. You'll top out in a shallow bowl that resembles a sinkhole, but isn't one. Cross the bowl and climb the far rim, then turn left, following the sign pointing to the overlook.

You'll top out on a narrow ridge at mile .24, at a trail sign that points left to the overlook, or right for the loop trail **[4]**. Go left to the overlook, which you'll reach at mile .27.

The overlook is a point of conglomerate projecting like the prow of a ship. Deep hardwood forests grow below you on three sides. As the forest climbs the ridge, tree age increases, and there is some old growth visible. Return to the trail junction **[4]** and go straight. You'll reach a Y at mile .4, which is the start of the loop **[5]**. Go left.

After descending to a feeder creek and ascending out of its valley, you'll top out at a trail marker at mile .5. Across from the marker is a climax beech **[6]**. In the roots on the uptrail side you'll find beech drops growing. These are nongreen flowering plants, which look like a dried floral arrangement.

The trail follows ridges now, with many deep hardwood hollows on either side. During the fall color season, these hollows are a mass of yellows, oranges, and golds, the autumn palette of a maple/beech forest. At mile 1.06 you'll reach an old-growth tree trunk that seems to block the trail **[7]**. The trail

actually turns hard left just before it. Sit and contemplate a moment the awesome power of the ice that carried rocks from Canada to form the cliffs through which you are passing.

As you leave the tree trunk behind, note the age and size differences between the old-growth forest in the hollow on your left, and the new, brushy growth on the right. Until recently, the area to the right was a farm field, which is being reclaimed by the forest.

You'll pass through a blowdown at mile 1.2 **[8]**. The trail has been cut through the trunks, which are rocklike in their hardness and texture. You can, during leafless months, just make out the cliff edge, the valley below, and the far ridges from the blowdown. The view improves as the trail moves closer to the edge. We watched a red-shouldered hawk soar in the thermals rising from the valley.

The trail descends steadily, but not steeply, from the cliff edge until rejoining the permanent creek, which it follows on the opposite bank. At mile 1.58 the trail steepens and climbs over rocks and erosion steps until mile 1.6, where you wade the creek **[9]** on rocks.

A few steps farther is Middle Creek Road. Turn left and follow it back to the trailhead.

1. Trailhead
2. Permanent creek
3. Fragile habitat gate
4. Overlook trail
5. Loop trail junction
6. Climax beech
7. Old-growth tree trunk
8. Blowdown
9. Creek crossing

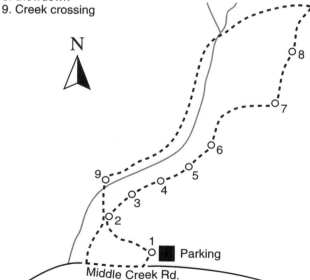

Short Loop Trail 🥾🥾🥾🥾

Distance Round-Trip: .68 miles

Estimated Hiking Time: 30 to 45 minutes

Cautions: The area has high cliffs, exposed rocks and roots, eroded sections, and logs across the trail.

Trail Directions: Although much shorter than the Long Loop Trail, the Short Loop Trail is more difficult. It is steeper, and you'll face technical difficulties not found on the Long Loop Trail.

The trailhead [1] is to the left of the parking lot. What appears to be a trailhead on the right is the return. There's an interpretive billboard and registration box at the trailhead.

Follow the trail through second-growth hardwoods until reaching the permanent creek that helped shape the park. Follow it to a fragile habitat gate that blocks access to the stream. Turn right and climb, steeply, to the bowl at mile .15 [2]. This shallow depression looks like a sinkhole, but isn't one. Cross the bowl, climb the far rim, and turn left. At mile .19 there are two trail signs. Between them is the crisscross tree [3], whose twin trunks cross each other, leaving a large viewing port. Peer through this window and you'll see climax beeches on the hill above you.

At mile .225 you'll see a shelf of exposed outwash conglomerate [4]. The cemented sand and gravel forming this outcrop were dropped by the glaciers 700,000 years ago. Some rocks traveled all the way from Canada. Talk about your free trade zone!

You'll reach a Y at mile .4, which is where the loops separate [5]. Go right, following the parking lot arrow. The trail descends, steeply, with several large tree trunks fallen across it. The trail makes a sharp right turn and becomes less steep at mile .42. Note the large grapevines along the way. You might be tempted to play Tarzan, but don't. It isn't safe.

An erosion ditch runs down the middle of the trail, causing unsure footing. Just watch your step, and you'll be okay. At mile .54 a wet-weather creek appears on the left [6]. The gorge it cut is deeper, and steeper, than the trail. Currently a shallow canyon, there will eventually be additional cliffs formed by the creek's cutting action. Come back in about 100,000 years and you'll see them.

The trail turns right at mile .62, descending parallel to Middle Creek Road until reaching the trailhead on the right of the parking lot.

1. Trailhead
2. Bowl
3. Crisscross tree
4. Conglomerate shelf
5. Loop trail junction
6. Gorge

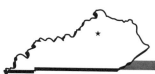

36. Clyde E. Buckley Wildlife Sanctuary

- Experience nature-oriented special events, such as wildflower searches, birdathons, and raptor exhibitions.
- Spend time in an all-weather bird blind, observing and photographing undisturbed songbirds.
- Explore diverse natural habitats—ranging from mature forests to ponds, meadows, open woods, and streams—and the wild creatures that live in them.

Park Information

Clyde E. Buckley Wildlife Sanctuary originated in 1967 when Mrs. Emma Buckley commemorated her late husband by placing their farm in a natural trust. The National Audubon Society and artist Ray Harm were invited to participate, and the area became the first sanctuary in the central United States to be managed by the Society.

The park preserves 275 acres of Kentucky's diverse natural habitats, including meadows, various deciduous forests, streams, and ponds. In addition, an all-weather bird blind, nature center, and display barn add to the experience.

Numerous wildflowers can be seen, especially in the spring. At any time, more than 30 wildflower varieties can be easily spotted from the trails. Wildlife, too, is plentiful. The park hosts deer, wild turkey, and numerous small mammals.

As wildlands diminish, this small, natural community in the heart of the Bluegrass country holds increasing importance for the education and enjoyment of future generations. Such natural spaces are especially important as the population centers of the Frankfort, Versailles, and Lexington spread.

Admission fees and donations are paid, on the honor system, in a special box located in the wishing well near the parking area. It takes more than $30,000 annually to operate the sanctuary, and no governmental funds are solicited or accepted. Thus, donations are an important part of the sanctuary's continued well-being.

Directions: From exit 58 off I-64 near Frankfort, Kentucky, go south on US-60, .3 mile to KY-1681. Make a right and go 2.5 miles to KY-1659. Turn left 1.6 miles to KY-1964. Turn right, going 1.3 miles to Germany Road. Go right again, 1.3 miles to park entrance on the left. Enter the park and go .3 mile to the parking area by the wishing well.

Hours Open: Open year-round, Wednesday through Sunday. Weekend and weekday hours vary.

Facilities: Nature Center and gift shop, picnic area, display barn, and an all-weather bird blind.

Permits and Rules: Only foot travel allowed on trails; do not collect anything; no hunting, fishing, or camping; picnicking in designated areas only; no pets; admission fee charged on weekends and for some special events.

Further Information: Clyde E. Buckley Wildlife Sanctuary, 1305 Germany Road, Frankfort, KY 40601; 606-873-5711.

Other Points of Interest

Raven Run Nature Sanctuary (see park #32), **City of Lexington** (see park #33), and **Taylorsville Lake State Park** (see park #38) are within 45 minutes of Clyde E. Buckley Wildlife Sanctuary.

Nearby **Frankfort** has numerous cultural and historic sites. Contact Frankfort-Franklin County Tourism and Convention Commission, 100 Capital Avenue, Frankfort, KY 40601; 502-875-8687 for details.

Nearby **Versailles** also provides cultural and historic sites of interest. For information, contact Woodford County Chamber of Commerce, 110 North Main Street, Versailles, KY 40383; 606-873-5122.

Park Trails

There are three well-groomed trails in the park, each lined with interpretive information. Guidebooks to each trail can be picked up at the billboard near the wishing well or in the display barn. Please return these booklets when finished.

White Trail 👢👢—.25-mile loop—is the shortest trail in the park, with some interpretive markers that go far beyond the usual tree identification typical of nature trails.

Clyde E. Buckley Wildlife Sanctuary

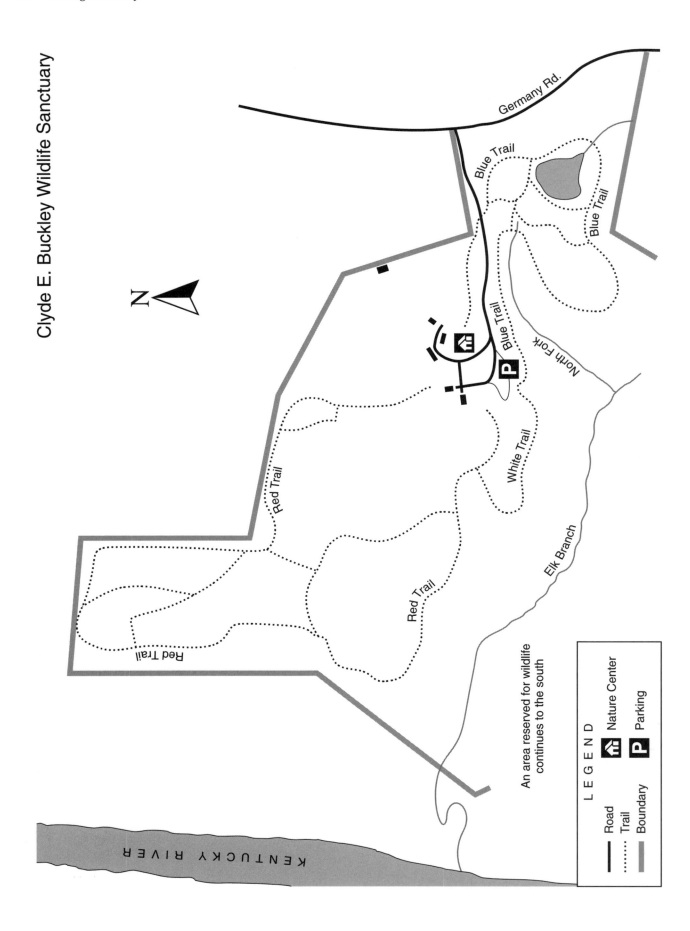

Red Trail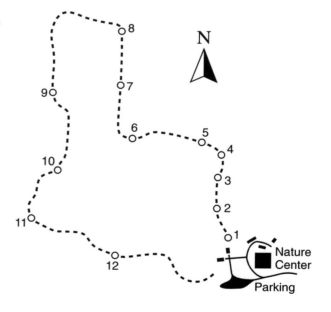

Distance Round-Trip: 1.5 miles

Estimated Hiking Time: 1.25 to 1.5 hours

Cautions: The area has exposed rocks and roots and high bluffs.

Trail Directions: The Red Trail is the longest hike in the park, taking you through the various ecosystems found on the property. Several alternative trails let you shorten the trip if you wish.

The trailhead **[1]** is .07 miles from the wishing well. Walk through the display barn and follow the edge of the woods to the trailhead, which comes in on your left. Right at the trailhead are several small, dead black locust trees, which now provide homes for woodpeckers and small mammals.

The trail is well marked, with 25 interpreted sites ranging from poison ivy to rock piles. It descends gradually from the trailhead to mile .049, where an old stone fence **[2]** is visible through the trees. Known locally as slave fences, they were actually built by Irish immigrants in the late 1800s.

At mile .09 you'll pass the first of several sinkholes **[3]** found along the trail. Sinkholes are formed when underground caves collapse. Some of them are large enough to be farm fields.

You'll reach an unmarked Y at mile .15 **[4]**. Go left and climb until reaching the meadow at mile .19 **[5]**. A sign here discusses habitat diversity and how the needs of many species are met along these habitat edges.

Cross the meadow following the fence line until you reenter the woods at mile .29 **[6]** on an old farm road. You'll be crossing a narrow strip of woods. Halfway across notice the moss-covered slave fence that used to separate two farm fields. Turn right when you reach the second meadow, and follow the thin tree line between the two fields. Notice that the meadow you just entered is filled with islands of trees **[7]**. If you want a short hike, the first alternate trail goes left here.

You'll reenter woods again at mile .48 **[8]** with another alternate trail picking up here. Watch for deer, who use this forest point as a resting area between forays into the field to feed. The trail turns left, off the old farm road, and meanders through the woods.

You'll circle the head of a minicanyon at mile .62 **[9]**. The stream forming it is barely a rivulet where you cross, but it suddenly drops into a deep, multi-armed V-valley. V-valleys form when stream banks erode wider than the stream itself. In cross section they look like the letter V.

The trail leapfrogs fields and woods until mile .98 where you reach a cliff line on the right **[10]**. You'll follow this ridgeline for awhile, until crossing the power line right-of-way at mile 1.17 **[11]**. From there you have a spectacular view into the gorge cut by the creek, which has flowed below the ridge this whole distance.

A rock pile appears at mile 1.23 **[12]**. This is not a natural formation. These rocks were moved here by farmers, but now provide safe homes for small mammals.

At mile 1.29 you'll merge into the White Trail. Follow it back to the wishing well. If you prefer a longer hike, turn right where the trails merge and follow the White Trail its full length.

1. Trailhead
2. Slave fence
3. Sinkhole
4. Unmarked Y
5. Meadow
6. Reenter woods
7. Tree islands
8. Reenter woods again
9. Minicanyon
10. Cliff line
11. Power line right-of-way
12. Rock pile

Blue Trail 👢👢

Distance Round-Trip: 1.06 miles

Estimated Hiking Time: 45 to 60 minutes

Cautions: Be careful of exposed rocks and roots.

Trail Directions: The Blue Trail is an easy, well-interpreted and maintained walk that explores the environment of a deciduous forest and pond community. There are 25 interpretive signs that examine the flora, fauna, and geology of this ecosystem.

The trailhead [1] is south of the wishing well, across the park road. The trailhead for the Blue Trail shares an opening in the woods with the terminus of the White Trail. Blue is on the left. An interpretive sign explains the succession from farmland to forest.

After a gentle slope, the trail flattens along a ridgeline, which drops down steeply to a creek. At mile .08 you enter a power line right-of-way [2] where a sign discusses sunlight in the woods. Notice that the ground here, where sunlight penetrates, bears different plants from the shaded area behind you. Dandelions, mustards, clovers, goldenrods, asters, and daisies are common here.

The right-of-way continues, but the trail turns right at mile .18, reentering the woods on a level path, which backtracks to the west and descends gently [3] until crossing a creek on rocks at mile .19 [4].

At mile .23 you'll pass a sugar maple [5]. Due to climactic conditions, there is no commercial sugaring in Kentucky. However, many landowners tap the sugar maples to make their own syrup and sugar.

There is a great diversity of tree types along the Blue Trail, including buckeyes, honey locusts, black walnuts, Osage oranges, hackberries, and elms, along with the more typical maples, oaks, and hickories.

Watch for the stone fence at mile .46 [6]. Commonly called slave fences, they were actually built by Irish immigrants in the late 1800s to separate fields and property lines.

You'll come to an unmarked Y at mile .51, marked by both multiflora rose and an American elm [7]. The elm is just a dead stump, used now as a den tree by birds and small mammals. Bear right at the Y.

At mile .57 you'll come to a small pond [8]. Be alert for fleeing deer, ducks, and wading birds who spook at your approach. Red-winged blackbirds, their ruby wing patches flashing in the sun, nest in the cattails lining the 1-1/2-acre pond. You may spot muskrats as well.

Follow the south shore of the pond. At the eastern edge the trail enters the woods, climbing around a marshy inlet, before rejoining the pond along its eastern shore. At mile .8 you'll reach a power line right-of-way [9]. Follow it a short distance until reaching a dirt road at mile .85 [10]. This road is used by the park to access the tobacco fields it plants to raise operating money. Turn right, and, in less than 100 feet, you'll reach the park road. Follow it left, crossing under the large black barn on the hill to the north.

Pause in the driveway leading to the barn at mile .9 to watch for raptors [11]. Red-tailed hawks are the most common birds of prey here, but other hawks are often sighted as well. Do not confuse raptors with the buzzards and vultures that also are here. They are scavengers who feed on dead animals rather than hunting their prey as the raptors do.

Turn left inside the driveway and follow the edge of the field toward an opening in the woods, where the trail ends east of the Nature Center at mile .99 [12]. Cross the lawn and return to the wishing well.

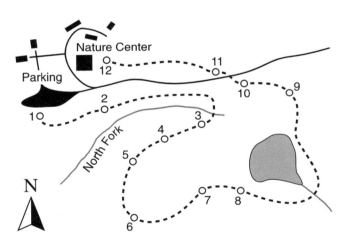

1. Trailhead
2. Power line right-of-way
3. Gentle descent
4. Creek crossing
5. Sugar maple
6. Slave fence
7. American elm
8. Pond
9. Power line right-of-way
10. Dirt road
11. Barn driveway
12. Nature Center

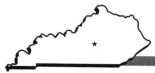

37. Central Kentucky Wildlife Refuge

- Explore the biodiversity and topography of the Knobs.
- Take part in special stargazing, listen to night sounds, and take wildflower walks in season.
- See a relatively unknown waterfall in central Kentucky.

Park Information

Central Kentucky Wildlife Refuge was established in 1965 by a concerned group of Boyle County residents who realized that the Knoblands and its diverse habitats were quickly disappearing. Using no public monies, they purchased an old farm with 100 acres of fields and 400 acres of forest. Miles of creeks flow through the property.

The forested ridges were left in their natural state. The fields are leased as farmland, providing a steady income to supplement the donations that keep this unique nature preserve afloat.

Selected improvements have been made, and continue. Many of these improvements have resulted from the efforts of the Eagle Scouts, who have adopted the refuge as an ongoing project. Four ponds have been built to increase habitat diversity. The Check Wetlands Area is an addition, and it continues to be developed. In 1975 a bird blind was built. This has become very popular with birders and photographers.

Directions: The refuge is located 13 miles from Danville, Kentucky. From Danville, follow US-127 south to Junction City. Take KY-300 west through Junction City to KY-37. Follow that for several miles to Carpenter Creek Road. Almost immediately you'll cross the North Branch of Rolling Fork River. The entrance and parking lot are about .5 miles further, on the left.

Hours Open: Open year-round, from dawn to dusk.

Facilities: There is a picnic table, but there are no other facilities. A port-a-pot is located near the parking area.

Permits and Rules: No permit is required. There is no fee to use the refuge, but donations are encouraged. Hunting, camping, fishing, athletic games, and big picnics are prohibited. Staying on trails to protect the habitat is encouraged.

Further Information: Contact Central Kentucky Wildlife Refuge, P.O. Box 152, Danville, KY 40422. Caretakers James and Rose-Marie Roessler can be reached at 606-332-7333.

Other Points of Interest

Herrington Lake, a 1,800-acre impoundment formed by the damming of the Dix River lies just north of Danville. All water sports are available there, but the lake is most known for fishing. Below the dam, on the lower Dix River, is Kentucky's only trophy trout water.

Fifteen miles from the refuge, near Gravel Switch, is **Penn's Store** (606-332-7715). This is an old-fashioned country store, considered to be the oldest store in the nation that has been run by one family. It's currently operated by the fifth generation, who still use a cigar box as a cash drawer. In the fall, this is the scene of an outhouse race and other activities, such as mountain music pickin' and pluckin'.

Constitution Square (606-239-7089), in downtown Danville, is the site where Kentucky became a state. A self-guided walk takes you through original and reconstructed buildings from the years around 1792. Across from the square is the **McDowell House and Apothecary** (606-236-2804), where Dr. McDowell performed the first abdominal surgery in history, back in the early 1800s.

Park Trails

There are six trails in the refuge, ranging from easy to strenuous. Except for the Wildflower Trail, they are all accessed from the split-rail gate near the interpretive billboard, or from other trails.

Deer Trail 👢—.5 miles—provides a pleasant, easy walk through woods and fields.

Ridge Trail 👢👢👢—.6 miles—takes you up and down three peaks. In the spring, the grassy ridge crest is full of wildflowers.

Blue Trail 👢👢—.5 miles—is a short path off Circle Trail on a shady ridge. This was the first trail established in the refuge.

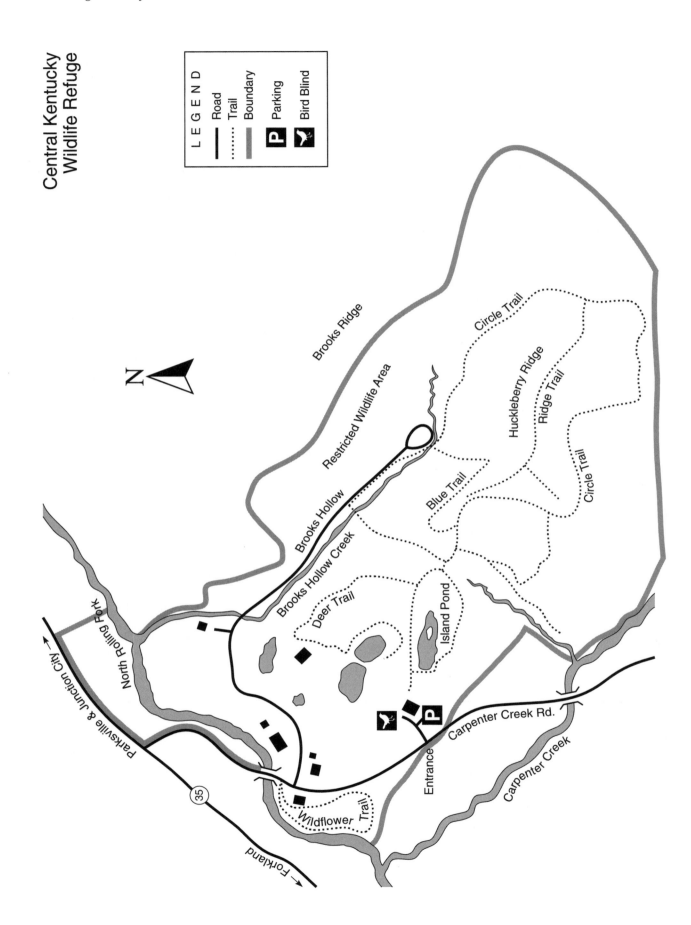

Central Kentucky
Wildlife Refuge

N

LEGEND

Road
Trail
Boundary
P Parking
Bird Blind

Brooks Ridge

Restricted Wildlife Area

Circle Trail

Huckleberry Ridge

Ridge Trail

Circle Trail

Brooks Hollow

Blue Trail

Brooks Hollow Creek

Deer Trail

Island Pond

North Rolling Fork

Parksville & Junction City

Carpenter Creek Rd.

Entrance

Carpenter Creek

35

Forkland

Wildflower Trail

Circle Trail 👢👢👢👢

Distance Round-Trip: 2.8 miles

Estimated Hiking Time: 2.5 hours

Cautions: You will encounter some loose and washed-out rock on the trail.

Trail Directions: Circle Trail is a rather strenuous hike across three ridges that provides a good overview of Knobs topography, flora, and fauna. The Knobs are a series of low-lying, rounded hills forming a line to the west of the mountains, from Berea, Kentucky, southward.

Access to trails is via a short path from the interpretive sign near the caretaker's cottage. Follow this path past Island Pond to the wood line. Turn right to the trailhead **[1]**, which is .33 miles from the gate. Do not confuse Circle Trail with Cross Trail, which starts at the same point. After an easy walk, you'll intersect the Waterfall Trail **[2]** on the right at mile .06. This is a nice .5-mile side trip to a seasonal waterfall that cascades over a sharp lip and drops 30 feet. A natural amphitheater has been carved in the banks behind the fall. Check with the caretaker ahead of time to find out whether or not the waterfall is running.

From the Waterfall Trail junction, Circle Trail climbs 668 linear feet, with one fairly steep pitch, to the first ridge. A thousand feet later, trail #2 comes in on the right. If you took the side trip to the waterfall, you could have used this connector to reach the ridge here at mile .34 **[3]**.

In another 1,000 feet, the trail narrows to shoulder width; then, 500 feet further, it descends sharply 250 linear feet and continues downward less steeply. After about 700 feet it bottoms out at a creek at mile .8 **[4]**, jogs left a short distance, then crosses the creek and ascends to the right. In 650 feet you'll cross the creek again; then in a few steps you'll cross a tributary to the creek and start climbing again—ascending gently 650 feet before the climb steepens. After another 300 feet, you top out on another ridge.

In .1 miles, the Ridge Trail comes in on the left. Ridge Trail follows the crest of this knob, while Circle Trail continues up and over it. The trail descends steadily, crossing over a fallen tree and then entering a fern garden at mile 1.25 **[5]**. In another .1 mile it levels out before descending to the creek 300 feet farther.

Circle Trail roughly follows the creek for .2 miles, then crosses it. After crossing the bridge, turn left. Follow the creek until you reach the wood line; then turn right. After 400 feet the trail widens and becomes a grassy swale similar to the path leading to the trailhead. Follow the swale for .2 miles. The swale continues, but at mile 1.65, the trail turns off it to the left **[6]**. Watch for the trail sign on the left that says "lodge" and shows an arrow; it's easy to miss.

Almost immediately you'll cross the creek on another new bridge; you'll follow the edge of a small meadow at mile 1.7 **[7]**. This is often a good spot to see wild turkey, so approach it carefully. The trail picks up halfway around the meadow, with another arrowed sign saying "lodge."

The trail now enters the woods and climbs gently. After .2 miles you'll reach the trailhead and meadow. Continue across the meadow on the mowed path for .1 miles. You'll then reenter the woods on a grassy swale. (Caution: There are no trail markers here.) In a short distance you'll enter some pine woods and then, at mile 2.13, make a sharp drop to the dam forming Island Pond **[8]**. Crossing the dam puts you on the entry path. Make a left to return to the interpretive sign and parking lot.

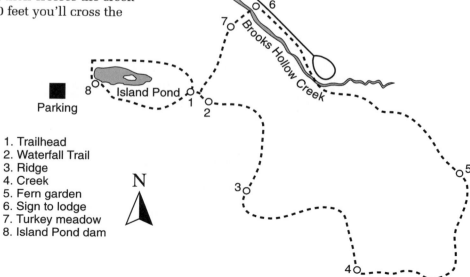

1. Trailhead
2. Waterfall Trail
3. Ridge
4. Creek
5. Fern garden
6. Sign to lodge
7. Turkey meadow
8. Island Pond dam

N

Wildflower Trail 🥾

Distance Round-Trip: .5 miles

Estimated Hiking Time: 15 to 20 minutes

Cautions: You will encounter wet rocks; after rains, there may be flowing water.

Trail Directions: The Wildflower Trail is a short, flat nature trail, framed by Carpenter Creek and the North Branch of Rolling Fork River, that follows the wooded edge along a large meadow. Wildflowers are especially prevalent in the spring, so if you're here then, allow more time, as you'll lose track of the clock while gazing at the blossoms.

From the main parking lot, turn right onto Carpenter Creek Road. You can either drive on this road or walk to the trailhead. In less than .5 miles, you'll pass an old barn on the left. A short distance further is a farm gate, just before you reach the highway bridge. If you've driven, park by the gate.

The trailhead is just three or four steps from the gate, on the left **[1]**. In about 100 feet, at mile .018, you'll pass by some undercut cliffs on the left. The old barn sits atop those cliffs **[2]**. These cliffs will remain on your left for the first half of the hike.

At mile .20, the trail junctions with a drain coming off the cliffs **[3]**. This drain becomes the trail, which turns 90 degrees right at the junction. During periods of heavy rain, there can be water flowing down the drain or wet, slippery rocks in it. Follow the drain to mile .204, where it terminates at Carpenter Creek **[4]**. There will be some interesting cliffs and rock formations upstream on your left.

Turn right and follow the creek edge through the brush to the meadow. There is no distinct trail here. Enter the meadow as soon as possible. Follow the meadow edge about 250 feet, where, at mile .207, it reenters the woods **[5]**. There is neither a sign nor a colored flash, however, so you need to watch for a well-beaten path.

The trail passes through a slightly different type of forest edge as it follows a stream instead of a cliff. You'll find different types of plants and wildflowers and may even see raccoons, mink, and other small mammals. At mile .27, the trail enters the meadow again, where Carpenter Creek junctions with the North Branch of Rolling Fork River **[6]**. Follow the river back to the gate.

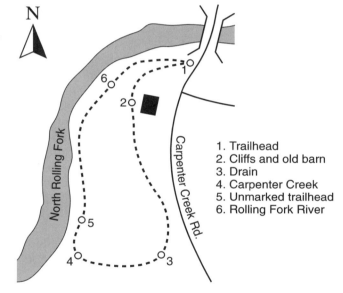

1. Trailhead
2. Cliffs and old barn
3. Drain
4. Carpenter Creek
5. Unmarked trailhead
6. Rolling Fork River

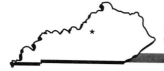

38. Taylorsville Lake State Park

- Explore the special environment of a backwater floodplain.
- See how plants and trees secede themselves to eventually form a mature forest.
- Learn firsthand why horses and hikers shouldn't mix on the same trails.

Park Information

Taylorsville Lake is a 3,050-acre, flood-control reservoir in the hill country of north central Kentucky, about 25 miles from Louisville.

Impounded from the Salt River, the lake was opened in 1983 and has been attracting anglers ever since. Until then, rivers in Kentucky had been impounded hand over fist, with little thought to recreational management. This changed with Taylorsville, where fisheries-management strategies were integral to the planning process. Special fish-attractor sites were established, and bass were stocked on a year-class basis—that is, both fry and subadults were stocked. Along with the resident adults, this provided a mixed group from the start. A 15-inch size limit was imposed as well. Anglers are still reaping the benefits of this intense management.

Taylorsville Lake State Park, which sprawls over 2,500 acres on the north shore of the lake, primarily appeals to those who use the marina to access the lake. Until recently there was no camping, but a new campground is slated to open this year (1998), which should make the park more attractive to anglers.

Horseback riding is the second big draw of the park. Although there is no rental stable, the park's proximity to both Louisville and Lexington—it's less than 50 miles from each city—makes it attractive to riders who trailer their own mounts.

Most of the park's topography is wild, consisting of several ridges and valleys, and the floodplains of Beech Creek, Little Beech Creek, and the Salt River.

There are few mature trees in the park, which had been heavily logged and farmed, but second-growth forests (those that have grown up since the land was logged) are thick.

In the floodplains, specialized flora and fauna have grown up, adapted to the periodic flooding of these backwater areas. White-tailed deer and wild turkey are plentiful.

Directions: From Taylorsville go east on KY-44, 5.9 miles until it merges into KY-248. Continue east 2 miles to the park entrance, turn left, and go 1.2 miles to the Visitor Center.

Hours Open: Open year-round during daylight hours.

Facilities: Boat ramp, picnic area, campground scheduled to open in 1998.

Permits and Rules: No bicycles or motor vehicles on trails; hikers must yield to horses.

Further Information: Taylorsville Lake State Park, P.O. Box 509, Taylorsville, KY 40071; 502-477-8713.

Other Points of Interest

E.P. "Tom" Sawyer State Park (see park #39), **City of Louisville** (see park #41), **Bernheim Arboretum and Research Forest** (see park #40), and **Freeman Lake Park** (see park #42) are within one hour of Taylorsville Lake State Park.

Park Trails

There are more than 17 miles of trails at Taylorsville Lake State Park. However, because they are used heavily by horses, they are unsuitable for hiking—being rutted and torn up almost as if a plow had chattered down them. Trail signs are confusing or nonexistent.

Possum Ridge Loop 👢👢👢👢—3.7 miles round-trip—connects from Beech Creek Loop A.

Little Beech Creek Loop 👢👢👢👢👢—4.6 miles round-trip—follows Possum Ridge, with side trails to the Little Beech Creek bottoms.

Snyder Hollow Loop 👢👢👢👢👢—1.7 miles round-trip—is the shortest hike in the park.

Beech Creek Loop A 👢👢👢👢👢

Distance Round-Trip: 2.6 miles

Estimated Hiking Time: 1.5 to 2 hours

Cautions: The area has high cliffs, loose rocks, eroded sections, mud, and unmarked and mismarked trail junctions. There are also horses and extensive horse damage to the trail.

Trail Directions: Beech Creek Loop A was not a loop when we measured it. Because of work on the new campground, the return leg was closed. So, think of it as a one-way hike.

The trailhead **[1]** is at the wildlife viewing station east of the Visitors Center. Several unmarked trails converge here. Go due east, parallel to the park road. You'll pass through young hardwoods, then run along their edge, until crossing the park road. Continue east a few steps to the horse trailer parking lot at mile .18 **[2]**, where the trail continues. At mile .23 a trail sign directs you straight to the Snyder Hollow Trail or left to Beech Creek **[3]**. Go left. On your left, at mile .31, is a secession field **[4]**.

You'll pass an old stock pond at mile .42 **[5]**, which is now a watering hole for wildlife. A bit farther, at mile .46, you'll enter an older hardwood forest, which had been a farmer's woodlot.

You'll reach a cliff edge at mile .6 **[6]**, overlooking what appears to be a giant meadow. You are looking at a backwater floodplain. Periodically, the rising waters of Beech Creek and its tributaries flood these bottoms. The vegetation growing there has adapted to these annual (sometimes more often) inundations.

The trail turns rocky as it drops into these bottoms and is torn up by horse traffic. After two steep descents, you'll reach a creek at mile .93 **[7]**. On the far bank is a moss-covered stone fence. Turn right, following the creek bank, to mile .95 where the trail seems to disappear in the creek **[8]**. Actually, it crosses diagonally to the right, but a large sycamore blocks your view. Go around the tree and you'll see the trail.

You'll reach a T at mile .96 at an ambiguous trail sign **[9]**. The sign bears a horse trail logo and an arrow pointing right. In fact, the trail describes a large oval around the edge of the backwater area. You can go in either direction. We chose left.

The trail will almost always be muddy as it skirts the backwater. On your left is a brushy border along a creek. On your right is the specialized flora of the floodplain. You are likely to see deer feeding, especially early and late in the day.

At the far end of this bottom you'll enter a cedar thicket at mile 1.05 **[10]**. A few hundred feet farther, at mile 1.1, a large bowl-like meadow appears on the right **[11]**, which looks like a dried-up lake bed being reclaimed by the forest.

At mile 1.29 you'll enter some young hardwoods in a boggy area. This is the head of the Beech Creek inlet **[12]** and is the first ground to flood when waters rise. Shortly after that, at mile 1.3, you'll juncture with the other loop of the oval **[13]** at a trail sign that points in both directions.

If the loop is still closed, this is the place to turn back. For the sake of diversity, follow the other half of the oval, and return to the trailhead.

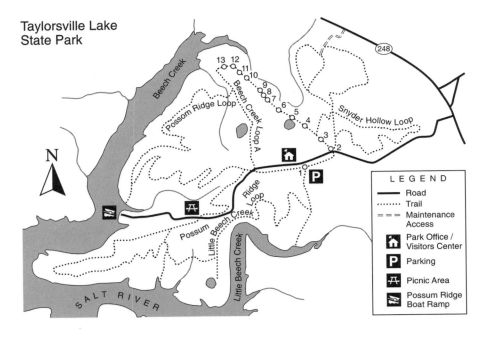

Taylorsville Lake
State Park

N

1. Trailhead
2. Horse trailer parking lot
3. Trails diverge
4. Secession field
5. Stock pond
6. Cliff
7. Creek
8. Creek crossing
9. Ambiguous trail sign
10. Cedar thicket
11. Dry lake bed
12. Beech Creek inlet
13. Junction with oval loop

LEGEND

—— Road
········· Trail
= = = Maintenance Access
🏠 Park Office / Visitors Center
🅿 Parking
🅰 Picnic Area
〰 Possum Ridge Boat Ramp

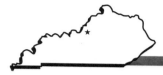

39. E.P. "Tom" Sawyer State Park

- Work out at some of the finest fitness and recreational facilities in Kentucky.
- Watch model aircraft enthusiasts fly their planes from a 400-foot runway.
- Explore the flora and fauna of a prairie environment.

Park Information

E.P. "Tom" Sawyer State Park is a 369-acre oasis on the outskirts of the Louisville metropolitan area. Its rolling hills and streams were once farmland. Now they are the site of both indoor and outdoor recreational facilities second to none.

Included in the complex are an Olympic-sized swimming pool; athletic fields for soccer and softball; tennis courts; an activities center housing a 600-seat gymnasium, offering indoor courts for basketball, volleyball, badminton, and a weight room; and fitness and nature trails.

The Steve Henry Radio-Controlled Airfield features a 400-foot-by-35-foot runway for flying model airplanes. Also, there's a BMX bicycle track considered one of the best in the country.

The park is named in honor of Erbon Powers "Tom" Sawyer, a Louisville leader. His daughter, Diane, is coanchor of ABC's *Prime Time Live* television show.

Directions: From Louisville take I-64 east 14 miles to I-265 north. Go 7.6 miles to Westpoint Road (exit 22), then right .8 miles to Frey's Hill Road, then left .4 miles to the park entrance.

Hours Open: Open year-round; some facilities are seasonal or have special operating hours.

Facilities: Complete indoor and outdoor recreational facilities plus picnic areas. The Corn Island Storytelling Festival is held annually in September.

Permits and Rules: Hiking trails open during daylight hours; foot travel only on trails.

Further Information: E.P. "Tom" Sawyer State Park, 3000 Freys Hill Road, Louisville, KY 40241; 502-426-8950.

E.P. "Tom" Sawyer State Park

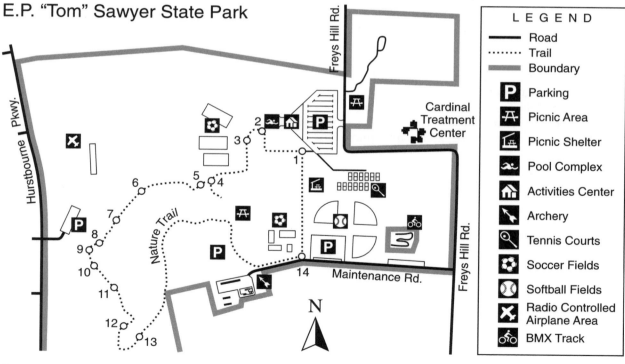

1. Trailhead
2. Cattail marshes
3. Exercise area
4. Old fitness trail
5. Goose Creek tNature Trail
6. Left turn
7. Sinkholes
8. Young hardwood forest
9. Second side trail
10. Goose Creek
11. Living arch
12. Monster tree
13. Rejoin old road
14. Unmarked Y

Goose Creek Nature Trail 👢👢

Distance Round-Trip: 2.1 miles

Estimated Hiking Time: 1 to 1.5 hours

Cautions: None.

Trail Directions: The Goose Creek Nature Trail, which now includes what had been the Fitness Trail, is an easy walk through various ecosystems, including prairie and riverine environments.

The trailhead **[1]** is on the left (west) side of the parking lot, near the maintenance road sign. The trail, which is crushed limestone at this point, forks right at the trailhead. Take the right-hand path, toward the visitor's center.

At mile .16, you'll pass behind the pool. Several small, cattail-filled marshy patches line the trail **[2]** behind the pool, and you are likely to see red-wing blackbirds perched on the reeds, their scarlet wing patches glinting like rubies in the sun.

The exercise area comes up at mile .2 **[3]**. At one time, these 12 fitness stations were spread out along the trail, but the park decided it was better to concentrate them in one spot. The return loop (a gravel road) for the old fitness trail comes up at mile .27 **[4]**, and the nature trail seems to cross it. This is incorrect. Turn right on the old road. Just after crossing a bridge, the nature trail comes in from the left at mile .35 **[5]**. Goose Creek Nature Trail is chipped bark, as it passes through a recovering farm field that looks like a prairie.

In addition to native grasses, the field is filled with young trees, thick ground cover, and wildflowers. You'll likely see blue jays here, along with other songbirds. For some years, these raucous birds had all but disappeared from Kentucky but are now plentiful once more.

The trail parallels the old road until mile .54, where it turns left **[6]**. That persistent buzzing you hear isn't in your head. The model plane airport is just across the meadow, on your right, and the Tom Sawyer Model Aircraft Association is probably flying.

The trail skirts several bowl-shaped depressions on both sides at mile .62 **[7]**. Although the park is outside the karst district found farther west, these are sinkholes, caused when underground caves collapse. Shortly after passing the sinkholes, a thin band of creek side trees appears on the left. Follow them until mile .79, where the trail—now a mowed path on an old road—enters young and thick bottomland hardwoods **[8]**.

Almost immediately you'll pass a side trail, then, at mile .86, reach a second one **[9]**. If you want a shorter walk, stay on the road, but the prettiest part of the trail is through the woods, along the side trail.

You'll reach Goose Creek at mile 1.02 **[10]**. The trail will be sandwiched between the creek and the old road. A little farther, at mile 1.18, you'll pass under a living arch **[11]**. The tree canopy here has folded over the trail, forming an arch about 12 feet high.

When you hit the upgrade at mile 1.24, watch for the "monster" tree on the right **[12]**. Sometime in the past a major, low-growing limb had torn free. It now extends like the groping finger of a monster. Despite this damage, the tree healed itself, and both parts are alive.

You'll rejoin the old road at mile 1.29 **[13]**, and follow it on the far side of the overgrown meadow, which is thickly filled with young growth and songbirds. A little farther the trail crosses a maintenance road and a fenced paddock, which, when we were there, held no animals even though the grass was closely cropped.

At mile 1.59 you'll come to an unmarked Y **[14]**. Go right until reaching a T at the old Fitness Trail. Go right again, circling the soccer fields, and continue back to the trailhead.

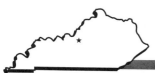

40. Bernheim Arboretum and Research Forest

- Observe more than 1,800 labeled varieties of trees, shrubs, and other plants.
- See the spectacular floral views from overlooks at Tablet Hill and Big Meadow.
- Watch hundreds of resident and migrating bird species.

Park Information

This 240-acre park, Kentucky's official arboretum, contains more than 1,800 labeled varieties of trees, shrubs, and other plants, as well as a separate wilderness area containing native trees and shrubbery.

Bernheim's formal plantings include several impressive collections, among them the largest group of American holly in North America. More than 250 varieties can be seen in the collection.

Other collections include maples, crab apples, dwarf conifers, and dogwoods, as well as a labeled collection of water lilies and other aquatic plants in the pool by the Arboretum Center.

There are four lakes within the park, each bordered by walking paths. Cedar Lakes are a good place to see waterfowl, and the 32-acre Lake Nevin is open to fishing from designated sections of the bank.

The arboretum was a gift of German immigrant Isaac W. Bernheim, who settled in Kentucky as a peddler. Later he became successful distilling bourbon under the I.W. Harper brand. Grateful for his good fortune, he founded Bernheim Arboretum and Research Forest as a gift to the people of Kentucky. In 1992, the Kentucky legislature named it the state's official arboretum.

Directions: Take exit 112 (Bardstown-Clermont) off I-65. Go east one mile on KY-245 to the arboretum entrance. Bernheim is 18 miles south of Louisville, 20 miles north of Elizabethtown, and 15 miles west of Bardstown.

Hours Open: Open year-round from 7:00 A.M. until sunset.

Facilities: Nature and Visitors Centers, picnic areas, and fishing.

Permits and Rules: No collecting plants or animals on arboretum property; free admission weekdays, but a fee is charged on weekends and holidays.

Further Information: Bernheim Arboretum and Research Forest, Highway 245, Clermont, KY 40110; 502-955-8512.

Other Points of Interest

Taylorsville Lake State Park (see park #38), **E.P. "Tom" Sawyer State Park** (see park #39), **Tioga Trails** (see park #43), **Otter Creek Park** (see park #44), **Vernon Douglas State Nature Preserve** (see park #45), and **Freeman Lake Park** (see park #42) are all within one hour of Bernheim Arboretum and Research Forest.

Numerous historic and cultural attractions can be found in nearby **Bardstown** (502-348-4877) and **Louisville** (502-584-2121).

Park Trails

There are 35 miles of scenic trails and fire roads in the park, most located in the wilderness areas off Tower Hill Road and Guerilla Hollow Road. The trails loop through the knobs, valleys, ridges, and hollows of the region, and all climb up hills and down into hollows.

Bent Twig Trail 👢👢—.5 mile loop—is an interpreted nature trail near the Nature Center.

Log Cabin Ridge Trail 👢👢👢👢—5.25 miles one way—connects Guerilla Hollow Road with the Yoe Fire Road, using the Guerilla Hollow and Yoe Loops.

Cull Hollow Trail 👢👢👢—1.5 mile loop—is a good trail for viewing wildlife.

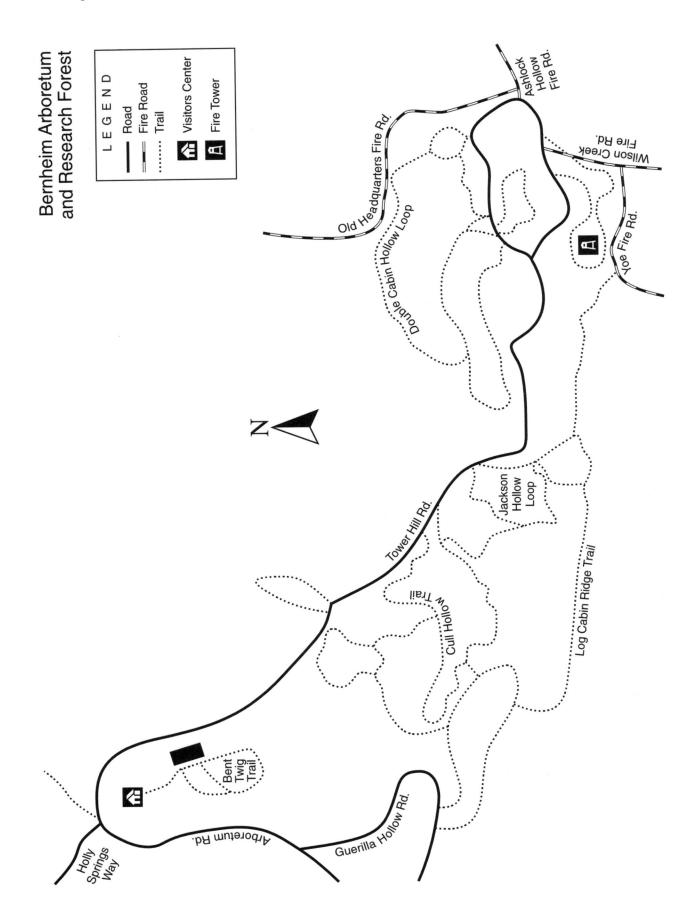

Bernheim Arboretum and Research Forest

LEGEND
Road
Fire Road
Trail
Visitors Center
Fire Tower

N

Holly Springs Way

Arboretum Rd.

Guerilla Hollow Rd.

Bent Twig Trail

Tower Hill Rd.

Cull Hollow Trail

Jackson Hollow Loop

Log Cabin Ridge Trail

Double Cabin Hollow Loop

Old Headquarters Fire Rd.

Ashlock Hollow Fire Rd.

Wilson Creek Fire Rd.

Yoe Fire Rd.

Jackson Hollow Loop 👢👢👢

Distance Round-Trip: .88 miles

Estimated Hiking Time: 40 to 60 minutes

Cautions: Be careful of unbridged creek crossings and exposed rocks and roots.

Trail Directions: Jackson Hollow serves as a good introduction to the topography of Bernheim's wilderness area.

The trailhead [1] is on the south end of a picnic area on Tower Hill Road, just behind the restrooms. Initially grass, the trail turns to hardwoods almost immediately.

When we visited, a tom turkey was strutting and gobbling just past the trailhead. This is not unusual, as Bernheim was deeply involved with the wild turkey restoration project in Kentucky. Thus, the big birds are plentiful. What made it special was the time of year. Wild turkey normally display in April and May, not in July.

Several other trails intersect with Jackson Hollow, so be sure to follow the red blazes. The trail follows a creek for the first couple hundred feet. Take note of the rotten sedimentary limestone shelves and scree on your right. You might find fossils if you look.

After crossing the creek twice at about mile .17 [2], you'll start climbing gradually, then more steeply, with several switchbacks. At mile .39, look for Bandit Rock on the right [3]. This is a large boulder whose natural holes and cracks leave the impression of a face with masked eyes. One of us thought it was a bandit-faced raccoon, the other thought it might be a Neanderthal man. Either way, it shows how reading eroded rock can be as much fun as dreaming the clouds.

The trail continues climbing, until it tops out on a ridge and runs level through a tunnel of sassafras on both sides at mile .51 [4]. You can't mistake these mitten-shaped leaves for anything else. It's the only tree whose leaves come in three forms. Sassafras was a major culinary and medicinal plant in the old days. Crush a leaf between your hands and you'll smell root beer.

A few feet farther, at mile .59, are twin benches overlooking Jackson Hollow [5]. This is a wonderful spot in which to rest and watch for wildlife. Deer and wild turkey, as well as small mammals and birds, are likely targets for your camera.

The trail Ys at mile .60. Take the right fork, and descend steeply to mile .69. The hollows on both sides [6] still show the effects of the tornado that swept through the region in 1974. Trees lie scattered like jackstraws thrown by a giant playing pick-up-sticks.

The trail continues downward until bottoming out at a deep drain, which you'll cross on a culvert. Then, at mile .82 is the main creek, which you'll have to wade [7] to reach the picnic area and return to the trailhead.

1. Trailhead
2. Creek crossing
3. Bandit Rock
4. Sassafras tunnel
5. Benches
6. Tornado hollows
7. Creek crossing

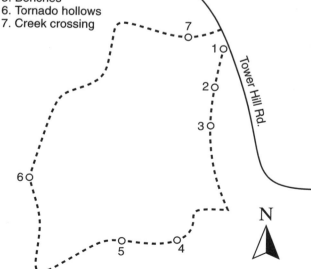

Double Cabin Hollow Loop

Distance Round-Trip: 2.25 miles

Estimated Hiking Time: 1.5 to 2 hours

Cautions: Be aware of exposed rocks and roots, loose rock, washed-out sections, and running water on the trail.

Trail Directions: Double Cabin Hollow Trail is a longish loop, with lots of climbing, that interprets the natural and human history of the area. Unfortunately, many interpretive signs have been broken or removed by vandals. Even so, the trail provides a good overview of the Highland Rim topography of Kentucky.

The trailhead [1] is off Paul's Point Loop, which anchors Tower Hill Road. Go about three quarters around the loop to find the trailhead, directly across the road from a parking area.

There are two entrances, about 20 feet apart. Take the one on the right, following the blue blazes, through a second-growth hardwood forest. After roller-coastering for 400 feet, the trail descends steeply, with erosion gullies cutting it up. It then levels out, and follows the rim of a bowl-like hollow on the left—a great place during fall color.

At mile .25 you'll descend into an oak/hickory hollow [2]. The interpretive signs pick up here. It's too bad that so many are missing, as the information they provide is useful.

The trail, from here on, is a series of climbs, descents, and roller-coaster hills and dips. At mile .67 there's a large downed poplar along the trail at a perfect height for sitting [3]. This is a good place to catch your breath from all the climbing. There's a steady descent from there, until you rejoin the creek, crossing and following it until mile .83, where the trail enters the creek bed [4] and follows it for 90 feet. Two hundred feet farther, you'll again be wading as the trail and creek bed are the same for 100 feet. Don't bother changing your socks, because you'll be wading the creek several more times, during wet seasons, over the next .2 miles. Finally, you'll come even with a large fern garden [5] across the creek at mile 1.08.

Now, while enjoying the cool serenity of the emerald fronds, you can change socks, because it's the last time you'll have to cross water.

The worst of the climbing is still in front of you, however, as the trail climbs and descends steeply several more times. At mile 1.27 the Iron Ore Hill Trail enters from the right [6], and the two run together for some time. Remember, you are following the blue blazes, not the white ones. The trail levels out for awhile after the trail junction, then descends steeply, and climbs again, still more steeply.

At mile 1.63 there is a view into Old Headquarters Hollow, 250 feet below on the left [7]. This is where two cabins, which the trail is named for, stood in earlier times. Nothing remains of the cabins, but the view, especially during fall color time, is spectacular.

Iron Ore Hill and Double Cabin Hollow Trails diverge again at mile 1.91 [8], and the trail turns parallel to Paul's Loop Road. You'll think the trailhead is just around the next curve, but, in fact, it descends away from the road, then climbs steeply again toward it, before reaching the trailhead at the second of the two entrances.

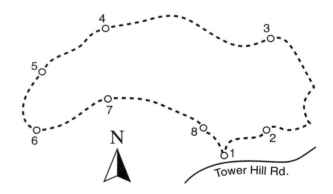

1. Trailhead
2. Oak/hickory hollow
3. Downed poplar
4. Enter creek bed
5. Fern garden
6. Iron Ore Hill Trail junction
7. Old Headquarters Hollow
8. Trails diverge

41. City of Louisville

- Tour the second largest cast-iron building district in the world.
- Visit the museum that commemorates the run for the roses—the Kentucky Derby.
- See the largest floating fountain ever built.

Park Information

Does anyone know how to pronounce "Louisville?" Some say "Looeyville." Others insist it's "Lewisville." Still another group corrects anybody who doesn't say,"Louahvul."

No matter how you say it, Kentucky's largest city has a lot more going for it than the Kentucky Derby—which is what most people think of when the town is mentioned.

The city was founded by George Rogers Clark as a base of operations during the American Revolution. Headquartering on Corn Island (now submerged beneath the Ohio River), Clark waged the war in the west successfully and would have likely captured Fort Detroit if he hadn't been held back.

The Ohio River played a continuing role in the city's history and development. The Falls of the Ohio, directly across the river from downtown, marked the head of navigation until the locks and dams were built this century. At the falls, you can now see, and walk out on, the largest known Devonian fossil bed. This raised rock bed is more than 400 million years old.

At the McAlpine Lock and Dam you can see how the river was changed. Watch barge traffic as it locks through on the way to Cincinnati and points east. Then visit the nearby Portland Museum, which showcases the city's river heritage, including newsreels of the devastating flood of 1937.

Louisville's Main Street contains the second largest grouping of cast-iron buildings in the world. Only New York's SoHo district has more of them. Louisville's are being restored and refurbished, and a walk downtown is an exciting adventure. Note,

especially, the walking-stick surrounded ironwood trees that mark each cast-iron structure.

Directions: Louisville lies at the crossroads of I-65 and I-64. The riverfront is accessible off either one.

Hours Open: Open year-round.

Facilities: Hotels, restaurants, picnic areas, and all amenities are available in the downtown area.

Permits and Rules: None.

Further Information: Louisville Convention and Visitors Bureau, 400 South First Street, Louisville, KY 40202; 502-584-2121.

Other Points of Interest

The Louisville area has numerous cultural and historic sites. Among the highlights are **The Falls of Ohio Interpretive Center** (812-280-8689), which houses an interactive gallery, observation rooms, and theater. The **Louisville Slugger Museum** (502-588-7228), which traces the history of baseball, includes a tour of the factory where the world-famous bats are made. The **Kentucky Derby Museum** (502-637-1111) celebrates the history and culture surrounding the Run for the Roses.

E.P. "Tom" Sawyer State Park (see park #39), **Taylorsville Lake State Park** (see park #38), **Bernheim Arboretum and Research Forest** (see park #40), **Freeman Lake Park** (see park #42), **Vernon Douglas State Nature Preserve** (see park #45), **Otter Creek Park** (see park #44), and **Tioga Trails** (see park #43) are all within one hour of Louisville.

For experienced hikers, well versed in trail finding, the **Jefferson County Memorial Forest** (502-368-5404) has a network of trails through strenuous country that may require map and compass work to follow.

At **Fort Hill Park** (502-922-4574), near West Point, several poorly maintained trails lead to Fort Duffield—the largest and best preserved Civil War earthworks in Kentucky. The fort interpretive trail, however, is well maintained and worth walking.

Louisville Riverwalk 🥾

Distance Round-Trip: 5.1 miles

Estimated Hiking Time: 2 hours

Cautions: Watch out for bicyclists.

Trail Directions: The Riverwalk is a paved, walking and cycling trail that extends 7 miles from the River Authority Headquarters to Chickasaw Park. Just over 2.5 miles follow the downtown riverfront.

The trailhead [1] is at the wharf, at the Louisville Authority Headquarters. The trail moves west from there.

The Star of Louisville paddlewheeler [2] is moored at mile .12. The Star offers river excursions, including dinner cruises. A few steps farther, at mile .128, is the Belle of Louisville [3], the oldest sternwheeler still in service. The Belle offers scheduled sightseeing tours.

You'll reach a set of concrete stairs at mile .176 leading to Belvedere Plaza [4]. If you aren't up to climbing, there's an elevator available.

Imbedded in the bricks is a blue tile representation of the Ohio River. On the western end is a statue of George Rogers Clark, looking out at the bridges to Indiana, and the Louisville Falls Fountain, the world's largest floating fountain.

Return to the Riverwalk and go west. About 200 feet farther, at mile .21 is the first in a string of large, corrugated metal cylinders [5], each crowned with shrubbery. They look like giant flowerpots, but are actually a safety net to prevent any run-away barges from hitting the Interstate.

At mile .43 you'll come to the first of several platform overlooks [6]. This one is directly across from The Falls of Ohio. The Louisville Ship Canal, which extended shipping past the falls, joins the river here.

Another overlook, at mile .67, stands across from the site of Corn Island, where Louisville was first settled [7].

The Lock Keeper's bridge—an iron grillwork structure that's a cross between a bridge and a cargo crane—appears overhead at mile 1.06 [8]. It's used by maintenance and operations people to reach the lock controls.

For awhile you'll be traveling along the river, with the never-ending boat traffic the only point of interest.

Note, at mile 1.58, the abandoned factory building on your left [9]. There is an interesting art deco tile design imbedded in the bricks of the eastern most wall.

You'll cross the railroad tracks at mile 1.83 [10], and climb up on a levy. Be careful! This is a live railroad track. The trail becomes blacktop, and continues westward, past a playground and trail sign. Then watch your feet at mile 2.05. A set of imbedded interpretive signs [11] called "Boats Plied the River" appears. Separate tiles tick off the types of boats that used the river as a road.

At mile 2.09 a second set of tiles is inlet into the trail [12]. These talk about ways of measuring river depth.

You'll reach the McAlpine Lock and Dam at mile 2.56 [13]. This marks the end of the Ship Canal and the completion of the downtown part of the trail.

After walking out on the maintenance road to watch the barges lock through, retrace your footsteps back to the trailhead.

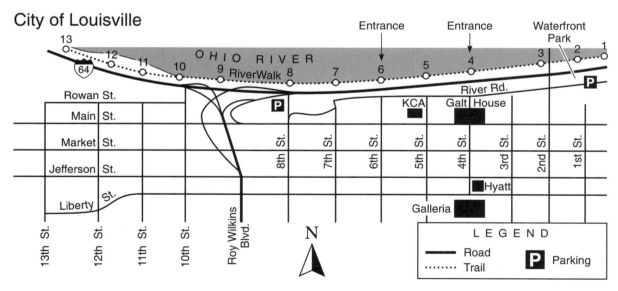

City of Louisville

1. Trailhead
2. Star of Louisville
3. Belle of Louisville
4. Belvedere Plaza
5. Giant flowerpots
6. First overlook
7. Second overlook
8. Lock Keeper's bridge
9. Abandoned factory
10. Railroad tracks
11. Boats Plied the River
12. Measuring river depth
13. McAlpine Lock and Dam

42. Freeman Lake Park

- Step onto broad, sweeping lawns reminiscent of the Great Gatsby period.
- Fish for bass, bluegill, catfish, and crappie in a 120-acre man-made lake.
- Enjoy the rejuvenating effects of the Emerald Cathedral—a natural amphitheater along the banks of General Braddock Creek.

Park Information

Freeman Lake Park is the centerpiece of the Elizabethtown parks and recreation system. In addition to celebrating and memorializing the human history of the area, it provides a wild space in the heart of a major metropolitan center.

The heart of the park is the 120-acre Freeman Lake, which provides fishing and boating opportunities. In addition to appropriate state licenses, a lake permit is required to fish for the lake's bass, bluegill, catfish, and crappie. Rowboats and paddleboats are available for rent, or you can launch your own boat. Only electric motors are permitted.

Freeman Lake Park hosts several special events throughout the year. These include Pops in the Park, the Heartland Festival (a summer concert series), and Christmas in the Park.

Be sure and visit the Lincoln Heritage House, near the park headquarters. Abraham Lincoln's father did the carpentry and cabinet work on this four-room log house, built circa 1805.

Directions: From Elizabethtown go 2 miles north on US-31W to the park entrance road. The trailhead for the Freeman Lake Trail is .6 miles farther north, to Nalls Road, then .6 miles to trailhead. For the John Cox Pirtle Nature Trail, continue to Ring Road. Go right 1 mile to Pear Orchard Road, then right again about a half mile to the parking lot.

Hours Open: Open year-round during daylight hours; some facilities are seasonal.

Facilities: Picnic grounds and pavilions, bandstand, and boat rentals.

Permits and Rules: Foot travel only on trails; no swimming, no alcoholic beverages, no parking on grass; special lake permit necessary for fishing.

Further Information: Freeman Lake Park, 140 Freeman Lake Park Road, Elizabethtown, KY 42701; 502-769-3916.

Other Points of Interest

Vernon Douglas State Nature Preserve (see park #45), **Otter Creek Park** (see park #44), **Tioga Trails** (see park #43), **City of Louisville** (see park #41), **E.P. "Tom" Sawyer State Park** (see park #39), **Taylorsville Lake State Park** (see park #38), and **Bernheim Arboretum and Research Forest** (see park #40) are all within one hour of Freeman Lake Park.

Schmidt's Coca-Cola Museum (502-737-4000), in Elizabethtown, displays the world's largest privately owned collection of Coca-Cola memorabilia.

Also in Elizabethtown is the **Emma Reno Connor Black History Gallery** (502-769-5204), where you can learn about such notables as Josephine Baker, Langston Hughes, and Martin Luther King, Jr.

There are numerous historic and cultural attractions in **Bardstown**, 25 miles east. Contact the Bardstown-Nelson County Tourist and Convention Commission (502-348-4877) for details.

Park Trails

There are 7 miles of hiking trails at Freeman Lake Park—a 5-mile trail circling the lake, with three short loops off it—all part of the Elizabethtown Greenbelt System. Comparatively flat, they are suitable for all levels but are not barrier free.

Freeman Lake Park

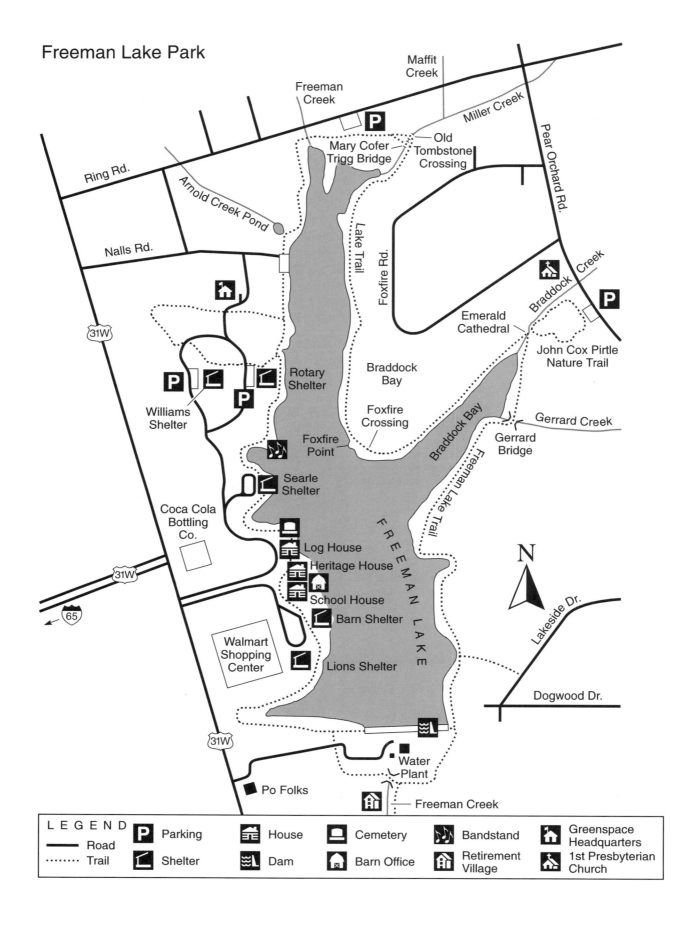

Maffit Creek

Freeman Creek

Miller Creek

Pear Orchard Rd.

Ring Rd.

Arnold Creek Pond

Nalls Rd.

Old Tombstone Crossing

Mary Cofer Trigg Bridge

Lake Trail

Braddock Creek

31W

Foxfire Rd.

Emerald Cathedral

John Cox Pirtle Nature Trail

Rotary Shelter

Braddock Bay

Williams Shelter

P

P

P

Foxfire Crossing

Gerrard Creek

Braddock Bay

Gerrard Bridge

Foxfire Point

Searle Shelter

Freeman Lake Trail

Coca Cola Bottling Co.

Log House

Heritage House

F R E E M A N   L A K E

N

31W

65

School House

Lakeside Dr.

Barn Shelter

Walmart Shopping Center

Dogwood Dr.

Lions Shelter

31W

Water Plant

Po Folks

Freeman Creek

LEGEND

P Parking	House	Cemetery	Bandstand	Greenspace Headquarters	
—— Road	Shelter	Dam	Retirement Village	1st Presbyterian Church	
···· Trail		Barn Office			

Freeman Lake Trail 👢👢

Distance Round-Trip: 4.47 miles

Estimated Hiking Time: 2 to 2.5 hours

Cautions: The area has some exposed roots and muddy patches.

Trail Directions: The Freeman Lake Trail is a long, but easy hike, which follows the shoreline of Freeman Lake. Several access points allow you to create shorter hikes.

The trailhead **[1]** is at the end of Nalls Road, .6 miles from the park headquarters, at the head of a small bay. You'll enter mixed second-growth hardwoods and cedars.

The trail turns right at mile .25, circling the end of the lake parallel to Ring Road **[2]**. You're at the tip of a long arm of the lake. Reentering the woods, you'll turn right, following the east shore of the lake, until coming to a Y at mile .87 **[3]**. You can take either leg—they both lead to Chris Miller Creek. Going left, however, means you have to wade the creek. Go right instead, and you can cross on a footbridge.

On your left are large houses, with broad, sweeping lawns running down to the lake. With a little imagination, you can picture ladies in hoopskirts chasing croquette balls at a 19th-century lawn party.

You'll hopscotch lawns and patches of woods, until leaving the subdivision behind at mile 1.4 and reentering the woods. Then, at mile 2.1 you'll cross General Braddock Creek and enter the Emerald Cathedral **[4]**.

The creek is not named for General Braddock of the French and Indian War fame, but for a slave who was emancipated in 1796.

At the Emerald Cathedral, a natural amphitheater surrounded by towering hardwoods, you'll intersect with the John Cox Pirtle Nature Trail. The junctions can be confusing. Just take any trail turning right— one goes above the amphitheater, the other past the site of the old Patterson limestone quarry (of which nothing remains). The Pattersons, early settlers, ran the quarry and farmed nearby.

The trail continues following the lake, passing an occasional private dwelling, until mile 3.2, where you turn right onto the dam **[5]**, following a mowed path across the earthen structure. About halfway across is a short causeway leading to the pumping station and stairs that go down to the waterworks. Keep going straight. You'll soon reach a blacktop road going to the waterworks. Follow it straight, until reaching the waterworks sign. On your right, across a lawn, you'll see a footbridge. Cross the meadow to it. On the far side the trail, as such, peters out. Follow along the lakeshore from there. You'll have to almost push ducks and geese out of your way. They are thick between here and the headquarters area, which you'll reach at mile 3.7 **[6]**.

In addition to picnic areas, a boat dock, and snack bar, you'll find the Lincoln Heritage House at headquarters. Abraham Lincoln's father did the carpentry and cabinet work on this four-room log house, built around 1805. Continue following the shoreline, past the butterfly garden, to mile 3.8. There's an old graveyard there and two totem poles **[7]** carved from storm-damaged trees. From there, you can follow either the shoreline or the park road through the Cub Scout Camp.

The trail resumes at the end of the scout camp parking lot, at mile 4.2 **[8]**. Follow it back to the trailhead.

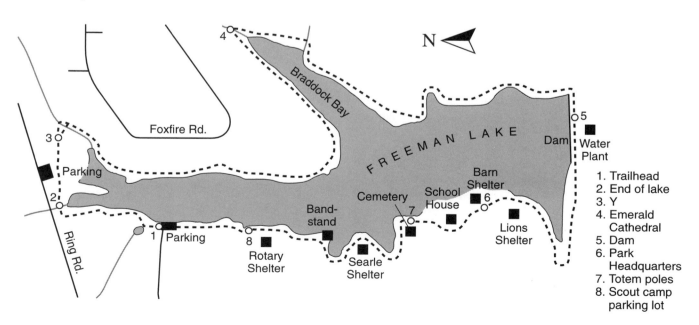

Foxfire Rd.

Braddock Bay

N

3

Parking

2

Ring Rd.

1   Parking

8

Rotary Shelter

Band-stand

Searle Shelter

Cemetery

7

School House

Barn Shelter

6

Lions Shelter

FREEMAN LAKE

Dam

5

Water Plant

1. Trailhead
2. End of lake
3. Y
4. Emerald Cathedral
5. Dam
6. Park Headquarters
7. Totem poles
8. Scout camp parking lot

4

John Cox Pirtle Nature Trail

Distance Round-Trip: .38 miles

Estimated Hiking Time: 20 to 35 minutes

Cautions: The area has some exposed roots.

Trail Directions: The John Cox Pirtle Nature Trail is a short, easy loop that explores and interprets the natural and human history of the area. It is named for John Cox Pirtle, perhaps the foremost advocate of public education in Hardin County in the late 1800s.

The trailhead **[1]** is at a small parking area on Pear Orchard Road. From the park entrance go north on 31W to Ring Road. Turn right, drive about a mile to Pear Orchard Road, then turn right again and go about .6 miles. The trail, which is graveled, starts at an interpretive post next to a billboard. Go left, ignoring all false trails—of which there are several.

At mile .07 you'll reach a hump across the trail **[2]** resembling a speed bump for a giant's car. In the old days, a fence separating two fields had run here, creating this low, artificial ridge that flanks and crosses the trail. Plant secession from field to forest is evident at this spot.

Visible at mile .1 is damage from a windstorm that swept the area in 1993 **[3]**. Numerous trees and limbs scatter the ground, like so many jackstraws.

The John Cox Pirtle Nature Trail passes through several distinct ecosystems. At mile .14 you'll come to the border of two of them **[4]**. Uphill, in the moister ground, are yellow (tulip) poplars. On the drier downslope you'll see a typical oak/hickory upland forest.

The trail descends gradually, until reaching the floodplain of General Braddock Creek and the Emerald Cathedral at mile .18 **[5]**. The Emerald Cathedral is a natural amphitheater surrounded by large, towering hardwoods. Below it, at the creek bank, there used to be a limestone quarry operated by the Patterson family—early settlers and farmers of the area.

Several trails intersect here. Take the right turn at the bottom of the hill. The trail will be as level as a pool table. Almost immediately, at mile .22, you'll cross another ecoborder **[6]**. The oak/hickory forest on the right gives way to bottomland hardwoods—

sycamore, walnut, slippery elm, and so on—on the left, along the creek. It's rare, indeed, that you can see so many distinct environments in so short a distance.

Grapevines sinuously climb a black walnut at mile .26 **[7]**. Notice how smooth skinned the vines are. This differentiates them from the hairy, vinelike version of poison ivy, which is common in these woods.

The Braddock Creek Loop/Wildflower Meadow Trail enters from the left at mile .29 **[8]**. During the spring, this short detour is worthwhile because of the many wildflowers you'll see there. The rest of the year you'll miss nothing by skipping it.

You'll reach a large, storm-damaged, old-growth sugar maple at mile .31 **[9]**. This marks the spot, like a natural gatepost, of an old, rock-lined spring, which was the only water supply for the Patterson family when they farmed here. Lining springs with rocks or trimmed stone was a common way of assuring it stayed clean and free flowing in olden days.

The trail climbs gently from the spring. Along the way you'll pass numerous autumn olive bushes, planted in 1976 by the Junior Soil Conservationists of the county. Behind them you can still pick out pear trees—reminders of the orchard that once thrived here. Pear Orchard Road is named for them.

Continue past the autumn olives to the trailhead.

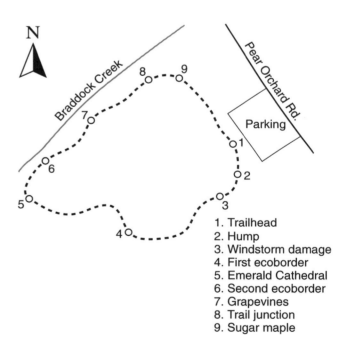

1. Trailhead
2. Hump
3. Windstorm damage
4. First ecoborder
5. Emerald Cathedral
6. Second ecoborder
7. Grapevines
8. Trail junction
9. Sugar maple

43. Tioga Trails

- Cross into history on stone bridges, some of the oldest in Kentucky, dating back more than 150 years.
- Watch water cascade down 130-foot Tioga Falls.
- Examine the forest damage caused in 1991 by a windthrow—which can be as destructive as a tornado.
- See several late 19th-century high trestles that still carry trains.

Park Information

Tioga Trails, located on a portion of Fort Knox used for military training, was developed to display an area with a unique combination of natural beauty and 19th-century history.

The major north and south transportation link, in the mid-19th century, was the L & N Turnpike, which joined Louisville, Kentucky, with Nashville, Tennessee. That road was taken out of public service in 1919, and the route relocated 10 miles west, when Camp Knox became the expanded Fort Knox.

The area was a popular resort destination, too, before the Civil War. Wealthy planters came north, fleeing the malaria epidemics common in the deep south's summer months. This was as far north as they could come, however, and still bring their slaves along. Several hotels, now gone, prospered from such trade.

In the years since the army took over this area, second-growth hardwoods have slowly reclaimed the land. A tree guide, available at the trailhead kiosk, identifies 35 trees and shrubs that now grow along the trails. A second booklet provides the historical background of the L & N Turnpike.

Directions: From Dixie Highway (US-31W) in West Point take the old L & N Turnpike .7 miles to the small picnic area. Trailheads start at information kiosks near the picnic area.

Hours Open: Open year-round, daylight hours only.

Facilities: Picnic tables.

Permits and Rules: No mechanized vehicles (wheelchairs excepted) on trails; collecting archeological or historic items, plants, or fossils prohibited; no alcohol, firearms, metal detectors, fireworks, or glass containers allowed.

Further Information: Fish and Wildlife Division, DPW, Building #112, Fort Knox, KY 40121; 502-624-8674.

Other Points of Interest

Otter Creek Park (see park #44) and **City of Louisville** (see park #41) are within 40 minutes of Tioga Trails.

The Patton Museum of Cavalry and Armor (502-624-3812), just inside the main gate of Fort Knox, commemorates the history and use of armor in warfare.

The Kentucky Derby Museum (502-637-1111), less than 30 minutes north, celebrates the history of the most famous horse race in the world.

Park Trails

The two trails comprising Tioga Trails recreation area rank among the most well-interpreted hiking paths in Kentucky. Pamphlets and trail guides available at the trailhead kiosk combine with on-site signage to provide an in-depth explanation of the area's human and natural history.

Because the trails are located on a part of Fort Knox used for training, they are sometimes closed to public visitation. They are also closed during some hunting seasons. Check with the Fort Knox Hunt Control Office (502-624-7311) to assure the trails are open.

Tioga Trails

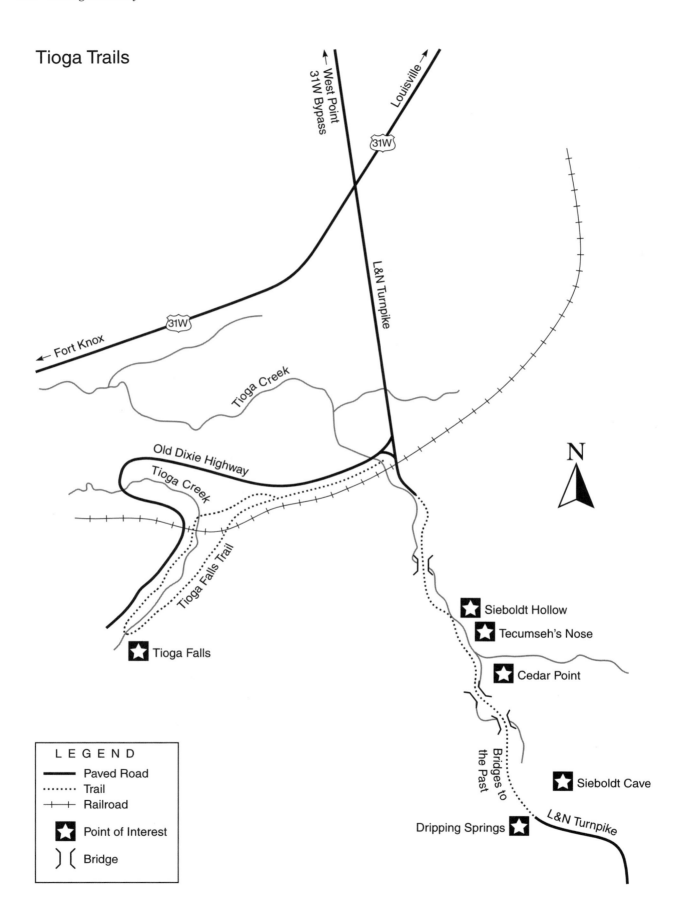

West Point
31W Bypass →

Louisville →

31W

L&N Turnpike

← Fort Knox   31W

Tioga Creek

Old Dixie Highway

Tioga Creek

Tioga Falls Trail

N

⭐ Tioga Falls

⭐ Sieboldt Hollow

⭐ Tecumseh's Nose

⭐ Cedar Point

Bridges to
the Past

⭐ Sieboldt Cave

Dripping Springs ⭐

L&N Turnpike

L E G E N D
━━━ Paved Road
••••• Trail
+–+ Railroad
⭐ Point of Interest
) (Bridge

Tioga Falls Trail 👢👢👢

Distance Round-Trip: 2.1 miles

Estimated Hiking Time: 1.5 to 2 hours

Cautions: Be careful of exposed rocks and roots and difficult stream crossings.

Trail Directions: Arguably the most well-interpreted trail in Kentucky, with 33 sites in the army's trail guide, 35 identified trees, and numerous interpretive signs along the way, Tioga Trails brings the human and natural history of the area alive. The dramatic Tioga Falls is just icing on this rich outdoor cake.

The trailhead **[1]** is at the kiosk near the picnic area. You'll immediately cross a footbridge. To your left is the Paducah and Louisville Railroad trestle, built in 1873. It towers 85 feet high, and stretches 578 feet. The trail climbs from here, passing exposed limestone outcrops rich in fossil shells, coral, and bryozoans.

The first 2,500 feet of trail follows the route of the now extinct Muldraugh Road, which led to Garnettsville. You are climbing part of Muldraugh Hill, an escarpment that runs from the Ohio River deep into the central portion of Kentucky.

At mile .43 you'll cross the railroad tracks, at the site of the old Tioga Railroad Station **[2]**, now gone. Eight trains a day loaded and discharged passengers and freight when the station was active. Caution: These are live tracks, still used by train traffic. To the west is another trestle. This is larger than the first, and you'll pass under it later.

A bit farther you'll see a stone wall about 100 yards downslope **[3]** at mile .48. The wall retains an old wagon road, also still visible.

You'll top out at mile .56, then descend gradually with a drop-off into a deep hollow on the right. Then, at mile .77, there's a stone wall with six steps on the outside **[4]** that seem to lead nowhere. In the old days, passengers could alight from their carriages and walk to the creek below, where a spring house was located, and get themselves a cool drink. Like all other surface water, it is no longer safe to drink untreated.

You'll reach, and cross, Tioga Creek at mile .98. Upstream are the falls **[5]**, which plunge 130 feet over limestone steps, from their source at Tioga Springs. At the top of the falls used to be a hotel used by southern planters fleeing malaria epidemics.

As you wade Tioga Creek, pause in midstream and look below you, where there is a miniature fall that almost replicates Tioga Falls itself. On the far side of the creek you'll find, with a bit of searching, remnants of a dam that created a swimming pond for guests of the Tioga Hotel.

The trail turns right and follows the creek, crossing it several times on footbridges that resemble ladders laid flat.

At mile 1.13 is the old stone spring house noted above **[6]**. The spring no longer flows, but the stone walls of the house remain. Above the spring house you can see the stonework used to contain the wagon road to Tioga Falls.

As you follow the trail, note the fallen trees and limbs, all of which point in the same direction. This is damage remaining from the 1991 windthrow. Winds funneled from a storm travel in one direction but can cause the same kind of damage as a tornado.

You'll pass under the high trestle at mile 1.43 **[7]**. Built more than 100 years ago, it towers 130 feet over our heads and is 707 feet long. The trail climbs left at the trestle, looping back on itself at mile 1.7 **[8]**. The building below you was built in the 1930s as a telephone relay station. It is now a private residence.

Turn left at the trail junction and return to the trailhead.

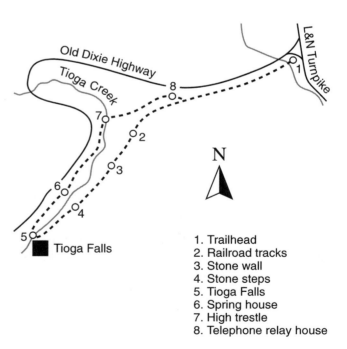

1. Trailhead
2. Railroad tracks
3. Stone wall
4. Stone steps
5. Tioga Falls
6. Spring house
7. High trestle
8. Telephone relay house

Bridges to the Past 👢👢

Distance Round Trip: 2.1 miles

Estimated Hiking Time: 60 to 90 minutes

Cautions: None.

Trail Directions: Bridges to the Past is a section of the old L & N Turnpike, with the original cobblestones paved over. Although the trail is barrier free, the slope is such that people in wheelchairs may require assistance.

The trail passes over several stone bridges built more than 150 years ago. As such, they rank among the oldest in the state. Side trails, at every bridge, lead down to the creek, so you can examine the old stonework. During World War II, German POWs were used to repoint the stonework, and you can still find where some signed their names in the fresh mortar.

Although human history is the main appeal of this trail, don't overlook the natural history of the area, which includes wildflowers, limestone gorges, seasonal waterfalls, and caves.

The trailhead [1] is at a stone traffic barrier south of the picnic area. You'll pass under the L & N Railroad trestle, then, at mile .07, go through a chain-link fence to reach an information kiosk inside the gate [2]. Pick up trail brochures there.

Beyond the kiosk is an old farm road that serviced farms there before World War I. The flats along the creek, known as Poplar Spring, once served as a gypsy camp.

At about mile .09 you can see remnants of the old turnpike at an eroded spot. Below the blacktop are the cobblestones and crushed rock of the original roadbed [3].

You'll reach the site of an old, seasonal mill [4] at mile .15. Built in the early 1800s by Ezekiel Field, it could be operated only a few months of the year, when rains provided a heavy water flow in the creek. Now only slabs of stone mark the site. Field, by the way, had two brothers who were members of the Lewis and Clark Expedition in 1803.

Another old road climbs to the right at mile .4 [5]. It once led to a one-room schoolhouse. There's nothing left of the school, however, so don't climb the hill.

The road follows a limestone gorge, until mile .7, where it crosses the second stone bridge. A bit farther, at mile .73 there's a path leading to the creek [6], which puts you halfway between two bridges. You can examine both of them easily by walking the creek bed.

On your left, at mile .84, is the entrance to Sieboldt Cave [7]. It's now off-limits to visitors, but before the army took over the land, area farmers would cool their milk, cream, and butter in this cave before taking it to market in West Point.

The trail ends at a chain-link fence at mile .88 [8]. To your right is Dripping Springs, a waterfall that sheets down the hillside from a cave in the ridge. This section of the road was often called Dripping Springs Road by natives. Drovers, in the 1800s, often camped here with their livestock on the way to the stockyards in Louisville.

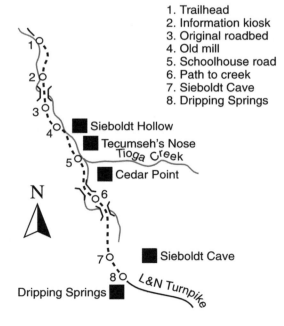

1. Trailhead
2. Information kiosk
3. Original roadbed
4. Old mill
5. Schoolhouse road
6. Path to creek
7. Sieboldt Cave
8. Dripping Springs

Sieboldt Hollow

Tecumseh's Nose

Tioga Creek

Cedar Point

N

Sieboldt Cave

Dripping Springs

L&N Turnpike

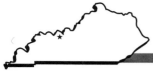

44. Otter Creek Park

- Visually contrast the wilderness-like hill country on the Kentucky side of the Ohio River with the cultivated bottomland of Indiana.
- Watch wildlife such as deer, wild turkey, and songbirds and see a diversity of wildflowers in an area surrounded by exurban sprawl.
- See how riverine systems interconnect to drain vast land areas.

Park Information

Otter Creek is a 26,000-acre park owned by the City of Louisville that provides a diversity of outdoor and nature-study opportunities. In addition to the trails and outdoor camps, the park offers a Nature Center and an astronomical observatory. Special naturalist programs every weekend provide insights into the green world, with activities like watching the night skies, wildflower walks, guided day hikes, and mountain bike rides.

Otter Creek, which forms the eastern boundary of the park, offers fishing, swimming, and the opportunity to explore a gorge for its entire length, from the Fort Knox reserve to the mouth of the creek at the Ohio River.

Sprawling across several ridges and valleys of second-growth forest, the park offers wilderness-like experiences despite widespread development. In addition to the campground, lodge, and cabins, "resident" camps are scattered through the area. These sites are used by youth groups and other organizations for both day and overnight camps.

Despite the popularity of the park and its proximity to population centers, you can still get away from it all in the park's backcountry—especially on weekdays. One cautionary note: The trails in Otter Park are multiuse. Horse riders are supposed to stay on their own specified trails, but some don't. You'll likely encounter horses or their leavings on all the trails. In addition, one mountain biking organization has identi-

fied Otter Creek as the best place to ride in Kentucky and one of the best places in the East. So there are times when bikers outnumber hikers by a large percentage.

Orienteering clubs also use the park. Unfortunately, some of them have neglected to remove their trail markers after the events, further confusing the park's sometimes vague and misleading markers.

Directions: From Louisville, go south on US-31W 30 miles to KY-1638. Turn right (west) and go 3 miles to the park entrance.

Hours Open: Open year-round, sunrise to sunset.

Facilities: Lodging in a lodge and cabins, campground, Nature Center, observatory, and picnic grounds.

Permits and Rules: A modest day-use fee is charged for use of the picnic areas; horses are not allowed on hiking trails.

Further Information: Contact Park Manager, Otter Creek Park, 850 Otter Creek Park Road, Brandenburg, KY 40175; 502-583-3577.

Other Points of Interest

Tioga Falls and **Bridges to the Past** (see park #43), two trails maintained by Fort Knox, are 6 miles north on US-31W. **Jefferson County Memorial Forest, E.P. "Tom" Sawyer State Park** (see park #39), **Bernheim Arboretum and Research Forest** (see park #40), and **Freeman Lake Park** (see park #42) all lie within 45 minutes of Otter Creek.

Twelve miles south, on the Fort Knox Reservation, is the **Patton Museum of Cavalry and Armor** (502-624-3812), which traces the history and development of armored warfare.

Louisville offers many attractions. Particularly noteworthy is the downtown "iron" district, which contains the second-largest collection of cast-iron buildings in the world, many of which have been preserved and restored. Contact the Louisville Convention and Visitors Bureau (502-584-2121).

Park Trails

There are about 20 total miles of trail in the park, including 5 miles of horse trail. Although the trails are generally well blazed, there are several confusing, badly marked, or unmarked trail junctures. You are likely to meet mountain bikers on all trails.

Blue Trail —8.1 miles—circles the entire park. Of all the trails in the park, this one offers the experience that is the most wilderness-like.

Horse Trail —5.3 miles—meanders through most sections of the park, but there are better hiking trails.

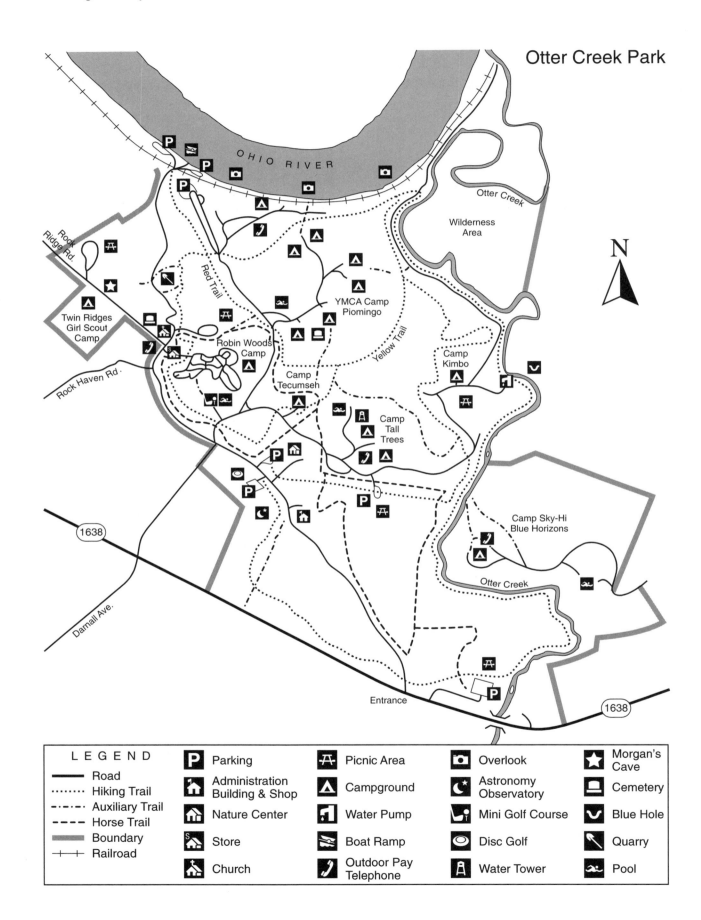

Otter Creek Park

OHIO RIVER

Otter Creek

Wilderness Area

Red Trail

Twin Ridges Girl Scout Camp

Rock Ridge Rd.

Rock Haven Rd.

Robin Woods Camp

YMCA Camp Piomingo

Yellow Trail

Camp Kimbo

Camp Tecumseh

Camp Tall Trees

Camp Sky-Hi Blue Horizons

Otter Creek

1638

Darnall Ave.

Entrance

1638

N

LEGEND
— Road
..... Hiking Trail
-.-.- Auxiliary Trail
- - - Horse Trail
— Boundary
+—+ Railroad

P Parking
Administration Building & Shop
Nature Center
S Store
Church

Picnic Area
Campground
Water Pump
Boat Ramp
Outdoor Pay Telephone

Overlook
Astronomy Observatory
Mini Golf Course
Disc Golf
Water Tower

Morgan's Cave
Cemetery
Blue Hole
Quarry
Pool

Yellow Trail 👢👢👢👢👢

Distance Round-Trip: 3.8 miles

Estimated Hiking Time: 2.5 to 3.5 hours

Cautions: You will encounter exposed rocks and roots, loose rock, water crossing the trail, rickety footbridges, and poorly marked trail junctions.

Trail Directions: The trail offers a challenging hike over several ridges and into deep hollows, with steep climbs and descents, and several natural overlooks into the Otter Creek Valley. The trailhead **[1]** is behind the Nature Center. You'll cross an open meadow on a mowed path, toward a wooden footbridge. Before crossing it, turn left into the woods on an unmarked trail. In about 500 feet you'll T into another trail. Go right, crossing a blacktop road.

You'll T again at mile .35. Off the trail are the foundations of some old cabins and the remains of a chimney **[2]**. Go right. You'll soon come to a confusing trail juncture at mile .45 **[3]**. Follow the sign to the YMCA Camp and River Overlook.

The trail roller-coasters through second-growth hardwoods until it Ts once more at mile 1.05 **[4]**. The Yellow Trail makes a double right turn here. Two hundred feet further it descends steeply, with a marker cautioning "Slower—Danger." The trail is rutted, and it has many exposed roots and rocks for the next 500 feet; it then levels out at a broken and washed-out footbridge. Do not attempt to cross here! There's a second bridge only 30 feet further.

After another 500 feet, a second sign cautions "Slower—Danger," and you repeat the process, this time bottoming out in a gas line right-of-way at mile 1.34 **[5]**. Notice the differences in vegetation as you pass from a woodland into a meadow/prairie environment, with tall grasses, different wildflowers, and the cloud shadows playing leapfrog downhill.

On the far side of the right-of-way the trail starts descending, then steepens as you reenter the woods. Fifty feet into the trees, you'll T into an unmarked trail. Go left, downhill. A hundred feet later you'll bottom out at a creek and an old road, where the trail markers seem to disappear. Bear hard right along the roadbed for about 100 feet, and the trail enters the woods, following the creek and climbing steeply. At mile 1.83 you'll cross a second rickety footbridge **[6]**. The trail bears right, circling a huge hollow. When the foliage is thick, you sense great depth, though you can't see much.

For the next .5 miles there will be more human encroachment as you descend gradually. You'll pass another gas line right-of-way and hear the sounds of campers below you at Camp Kimbo before bottoming out at a pumping station. Cross the new footbridge there, and follow the trail as it parallels the camp access road. You'll cross yet another rickety footbridge, then start climbing again at mile 2.47. A few feet further, the trail Ts. Go left.

After crossing a broken blacktop road, you'll follow the edge of a canyon carved by Otter Creek. The trail is very steep, with high cliffs on the left. Finally, you'll top out at a natural limestone overlook **[7]** at mile 2.75.

From this perch you become one with the processes that shaped the canyon. Perhaps, as we did, you'll gain a sense of geologic time and feel the creek cutting the gorge ever deeper.

The overlook itself is a set of mini-limestone ridges, forming a set of steps. There is no safety rail, and there is a dangerous drop below the lowest step. Obey the "stop" sign painted on the rock, and mind youngsters carefully.

The trail follows the cliff edge, ascending gradually and providing periodic glimpses into the canyon. It then Ts into a power line right-of-way and turns downhill with it, passing the Pine Grove picnic area at mile 3.2. Continue down the right-of-way to a gravel road, where the trail ends. The Nature Center is across the field in front of you.

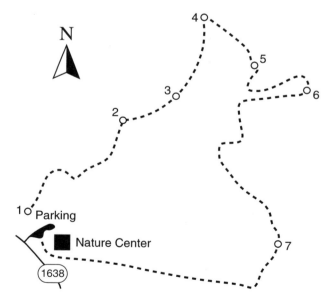

1. Trailhead
2. Remains of old cabins
3. Confusing trail junction
4. Double right turn
5. Gas line right-of-way
6. Rickety footbridge and hollow
7. Overlook

Red Trail 👢👢👢 or 👢👢👢👢 with alternate trailhead

Distance Round-Trip: 3.3 miles; 4.25 miles with alternate trailhead

Estimated Hiking Time: 2.5 to 3 hours

Cautions: You will encounter high cliffs, exposed roots and rocks, loose rocks, muddy patches, and poorly marked trail junctions. Keep in mind that mountain bikes and horses are allowed on the trail.

Trail Directions: This is a shorter version of the Yellow Trail, with less climbing and with overlooks along the Ohio River.

The hike can be extended if you use an alternative trailhead at the Ohio River picnic area. This involves a strenuous uphill climb and adds almost 1 mile to the trip. You can avoid the climb by parking at the lodge instead. You'll have a short, easy hike if you follow the trail from the lodge to the overlook and back.

The trailhead [1] starts behind the Nature Center, through an open meadow on a mowed path. When you reach a footbridge, turn left and enter the woods on an unmarked trail. You'll soon T. Go right, cross a blacktop road, and follow the trail until it Ts again above Camp Tecumseh at mile .35 [2]. In front of you are the foundations and a chimney of some old cabins. Turn right. At mile .45 you'll reach a confusing junction of several trails [3]. Go left, following the sign that says "YMCA Camp Piomingo—Main Gate— Lodge—River."

You'll cross a boggy area on a beam walkway and then reach a blacktop road a little further. Angle slightly left as you cross the road. The trail is unmarked, but obvious. It will intersect with a trail from the YMCA camp. Go straight, descending gradually. Ignore false trails on the right and left. At the Y, go right, uphill. You'll cross a creek, then come to open woods with a shallow hollow on the left at mile .87 [4].

In the hollow, laid helter-skelter like jackstraws in a wind, are several large downed trees. These trees went down in 1974 when a tornado swept through the region. Even deep in the woods, wind can have a damaging effect on the forest.

In 600 feet, you'll T with the Blue Trail. Go right here. Then, 100 feet farther, is a very confusing trail juncture. Red blazes go left. Ignore them: they lead to the lodge and alternative trailhead. Instead, go right,

following the sign saying "cabins 1-10." A little farther you'll cross the blacktop road leading to the lodge, then cross a gravel road, and eventually a power line right-of-way. There are only blue blazes in this stretch, but you're on the right trail. A little further on, you pass a trail to the cabins, and the red blazes start again.

At mile 1.5 [5], the Ohio River comes into view, below on your right. The trail follows the river until you reach a three-way junction at mile 1.6 [6]. On the right is the opening into a small cave that drops straight down to the river. It appears like a narrow, rough-hewn well, or maybe a gateway to Hades. Although it serves as a drain here, you'd think it was a spring where it emerges on the banks of the Ohio.

The middle path is a false trail leading uphill. Go left, following the river. At mile 1.7 you'll reach a natural rock overlook [7]. From here the river curves right and left. On the Kentucky side is only wilderness, with regiments of trees marching down to the river's edge. Across the river are the rich, cultivated bottoms of Indiana.

The trail now follows the ridge overlooking Otter Creek Valley. If the foliage is thin, you can see the confluence of Otter Creek and the Ohio River. At mile 2.0, the Red Trail merges with the Yellow Trail. Go right, following red and yellow blazes until reaching the multi-trail junction above Camp Tecumseh. From there, retrace your steps to the Nature Center.

1. Trailhead
2. Cabin remains
3. Confusing trail junction
4. Tornado hollow
5. Ohio River views
6. Three-way junction and cave
7. Overlook

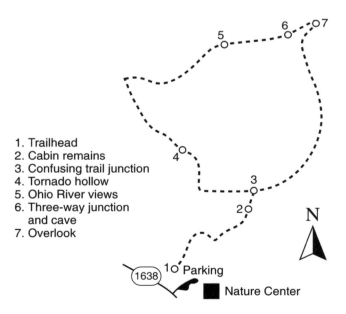

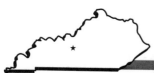

45. Vernon Douglas State Nature Preserve

- Walk through one of the most mature second-growth forests in the Knobs Physiographic Region.
- Stand on the pinnacle, an overlook projecting out over the Younger Creek valley.
- See one of the most profuse displays of spring wildflowers in Kentucky.

Park Information

A new preserve, dedicated in 1992, Vernon Douglas State Nature Preserve protects one of the most mature second-growth forests in the Knobs Physiographic Region. Although commonly thought of as part of the Appalachians, the Knobs are a distinct geologic formation that resulted from the erosion of a sedimentary plateau.

The 730-acre preserve is located within a rugged, steep, forested section of Hardin County, where you'll see stands of sugar maple, beech, and tulip poplar. Many trees resemble old-growth in their size and diameter, but they are mature second-growth.

You can see numerous wildflowers throughout the growing season, with the springtime period (March-May) showing the most diversity. At any time, 30 to 40 varieties may be blooming.

Several ecosystems are encompassed by the preserve, from the moist valley bottom to dry ridges.

Directions: From Elizabethtown, Kentucky, take US-62 east 9 miles to KY-583. Turn right after 4 miles. Immediately after crossing the Bluegrass Parkway, turn right onto Audubon Trace Road, a gravel road. Go .7 miles to parking area on left.

Hours Open: Open year-round during daylight hours.

Facilities: None.

Permits and Rules: Foot travel only on trail; no fires, camping, alcoholic beverages, or firearms.

Further Information: Kentucky State Nature Preserves Commission, 801 Schenkel Lane, Frankfort, KY 40601; 502-573-2886.

Other Points of Interest

Rough River Dam State Resort Park (see park #46), **Freeman Lake Park** (see park #42), **Otter Creek Park** (see park #44), and **Tioga Trails** (see park #43) are within one hour of Vernon Douglas State Nature Preserve.

Schmidt's Coca-Cola Museum (502-737-4000), in Elizabethtown, displays the world's second largest privately owned collection of Coca-Cola memorabilia.

Also in Elizabethtown is the **Emma Reno Connor Black History Gallery** (502-769-5204), where you can learn about such notables as Josephine Baker, Langston Hughes, and Martin Luther King, Jr.

Park Trails

Although there is only one trail, it crosses all the ecosystems in the preserve. Off-trail travel for wildflower, bird, and wildlife watching is not permitted. The countryside is rough and steep, and rattlesnakes and poison ivy are possible hazards off the trail.

Vernon Douglas Nature Trail

👢👢👢

Distance Round-Trip: 3.4 miles

Estimated Hiking Time: 2 to 2.5 hours

Cautions: There are tree trunks across trail and exposed rocks and roots.

Trail Directions: The trailhead **[1]** is at the post and cable fence at the rear of the parking lot. The young second-growth and older cedars you initially pass through belie the mature forest that highlights the preserve.

The trail climbs gradually. At mile .05 a blow-down jungle lines the trail **[2]**. As you climb, the hardwoods increase in size, because you are entering a mature forest of sugar maple, beech, and tulip poplar.

The trail steepens slightly until you cross a drain by bridge, then descends gradually, following the edge of a hollow. At mile .33 you cross a drain on puncheons made by splitting a single cedar and setting it in place, round side down **[3]**.

The trail steepens at mile .38 as it climbs around a large hollow on the left **[4]**. Stay alert, as there are likely to be wild turkey in the hollow, as well as other wildlife. A little farther you'll come to a steep pitch, until reaching a T at mile .59 **[5]**. A trail post marker says "Loop 2.5 miles" with an arrow pointing both

ways. Go left, uphill. The trail—which has much loose and exposed rock in this section—is a finger of ridge between two hollows.

You'll top out on a ridge at mile .71 **[6]**. The trail will be level along the ridgetop, as it skirts hollows on one or both sides.

At mile 1.1, after passing a privately owned meadow that may have deer feeding in it, you'll reach several beeches **[7]**. Look among their roots for beech drops, which are nongreen flowering plants that look like dried flower arrangements.

Continue along the ridge to mile 1.3. On the left is a large cedar stump, sanded and polished by wind and water until it looks like a sculpture you'd expect to find in a museum **[8]**.

The trail starts descending soon, gradually at first, then more steeply, until mile 1.8, where it doglegs left at a trail marker **[9]** and false trail on the right. The trail narrows here, becoming a foot-wide ledge along the sidehill, parallel to the parkway. Then, at mile 2.1, it seems to disappear **[10]**.

In actuality, the trail is faint, and may be covered with leaves, as it switches back left a full 180 degrees and descends like a snake, until bottoming out at mile 2.0 **[11]**.

After steepening somewhat, the trail follows an old dirt road uphill. This will be a long haul, but emerald mosses and parti-colored wildflowers smile you on your way, until mile 2.7, where you'll rejoin the original trail junction **[5]**. Turn left and follow it to the trailhead.

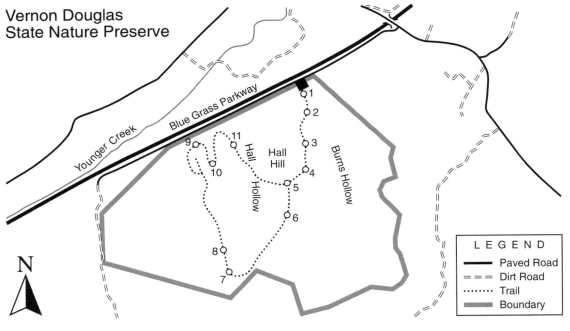

1. Trailhead
2. Blow-down jungle
3. Cedar puncheons
4. Large hollow
5. T
6. Top out on ridge
7. Climax beeches
8. Sculptured stump
9. Trail marker
10. Trail disappears
11. Bottom out

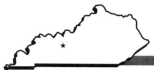

46. Rough River Dam State Resort Park

- Check out the fishing in 4,860-acre Rough River Lake.
- Enjoy the music at the annual Kentucky Championship Old-Time Fiddler's Contest.
- See the effects of artificial tides on the limestone of the Highland Rim.

Park Information

Rough River Dam State Resort Park sprawls along the western shore of 4,860-acre Rough River Lake, a flood-control impoundment in the Highland Rim country. When the lake filled in 1961, it created a multipurpose marine environment that provides flood control, water supply, and recreation.

The marina at Rough River Dam State Resort Park, with more than 200 covered and open slips, offers unparalleled opportunities for boating and fishing. Rental boats are available as well as a boat launch.

One of only two facilities in the state park system with its own airstrip, the park hosts the Kentucky Championship Old-Time Fiddler's Contest the third weekend each July. Hundreds of fiddlers play Bluegrass and mountain music as they compete for the coveted state champion title.

Because Rough River Lake is a flood-control facility, there can be extreme differences in water levels between summer and winter pools. These artificial tides have affected the exposed limestones of the shore, softening and rotting the stone, and exposing numerous fossils—which you can see, but not collect. They're protected under the National Antiquities Act.

Directions: From exit 94 on the Western Kentucky Parkway, take KY-79 north 15 miles to the second park entrance, then .5 miles to the lodge.

Hours Open: Open year-round; some facilities are seasonal.

Facilities: Lodge, cottages, camping, airport, golf, swimming pool, picnic grounds, marina, 10-station fitness trail.

Permits and Rules: Foot travel only on trails.

Further Information: Rough River Dam State Resort Park, 450 Lodge Road, Falls of Rough, KY 40119; 502-257-2311.

Other Points of Interest

Pine Knob Outdoor Theater (502-879-8190) offers *Doc Brown* and other productions about the history and folklore of the area during the summer. Performances are given on Friday and Saturday evenings, under the stars, June through September.

Falls of Rough (502-257-8160) is a National Register of Historic Places site that was a plantation and business community owned by one family. Currently undergoing restoration, only the **Green Farms General Store Museum** is open for visitation, but you can see the mill and manor house from the outside. The mill is slated for restoration soon.

Park Trails

Trails in the park are easy, with occasional steeper pitches that throw them into higher difficulty categories than may be warranted.

Rough River Dam State Resort Park

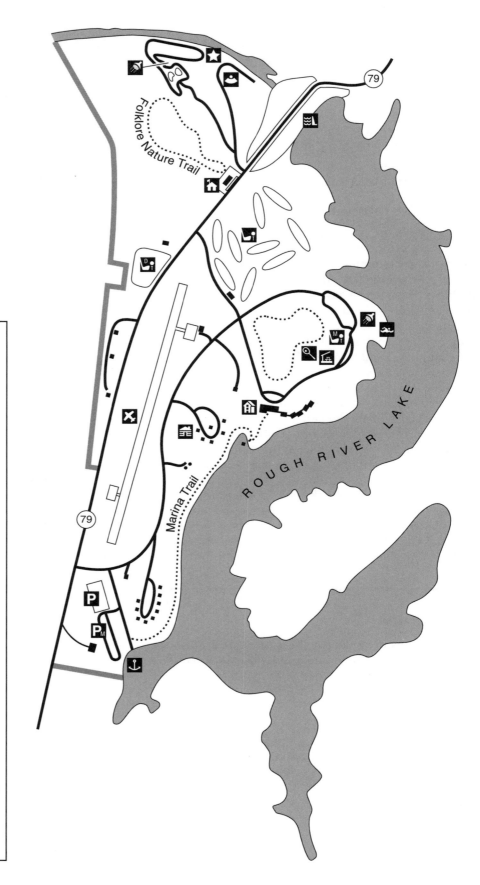

Marina Trail 👢👢👢

Distance Round-Trip: 1.49 miles

Estimated Hiking Time: 1 hour

Cautions: The area includes high cliffs and some exposed rock.

Trail Directions: The one-way Marina Trail offers almost continuous vistas of Rough River Dam Lake, as it follows a bluff along the shoreline. Although a short, easy path, the views are worthwhile, especially during the peak foliage of late October.

The trailhead **[1]** is a gravel path behind and below the lodge. You'll descend a series of broad erosion-control platforms that are so flat the incline is almost imperceptible. It's quite a drop to the lakeshore, where you bottom out, at mile .06, at the head of an inlet to a large bay **[2]**. During the fall months, multicolored trees draw your eye along the sinuous shoreline to the main lake and the hills beyond.

After crossing the inlet on a wooden footbridge at mile .12 **[3]** make a hard left, on a hard-packed sand trail. Take some time to explore the shoreline here. The rocks and shingle that pave the water's edge result from the artificial tides created by the Corps of Engineers as they raise and lower the lake level with the seasons.

You may come across several fossils while you're at it. This area was once the bed of a shallow sea.

At mile .21 you'll cross a creek on a cement slab, then climb through thick, second-growth bottomland hardwoods. Mixed with them, however, are several large climax beeches, which dominate the woods with their size.

Don't be surprised, at mile .33, if the air is suddenly and silently filled with winged shadows **[4]**. There's a buzzard roosting area on your left, and, when spooked by your presence, they take flight with barely a sound. A whisper of wide, black wings brushing a branch, then a couple wing beats, and they catch thermals coming off the lake, soaring in wide circles until your disturbance settles.

At mile .46 a false trail, used by park maintenance people, leads down to the lake **[5]**. You can take it, if you like, but there's not much down there that you can't see better elsewhere. Also, it can be a thigh-busting climb back up. Better skip it.

You'll pass a set of stairs leading uphill to the park playground, then, at mile .57, reach a natural stone overlook **[6]**. From here, especially during the leafless months, there's a panoramic view of the main lake. The landmass to your left is an island, not the far shore. This view is especially appealing during fall color, although it's partially obscured by the foliage.

The trail descends gently at mile .67 below the cabins. You'll step across a V-shaped cement drain. A few feet farther the trail ends on a cliff overlooking the marina, at mile .74 **[7]**.

Retrace your steps to return to the trailhead.

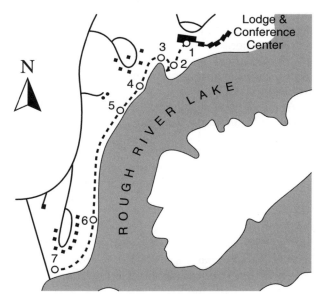

1. Trailhead
2. Inlet
3. Footbridge
4. Buzzard roost
5. False trail to lake
6. Stone overlook
7. Cliff overlook

Folklore Nature Trail 👢👢👢

Distance Round-Trip: .71 miles

Estimated Hiking Time: 35 to 50 minutes

Cautions: The area includes some exposed rock.

Trail Directions: The Folklore Nature Trail is a well-interpreted trail with 27 marked sites that highlight and identify the natural and human history of the area.

The trailhead **[1]** is at a billboard near the west end of the Corps of Engineers parking lot, across KY-79 from the park entrance. Trail guides to the 27 sites are in a box there. Unfortunately, several of the numbered posts are missing or rotted away.

You'll start on a paved, barrier-free sidewalk that leads behind the headquarters building. In just a few steps the trail takes off to the right, descending through mixed cedars and second-growth hardwoods. At the bottom of the hill, at mile .02, is the remains of a moonshiner's still **[2]**. Now only decayed barrel staves and metal hoops remain from what had been (and, in some sections, remains) a thriving industry in rural Kentucky.

At about mile .07 (the post is missing) is site 3, referring to sassafras. You can't miss this plant with the mitten-shaped leaves, though, because there are three variations of the leaves on the same plant. Sassafras was an important medicinal and culinary plant for early settlers, who used it to cure fevers, skin troubles, gout, and stomach problems. It was also made into tea, candy, and jelly.

You'll cross the first of several footbridges at mile .12 **[3]**. This one goes over a V-valley, at the mouth of a creek. Erosion causes the banks of creeks to widen much farther than the stream itself. In cross section, they look like the letter V.

Site 7, at mile .16, is a small cave **[4]**, typical of those found in karst topography. Karsts are soluble limestones under a protective sandstone cap. Groundwater dissolves portions of the limestone, creating caves and sinkholes.

At mile .18 you'll come to the only unmarked junction on the trail **[5]**. Take the left arm of the Y, descending across exposed rock slabs and erosion steps. The trail levels out, until mile .29, where you'll T into a footbridge **[6]**. The campground is on the right. Go left for the trail. A couple hundred feet farther, at mile .34, you'll enter an area of old, second-growth hardwoods. These trees tower above you, like a green cathedral, while the sun dapples the understory, which is only knee-high to these giants.

The trail Ys again at mile .36. On the left is a side trail leading to a spring at mile .37 **[7]**. Sometime in the past, a settler lined the spring with limestone blocks, which now are covered thickly with moss. This is surrounded by a semicircular rock grotto.

Climb back to the main trail, which itself climbs steeply up erosion steps. You'll top out at some benches, which couldn't be located at a handier place. After catching your breath, continue about 100 feet where, at mile .45, you'll see some large, multilimbed climax beeches **[8]**.

Site 23, at mile .58, is a shagbark hickory **[9]**, one of the most useful trees for pioneers, who preferred it for heating, smoking food, furniture, and wagon beds. Hickory withes (thin, flexible branches) were used for hanging dried and smoked foods, and, as switches in the classroom. To your right are some cedars. Beyond them is a wildlife clearing, where you are likely to spot deer early in the morning or late in the afternoon.

You'll T onto the barrier-free sidewalk at mile .63. Go left a few feet to the settler's cabin (site 27) **[10]**, which you can examine to your heart's content. When finished, return to the trailhead on the sidewalk.

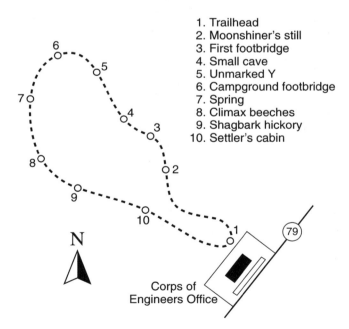

1. Trailhead
2. Moonshiner's still
3. First footbridge
4. Small cave
5. Unmarked Y
6. Campground footbridge
7. Spring
8. Climax beeches
9. Shagbark hickory
10. Settler's cabin

N

Corps of
Engineers Office

Western Waterlands

Geologically, there are two Kentuckies. Nine-tenths of the state was formed by carboniferous sediments deposited in shallow seas, lakes, and streambeds during the Mississippian and Pennsylvanian periods. The final, and youngest, part was formed when a northern arm of the Gulf of Mexico covered extreme western Kentucky during the Mesozoic and Cenozoic Eras.

The Tennessee River marks the boundary between these two provinces. East of the river lie the sediments and eroded hillsides of the Interior Low Plateaus. West of the river are the sandy soil and poorly compacted gravels of the Gulf Coastal Plain.

The Western Waterlands are bordered by the Ohio River on the north, the Mississippi River on the west, Tennessee on the south, and an imaginary line going south to north from Guthrie to Hawesville.

Topography

Along the Ohio River is the western portion of the Shawnee Hills, composed of eroded limestones and sandstones but lacking the high cliffs and scarps of the Eastern Highlands.

South and west of the hills are the rolling plains of the Pennyrile, a limestone karst plain with few surface streams and numerous sinkholes formed when underground caves and fissures collapsed.

Because early settlers found no trees here, they thought the land was infertile and referred to it as the barrens. The rich, limestone soils of the area, in reality, make first-rate farmland.

West of the Tennessee River is the Gulf Coastal Plain, the youngest part of Kentucky. Here you'll find a low, flat landscape, typified by sandy soils and few rock formations. Poorly compacted tertiary sandstones and loose quarternary gravels are found under the thin soil, most of which is floodplain.

Major Rivers and Lakes

Four major rivers not only flow through, but define, the Western Waterlands: the Ohio River to the north, the Mississippi River to the west, and the Tennessee and Cumberland Rivers, which divide the area on a north to south axis.

The Tennessee and Cumberland Rivers parallel each other, flowing north out of Tennessee. The isolated country between them was known as "the land between the rivers" until the Tennessee Valley Authority (TVA) dammed the flows to create two huge impoundments. Lake Barkley was formed in the Cumberland River, and Kentucky Lake was impounded from the Tennessee River. The landmass surrounded by the impoundments is now known as Land Between the Lakes (LBL).

The Tennessee River is navigable its entire length. In fact, barge traffic, using a series of locks, dams, and canals, can travel from Paducah to the Gulf of Mexico near the Alabama and Mississippi border.

Other rivers in the area include the Green, Rough, and Tradewater, east of Land Between the Lakes, and the Mayfield and Obion to the west.

West of Land Between the Lakes is the Gulf Coastal Plain, which is flat and marshy. Unique to Kentucky are the small, natural lakes found here. Everywhere else in the state, lakes and ponds are formed by damming rivers and streams.

Common Plant Life

Although primarily agricultural lands, much of the Western Waterlands remains forested. Indeed, all 84 species of trees native to Kentucky can be found here.

Surprisingly, there are tracts of old-growth forest in the region, especially along the Ohio River. John James Audubon State Park, which is located in downtown Henderson, contains many examples of such old-growth, including oaks, hickories, and beeches.

Some of the largest, and oldest, grapevines in the state are located in the Western Waterlands. Grapevines five inches thick are not unusual, and hikers can pass vines nearly a foot in diameter on some trails.

The diverse habitats of the Western Waterlands support numerous wildflowers. Nearly 400 species can be found here, with the festively colored blooms succeeding each other from March through November. Many of the lilies—such as the white trout lily and the spider lily, absent or infrequent in eastern Kentucky—can be found here. The recurved trillium is another species restricted to the western third of the state.

Poison ivy, although encountered less frequently along hiking trails than farther east, is still common.

Because of differences in the soil, less tobacco is grown here than elsewhere in the state. Agriculture is based more on corn and soybeans, and recent attempts at viniculture seem to be working.

Common Birds and Mammals

As in the rest of the state, white-tailed deer are common throughout the Western Waterlands. However, thanks to native species restoration work at Land Between the Lakes, you can see other large game animals as well. Bison and elk herds, for instance, are maintained in a special 700-acre enclosure.

Fallow deer run wild at Land Between the Lakes as well. Originally introduced on private property before TVA took over, the fallow escaped and have thrived. You can recognize them from their palmated, mooselike antlers.

Swamp rabbits, a subspecies of the cottontail, can be found in some marshy backwaters. Their webby feet—actually stiff hairs growing between their toes—allow them to move about in the muck as if they were wearing snowshoes.

Birdlife is abundant and varied. It was no accident that John James Audubon chose Henderson when he painted *Birds of America*. It was, and remains, a haven for more than 250 species—although some present when he lived are now gone and others have moved in that did not share Kentucky when he worked here.

Of special note are the twice-annual warbler migrations that pass through. As many as 20 species rest in western Kentucky on their way south in the winter and north in the summer.

Wild turkey can be found throughout the region. In fact, much of the early restoration work was done in Land Between the Lakes. Birds raised there were used to stock other parts of Kentucky.

The confluence region, where the Ohio and Mississippi Rivers meet, is a magnet for waterfowl. Several refuges provide safe nesting and wintering areas for vast flocks of ducks and Canada geese. In recent years, snow geese also have been stopping at these refuges during the winter months.

Thanks to enlightened management practices, bald eagles have made a comeback in the Bluegrass state and are commonly seen in Land Between the Lakes and along the rivers.

Climate

Although classified as temperate, the weather of western Kentucky approaches subtropical at times, thanks to the moderating influence of the major rivers and the weather systems that sweep up from the southwest.

By and large, expect average temperatures to be five degrees warmer than the rest of the state and the humidity to be at least as high. Summer highs in the upper 90s are common, along with humidity hovering around 95 percent. Winters, on the other hand, usually are mild, with lows in the upper 20s to mid-50s. Even in winter, rain is more likely than snow.

Best Features

- Land Between the Lakes, a 170,000-acre outdoor recreation area sandwiched between Lake Barkley and Kentucky Lake.
- Sloughs Wildlife Management Area, where as many as 60,000 Canada geese can be seen wintering over.
- Cypress swamps and natural lakes edged by these seemingly out-of-place trees.
- Wickliffe Mounds and museum, where you can explore the artifacts left behind by a prehistoric native civilization.

47. Yellow Creek Park

- Visit a restored one-room schoolhouse used by the Black community of Daviess County.
- See 36 identified tree species, including some uncommon in Kentucky, such as bald cypress.
- Visually explore the park from the top of a restored 1960 fire lookout tower.

Park Information

Nestled along the wooded banks of Yellow Creek, the park provides 110 acres of multipurpose outdoor recreation.

One highlight is the diversity of bridges in Yellow Creek Park. There are two reconstructed covered bridges over Yellow Creek, for instance, and a circa 1800s iron bridge that once spanned the larger Panther Creek west of Owensboro.

The park's Nature Center, an outdoor classroom for nature studies, is a young oak/hickory forest, interspersed with Scotch pine and red maple. Three dozen tree species are identified in the Nature Center. However, because the canopy of this young forest is open, vines such as Virginia creeper and bittersweet grow in profusion.

Rich in wildflowers, more than 60 varieties have been identified in the park, along with about 100 species of birds. Wildlife includes deer, coyote, fox, raccoon, and several species of bat. Waterfowl, shorebirds, and turtles are abundant on the two-acre lake. Fishing for bass, bluegill, and catfish is permitted for youngsters and seniors only.

A restored 1960 fire tower provides an aerial view of the park and its wild areas.

As you explore Yellow Creek Park, note that the picnic tables, benches, and other seating are made from large limestone blocks. These were quarried locally long before the War Between the States, and were moved here to provide rustic and historic seating areas.

One seating area, along with a tree-finder compass, sits beside a waterfall just after entering the Nature Center over the iron bridge.

Directions: From Owensboro take US-60 east about 4 miles to KY-144. Follow it 1.7 miles to the park entrance. Turn right and go .8 miles on the park road to the Nature Center.

Hours Open: Open year-round, 7:00 A.M. to dusk.

Facilities: Events gazebo, roofed barbecue pit, athletic fields, picnic area, fishing for youngsters and seniors, restored one-room schoolhouse.

Permits and Rules: Foot travel only on trails.

Further Information: Daviess County Parks and Recreation Department, 5620 Highway 144, Owensboro, KY 42303; 502-281-5346.

Other Points of Interest

Panther Creek Park (see park #48) is just west of Owensboro. **John James Audubon State Park** (see park #49) is 25 miles west in Henderson.

Ben Hawes State Park (502-684-9808), 4 miles west of Owensboro, is said to have the best golf course in Kentucky.

There are numerous cultural and historic sites in **Owensboro and Daviess County**. For information, contact Owensboro-Daviess County Tourism Commission, 215 East Second Street, Owensboro, KY 42301; 502-926-1100.

Park Trails

Yellow Creek Park offers almost 4 miles of hiking trails, all of them accessible off the 2-mile Adventure Trail loop. You can combine them in various ways to provide longer hikes that pass through all the park's ecosystems.

Challenge Trail —.02 miles round-trip—is a paved, barrier-free trail leading to a decked platform overlooking Yellow Creek.

Creek Trail —1 mile round-trip—follows Yellow Creek. Creek Trail overlays the Adventure Trail its entire length.

Yellow Creek Park

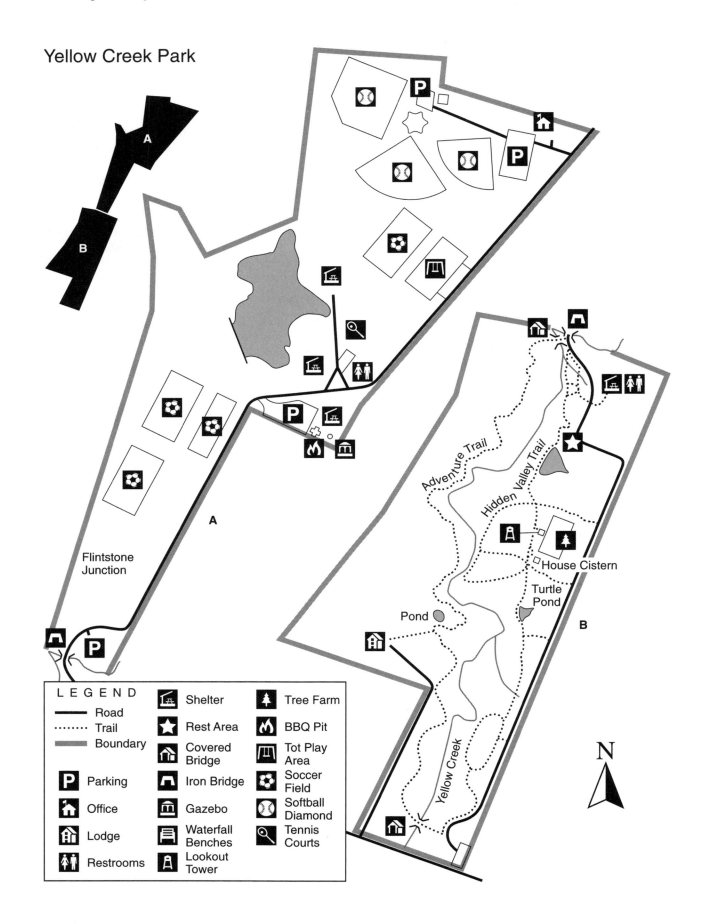

Flintstone
Junction

A

B

Adventure Trail

Hidden Valley Trail

House Cistern

Turtle
Pond

Pond

Yellow Creek

N

L E G E N D
—— Road
········ Trail
▬▬ Boundary

P Parking
🏠 Office
🏠 Lodge
🚻 Restrooms

Shelter
⭐ Rest Area
Covered Bridge
Iron Bridge
Gazebo
Waterfall Benches
Lookout Tower

🌲 Tree Farm
🔥 BBQ Pit
Tot Play Area
⚽ Soccer Field
⚾ Softball Diamond
🔍 Tennis Courts

Adventure Trail (Blue) 👢👢

Distance Round-Trip: 1.2 miles

Estimated Hiking Time: 1 to 1.25 hours

Cautions: The area includes high creek banks and some exposed roots.

Trail Directions: Reach the trailhead **[1]** by crossing the iron bridge. On your left is a seating area, waterfall, and tree-finder compass. On your right is a covered bridge.

Although the trail is designed as a clockwise loop, most hikers run it backward, starting at the covered bridge. Cross the covered bridge and follow the trail through young second-growth hardwoods to Wildflower Hill **[2]** at mile .10. Park naturalists have identified as many as 20 species of wildflowers growing here at any time.

The trail runs level, crossing tributary creeks and drains. At mile .36 there's a railed overlook on the left **[3]**. From here, the creek's seasonal personality is revealed—a brawling slugger in the spring, full but placid in the summer, and gentle in the fall.

A few feet farther, at mile .38, is another railed overlook **[4]**. What appears to be a sinkhole is, in reality, a dried-up pond. During wet weather the depression turns marshy but never holds water. There's enough wetness, however, for it to have earned its name, "Mosquito Pond."

There's a living den tree at mile .56 **[5]**, where a huge old-growth tree trunk, twisted and hollow, provides nesting areas for birds and small mammals. Although it's been lightning struck several times, the tree still lives.

You'll reach the park's second covered bridge at mile .60 **[6]**. Traditionally, lovers would pause to spoon within the privacy of covered bridges, leading to the generic title, kissing bridges. This one takes its name from that idea.

You'll cross an open meadow on the far side of Kissing Bridge, then begin the return loop, following the other bank of Yellow Creek. At mile .74 you'll come to a swinging bridge **[7]**. Fashioned after those in common use in the 1800s, this one is short—but bouncy. If you have kids with you, better figure on some extra time. They'll want to cross back and forth several times.

At mile .89 there's a turtle pond **[8]**. In addition to turtles and frogs, expect to see muskrats or, at least, their bankside burrows. Parti-colored dragon- and damselflies give the pond a festive air as they dart about like living jewels.

Watch for the giant grapevine growing up a maple at mile .94 **[9]**. At its base, it's about eight inches in diameter. Some of the largest, and oldest, grapes found in Kentucky are in the Owensboro and Henderson area. However, this is a particularly large example. Go right at the Y 10 feet past the grapevine and right again at the Y 100 feet farther. You'll climb, gently, to mile .97 and the site of an old well **[10]**, all that is left of a homestead that once thrived here.

At mile .99 you'll reach the restored 1960 fire tower **[11]**. During the leafless months, you can see all the way to the Green River from its platform. A little farther you'll reach a trail junction and sign. Continue straight to the wooden compass ring at mile 1.0 **[12]**. You can check your own azimuth, or teach kids the fine points of finding their way in the woods.

You'll come to an unmarked Y at mile 1.1 **[13]**. Follow the rail fence that lines the creek bank, cross a footbridge, and descend six steps. Turn left, and you'll come to a decked platform built out over Yellow Creek. Below you, the stream flows through a canyon it has cut. To the right is the first covered bridge.

Retrace your steps to the trail and turn left on the paved, barrier-free Challenge Trail to return to the trailhead.

1. Trailhead
2. Wildflower Hill
3. Creek overlook
4. Mosquito Pond
5. Living den tree
6. Kissing Bridge
7. Swinging bridge
8. Turtle pond
9. Giant grapevine
10. Old well
11. Fire tower
12. Wooden compass ring
13. Unmarked Y

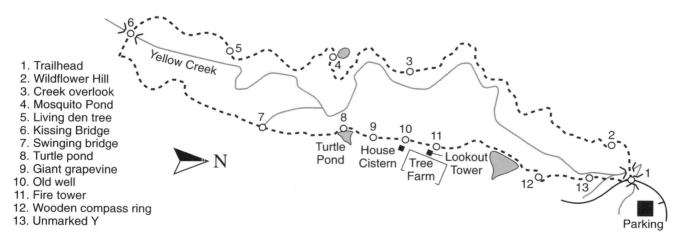

Hidden Valley Trail 👢👢

Distance Round-Trip: .58 miles

Estimated Hiking Time: 20 to 30 minutes

Cautions: Be aware of high banks and some exposed roots.

Trail Directions: Hidden Valley Trail is a double loop that drops from the hills above Yellow Creek to its banks, then returns to the ridge via one of two trails. To enjoy the natural sights fully, take the longer of the two routes.

The trailhead **[1]** is at the end of the iron bridge. On your left is a small seating area made of 150-year-old limestone blocks, along with a tree-finder compass. There's also a small waterfall for you to enjoy. Go straight, following the road.

At mile .06 you'll come to a white clapboard building **[2]**. This is the restored Pleasant Ridge Rosenwald one-room schoolhouse, a Black school that served the African-American community in Daviess County from 1919 to 1932. It was moved to this sight in 1992.

Follow the cement path south of the schoolhouse until the trail leaves it to the left. Going right returns you to the trailhead on the Challenge Trail. The Hidden Valley Trail will T at the rail fence along Yellow Creek. Go left, passing the wooden compass and stone block benches at mile .15 **[3]**.

You'll cross a deep V-valley on a footbridge at mile .18 **[4]**. A V-valley forms when the banks of a downcutting stream erode wider than the streambed. In cross-section, the letter V is formed.

At mile .21 the trail is blocked by a climax beech **[5]**. Just behind it is the trail sign for the three trails that converge here. Go right, downhill, on the Hidden Valley Trail, descending to the creek bottom. The trail will be level, following Yellow Creek.

Watch for the large, dead den tree on the left at mile .26 **[6]**. It was a climax beech. Now it's a favorite site for pileated woodpeckers.

At mile .28 the trail converges with the edge of the creek bank **[7]**. This is an unprotected sharp drop to the water, so if you have kids along you may want to watch them here. The trail climbs gradually, until it Ts into the Adventure Trail. Go left, following it to the unmarked Y at mile .33 **[8]**. Take the left fork. Be careful of the underbrush on the left of the trail. That's a large patch of stinging nettle.

Adventure Trail and Hidden Valley Trail run together from here on. You'll reach the T at the rail fence along the high creek bank. Stay left, following the fence across a footbridge and down six steps. Go left to the decked platform extending into the Yellow Creek Canyon at mile .52 **[9]**.

From here you can see the erosional action of the creek and the canyon it continues cutting. To the left is a covered bridge, terminus of the Adventure Trail. Backtrack to the steps, and use the paved Challenge Trail to return to the trailhead.

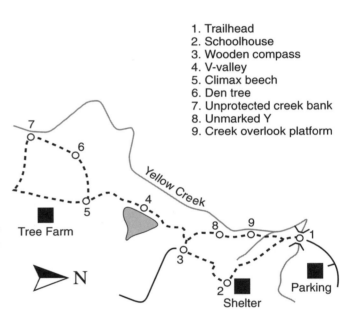

1. Trailhead
2. Schoolhouse
3. Wooden compass
4. V-valley
5. Climax beech
6. Den tree
7. Unprotected creek bank
8. Unmarked Y
9. Creek overlook platform

48. Panther Creek Park

- Cool your feet in an artificial creek.
- Cross Panther Creek on a bouncing, swaying, swinging bridge fashioned after those common in 1800.
- See more than 60 varieties of wildflowers.

Park Information

Panther Creek is a Daviess County park, providing recreational facilities to the people of the area. Included is the Nature Center, a 50-acre wild area billed as an "open air" classroom for nature studies.

In 1993, Panther Creek Park received an "Enjoy Outdoors America" award for its Nature Trail. It was the first trail in the nation to receive this prestigious award.

The park is named for Panther Creek, which flows westward through the property. Although it is the major drainage system in Daviess County, the portion flowing through the park is artificial. It was dug to facilitate drainage of southern Owensboro and the surrounding area.

A smaller creek, known as Clear Creek, flows north to south. Most wildflowers and the bird and animal life can be seen in the Clear Creek flowage.

More than 100 bird species have been sighted in the park, and wildlife includes several species of bat, beaver, deer, mink, raccoon, skunk, and weasel.

Of special interest is the solar-energy lighted fountain. The fountain and waterfall were built of creek stones from Falls of Rough, near Paddyville,

Kentucky, to add a geological and fossil background to park tours. The waterfall's motor and lighting are powered by nine solar panels on the roof of the park information center.

Directions: From Owensboro take US-60 west to the US-60 Bypass. Go 2.3 miles to Key 81 (exit 2), and follow it 2 miles to the park entrance. The Nature Center and trailheads are .4 miles into the park.

Hours Open: Open year-round, 7:00 A.M. until dusk.

Facilities: Picnic shelters, ball fields, fishing lake (for kids and seniors only), lookout tower, solar fountain.

Permits and Rules: Foot travel only on trails.

Further Information: Daviess County Parks and Recreation Dept., 5620 Highway 144, Owensboro, KY 42303; 502-281-5346.

Other Points of Interest

Yellow Creek Park (see park #47) is east of Owensboro on KY-144. **John James Audubon State Park** (see park #49) is 21 miles west in Henderson, Kentucky.

Ben Hawes State Park (502-684-9808), 4 miles west of Owensboro, is said to have the finest golf course in Kentucky.

Numerous cultural and historic sites can be found in **Owensboro and Daviess County**. For information, contact Owensboro-Daviess County Tourist Commission, 215 East Second Street, Owensboro, KY 42301; 502-926-1100.

Park Trails

New trails were under construction when we visited, so check with park officials for updates.

Nature Center Trail 👢

Distance Round-Trip: .61 miles

Estimated Hiking Time: 25 to 45 minutes

Cautions: None.

Trail Directions: The Nature Center Trail is a hub and spoke system of barrier-free elevated boardwalks. In the center is the Nature's Lair gazebo, from which four boardwalks radiate like the spokes of a wheel. Trailheads are at the end of each spoke.

You can follow any trail independently, or combine them in a series of loops. Alternatively, you can follow one large loop.

The trailhead **[1]** for the loop walk is at the Nature Center shelter, at the northwest corner of the parking lot. You'll enter through a gateway made of welded train rails. Along the way are many identified trees.

At mile .06 you'll pass over Clear Creek **[2]**. Note the profusion of wildflowers found in the low-lying, moist bottom. You'll also see several birdhouses, erected to provide nesting sites for resident and migratory birds.

You'll reach Nature's Lair at mile .17 **[3]**. This is a roofed pavilion, with a bench for resting and contemplating nature. Three other trails radiate from it. Go right on Cool Springs Trail. At mile .20 a covered bridge **[4]** carries you over Panther Creek. Windows in the bridge sides provide views of wildlife.

Panther Creek, here, is artificial. It was dug to provide drainage for Owensboro, but it looks as natural as any wild stream in the state.

At mile .23 the boardwalk ends, and the trail becomes hard packed **[5]**. Wheelchairs might need assistance here, as the trail ascends, until leveling out by the Swinger at mile .25 **[6]**. The Swinger is a 180-foot long suspension (swinging) bridge, modeled off those found in eastern Kentucky during the 1800s.

The Swinger ends at the park road. Go left, following it to the Sycamore Hill trailhead **[7]**, which you'll reach at mile .46.

Sycamore Hill descends down a half dozen wide, stone steps. Wheelchairs will definitely need assistance here. At the base of the stairs, you pick up the boardwalk again. Follow it to Nature's Lair **[2]**, at mile .5, and turn right onto Tall Timber Trail. The boardwalk ends at mile .56, at the base of a large honey locust tree **[8]**, and climbs. Here, again, wheelchairs might need some help.

The trail ends at an old L & N railcar, at mile .61 **[9]**. Turn left on the park road to return to the trailhead.

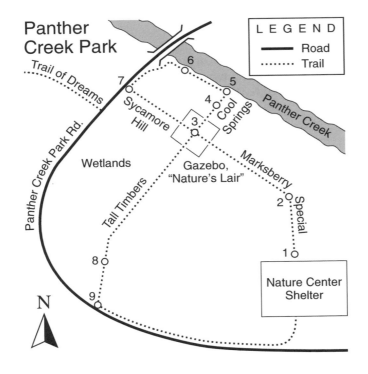

1. Trailhead
2. Clear Creek crossing
3. Nature's Lair
4. Covered bridge
5. Boardwalk ends
6. Swinging bridge
7. Sycamore Hill trailhead
8. Honey locust tree
9. Railcar

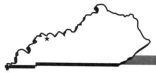

49. John James Audubon State Park

- See original Audubon paintings in the John James Audubon Museum.
- Explore a climax forest containing more than 160 bird species, nearly 300 species of wildflowers and herbs, and 61 varieties of trees.
- Observe beavers at work.

Park Information

The hilly terrain lying south of the Ohio River and east of US-41 is known as the "Wolf Hills." The 692 acres of John James Audubon State Park lie smack in the middle of them.

This is the area where John James Audubon lived and created many paintings that would make him world famous when *Birds of America* was first published. A museum and nature center commemorating his work and life has many original paintings on display, and includes at least two folio-version first editions of his book.

Surrounding the museum complex is a climax forest. There are two primary forest communities, beech/sugar maple/basswood in the moist, rich northern portion of the park, and oak/sugar maple/tulip tree in the drier southern portion.

Best known as a bird sanctuary where 169 species have been clearly observed, the park is a haven for all nature enthusiasts. There are 61 species of trees, some more than 200 years old; 280 varieties of wildflowers, including the rare white trillium; 14 different ferns; and numerous mammals, including beaver in the ponds and streams of the preserve.

Thick with huge, old trees laced with large grapevines (some of the oldest and largest grapevines in Kentucky are in the park), Audubon resembles an Old-World forest, perhaps as designed by the Brothers Grimm or maybe J.R.R. Tolkien.

Directions: From Henderson follow US-41 Alternate, then US-41 nine miles to the park entrance.

Caution: The entrance comes up suddenly in the midst of the fast-food restaurants, used car lots, and similar urban sprawl that lines the highway.

Hours Open: Open year-round; some facilities have daily or seasonal hours.

Facilities: Museum and nature center, cottages, campground, boat dock and beach, golf course, picnic shelters.

Permits and Rules: Foot travel only on trails; no dogs in nature preserve.

Further Information: John James Audubon State Park, P.O. Box 576, Henderson, KY 42420; 502-826-2247.

Other Points of Interest

Panther Creek Park (see park #48) and **Yellow Creek Park** (see park #47) are half an hour east in Owensboro.

There are numerous cultural and historic sites in **Henderson**. For information, contact the Henderson County Tourist Commission, 2961 U.S. 41 North, Henderson, KY 42420; 502-826-3128.

Park Trails

Most trails in the park are accessed off Warbler Road, itself a declared hiking trail. Mileage figures do not include the distance you walk on Warbler Road to reach the trailheads. Using Warbler Road, you can construct numerous loop hikes of your own.

Museum Trail 👢—.25 mile loop—is a barrier-free trail near the museum complex.

Wilderness Lake Trail 👢👢—1 mile round-trip—is a post and loop trail circling Wilderness Lake.

King Benson Trail 👢👢—.3 mile loop—is an interpreted nature trail on both sides of Warbler Road.

John James Audubon
State Park

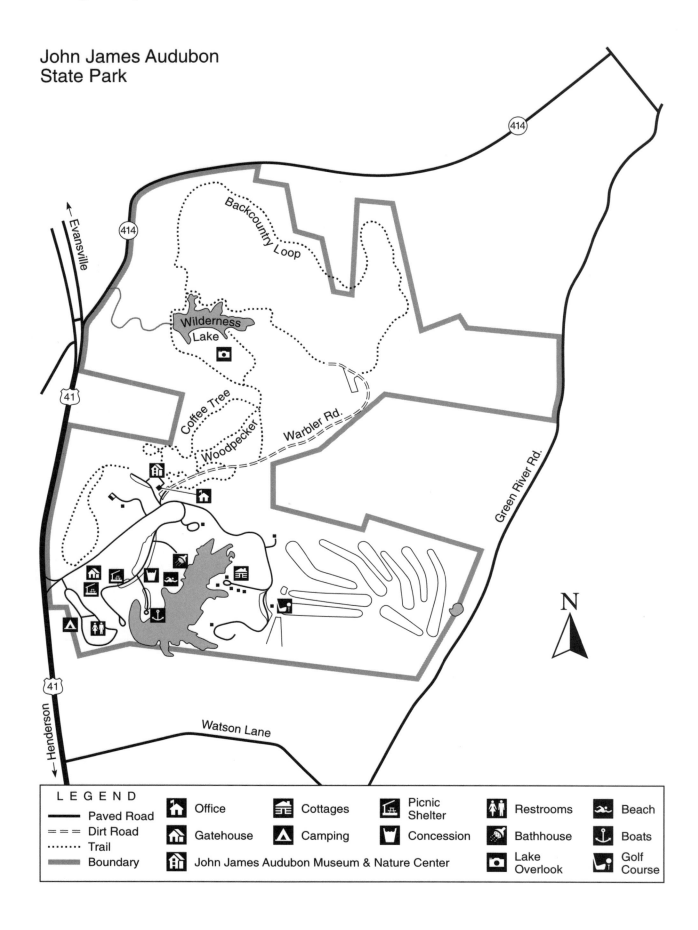

414

Evansville

414

Backcountry Loop

Wilderness Lake

41

Coffee Tree

Woodpecker

Warbler Rd.

Green River Rd.

41

Henderson

Watson Lane

N

L E G E N D

▬▬ Paved Road	
═══ Dirt Road	
⋯⋯ Trail	
▬ Boundary	

🏠 Office   🏘 Cottages   🏕 Picnic Shelter   🚻 Restrooms   🏊 Beach

🏠 Gatehouse   ⛺ Camping   🛒 Concession   🚿 Bathhouse   ⚓ Boats

🏛 John James Audubon Museum & Nature Center   📷 Lake Overlook   ⛳ Golf Course

Backcountry Loop

Distance Round-Trip: 2 miles plus 1.4 miles on Warbler Road

Estimated Hiking Time: 1.5 to 2 hours

Cautions: Watch out for exposed roots, fallen trees, and thick vines across the trail.

Trail Directions: The Backcountry Loop is a hilly walk through a climax forest. Thick-boled beeches, maples, basswoods, and oaks fill the woods, laced together with heavy grapevines. The canopy is so thick that, even on a sunny day, the forest floor can be dark and oppressive. Leaving a trail of bread crumbs through this Brothers Grimm woods won't help. The myriad of birds and small mammals found here are sure to eat the crumbs as soon as you strew them about.

The trailhead **[1]** is at the end of a .7-mile walk along Warbler Road. Just before the road dead-ends against the wall of forest, the trailhead opens on your right, backtracking parallel to the road, but angling slightly away from it.

You'll descend into a hollow, toward a dressed-stone building at mile .17 that looks like a fairy-tale house **[2]**. The Hansel and Gretel idea is reinforced when you look inside. The building was an incinerator, built by the Civilian Conservation Corps in the 1930s. In short, it houses an oven!

The trail necks down to a thin causeway, then descends in a long, lazy switchback to mile .32 and an old-growth oak festooned with grapevines **[3]**. Some of the oldest, thickest grapevines in Kentucky are in these woods. Another old-growth tree, this one a shagbark hickory, comes into view at mile .49 **[4]**. Look beyond it, and a line of sycamores along a creek suggest a Japanese minimalist painting.

At mile .51 you'll circle the corpse of a forest giant whose splintered stump stands 12 feet tall, pointing, like a many-fingered sentinel, at the sky **[5]**. From here, you'll climb steadily, topping out at mile .68. You can just make out, during the leafless months, a cypress swamp in front of you.

You'll climb and descend several ridges and hills, reaching a climax beech at mile 1.1 **[6]**. You'll likely find beech drops in its roots. These are nongreen flowering plants that resemble dried floral arrangements.

Shortly after the beech you'll start a long, gradual descent. Notice, at mile 1.3, the large hole on your left **[7]**. Twenty feet wide and about half that across, this

is the hole left by the root ball of a single forest giant. The tree is long rotted away, but a dirt wall on the far side of the hole marks where the root ball stood.

Wilderness Lake comes into view at mile 1.5, and you'll reach the lake and the end of the trail at mile 1.58 **[8]**. We found it hard to shake the mood of the Brother's Grimm forest. The lake was flat gray and oppressive. Momentarily we expected some creature of the darkness to reach out a slimy tentacle.

In fact, the largest creatures in the lake are beavers, which you may see. During the spring, their activities often cause the upcoming bridges and boardwalks to flood. If they are under water, it will only be ankle deep, so they are not dangerous.

Turn left on the Wilderness Lake Trail, which follows the east side of the lake. Immediately you'll cross a boardwalk, then climb above the lake on a rough trail. At mile 1.6 you'll cross a second boardwalk, this one through a cattail marsh **[9]**. Those large birdhouses you see are wood duck nesting boxes.

After crossing a deep drain on a footbridge, you'll come to another boardwalk at mile 1.8 **[10]**. This one crosses a marshy backwater. Circling that backwater, you'll reenter the woods, and, about 1,000 feet farther, reach the end of Warbler Road at mile 2.0 **[11]**. Follow it back to the museum complex.

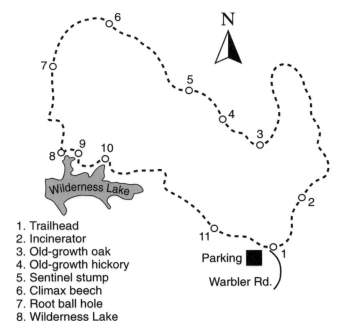

1. Trailhead
2. Incinerator
3. Old-growth oak
4. Old-growth hickory
5. Sentinel stump
6. Climax beech
7. Root ball hole
8. Wilderness Lake
9. Second boardwalk
10. Third boardwalk
11. Juncture with Warbler Road

Coffeetree/Woodpecker/ Warbler Road Loop 👢👢👢

Distance Round-Trip: .96 miles

Estimated Hiking Time: 45-60 minutes

Cautions: Be careful of exposed roots.

Trail Directions: This loop is an abbreviated version of the Backcountry Loop, through a more open climax forest. The trailhead [1] is off the Museum Trail, behind the museum building. You'll start on that paved, barrier-free trail, which has interpretive signs in both English and Braille.

Sixty feet from the trailhead, at mile .01, you'll pass the wildlife observation garden [2], which has a pool, plantings, and feeders to attract birds and wildlife. Do not enter the garden! In fact, to really appreciate it, do your wildlife watching from the special observation deck inside the nature center.

The Kentucky Coffeetree Trail leaves the Museum Trail at mile .06 [3], descending gradually. You'll cross a drain on planks, go up and over a small rise, descending to a second crossing of the same drain. There's a small fern garden on the far side of this crossing.

Notice the dead tree [4] on your left at mile .18. Those hieroglyphics were left by wood-borers and other insects before the bark peeled away. With a little imagination, you'll convince yourself you can read a message in the carvings.

At mile .19 you'll bottom out at a confusing three-way trail junction [5]. All three trails are pointed to from two directions. Go left, over a plank bridge, for the correct trail.

A little farther, at mile .2, you'll go through a gate of living beeches [6]. Both are seriously scarred by initials and other messages carved by thoughtless people. However, the carvings are weathered enough to look arty, rather than damaging. The trail Ys immediately after this natural gateway. Take the left fork, following the creek bottom until the trail makes a sharp right turn and starts climbing steeply.

You'll come to a foundation of dressed stones at mile .37 [7], all that's left of a CCC structure of some kind. Nobody could tell us what it was. The trail is less steep.

A large grapevine loops across the trail at mile .47 [8]. Look about 20 degrees to the left, and an even more massive vine—about 9 inches in diameter—has tied itself into a free-hanging figure eight knot.

After a steady climb, you'll top out at the hub of the "wagon wheel" knob, at mile .57 [9]. Four ridges (one of which you just climbed) radiate like the spokes of a wagon wheel. Less than 100 feet farther you'll T into the Woodpecker Trail. Go right, passing the remains of a stone water fountain built before the area became a preserve. At mile .7 you'll T at Warbler Road [10]. Turn right and follow it toward the museum complex.

You'll reach an interpretive sign at mile .85 [11], which explains grapevines. Next to it is a small loop, part of the King Benson Trail. If you follow it, you can learn the relationship of flowering dogwoods to the crucifixion. Among other things, their petals form crosses with rusty nail prints at the edges, or so the legend says.

The loop rejoins Warbler Road at mile .88 [12]. Turn right and return to the museum complex.

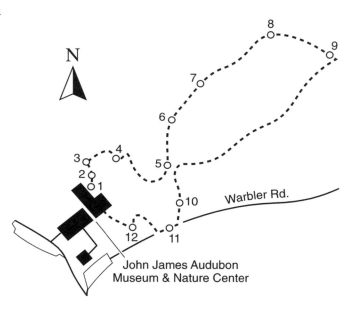

John James Audubon
Museum & Nature Center

1. Trailhead	7. Old foundation
2. Wildlife garden	8. Grapevine loops
3. Coffeetree Trail	9. Wagon wheel knob
4. Dead tree	10. T
5. Three-way trail junction	11. Interpretive sign
6. Living gate	12. Warbler Road

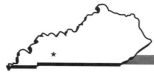

50. Pennyrile Forest State Resort Park

- Find vestiges of the rare American pennyroyal, a medicinal mint for which the park is named.
- See stands of wild cane, said by settlers to provide the most nourishing fodder available for cattle and horses.
- Explore the human history of an area settled for the same reasons Daniel Boone opened the Bluegrass country—people looking for elbow room.

Park Information

The 863-acre Pennyrile Forest State Resort Park is surrounded by the Pennyrile State Forest, 15,331 acres of what is considered by many to be the most beautiful woods in western Kentucky.

Both are named for the American pennyroyal, a member of the mint family used medicinally by early settlers. Modern herbalists still use it to produce aromatic and essential oils. Locally the plant is called pennyrile. Pennyrile once blanketed the area but is now becoming rare in the park. Still, you are likely to come across it, especially in dry fields and in creek bottoms.

A pungent aromatic annual, growing 4 to 16 inches high, pennyrile has elliptic leaves and bears pale violet flowers from August through September.

A major portion of the Mississippian Plateau of western Kentucky also takes its name from this plant, with the whole region popularly called the Pennyrile.

The area now occupied by the park was settled in 1808, when John Thompson, the first settler, traveled here looking for wild game. He took up residence in a fair-sized rock-shelter, which can still be visited.

Within a few years a thriving community grew, called Concord. Numerous remains of the settlement and human occupation can be found in the park and surrounding state forest.

Most modern human encroachments– including the cabins, the lodge, and other buildings, along with Pennyrile Lake– were constructed by the Works Progress Administration in the 1930s.

Directions: From Hopkinsville, Kentucky, take KY-109 north about 21 miles to the park entrance, then right 1.5 miles to the lodge.

Hours Open: Open year-round; some facilities are seasonal.

Facilities: Lodge, cottages, campground, golf, boating, fishing, swimming pool and beach, picnic grounds.

Further Information: Pennyrile Forest State Resort Park, 20781 Pennyrile Lodge Road, Dawson Springs, KY 42408; 502-797-3421.

Other Points of Interest

Lake Barkley State Resort Park (see park #51) and **Land Between the Lakes National Recreation Area** (see park #52) are less than one hour southwest.

Hopkinsville has numerous cultural and historic sites. For information contact Hopkinsville-Christian County Tourism Commission, 1209 South Virginia Street, Hopkinsville, KY 42241; 502-885-9096.

The **Jefferson Davis Monument** (502-886-1765), in Fairvew, celebrates the President of the Confederate States with a 351-foot obelisk. Elevator service carries you to the top for panoramic views of the countryside.

Park Trails

There are more than eight miles of hiking and nature study trails in the park, ranging from easy to very difficult.

Pennyroyal Trail 👢👢👢👢—.75 miles each way—is a strenuous horseshoe that connects with the Lake Trail and can be combined with it for a long, double-loop hike.

Thompson's Hollow Trail 👢👢👢👢—.16 mile each way—is a steep, strenuous trail named for the first pioneer family to settle in the area. It connects the campground with both the Lake and Pennyroyal Trails.

Cane Trail 👢👢👢—a 1.25 mile loop—provides a second double-loop hike using the Lake Trail. Patches of wild cane—for which it is named—can still be found along the streamside at the lower end of the trail.

Pennyrile Forest State Resort Park

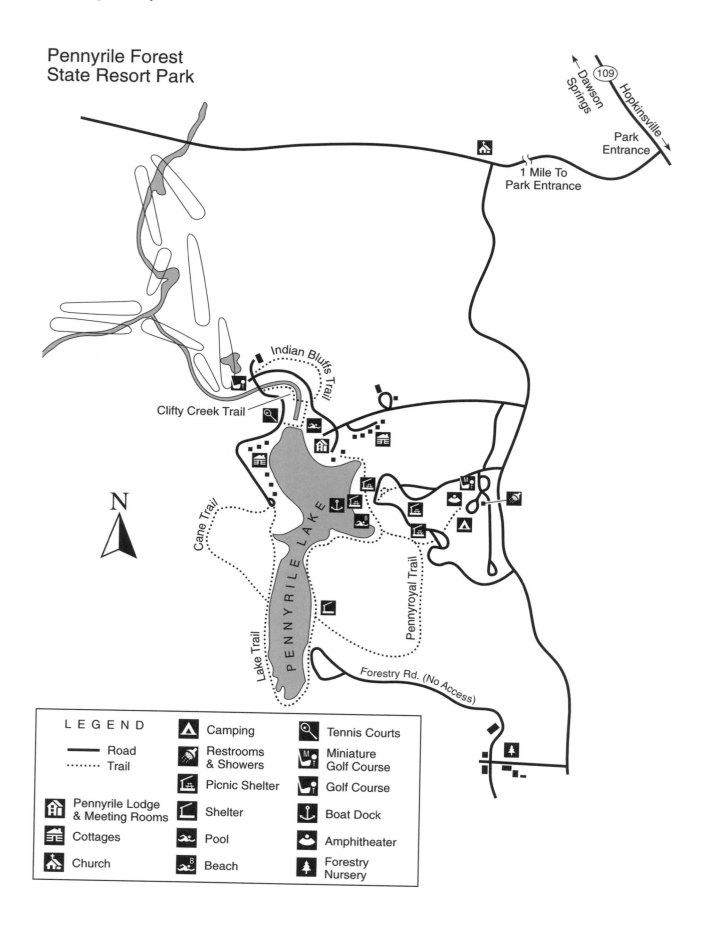

Dawson Springs
109
Hopkinsville →

Park Entrance

1 Mile To Park Entrance

Indian Bluffs Trail

Clifty Creek Trail

Cane Trail

PENNYRILE LAKE

Lake Trail

Pennyroyal Trail

Forestry Rd. (No Access)

N

LEGEND

── Road
······· Trail

Pennyrile Lodge & Meeting Rooms

Cottages

Church

Camping

Restrooms & Showers

Picnic Shelter

Shelter

Pool

Beach

Tennis Courts

Miniature Golf Course

Golf Course

Boat Dock

Amphitheater

Forestry Nursery

Lake Trail 👢👢👢

Distance Round-Trip: 2.7 miles

Estimated Hiking Time: 1.5 to 2 hours

Cautions: The area has high cliffs, poorly marked trail junctions, exposed rocks and roots, and some muddy patches.

Trail Directions: Lake Trail circles 56-acre Pennyrile Lake, which offers fishing for largemouth bass, bluegill, catfish, and crappie. Along the way you'll pass through several ecosystems, and connections for both the Cane Trail and Pennyroyal Trail, where additional environments will be encountered.

The trailhead [1] is on the left of the lodge. Descend cement steps and follow the blacktop road to the cottage access road. Go left to the cottages where you'll find more stone and cement steps and a walkway through hardwoods, past a private residence. At mile .07 you'll cross a wooden footbridge [2] to the trail.

The trail passes through second-growth hardwoods, with the lake on your right, crossing several more footbridges until mile .29, where you'll reach the boat dock and beach [3]. The trail sign is confusing here. Just follow the seawall along the beach. At mile .38 the beach ends at an eroded cliff. This is a sandstone ridge, an anomaly in western Kentucky, where limestone is the prevailing rock. Note the ferns, wild ginger, and other plants growing, like hanging gardens, from the water-cut ledges.

The trail climbs the ridge to the left. Watch carefully, as there are several unmarked false trails. You climb some stone steps, and reach another unmarked juncture. Go right following the switchback. At mile .43 you'll reach the base of some stairs [4]. The trail seems to continue, but that's a false trail leading to high, dangerous cliffs. Climb the stairs instead. At the top, several false trails converge. Take the second right.

You'll reach a slump-block canyon at mile .53 [5]. Slump blocks are large chunks of rock that have fallen from the cliffs and migrated. Below you is a jungle of them in a canyon leading to the lake. The trail descends from here, bottoming out at a T. Go left and ascend over and around an arm of the lake.

The Pennyroyal Trail comes in on the left, at mile .92 [6]. Shortly after that the trail merges with an old gravel road, now overgrown, leaving it a couple hundred feet farther.

At mile 1.0 you'll reach a back bay, covered with lily pads [7]. Most of the time, the park's resident flock of Canada geese can be found here, resting on the water and gabbling softly to each other. In the spring, when the young are first swimming, they look like dirty, yellow hair balls. Only later, when their feathers come in, do they acquire the banker's-gray dignity of the adults.

You'll circle the back bay, which may be boggy and muddy, passing an abandoned pumping station used by the state forest service before the park came into being. At mile 1.20 the trail edges the lakeshore [8]. Patches of cane appear. Looking like thin bamboo, they served many purposes for pioneers, who used them for everything from pipe stems to torches.

Cane Trail [9] enters from the left at mile 1.4. From there the trail roller-coasters through mixed pines and hardwoods until reaching a side trail at mile 1.7 [10], which leads to a natural rock overlook.

The trail ends at mile 1.85 at a loop in the cottage access road [11]. Follow it back to the lodge.

If you feel like more hiking, follow Cane Trail, whose trailhead is at the same loop, intersecting Lake Trail 1.25 miles farther at [9].

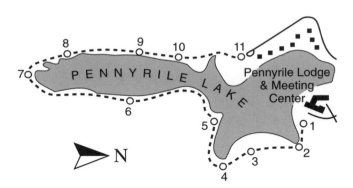

1. Trailhead
2. Wooden footbridge
3. Boat dock and beach
4. Stairs
5. Slump-block canyon
6. Pennyroyal Trail junction
7. Back bay
8. Lakeshore edge
9. Cane Trail junction
10. Side trail to overlook
11. Trailhead of Cane Trail

Indian Bluffs/Clifty Creek Combined Loop 👢👢👢

Distance Round-Trip: .93 miles

Estimated Hiking Time: 35 to 60 minutes

Cautions: Be careful of exposed rocks and roots, and of one steep set of stairs.

Trail Directions: These two short trails take you through some of the best of the human and natural history in Pennyrile Forest State Resort Park. Park near the pool and follow the blacktop road 187 feet toward the golf course to find the trailhead [1] for Indian Bluffs Trail. You'll climb five steps, then climb through an oak/hickory forest until topping out on a ridge at mile .11 [2].

A short distance later, at mile .13, a large sandstone outcrop comes into view on the right [3]. Sandstone is unusual in the Pennyroyal, where the predominant rock is limestone. The trail will follow this spine of stone until it descends later. This particular ridge has a long history of human use. Both Native Americans and early settlers used the natural shelters formed in the sandstone as dwellings.

Shortly after leveling off, there is a lighthouse (a small hole passing completely through the cliff) in the ridge, called Indian Window. This is the only natural arch in the park, but it's hard to locate, so you'll have to search.

At mile .24 you'll pass through a large sandstone rock-shelter [4], the biggest in the park. Eight to 12 people once lived in this shelter.

You'll leave the bluff line and start descending gradually at mile .33 [5], until reaching the blacktop road at the golf course. Follow it downhill, crossing the bridge over Clifty Creek. The Clifty Creek Trailhead [6] is just beyond the bridge, at mile .42, on the left. The trail is level, as it follows the creek.

Watch the far shore at mile .45. There's a large patch of cane growing there [7]. Cane was one of the most useful plants for pioneers, who used it for everything from pipe stems to torches. Its leaves are said to be the most nourishing fodder cattle can eat. Native Americans used this cane to weave baskets and make arrow shafts.

There'll be a seep running across the trail at mile .6 [8]. The water flows even in the driest weather, but note the distinctive perfume of chlorine. This isn't a spring, as you may first have thought, but a drain from the swimming pool, which is on the cliff above you.

You'll cross the creek on a wooden bridge below the lake dam at mile .64 [9]. The dam was built by the WPA in the 1930s from sandstone block. There used to be a mill on this site, and the millstones were incorporated into the dam. There are two of them in the dam face.

From the bridge the trail turns back along the creek and climbs to the blacktop road. Turn left and follow it to a small parking area, where a paved path leads to the dam. You'll reach the catwalk over the dam at mile .81 [10]. On the far side are three sets of stone steps leading up the hillside. The trail reaches the pool at mile .88 [11], where a wood chip path leads to the back of the lodge. Follow it to the cement walk and stairs, which take you to the trailhead.

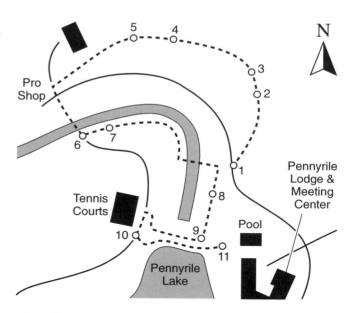

1. Trailhead
2. Ridgetop
3. Sandstone outcrop
4. Large rock-shelter
5. Leave bluff line
6. Clifty Creek trailhead
7. Cane patch
8. Drain from pool
9. Wooden bridge
10. Dam catwalk
11. Pool

51. Lake Barkley State Resort Park

- Fish for largemouth bass, white bass, bluegill, crappie, or catfish in one of the largest man-made lakes in Kentucky.
- Watch numerous species of shorebirds and waterfowl in the bays and backwaters of Lake Barkley.
- See the incredible display of spring wildflowers in the diverse habitats of the park.
- Observe uncommon trees, including bald cypress, sweet gum, and water tupelo, typical of southern swamps.

Park Information

Nestled on the shore of 57,900-acre Lake Barkley, formed when the Tennessee Valley Authority (TVA) dammed the Cumberland River, Lake Barkley State Resort Park provides an array of outdoor activities ranging from fishing and boating, to golf, swimming, and hiking. There's even a trap range, one of the few shooting facilities at a state park. If you didn't bring your shotgun, not to worry. There are 12-gauge guns available for rent, along with shotshells and clay targets for sale.

One of only two facilities in the state park system with its own airfield, the park provides a paved, lighted landing strip almost 5,000 feet long.

Fishing is a major draw of Lake Barkley, especially in the spring when the huge slab crappie make their runs. Many anglers release any fish weighing less than a pound—which is a good size crappie anywhere else. Largemouth bass fishing is another big draw, and there are many large bass-fishing tournaments held on the lake. Rental fishing boats are available at the park's marina.

Although the pool is only open to lodge and cottage guests, you can cool off in the lake at the public beach.

The fields and woods of the park provide diverse ecosystems and forest communities, including prairie and meadow, upland oak/hickory woods, and bottomland hardwoods, along with the various marine habitats created by the lake. Thus, there is an incredible array of flora and fauna for the nature enthusiast to see.

Directions: From Cadiz, Kentucky, take US-68 west 9.4 miles to KY-1489, which is the park access road. Go north 3.5 miles to Barkley Lodge.

Hours Open: Open year-round; some facilities are seasonal.

Facilities: Two lodges, cottages, airstrip, campground, picnic areas, trap range, golf course, pool and beach swimming, tennis courts, fitness center.

Permits and Rules: Foot travel only on trails.

Further Information: Lake Barkley State Resort Park, Box 790, Cadiz, KY 42211; 502-924-1131.

Other Points of Interest

Land Between the Lakes National Recreation Area (see park #52) is 8 miles west. **Pennyrile Forest State Resort Park** (see park #50) is less than an hour to the northeast.

The **Woods and Wetlands Wildlife Center** (502-924-9107) in Cadiz is a wildlife park providing aquariums, a serpentarium, birds of prey, and wild mammals indigenous to Kentucky.

At the **National Scouting Museum** (502-762-3883) in Murray you can see displays and exhibits relating to the Boy Scouts, including the second largest collection of original Norman Rockwell paintings.

Numerous cultural and historic sites are found in **Hopkinsville,** 40 miles east. For information, contact the Hopkinsville-Christian County Tourism Commission, 1209 South Virginia Street, Hopkinsville, KY 42241; 502-885-9096.

Park Trails

Cedar Grove 🥾🥾🥾—2 miles each way—is the longest trail in the park. It is accessed from the Lena Madesin Phillips Trail.

Wilderness Trail 🥾🥾🥾—1.25 miles each way—climbs through the hill country surrounding the

riding stables. It, too, is accessed from the Lena Madesin Phillips Trail.

Wagon Wheel Trail 🥾🥾—3 miles each way—is a short woods walk connecting the campground with the public beach.

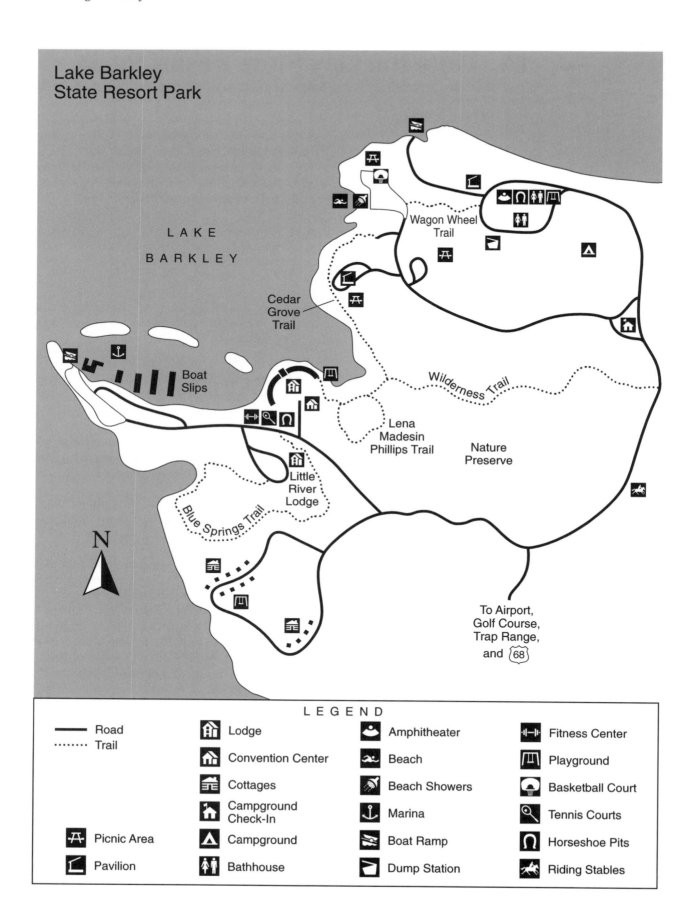

Lake Barkley
State Resort Park

LAKE

BARKLEY

Cedar
Grove
Trail

Boat
Slips

Wagon Wheel
Trail

Wilderness Trail

Lena
Madesin
Phillips Trail

Nature
Preserve

Little
River
Lodge

Blue Springs Trail

N

To Airport,
Golf Course,
Trap Range,
and 68

L E G E N D

—— Road	🏠 Lodge	Amphitheater	Fitness Center
···· Trail	Convention Center	Beach	Playground
	Cottages	Beach Showers	Basketball Court
	Campground Check-In	Marina	Tennis Courts
Picnic Area	Campground	Boat Ramp	Horseshoe Pits
Pavilion	Bathhouse	Dump Station	Riding Stables

Blue Springs Trail 👢👢👢

Distance Round-Trip: 1.6 miles

Estimated Hiking Time: 1.25 to 1.5 hours

Cautions: Watch for exposed roots, missing trail signs, false trails.

Trail Directions: Blue Springs Trail is a moderate loop that descends from the hills surrounding Lake Barkley to the shoreline and back up. None of the grades, however, are particularly steep. Along the way the trail passes through several distinct habitats and forest communities.

The trailhead [1] is at the intersection of the park road and the access road to Barkley Lodge. There is limited parking at the trailhead. A better bet is to park at the fitness center down the hill.

The trail initially roller-coasters through mixed, young second-growth hardwoods and cedars, paralleling the park road. Almost imperceptibly, the trail descends, until mile .18, where you'll cross a wet-weather stream [2] and level out. There are some old-growth trees mixed in with the young stuff here. Watch for deer, which are plentiful. Wild turkey also find these open woods to their liking. Also, you might, as we did, spook an owl who indignantly ghosted through the trees to find another perch.

At mile .34 there will be an open meadow on your right [3]. Here, in the blue gloaming of early evening, deer sightings are likely. A side trail across this meadow leads to an alternative trailhead.

After crossing the meadow you'll T into an unmarked old roadbed. Go left— reentering the woods at mile .37. The trail forms an ecoborder here [4], with upland oak/hickory woods on the left and young bottomland hardwoods on the right.

At mile .7 you'll come to a covered billboard explaining open-field habitat and succession forests [5]. You can clearly see the process here. Most of what had been a field is now grown over with brush, young cedars, and hardwoods. A few steps farther, at mile .72, is a wooden tree-finder compass. Unfortunately, when we were there it had been seriously vandalized and no longer operated.

For much of the time you've been following an old roadbed. At mile .82 the road continues straight, toward the lake, but the trail turns right [6]. Watch sharply, because the trail sign is missing.

The trail follows the lakeshore now. During leafless months especially, you'll have broad vistas of this inland sea, whose personality changes with the time and season. It might be a dull, slate gray one minute, and the next it is reflecting the blazing colors of autumn's palette. Note, starting at mile .89, the groups of sticks and poles forming rough circles in the water [7]. These are fish habitat structures. The sticks attract bait fish, who, in turn, attract prey fish— especially crappie. You may not see the fish habitats during high water. However, you can locate them easily by the fishing boats above them.

A marshy meadow at the head of an inlet usually holds numerous shorebirds [8] at mile .94. Among others are sure to be one or two great blue herons. As the meadow dries, grassland birds, such as killdeer, can be seen.

The trail turns sharply right here and climbs with several switchbacks, until reaching a short side trail at mile 1.26 leading to Little River Lodge [9]. Blue Springs Trail officially ends here, but, in fact, continues upward, circling the lodge and rejoining the main trail just before the trailhead. Unless you enjoy walking on blacktop, follow the trail extension rather than the road from the lodge.

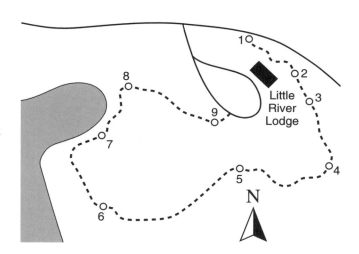

1. Trailhead
2. Wet-weather stream
3. Open meadow
4. Ecoborder
5. Succession forest
6. Right turn
7. Fish habitat structure
8. Meadow
9. Side trail

Lena Madesin Phillips Trail 👢 and 👢👢👢

Distance Round-Trip: 1.25 miles

Estimated Hiking Time: 40 to 60 minutes

Cautions: Watch for steep riprap banks along lake, exposed rocks and roots, eroded areas.

Trail Directions: The Lena Madesin Phillips Trail combines a paved interpretive nature walk along the lakeshore with a rough .75-mile hike through the woods above an embayment.

The first part is flat and level, and includes numerous benches as well as the interpretive signage. It would be an ideal barrier-free trail. Unfortunately, the only access is down some steep steps, making it difficult for wheelchairs to reach.

The trailhead **[1]** is below the lodge. There is a shellbark hickory and a red cypress at the start of the cement walkway. Considered a tree of the deep south, cypress actually are native as far north as southern Illinois. To your left is the marina, flanked by a series of artificial barrier islands.

There are 10 trees identified along the path, including some, like the red cypress, not likely to be seen anywhere else.

At mile .12 is the boat dock **[2]** serving the lodge. Above you is the swimming pool and, beyond that, the restaurant and activities center.

You'll reach a sweet gum at mile .19 **[3]**, then come to a bald cypress at mile .24 **[4]** and a water tupelo at mile .25 **[5]**. Though rarely seen, these trees are common in some areas of western Kentucky, especially around the lakes and ponds formed by the great New Madrid earthquake in 1813.

You'll reach the playground and end of the cement at mile .28. The Lena Madesin Phillips Trail **[6]** officially starts here.

Entering the woods, you'll find yourself in a mixed bottomlands and swamp forest. If you paid attention on the interpretive walk, you should be able to identify most trees you see.

You'll cross a marshy drain on planks at mile .3, then turn right and climb a speed bump ridge **[7]**. This is a low ridge, resembling a speed bump for the Jolly Green Giant. The bottoms here are cut and sculptured by flowing water, which produces these mini-ridges.

There's a Y and trail sign at mile .38 **[8]**. Straight ahead is the connector trail for the Cedar Grove and Wilderness Trails. The Lena Madesin Phillips Trail

goes right, climbing steeply through mixed hardwoods and cedars. The trail is rough and eroded.

You'll come to a recovering field at mile .43 **[9]**. You'll know it by the thick cedars that grow there. Cedar, along with redbud, are among the first succession trees to grow in an old field or clear-cut and are known as "pioneer trees" for that reason.

After crossing the power line right-of-way, the trail descends to mile .51, where you'll cross a creek **[10]** on a footbridge. To your right, two small tributaries flow, joining under your feet to form a single stream. Look upstream and you can see even smaller runs joining the creeks. This is the Mississippi River drainage in miniature. All watersheds, great and small, follow this pattern. The trail climbs again, until topping out at mile .57 **[11]**. Despite its proximity to the lodge, wildlife is common in these woods, and you're likely to see wild turkey and deer up on this ridge.

The trail descends to mile .67, where you'll reach a swinging bridge **[12]**. It carries you, bouncing and swaying, 37 feet across a deep V-valley. V-valleys are formed when the banks of down-cutting streams erode wider than the creek bed. In cross-section they form the letter V.

Continuing downward, you'll reach the trail junction **[8]** at mile .77. Go left and return to the trailhead.

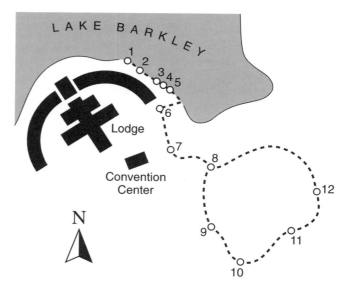

1. Trailhead
2. Boat dock
3. Sweet gum
4. Bald cypress
5. Water tupelo
6. Official trailhead
7. Speed bump ridge
8. Y
9. Recovering field
10. Creek confluence
11. Top out
12. Swinging bridge

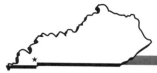

52. Land Between the Lakes

- See elk and bison in their native habitat at the 750-acre restoration of Kentucky's native barrens.
- Explore the natural and human history of the area that became the nation's first National Recreation Area.
- Watch undisturbed wildlife, ranging from bald eagles to fallow deer.
- Visit a recreated 19th-century living history farm.

Park Information

Land Between the Lakes National Recreation Area is a 170,000-acre natural area, sandwiched between Lake Barkley and Kentucky Lake.

Long known as the Land Between the Rivers, this spit of land extending across Kentucky and Tennessee epitomized 19th- and early 20th- century rural America. Towns were scattered, and the people earned their livelihoods from hardscrabble farming, logging, and mining.

Then the TVA (Tennessee Valley Authority) dammed the Tennessee and Cumberland Rivers, first removing all inhabitants. The resulting wild area between the two new lakes was declared a National Recreation Area in the mid-1960s, dedicated to providing outdoor recreational opportunities and to preserving the natural and human history of the region.

Flanked by the two huge impoundments, Land Between the Lakes has more than 300 miles of undeveloped shoreline, and its forests contain a rich diversity of wildlife—including fallow deer and white-tailed deer. The fallow, which now roam freely through the park, originated with a private herd stocked in the area in 1918. Land Between the Lakes was instrumental in wild turkey restocking programs in the state, and it maintains a large flock of its own.

Numerous smaller lakes dot the region, offering fishing, canoeing, and wildlife-watching opportunities away from the major impoundments.

Several special areas are maintained, including the Homeplace 1850 (a recreated 19th-century farm, using original buildings and costumed interpreters); the Elk and Bison Prairie (a restored native prairie on which elk and bison—both native species—roam free); the 2,500-acre Turkey Bay Off Highway Vehicles Area (an area set aside for all-terrain vehicle use); and The Nature Station (an educational facility where visitors can see native wildlife and learn ways of interacting with the natural world).

Most of the park remains wild, however, offering visitors hiking, hunting, fishing, camping, and wildlife-watching opportunities unequaled in the state.

Directions: From Cadiz, Kentucky, take US-68 west 17.5 miles to the Trace. Follow the Trace north a half mile to the Visitors Center at Golden Pond, 10 miles north to The Nature Station entrance road, then east 3.2 miles to The Nature Station.

Hours Open: Open year-round; some facilities have date and time restrictions.

Facilities: Camping, fishing, boating, Visitors Center, The Nature Station, living history farm, planetarium.

Permits and Rules: Special hunting regulations apply.

Further Information: TVA's Land Between the Lakes, 100 Van Morgan Drive, Golden Pond, KY 42211; 502-924-2000.

Other Points of Interest

Lake Barkley State Resort Park (see park #51) is eight miles east of Land Between the Lakes.

Woods and Wetlands Wildlife Center (502-924-9107) in Cadiz is a wildlife park with aquariums, a serpentarium, birds of prey, and wild mammals.

The National Scouting Museum (502-762-3383) in Murray commemorates the Boy Scout movement, and includes the world's second largest collection of original Norman Rockwell paintings.

Park Trails

There are hiking trails throughout the park, but most of them are more suitable for backpacking and mountain biking, ranging from 14 to 65 miles. The long trails are multiuse, so you're likely to see mountain bikes and horses on them, as well as hikers. Day hiking trails, confined to foot travel only, surround The Nature Station.

Honker Trail —4.5 mile loop—circles Honker Lake, where Canada geese can often be seen.

Long Creek Trail —.2 mile post and loop—is a paved, barrier-free trail along a creek.

Woodland Walk —1.0 mile loop—is an interpretive trail rich in wildlife-viewing opportunities.

Land Between the Lakes

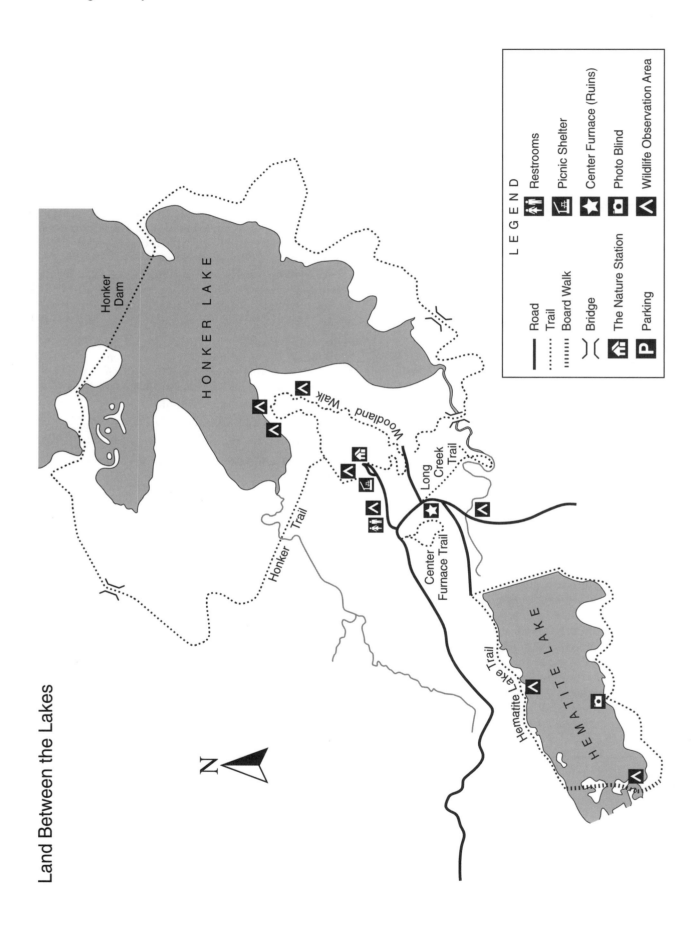

LEGEND

——	Road	👫	Restrooms
····	Trail	🏕	Picnic Shelter
|||||	Board Walk	★	Center Furnace (Ruins)
)(	Bridge	◻	Photo Blind
🏠	The Nature Station	◄	Wildlife Observation Area
P	Parking		

HONKER LAKE

Honker Dam

Woodland Walk

Honker Trail

Long Creek Trail

Center Furnace Trail

Hematite Lake Trail

HEMATITE LAKE

N

Hematite Lake Trail 👢👢👢

Distance Round-Trip: 2.4 miles

Estimated Hiking Time: 1.5 hours to all day

Cautions: The area includes exposed rocks and roots, slick gravel, possible water across the spillway.

Trail Directions: An easy hike around Hematite Lake, this trail provides some of the finest wildlife-viewing opportunities in the state. A mature fallow deer, with mooselike antlers, greeted us at the trailhead, and the wildlife watching got better after that. Expect to see deer, waterfowl, beaver, and bald eagles, among other birds and beasts.

Although you can walk this trail in a bare hour and a half, you might want to spend all day on it, viewing wildlife in its natural habitat.

The trailhead **[1]** is at the far end of the Hematite picnic area, near the dam spillway. The trail is graveled heavily at first, then the rocks thin out. You'll reach the lake **[2]** at mile .06. The lake is covered with lotus (at first you might think they are water lilies) and waterfowl—ducks and geese both. Even in the summer, resident flocks of mallards, wood ducks, and Canada geese call the lake home.

You'll climb a wooden ramp at mile .10, which may be slippery, then cross several tributary creeks on plank bridges before coming to a small bay at mile .26. Rock columns stand along shore, like sentinels guarding the lake's treasures **[3]**. If you're lucky you may, as we did, see an eagle hunting, while a cacophony of geese cry warnings.

At mile .32 a short side trail leads down steps to an observation platform and bench **[4]**. Here you can pause to watch the antics of the ducks. One moment they're as idle as a painted millpond. The next, for no discernible reason, they spring into the air to noisily circle the lake.

Stay alert as you approach mile .55. There's a beaver lodge below the trail there **[5]**. If you're stealthy enough you may get to see the large rodents. If not, the shot-like sound of a tail slapping the water, and a ring of wavelets on the surface, is all you'll know of them firsthand.

Shortly after the beaver den the trail descends to the lakeshore, which it follows to an unmarked Y at mile .76. **[6]**. Go left, following the boardwalk that leads through bottomland hardwoods and marshy backwater filled with wildflowers and river cane. A side trail—also a boardwalk—leads to a small loop and bench at mile .9. Although a good wildlife-viewing area, a better one is coming up.

The boardwalk ends at another unmarked Y. Again, go left, following the lakeshore. You'll reach a side trail to the duck blind at mile 1.4 and the blind itself 150 feet farther **[7]**. The blind, a small wooden shack, sits at the end of a short pier leading out into the lake. Designed as a photo blind, you can spend hours here, staring through the slit windows at the waterfowl and wildlife making their homes on and about the water.

When you've gazed until you're dazed, return to the main trail. This side of the lake is hillier than the north shore, so expect some gradual ups and downs. Just as on the north shore, you'll have to cross several drains and tributary creeks, and at least one low-lying marshy area. Wooden bridges carry you over all these wet spots, however.

You'll reach the dam at mile 2.1 **[8]**. Cross this earthen structure on a mowed path until reaching the concrete spillway at mile 2.3 **[9]**. When dry, you can cross the cement surface anywhere. If water is flowing, try to remain on the concrete-block stepping stones that form a line of cubes across the apron. After climbing the bank, turn right and return to the trailhead.

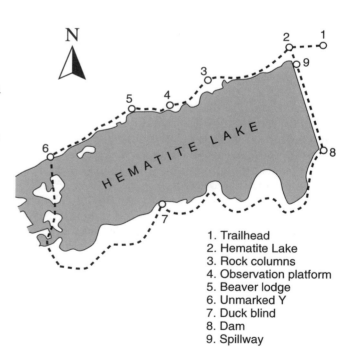

1. Trailhead
2. Hematite Lake
3. Rock columns
4. Observation platform
5. Beaver lodge
6. Unmarked Y
7. Duck blind
8. Dam
9. Spillway

Center Furnace Trail 👢👢👢

Distance Round-Trip: .3 miles

Estimated Hiking Time: 20 to 30 minutes

Cautions: None.

Trail Directions: Center Furnace is a short, easy trail that explores the site of Hematite, a town that grew up around the Center Furnace iron smelter, which operated from the mid-1800s to the early part of this century. Center Furnace was one of eight iron smelters that operated in the Land Between the Rivers, before the rivers were dammed.

The trailhead **[1]** is at a small parking lot, west of The Nature Station. You'll go up a couple of stairs, then reach the trail proper. Follow the loop counterclockwise, through mixed, young, second-growth hardwoods and cedars.

At mile .03 you'll see a large hole in the ground, filled with young trees **[2]**. This was the site of the Hematite General Store, of which nothing remains. While the store operated there were no trees here. The furnace had consumed all the forest in 15 to 20 square miles.

A few feet farther, at mile .04, is a fenced-in hole, lined with bricks **[3]**. This was a cistern, which was the sole water supply for the community. Gutters ran from the store roof to collect rainwater in the cistern. There was no other dependable drinking water for about 250 people who lived and worked here.

Not all the trees were cut for fuel. An old-growth white oak stands at mile .06 **[4]**. More than 150 years old, it is thought that it, and a few like it, were left standing to provide shade. You'll see another one at mile .11. From that tree the trail roller-coasters downward with two sets of steps, until mile .13 and the iron mine **[5]**. You'll see several mounds and pits along the trail, typical of the iron mining done in the region.

It took more than ore to make iron, though. At mile .16 is a reconstructed charcoal hearth **[6]**. Each batch of charcoal produced here could keep Center Furnace operating for 24 hours—which explains why so much of the forest had been cut to feed the hungry furnaces.

There's a display of slag at mile .18 **[7]**. When the ore was melted, limestone and other impurities floated on top of the "heat," producing these polished blue stones with darker streaks. Although they may look like pebbles, do not remove them. If you do, you'll be violating the National Antiquities Act. These "pebbles" are archeological artifacts.

The same goes for the iron products you'll see at mile .2 **[8]**, of which the large "sugar kettle" is the most dramatic. This bowl was part of the furnace operation.

You'll reach the ruins of Center Furnace at mile .22 **[9]**. The broken and twisted brick- and limestone-block walls make you think a war has been fought. However, the damage is just the effect of time and weather.

Shortly after the furnace you'll reach Watson's Monument, at mile .23 **[10]**. This is the gravesite of Dr. Thomas Tennessee Watson, who owned all this land before the furnace was built. His headstone—a tall, carved pillar—is in better condition than the furnace. "Look on my works, ye mighty, and despair!" said the king of kings.

Continue following the loop to reach the trailhead.

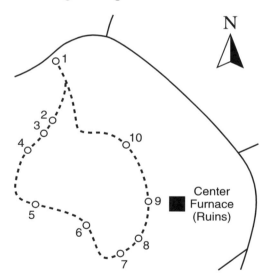

1. Trailhead
2. Hematite General Store site
3. Cistern
4. White oak
5. Iron mine
6. Charcoal hearth
7. Slag
8. Iron products
9. Center Furnace ruins
10. Watson's Monument

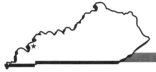

53. Mantle Rock Nature Preserve

- See a natural sandstone arch that once sheltered Cherokee Indians on their forced relocation along the "Trail of Tears."
- Explore the unique sandstone glades environment and the islands of special vegetation that grow there.
- Observe rare plants, such as June grass (which grows nowhere else in Kentucky), hairy lipfern, and prickly pear cactus.

Park Information

Mantle Rock Nature Preserve consists of 190 acres of fragile sandstone glades, interspersed through an upland forest community. In the glades, large exposed bedrock areas host islands of vegetation that can tolerate extreme physiological stress.

The centerpiece of the preserve is Mantle Rock, a 30-foot high, 188-foot long natural bridge. This arch, found in a Pennsylvanian Pounds sandstone outcrop, resulted from physical and chemical weathering of the fractures in the rock. Numerous bluffs, shelters, and honeycomb formations were created the same way.

During the icy winter of 1838 to 1839, when there was no ferry service on the Ohio River, Cherokees being relocated along the infamous Trail of Tears took shelter under Mantle Rock and nearby rockshelters. Many died there.

Soil building is evident in its various stages, from lichens growing on bare rock to mosses and vascular flowering plants growing in patches of thin soil. The thin soil, high temperatures, exposed bedrock, and constant exposure to the sun forces plants in this environment to adapt to extraordinarily dry conditions. Thus, you see the unusual vegetation.

Directions: From Smithland, Kentucky, take US-60 east 15 miles to KY-133 in Salem. Follow it north, passing through the crossroads village Joy, then 2.2 miles to the historic marker on the left. Take the gravel road next to the marker to the parking area.

Hours Open: Open year-round during daylight hours.

Facilities: None.

Permits and Rules: Foot travel only on trails; no cross-country travel allowed; no firearms, alcoholic beverages, fires, or camping in the park.

Further Information: The Nature Conservancy, 642 West Main Street, Lexington, KY 40508; 606-259-9655.

Other Points of Interest

There are numerous cultural and historic sites in and around **Paducah**, 40 miles to the west. For information, contact Paducah-McCracken County Tourist and Convention Bureau, 417 South Fourth Street, Paducah, KY 42002, 502-443-8783.

Metropolis Lake State Nature Preserve (see park #54) is on the western edge of Paducah. **Land Between the Lakes National Recreation Area** (see park #52) is about one hour south.

Mantle Rock Trail 👢👢👢

Distance Round-Trip: 1.9 miles

Estimated Hiking Time: 1.25 to 1.5 hours

Cautions: Be aware of high cliffs, exposed rocks and roots, possible water on trail; trail possibly obscured by fallen leaves.

Trail Directions: Mantle Rock is a post and loop trail through the sandstone glade country of Kentucky's Interior Low Plateaus. The trailhead [1] is a continuation of the gravel entry road. No vehicular traffic is allowed past the parking area!

Follow the gravel past prairie patches and meadows to the gate at mile .24 [2]. Just beyond it is a registration box. The trail descends from there, through a hardwood forest, with several large humps crossing it to prevent illegal motor traffic.

The trail bottoms out at a Y at mile .44. On your immediate left is Mantle Rock [3], a 30-foot high, 188-foot long natural sandstone bridge. During the winter of 1838 to 1839, Cherokees on the Trail of Tears took refuge under the arch and in some of the many rock-shelters around it.

Crawl into any of them. Now imagine yourself cold, wet, poorly fed, badly clothed, and exhausted by a forced march from Georgia, a guttering fire your only source of warmth. No wonder so many died that terrible winter.

After exploring the arch and rock-shelters, follow the trail right, paralleling the creek and cliff line.

During the leafless months especially, you'll see several more shelters.

At mile .48 you'll pass a den tree that forms its own buttress arch [4]. A major limb, broken when the tree still lived, seems to support the tree like the buttress of a bridge.

Cedars appear mixed with the hardwoods at mile .75 and get thicker as you climb. You'll top out at mile .87 on a cliff line [5]. The rock drops sheer for about 20 feet, then slopes down to the creek bottom. Watch for deer and wild turkey here.

There's an old-growth stump about 15 feet tall at mile .92 [6]. Did this tree bear witness to the misery of the huddled Cherokee? Did its branches provide fuel for their fires? Only the ghosts know, and they aren't talking.

Until now the trail has been an old road. At mile .99, however, it turns left and enters the woods at a trail marker [7]. From there it serpentines downward through the forest. The trail may be obscured by leaves, so stay alert for the Nature Conservancy trail arrows that point the way.

One thing they point to we call the Medusa tree [8], which you'll see at mile 1.15. It's an old, dead cedar whose branches twist and writhe in all directions like snakes—or maybe the tormented souls lost on the "Trail of Tears."

You'll T into the main trail at mile 1.25. Go right, descending to the Mantle Rock [3] Y, turn right, and return to the trailhead, which lies at the end of a long, steady climb.

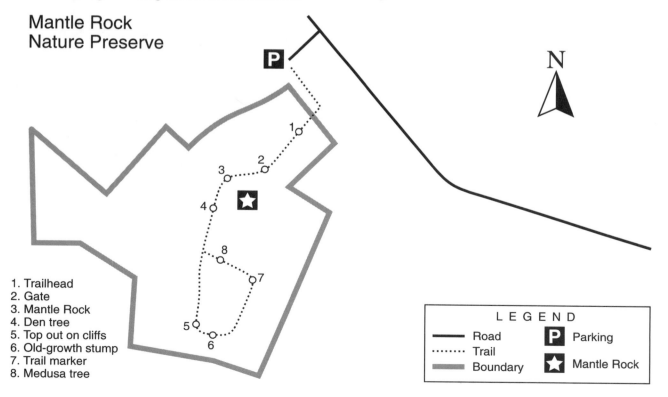

Mantle Rock
Nature Preserve

1. Trailhead
2. Gate
3. Mantle Rock
4. Den tree
5. Top out on cliffs
6. Old-growth stump
7. Trail marker
8. Medusa tree

LEGEND
—— Road
········· Trail
—— Boundary
P Parking
⭐ Mantle Rock

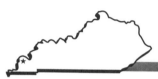

54. Metropolis Lake State Nature Preserve

- See one of the few undeveloped natural lakes in Kentucky.
- Explore the specialized environment of a cypress/tupelo forest.
- Discover rare wildflowers, such as the late-summer blooming cardinal flower.

Park Information

Metropolis Lake State Nature Preserve takes its name from the 50-acre natural lake in the center of this 123-acre nature preserve. The lake is ringed by bald cypress and swamp tupelo trees, mirrored in its calm surface.

Although there are few remaining signs, the preserve was once a recreation area run by a local family. There was a concession building, several rental cabins, and a lighted baseball diamond. Politicians spoke at rallies held on the grounds during the area's heyday.

An old-timer we met recalled those days. "All these trees were whitewashed to about head high," he pointed out, "to mark parking spaces. It was a great place for girling."

One of the few undeveloped natural waters in Kentucky, Metropolis Lake is open for fishing. The primary purpose of the preserve, though, is to protect seven rare species (mostly fish), so special regulations apply. Included are the following: electric motors only; rod and reel only; no gill nets, jugs, or trotlines. Camping and picnicking along the lake are prohibited to protect the rare aquatic species that live there.

Lake-oriented wildlife abounds, and you are likely to see beaver (or, at least, their fresh cuttings), turtles, and kingfishers at any time.

There's an array of wildflowers to see, mostly in the spring. During late summer, the infrequent cardinal flower can be found along the lake's edge.

Directions: From exit 3 off I-24 in Paducah, Kentucky, go west 3 miles on KY-305 to KY-388. Take it 2.5 miles to KY-996. Go north 4 miles to Stafford Drive, which becomes the park road leading to the boat ramp and parking lot .3 miles farther.

Stafford Drive is easy to miss, because it looks like somebody's driveway. When you see the sign saying "State Maintenance Ends," you need to turn right.

Hours Open: Open year-round during daylight hours.

Facilities: Boat ramp.

Permits and Rules: Foot travel only on trails; no camping, fires, alcoholic beverages, or firearms. Special fishing regulations are posted.

Further Information: Kentucky State Nature Preserves Commission, 801 Schenkel Lane, Frankfort, KY 40601; 502-573-2886.

Other Points of Interest

Paducah has numerous cultural and historic sites. For information contact the Paducah-McCracken County Tourist and Convention Bureau, 417 South Fourth Street, Paducah, KY 42002; 502-443-8783.

Metropolis Lake Nature Trail

Distance Round-Trip: .72 miles

Estimated Hiking Time: 40 to 60 minutes

Cautions: The area has exposed roots and possibly some water on the trail.

Trail Directions: The trail starts at the trailhead [1] and travels through the lake's bottomlands, composed of mixed hardwoods, and of the cypress and tupelo that line the lakeshore.

The large birdhouse on your left at mile .03 [2] is a wood duck nesting box. Once almost extinct, wood ducks are now the second most common duck in America, thanks to efforts like this.

At mile .05 you'll reach the first of 12 interpretive signs, this one discussing belted kingfishers [3]. Vandalitor Americanus seems to have not discovered this park. The signs, framed under glass, have not been defaced or damaged, as is, unfortunately, so often the case in our parks.

You'll come to an old cement foundation at mile .11 [4], the remains of a rental cabin that stood here when the park was a privately run recreation area. Note that the foundation has filled naturally, and there are trees that have taken root in it since the early 1960s. The trail circles the foundation, turns left, and climbs gently, passing several interpretive signs along the way.

Two wet-weather streams form a confluence across the trail at mile .27 [5]. During wet periods, you'll have no choice but to wade them. Most of the year, however, there is no water in these runs.

Note the interpretive sign for poison ivy at mile .32 [6]. It's the highest point on the trail. From here, you'll descend gently toward the lake, which you'll reach at mile .39 [7].

There are numerous tree species along the lake. However, the bald cypress so dominate that you won't notice them. The cypress are both unexpected (they're usually thought of as trees of the southern swamps) and intrusive. On calm days, their frothy green heads are perfectly reflected in the waters, while their knees form strange sculptures.

Although a conifer with needles and cones, cypress "leaves" turn brown and fall off in the winter. The woody bumps and fingers surrounding the trees are called knees.

There are, by the way, two theories regarding the function of cypress knees. One says they help stabilize the trees and prevent them from falling over. The other says they help the trees breathe during high water, when the roots are otherwise flooded.

About mile .4 you'll start seeing beaver signs [8]. Look for the distinctive sharp, pointed stumps of small trees and the paths leading from them to the lake. You might even see one of the large rodents swimming.

The trail climbs gently away from the lake, reaching the cabin foundation [4] at mile .6. Turn left, and return to the trailhead.

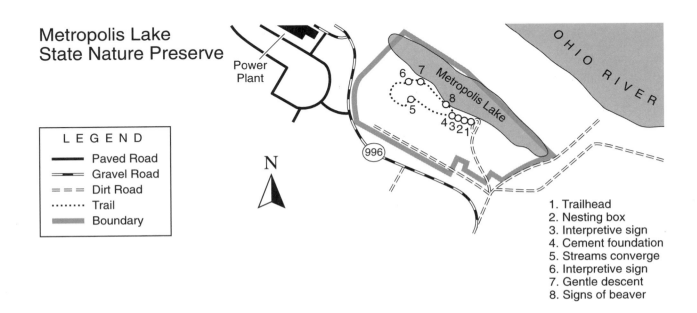

Metropolis Lake State Nature Preserve

Power Plant

OHIO RIVER

Metropolis Lake

996

N

LEGEND
— Paved Road
=== Gravel Road
= = = Dirt Road
······· Trail
▬ Boundary

1. Trailhead
2. Nesting box
3. Interpretive sign
4. Cement foundation
5. Streams converge
6. Interpretive sign
7. Gentle descent
8. Signs of beaver